Metropolis and Experience: Defoe, Dickens, Joyce

By

Hye-Joon Yoon

Metropolis and Experience:
Defoe, Dickens, Joyce,
by Hye-Joon Yoon

This book first published 2012

Cambridge Scholars Publishing

12 Back Chapman Street, Newcastle upon Tyne, NE6 2XX, UK

British Library Cataloguing in Publication Data
A catalogue record for this book is available from the British Library

ISBN (10): 1-4438-3455-6, ISBN (13): 978-1-4438-3455-1

TABLE OF CONTENTS

Part III: Joyce

ACKNOWLEDGEMENTS

This work was supported by the Korea Research Foundation Grant (KRF-2007-A00216) funded by the Ministry of Education and Human Resources Development of the Republic of Korea.

The research for the book has been conducted at the University Library Cambridge, British Library, Senate House Library London, and Yonsei University Library. These superb libraries have furnished vital material in the different phases of my work on this topic during the past decade or so. The idea of writing on the metropolis and experience was first conceived in Cambridge, some ten years ago, where I was spending my first sabbatical leave. It saw its final completion in London during my second sabbatical. The regular labour of teaching, reading, and writing for the ten years between these two recesses has been graced by various fellow travellers, above all my students at Yonsei, in whose company I articulated and refined a large part of what finally went into this book.

As this book comes out at the mid-point of my academic career, I find myself appreciating anew my old teachers during my scholarly apprenticeship at graduate schools, in particular, Rodolphe Gasché, Irving Massey, and John Dings at Buffalo, Sung-Won Lee and Nak-chung Paik at Seoul National. Of my friends who generously supported my work, I particularly thank Peter Grieco, who read and vastly improved the manuscript. I thank also Janet Sorensen, Simon Joyce, and So Young Park, for reading and commenting on the manuscript.

But above all, the greatest support has as ever come from my beloved wife Young-Mi, who with our daughters Wonhee and Wonah, has kept the soul and body of her husband together during all these years.

All human handiworks are bound to be faulty, this book being no exception. The many blemishes of this work I acknowledge as solely mine and confess *mea culpa.* On any merit any reader may find in it, I exclaim *soli Deo gloria.*

INTRODUCTION

At a time when life-long attachment to one's spouse has become decidedly unfashionable in the West, it is odd to find how in the world of English Studies constancy to one's chosen author (and period) seems to be the norm. Or so the writer of this book was told by certain publishers wincing at its subtitle: just Defoe (and his novel-inventors' club) or Dickens (and his earnest Victorian age) or Joyce (sufficient unto himself), but not two together, and surely never all three. The last time we have seen a triad of novelists celebrated memorably in concert was in F. R. Leavis' *The Great Tradition: George Eliot, Henry James, Joseph Conrad*. That was in 1948, more than half a century ago, when being faithful to your marital companion was better received. We change partners with lesser inhibition than the generation of the well-matched pair F. R. and Q. D. Leavis, but we jealously guard the bread-earning authors we first espoused as graduate students. This book challenges that professional monogamy, above all, by adding two more authors from two separate "fields" to the original author who helped its writer earn his doctorate and secure his salary.

Defoe, Dickens, Joyce, odd bedfellows as they may be, as members of a symposium (in Platonic style, without the flute girls) to which all three professional liars (as Plato might call them) are summoned in the name of the metropolitan modernity which affects us all, make up a party worth inviting oneself to, if for no other reason than its rarity.[1] We brought them together here not simply because they belong to some select club of "the few really great" novelists (Leavis 2)—in fact, all three failed Leavis' test of "sustained seriousness" (19)—but because of the historical relevance they bring to an inquiry into the vicissitudes of experience in the modern metropolis. The best reason to include all three in a single book is the vital span of historical urban experience which, when considered together, their works demark.

Novels have been studied, taught, and written about on a staggering scale since the mid-twentieth century, when literature departments, many of them less than half-a-century old, began to open up their curriculum to this most protean, multitudinous, and unwieldy genre. The novel's incorporation into the university curriculum, however, still poses practical problems. Unlike the eminently teachable genres of poetry, drama, or short stories, the bulky novels we discuss in this book may very well threaten to spell logistic disaster in classrooms when covered together in a single semester. The obverse side of this uneasy institutional tenure of the long novel is the minute, quasi-religious devotion given to a handful, or even to a single great novelist of one's choice. Defoe, Dickens, and Joyce, consequently, are separately mobilized for respective "industries" of scholarship built on their tomes and tombs.

On Defoe's works is erected the discourse of the "rise of the novel," whose axis of orthodoxy runs from Ian Watt's *The Rise of the Novel* to Michael McKeon's *The Origins of the English Novel, 1660-1740*. The title of the latter comes with a period marker, "1660-1740." The starting year reflects political history, but the closing year of "1740" is bound to remain a puzzle, whatever the author may have to say in his defence. Surely, "The Origins of the *English* Novel" is an improvement on the supreme contempt for non-English novels implied in Watt's "*The* Rise of *the* Novel," but Watt's spirit of academic territoriality is handed down to the later work undiminished. Ignoring the obvious historical and national borders, of course, has the danger (or advantage) of enabling a mythological narrative of the novel, such as Margaret Doody's *The True Story of the Novel*. The ancient Greek novels Doody eulogizes are no doubt fascinating relics, but one cannot jump centuries, peninsulas, mountains, and seas to establish an atavistic lineage from Chariton to *Clarissa*.

The mood becomes more strenuous and rigid as we move further down the centuries, for whereas eighteenth-century novels are often treated as a group (the subtitle of Watt's book being "Studies in Defoe, Richardson and Fielding"), Victorians and Modernists tend to inspire chronic dissension: either Dickens or George Eliot, either D. H. Lawrence or Joyce, but rarely both or more. The practices of distributing academic capital to new initiates being what they are, sticking to a narrow field is always safer than being expansive. But the problem is that the habit is hard to eradicate even in one's tenured security. A Dickensian would most likely remain a "Dickensian" to his blissful retirement, a George Eliot scholar would be happy to read nothing else. Lawrence, Joyce, and Woolf, contemporaries as they are, all have their respective groups of loyal followers who refuse to understand or respect the tastes of the other parties, replicating in their scholarship with compound interest the fierce individualist animus of the authors they are dedicated to.

Valuable as these works undoubtedly are, there is something in the excessive specialization verging on author-worship (of Joyce, in particular) that goes against the very nature of the novel itself. The novel belongs to a larger world outside English departments, as popular film and television adaptations of Jane Austen or even Henry James should remind us.

Moreover, the metropolitan condition of life, which has multiple links to the genre, and which has become utterly pervasive since Defoe's age, calls for a corresponding synthetic approach crossing the period boundaries set up by faculty meetings. The classics of metropolitan novels we discuss in this book address the challenges of modernity as embodied in an urbanized world. They can and should be read in conjunction, in concert, for the metropolitan experiences they articulate ignore academic border control.

Comparative studies sewn together by thematic threads, however, are beset with their own permanent problem of which authors or fields to select or shun. Robert Alter's *Imagined Cities: Urban Experience and the Language of the Novel* is an illustrative case. Alter begins with Flaubert and ends with Kafka. Why Flaubert? Why not Balzac, for instance, who wrote more than anyone else before and after him on Paris? Alter's answer that it is because Balzac is "more a mythographer of Paris than a realist witness to the experience of the city" (Alter 7) would convince few readers aware of Balzac's meticulous portrayal of Parisian life. Alter begins with Flaubert, whose representative work *Madame Bovary* deals with the "mœurs de province" (provincial manners or ways) as its subtitle states. Alter finds neither "urban panorama" nor any "overviewing narratorial presence" in Flaubert. Instead, the "reality of the city is intimated as it impinges on the senses of the characters" (15). This may sound convincing as a description of Flaubert's *L'éducation sentimentale*, his only Parisian novel, but this single one work cannot sustain Alter's campaign to make Flaubert the founder of a new tradition of urban writing. Or perhaps genealogy is none of Alter's concern. Dickens comes after Flaubert, even though Dickens is older than Flaubert and even though his technique would be considered more old-fashioned, dominated as it is by an "overviewing narratorial presence." Joyce precedes Kafka in Alter's order. Kafka was born in 1883 one year after Joyce but died in 1924, only two years after Joyce's *Ulysses* (1922). Joyce lived on and wrote something else, but *Ulysses* in itself surely has more forward-looking innovations than Kafka's works do, most of which were written before *Ulysses* and published posthumously.

Our choice and order have a clearer historical blueprint. From Defoe to Dickens, Londoners both, the metropolis becomes more complex and so do their novelistic devices. These culminate in Joyce's *Ulysses*, where the heritage of the English novel, having "risen" with Defoe, meets its joyous end. However, while history is the ultimate matrix of our inquiry, we cannot remain content with an analysis of each novel's representation of period scenes. Connecting these three writers through a merely historical approach, when they are as removed from one another in period, circumstance, and temperament, is virtually impossible and highly unwarranted. Defoe wrote in the early eighteenth-century London and was single-minded in his devotion to constructing fraudulent autobiographies. Dickens from the early to mid Victorian period was busy responding to and cashing in on an expanding print market. Joyce, the indigent exiled artificer, thought it worth his while to spend his time displaying his narrative and linguistic virtuosity, while painstakingly reconstructing Edwardian Dublin. No literary history would allow us to bridge the gaps between these three authors; no social history can be stretched far enough to tie them. History must be well-tempered or fine-tuned by a thematic focus, which their shared preoccupation with the urban experience offers.

But before we advance further, we have to answer a possible objection to our inherently Leavisite selection of the "great novelists." The question of why focus on these writers and their novels only and not others becomes quite a contentious issue when the "others" refer to the huge mass of novels produced, consumed, and generally forgotten. Apparently disgusted by those comparatists who underplay historical differences between novels and overplay their amenability to theoretical models of their choice, Franco Moretti has weaned himself of the more conventional notion of comparative "criticism" altogether and migrated into a quantitative terrain where maps and graphs are summoned to supersede the dubious task of close reading. In doing so, Moretti assaults the notion of the qualitative uniqueness of individual works:

> As in all serial history, my object is an artificial one, because a series is never "found," but always constructed—and constructed by focusing on what is *repeatable* and can therefore turn discrete objects into a series. And this, of course, is what makes quantitative methods so repugnant to literary critics: the fear that they may suppress the uniqueness of texts. Which indeed they do. But as I don't believe in the epistemological value of the unique, its suppression doesn't really bother me. (Moretti 1998: 143)

One cannot defend perhaps the "epistemological value of the unique" epistemologically, but repetition can hardly be a solid category, either. The novel as a genre, due to its keen attachment to the book market, does seem to merit a more sober approach not blinded by the charms of individual texts. Novels proliferate and repeat themselves indeed. But even due to the purely commercial requisite of having to be a recognizably new book-commodity that justifies copyright and price tag, a novel (or any other cultural commodity) can by no means be an exact replica of its rivals. Pure repetition is as vacuous a concept as pure uniqueness; repetitions are bound to display differences and degrees in the series. Differences in a series of cultural products call for selection and evaluation, for their shelf lives can vary considerably. However prolific the novel as a genre may be in its propagation, the works that truly matter have endured and survived many changes, promotions and denigrations. They do so, because they offer living experiences that supplement and expand our experience of living, above all, that of living in big cities, which has become the dominant mode of existence for the majority of the human kind. We have chosen the works of these three writers, each within a "constructed" series formed with other relevant writers, because, rather than simply "depicting" or "representing" urban life, they have invented distinctive modes of "experiencing" the city.

We inevitably experience the city everyday and everywhere, but we also fail to experience it. A bustling metropolis at once overwhelms and undermines its dwellers with its absolute excess of shocks and its sheer abundance of stimuli. To the depleted, dejected, disgusted subject living in a big city, these novels offer a reading experience which simulates an experience of the city as such, the city as a whole. Lewis Mumford believed that the city should be "the point of maximum concentration for the power and culture of a community," where "human experience is transformed into viable signs, symbols, patterns of conduct, systems of order" (Mumford 1938: 3). In the modern metropolis, however, human experience exceeds and eludes such communal articulations: it becomes inchoate, fleeting, schizophrenic. The very same street you pass by every day on your way to and from work you experience without fully experiencing, for you are literally a mere passer-by. The very same self you assume yourself to be falters as you move about your city. Your desire wanders away to unmentionable fantasies, transforming you into voyeur, burglar, murderer and what not in a matter of minutes or even seconds. When we attempt to conceive of the city as such, it often appears to us as a cluster of massive structures, machinery, artifacts. Those towering high-rise buildings and yellow cabs of Manhattan become the main protagonists of New York, for instance. It is in the novels that subjects can best come to terms with the problem of experiencing the metropolis, for the novels moderate between the excess and dearth of experience—the absolute overpowering of the subject by the city's grandeur and the chronic undermining of the subject by its velocity. Older literary forms such as poetry and drama can only have marginal roles to play in preserving humans as subjects in a metropolitan ambience, for they came to birth in earlier days when spatial and temporal parameters were different from those of the modern metropolis. Films merely deepen the chasm between the sensory and the intellectual capacities of the subject, as their maximized titillations drill the viewers into becoming mere passive receptacles taking in the cinematic stimuli, say, of seeing Manhattan regularly destroyed in Hollywood disaster films.

The novel, born along with modernity itself, partakes of that peculiar mode of isolation built into the big city, the "reserve" or "aversion," in Georg Simmel's analysis, manifested as "mutual strangeness and repulsion" (Simmel 1997: 179). The novel caters to the needs of the solitary reader, as Walter Benjamin observes in "The Storyteller" (1936):

> A man listening to a story is in the company of the storyteller; even a man reading one shares this companionship. The reader of a novel, however, is isolated, more so than any other reader. . . . In this solitude of his, the reader of a novel seizes upon his material more jealously than anyone else. He is ready to take it completely his own, to devour it, as it were. (Benjamin 2002: 156)

"The birthplace of the novel," wrote Benjamin in an earlier essay "The Crisis of the Novel" (1930), "is the individual in his isolation, the individual who can no longer speak of his concerns in exemplary fashion, who himself lacks counsel and can give none" (Benjamin 2004: 299). As solitude is nowhere more poignantly felt than in the crowded cities, the novel becomes the tenuous but indispensable link of communication simulating life to the individual in his or her isolation. You read the city and its lives, and in reading them, you "seize upon" the city, making it your own—even if it never comes with any edifying "counsel." The novel is notorious for its porous openness, for the "lack of limits in the novel," which according to Georg Lukács "has a 'bad' infinity about it" (Lukács 1971: 81). The inherent incompletion of the novel, in the metropolitan context, matches the fluctuation of individual lives, their "bad infinity" of constant movement, exemplified by Defoe's Roxana, from one place to another. Even wealth, as the case of Roxana illustrates, fails to guarantee being at home in the city, for the richer you are the more restless you grow. To quote Moretti before he turned quantitative, the novel's "weak form" reflecting its "contradictory, hybrid and compromising nature" is "intrinsic to that way of existence—everyday, normal, half-unaware and decidedly unheroic—that Western culture has tried incessantly to protect and expand, and has endowed with an ever-growing significance" (Moretti 1987: 12-13). One would only need to add the qualifier "metropolitan" to this "way of existence" to adapt Moretti's assertion to our context. The novel corresponds to the "half-unaware and decidedly unheroic" metropolitan civilization which has now become truly global. The solitary, insecure, contradictory features of metropolitan experience find their objective correlatives in the "weak" hybrid forms of *Bleak House* or *Ulysses*.

What do we precisely mean, however, by "experience" here? In what way can the isolated novelist, with no "counsel" to give, communicate to us any shared "experience"? To answer this question we need to look into the very word itself. It turns out that *experience* in English usage predominantly privileges one particular type of experience, namely experience in the sense of empirical validation of truth claims of propositions. *Oxford English Dictionary* gives the first three definitions of the word as,

> 1. The action of putting to the test; trial.
> 2. Proof by actual trial; practical demonstration.
> 3. The actual observation of facts or events, considered as a source of knowledge.

Experience in these senses has little to do with the experience novels present to the reader. This usage may be serviceable enough for business or science, but it is sorely inadequate for literary studies. In the discourse of the "rise of the novel," the "primacy of individual experience" or "apprehension of reality" based on "the immediate facts of consciousness" (Watt 15) is credited as what "formal realism" subscribes to in its claim to veracity. Defoe is granted the honour of being the first "realist" novelist, according to this criterion of experiential authorization that his narratives presumably adhere to. Yet inconsistencies and improbabilities abound in the memoirs fabricated by Defoe—just recall the sumptuous supply the wrecked ship bequeathed to Crusoe. The "individual experience" of Crusoe can never be tested experimentally, nor does the novel's "immediate facts of consciousness" square with psychological findings. We seek not knowledge, facts, or information in a novel. No one reads *Little Dorrit* to measure how quick a young girl can work with her needle, or use *Roxana* as a manual for enriching oneself as a kept mistress. *Ulysses* compares poorly with more user-friendly (and portable) guidebooks on Dublin. Most definitions of *experience* listed by *OED* are derived from this sense of gaining knowledge through trial or demonstration, but there are two significant exceptions:

> 4. a. The fact of being consciously the subject of a state or condition, or of being consciously affected by an event.
>
> b. In religious use: A state of mind or feeling forming part of the inner religious life; the mental history (of a person) with regard to religious emotion.

These subjective definitions are at odds with the dominant sense of tested knowledge, since they are bound to remain vague and their cognitive value dubious. For literary criticism this minority usage has obvious merits, but the dominant sense of *experience* being what it is, there is no guarantee that this particular sense will be conveyed, unless modifiers are added to guide their meaning each time (e.g. "the psychological experience of bereavement" or "the religious experience of conversion"). In this book, we choose to offset this scientific, empiricist bias of the English word by supplementing and at times replacing it with two German words for "experience": *Erfahrung* and *Erlebnis*.

Of the two, *Erfahrung* shares some terrain with the English *experience*, since by its very shape it implies something acquired through travel and journey (*fahren*) and therefore enjoys the authority of having been tested by experience, as in the common expressions such as "ich weiß aus Erfahrung" (I know by experience) or "sechsjährige schelchte Erfahrung" (six years' trying experience). But unlike *experience*, *Erfahrung* assumes a certain time qualification, something that one acquires through a given period of time. As the phrases above imply and as the first definition of the term in *Duden: Das Große Wörterbuch der deutschen Sprache* states, *Erfahrung* is "bei prakitscher Arbeit od. durch Wiederholen einer Sache gewonne Kenntnis" (to gain knowledge of something through practical work or through repetition). As Benjamin cautions us, "There is no greater error than the attempt to construe experience—in the sense of life experience [*Lebenserfahrung*]—according to the model on which the exact natural sciences are based. The decisive element here is not the causal connections established over the course of time, but the similarities that have been lived" (Benjamin 2005: 553 / Benjamin 1985: 89). This non-linear or non-mechanical temporality of *Erfahrung* has immediate implications for us, since they suggest a narrative of what one has gone through or repeated through a certain time span, which is what novels offer one way or another. But as we attempt to narrow our focus to literary representation of experience, we are detained by two further definitions in the same standard dictionary. The second and third definitions of the word are,

> 2. Erleben. Erlebnis, durch das man klüger wird.
> 3. (Phils.) durch Anschauung, Wahrnehmung, Empfindung gewonnes Wissen als Grundlage der Erkenntnis.
>
> (2. An experience through which one becomes more clever.
> (3. [Phil.] through conception, perception, sensation to gain knowledge of the foundation of cognition.)

How far *Erfahrung* can be interchangeable with *Erlebnis* is a question we shall examine a little while later, but one may point out at this stage that even in this second sense, *Erfahrung* implies a more practical kind of knowledge of particular actions: it makes one more clever and savvy (*klüger*) in getting things done. In this regard, it harmonizes with the "prakitscher Arbeit" of the first definition.

The philosophical definition of *Erfahrung*, however, demands a more detailed annotation, since it sounds quite abstruse as it stands. The time factor and the practical aspects of *Erfahrung* here have to do with the philosophical labour of investigating the basis of knowledge through reason and sensation—a very special and strange kind of work indeed. But it makes better sense when we place it in the context of the great labour of Immanuel Kant's critical philosophy. Kant describes in his introduction to *Critique of Judgement* how our cognitive faculty bids us make sense of the outside world, to turn into a "general empirical knowledge [*Erfahrungserkenntnisses überhaupt*]" or form "a consistent context of experience [*eine zusammenhängende Erfahrung*]." Experience as *Erfahrung* is the end product or the objective of our "conception, perception, sensation," but its foundation is as much subjective or conceptual as objective or empirical. For even as our cognitive faculty constructs "empirical knowledge" or a "context of experience," understanding nonetheless "recognizes it objectively as contingent, and it is merely judgement that attributes it to nature as transcendental purposiveness, i.e. a purposiveness in respect of the subject's faculty of cognition" (Kant 2008: 20-21 / Kant 1974: 95). In this picture of the subject's faculty of judgment (*Urteilskraft*), and not those of ambitious reason (*Vernunft*) or skeptical understanding (*Verstand*), presented by the great thinker's third and final *Critique*, experience is not in itself the foundation of knowledge but what is constructed as such, in full awareness of the inherent contingencies, exceptions and aberrations that may anytime dismantle it.

We are tempted here, once again, to assert how appropriate this view of *Erfahrung*, as experience constructed by the judging subject, is to a description of fiction writing and plot making. Accidental incidents are moulded in a novel to reveal a semblance of meaningful relationship and even knowledge or wisdom, based on the writer's power of judgement. One may add immediately that the metropolis and its motley crowd, through the indefatigable and sedulous labour of Balzac or Dickens are given recognizable form and semblance of "purposiveness." The later Marxist Lukács, in fact posits *Erfahrung* as a key criterion of critical distinction in his "Narrate or Describe?" (published in 1936, the same year as Benjamin's "The Storyteller").[2] In the novels of the great "realists" such as Balzac or Tolstoy, "we experience [*erfahren*] events which are inherently significant because of the direct involvement of the characters in the events," whereas in the works of the decadent naturalists such as Flaubert or Zola "the events themselves become only a tableau for the reader or, at best, a series of tableaux" (Lukács 1970: 116 / Lukács 1971b: 202).[3] A good narrative, in other words, must come up with a significant *Erfahrung*, both in the dictionary sense of time-worn practical life experience and in the Kantian sense of contextualized purposive judgement. Flaubert and his indecisive characters, such as Frédéric Moreau of *L'éducation sentimentale*, lack purposiveness and fail to transcend contingency, Lukács would say with Kant nodding behind him.

Novels and narrative, whether they appeal to Lukács' rather exacting palate or not, are before anything else linguistic constructs. Experience, however, under any name or in any national language, does not have to be necessarily verbal. More often than not, the most unforgettable or valuable kinds of experience are hard to put in words. Experience as *Erfahrung* in its definitions traced above is no exception. Practical work or repetition, becoming clever in handling things, contemplating on the mind's workings, all of that need not be verbal or verbose. Before we can further elaborate on the literary implications of *Erfahrung*, we have to find an answer to this legitimate objection. Giorgio Agamben's thoughts on the relationship or the lack thereof between language and experience may help us here. For Agamben, experience stands outside or on the outskirts of language as the latter's "transcendental limit," but it affects language as the mark of the "difference between the human and the linguistic" pointing not merely to the arbitrariness of language but to its failure, to what Agamben calls "infancy," or one's being without language. Experience that bears the marks of "infancy" denotes the limitation and insufficiency of language, but since it is a substantive presence (we know what we have experienced, though we cannot always translate it into words), it "commits the individual to speech," while "language constitutes truth as the destiny of experience" (Agamben 1993: 58). Language and experience prompt each other, by virtue of the rupture severing them, in a relationship of reciprocal causality. One leads another to go beyond itself, to approximate "truth," which can never be final or complete, given the shortcomings of language and the "infancy" or speechlessness of experience. Yet by the same token, temporal and partial truths can be produced between language and experience, in narratives, for instance, told, received, and shared in a community acknowledging their truth or significance.

We are now prepared to resume the task of employing *Erfahrung* as a category for discussing the novel as an interaction between potentially non-verbal experience and language. But another hurdle blocks us, for *Erfahrung* in Benjamin's "Storyteller" is strictly reserved for traditional narratives only, and not for the "solitary" and "isolated" world of writing and reading novels.

> Experience [*Erfahrung*] which is passed on from mouth to mouth is the source from which all storytellers have drawn. . . . "When someone goes on a trip, he has something to tell about," goes the German saying, and people imagine the storyteller as someone who has come from afar. But they enjoy no less listening to the man who has stayed at home, making an honest living, and who knows the local tales and traditions. (Benjamin 2002: 144 / Benjamin 1977: 440)

In an earlier text, "Experience and Poverty" (1933), Benjamin conceived *Erfahrung* in terms of inter-generational communication, as that which is "handed down" to younger generations "with the authority of age, in proverbs" or "as tales" or "sometimes as stories from foreign lands" which the young in their turn would "find out [*erfahren*]" through their own travels (Benjamin 2005: 731 / Benjamin 1977: 214). Benjamin's conception of *Erfahrung* thus has a distinctively communal and collective profile (Nägele 128). By sharing the experience of travelling geographically, or by having embarked on life's journey, the teller and the audience set up a community of shared knowledge. To define the novel as a non-communal individualistic genre, as does Benjamin, then, is to deny its capacity of imparting *Erfahrung*.

Not all novels could possibly be the same, one may object at this point, nor must Benjamin be, after all, the most trustworthy voice to heed on matters concerning novels, which he has no sympathy for.[4] Novels can rarely offer proper *Erfahrung*? Raymond Williams, a respected critic who also wrote novels, would beg to differ. "Most novels," Williams proposes, "are in some sense knowable communities" in that "the novelist offers to show people and their relationships in essentially knowable and communicable ways" (Williams 202). This statement would apply ideally to those works presenting a smaller community which the reader is invited to join, such as the regional country novels from Jane Austen to Thomas Hardy. Would it be also relevant to our authors, to Defoe's insistently anti-social first-person narratives, as well to the gregarious novels of Dickens and Joyce? The works of these latter do profess their intention to portray a "knowable community" and to communicate shared life experience. But there are forces counteracting such gesture or intention, forces that are built into the very fabric of modern metropolitan life their works depict and embody, as Williams himself admits. "The growth of towns and especially of cities and a metropolis" offers a stiff challenge to "any assumption of a knowable community" (Williams 202). Simmel's foundational essay on the "Metropolis and Mental Life" dissects how this is bound to be so:

> Lasting impressions, impressions which differ only slightly from one another, impressions which take a regular and habitual course and show regular and habitual contrasts—all these use up . . . less consciousness than does the rapid crowding of changing images, the sharp discontinuity in the grasp of a single glance, and the unexpectedness of onrushing impressions. These are the psychological conditions which the metropolis creates. With each crossing of the street, with the tempo and multiplicity of economic, occupational and social life, the city sets up a deep contrast with small town and rural life with reference to the sensory foundations of psychic life. The metropolis exacts from man as a discriminating creature a different amount of consciousness than does rural life. Here the rhythm of life and sensory mental imagery flows more slowly, more habitually, and more evenly. (Simmel 1997: 175)

The challenge such conditions offer to a novel seeking to construct a "knowable community" can be felt in Dickens, the most community-oriented among the urban novelists in English literature. The very fact that it takes such an elaborate (and often fortuitous) scaffolding to work out his typical plot of digging out hidden connections speaks for the difficulty of maintaining *Erfahrung* under the conditions of modern metropolitan life. Even in the relatively streamlined narrative of Pip acknowledging his indebtedness to Magwitch, the boundless gratitude the latter feels for the lad is based on inaccurate memory (young Pip was terrorized into bringing him food and file). Moreover, the first charitable encounter took place away from the capital in a rural setting. A warm heart is a rarity in London where enduring commitment has to cope with rapid, onrushing, unexpected contacts of busy living. The "psychological conditions" of the metropolis favors, in Simmel's analysis, the "heightened awareness and a predominance of intelligence" as vital means of preserving "subjective life against the overwhelming power" (Simmel 1997: 176) of the big city's "impersonalized spirit" (184). It is in testimony to their threatened subjectivity that Defoe's narrator-protagonists exemplify the vigilant self-interest of metropolitan psyche, as we shall show in our chapters on Defoe. This mental condition of the metropolitan subject also inspires Joyce to orchestrate the narratives of *Ulysses* in such a way as to have different episodes present differentiated views, at times almost different languages, exhibiting "sharp discontinuity," even though a semblance of "knowable community" forms part of the menu offered.

To understand the stakes and stances involved in the novel's confrontation of metropolitan modernity we need to bring in the second German word for experience, *Erlebnis*, as the dialectical counterpoint to *Erfahrung*. Experience as *Erlebnis* in *Duden*'s definition is, "von jmdm. als in einer bestimmten Weise beeindruckend erlebtes Geschehen (to impress in a distinct manner someone with a lived occurrence)." Its temporality is different from *Erfahrung* in that it is instantaneous and momentary rather than something spread through a period of time. In contrast to the continuous practical work *Erfahrung* implies, *Erlebnis* connotes a "lived (*erlebt*) moment," a distinctively memorable incident, typically accompanying a sensory, psychological, or physiological shock. If one becomes "more clever" from such experience, then it can be called "*Erfahrung*" (in the second *Duden* definition of *Erfahrung* given above). The experience in question remains an *Erlebnis* when the significance or value of the incident fails to be realized or assessed. This species of experience the metropolis never fails to supply to the individual. With "each crossing of the street, with the tempo and multiplicity of economic, occupational and social life," things happen that make us alert but not a bit wiser. The metropolis is the realm *par excellence* of experience as *Erlebnis*, as Benjamin admits in one of his last essays, "Some Motifs in Baudelaire" (1939):

> Baudelaire battled the crowd—with the impotent rage of someone fighting the rain or the wind. This is the nature of something lived through [*Erlebnis*] to which Baudelaire has given the weight of an experience [*Erfahrung*]. He indicated the price for which the sensation of the modern age may be had: the disintegration of the aura in the experience [*Erlebnis*] of the shock. (Benjamin 1983: 154)

The jostling, bustling, hostile crowd has nothing but *Erlebnis* to offer to the poet, which he heroically seeks to convert into *Erfahrung*, into something meaningful and communicable—against the odds, for "the city is the site of the rise of *Erlebnis* and the concomitant demise of *Erfahrung*" (Gilloch 144). That which is shocking, subjective, spurious, and hence lacks the "weight" or authority of *Erfahrung* Benjamin assigns to the domain of *Erlebnis*. For a poet who cannot do without the "aura" of subjectivity, as well as the authority and skill of rhyme, this bifurcation of experience in the city can be a tragic double bind. For the novel, however, the *Erlebnis* of the metropolis can be captured or even celebrated positively by its diffuse, disorderly, disparate prose, by the "living heteroglossia" the novel incorporates, according to Mikhail Bakhtin (Bakhtin 308). Yet as in Baudelaire's poems, *Erlebnis* and *Erfahrung* are mutually complementary as well as contrastive in the metropolitan novel. Without one the other cannot stand. Without the desire to attain a level of *Erfahrung* the very act of narration cannot be continued, without the constant encounter of *Erlebnis* the novelist has nothing to write about.[5]

In Benjamin's remarks on Baudelaire, and in those quoted earlier, we can easily see how he prefers *Erfahrung* to *Erlebnis*. This has to be put in the context of the intellectual history of the times. Thanks to the privileged status Wilhelm Dilthey granted the term in his lectures in Berlin University (where both Simmel and Benjamin, fellow Berliners of Dilthey, studied), *Erlebnis* had enjoyed a fairly respectable career from the late nineteenth to the early twentieth century.[6] After his death, onslaughts on the term were launched from different quarters. Martin Heidegger in "The Origin of the Work of Art" complained about the excessive use of the word, about how it became "the source that is standard not only for art appreciation and enjoyment but also for artistic creation." "Yet perhaps lived experience is the element in which art dies," he remonstrated (Heidegger, 204). More vociferous were those charges levelled at it by the Marxist Lukács. The subjectivism of the "cult" of *Erlebnis*, he claimed, is nothing but the flip side of bureaucratic objectivity (Lukács 1971b: 430-31). Dilthey, the author who boosted the status of *Erlebnis*, was attacked in *Destruction of Reason* as the "founder" of "the subjectivism of imperialist philosophy" (Lukács 1962: 373). Should we perhaps be wary of using this term burdened with such compromising allegations?

Whether Dilthey and his brainchild *Erlebnis* are culpable politically is a question we need not broach in this book, but we are obliged still to elucidate the specific meaning of *Erlebnis* as Dilthey uses it. For Dilthey, *Erlebnis* is something that is "inner," above all. It is not "the knowledge that comes from perception" but that which "receives its particular content from me through inner perception" (Dilthey 1989: 280). Such lived experiences as "sorrow *about* an event, striving *for* a good" constitute "inner relations clearly different from one another," grounded as they are in one's "psychic attitude" (Dilthey 2002: 36). Being an apprehension that is essentially "inner," it pertains to the subject's self-certainty, even though it can only be "displayed, but not defined" (Dilthey 2002: 37). It is "a distinctive and characteristic mode in which reality is there-for-me" (Dilthey 1985: 223), for the "structural unity of attitudes and contents" is what gives *Erlebnis* its coherence (Dilthey 2002: 47). That Dilthey wishes to protect the dignity of the individual subject through his concept of *Erlebnis*, in opposition to objective forces of technology and bureaucracy, seems unmistakable in these formulations. I can be estranged from the great impersonal systems of modern metropolis, or as in Dilthey's case, from the Prussian state machinery, but my "inner" *Erlebnis* can still be mine legitimately and exclusively.

Without hurling huge political charges at Dilthey, we can quietly admit that the lofty pretensions of reason, the unflinching analysis of understanding, and the purposive synthesis of judgement which in Kant constituted the order of human faculties, have all fallen into disarray in Dilthey's thinking, leaving the subject with only a "qualitatively determinate reality" in lived experience (Dilthey 1985: 226). This turn to subjectivism may be due to the influence of "neo-Kantianism" and its diminution of the status and scope of Kant's comprehensive and answerable subject (Hanssen 55), or it may be a symptom of bourgeois decadence. In either case, one can hardly describe Dilthey's logic as watertight, since questions are begged rather than answered as to how *Erlebnis* can be positively self-sufficient.[7] Closer to our topic, the entrenched and callous "psychic life" of the metropolitan subject, which Simmel speaks of, can have little hope of enjoying the fulfilling inner certainty of Dithey's *Erlebnis*. We can readily concede how *Erlebnis* can only be "displayed" but never "defined" in the novels, yet unlike lyric poetry, novels also display the foibles and failures of a character or narrator who fancies that some "reality" is "there-for-me." Dilthey privileged literature as the medium of communicating *Erlebnis*, understood as the "re-experiencing of a nexus of lived experience" (Dilthey 2002: 235) distilled by a poet's subjectivity. Yet a poet's *Erlebnis* can at best be reconstructed "in accordance with the principle of analogy" (Plantinga 47). The novel, however, offers "re-experiencing" far more diversely, since it is not constrained by the originating life experience of the author but can freely exhibit different modes of subjective experience.

In using *Erlebnis* in this book as a counterpoint to *Erfahrung* we critically adopt Dilthey's subjective determination of the term while rejecting its positive assertions: it is a form of subjective attitude to contents, which, however, has no guarantee of attaining "structural unity." It may be an "inner perception" not thanks to the protections provided by a more genuine or authentic psychic realm, but in the sense that it eludes universalizing rational reflections, which, therefore, can only be "displayed, but not defined." Such instability of *Erlebnis*, in fact, Dilthey was more than aware of. "The principle of lived experience is that everything that is there for us is so only as a given in the present," he concedes (Dilthey 2002: 250). The "present," moreover, is hardly a self-standing unit, for "what we experience as present always contains the memory of what has just been present," so much so that a "lived experience" has to be understood as a "temporal sequence in which every state is in flux"

(Dilthey 2002: 216). This fluid, open, "restless advance of the present" (Dilthey 2002: 93) of *Erlebnis* seems most apposite to the metropolitan novel, as much in the first-person voices of Moll's wavering narration as in Molly Bloom's interior monologues.[8] The temporality of incomplete precarious moments of the individual subject's experience, which bears on the subject's attitude and sentiments with no promise or possibility of their articulation into a "structural unity" or "inner relations"—this is how we define *Erlebnis* for our purpose. As Rudolf A. Makkreel states, "we can have an *Erlebnis* of the present, but no *Erfahrung* of its content as presented" (Makkreel 387-88). The temporality of *Erfahrung* fosters a retrospective reflection on that which one has gone through, and which inherently is amenable to communication and transmission. The very act of narrating, of addressing the reader, however abstruse its language (as in "Proteus" episode of *Ulysses*), implicitly gestures towards *Erfahrung* in this sense. This dialectic of *Erlebnis* and *Erfahrung* in novelistic discourse, which intends the latter by depicting the former, is most poignantly activated in the novels dealing with the metropolitan conditions of life marked by persistent contingency. This dialectic knows no synthesis other than the tentative gesture towards solution at each nodal point in the narrative, which is what we investigate in the following chapters, each in its specific historical context.

The "metropolis," compared with "experience," has been given less coverage thus far, in part because it needs little introduction (we are all too painfully familiar with its ways and woes) but more so because it is a topic demanding to be approached as specific historical and topographical problems. We move chronologically from Defoe through Dickens to Joyce, for the historical conditions of the modern metropolis find different and distinctive articulations in this order. Defoe's London and other European cities (in *Roxana*) brimming over with the hectic drive for capital accumulation show their advanced form of development in Dickens's sprawling Victorian London, whose idiosyncrasies the author vigilantly captures in his efforts to humanize the incongruous manifold of the metropolis. By contrast, the stalemate of subordinated subjects in Dublin, the famous "paralysis" of *Dubliners*, is uplifted and stirred through the technical exuberance of *Ulysses*. The thread that runs through these different authors, periods, and texts, we weave from the concept of experience as *Erlebnis*, understood in its dialectical pairing with *Erfahrung*.

Defoe for us is the supreme novelist of *Erlebnis*, turning even a collective *Erfahrung* into *Erlebnis* as in his *Journal of the Plague Year*, conveyed by his seamless first-person narrations. The ambiguity and complexity attending this subjective approach to modernity we shall trace from Samuel Pepys's monumental *Diary*, which presents a vivid picture of a Simmelian metropolitan psyche—calculative, restless, sensuous, self-divided—exemplified by Defoe's Moll and Roxana. What confronts and supplements Defoe's efforts to offer experience of the private subject to the reader is the numerical language of accounting and statistics (the body count in *A Journal of the Plague Year* and the money count in *Moll Flanders* or *Roxana*), which also has precedents in Pepys.

In Dickens, *Erlebnis* and *Erfahrung* compete with each other, at the level of style above all, which seeks to endear itself to the reader, as well as to astonish, entertain, and agitate. Writing of the crowd from the crowd, Boz creates a new platform for himself, which inherently harbours a "journalistic" tendency. Journalism, the twin or double of realist fiction for the journalist-novelists Defoe and Dickens, debilitates *Erfahrung* by its pseudo-objectivity of unreflective narration of the events. We therefore investigate extensively how the novel interacts with informative genres of journalism and travelogue in our chapters on Dickens.

Joyce's *Ulysses* confronts the fragmentation of the metropolitan subject (of Bloom and Stephen), which has grown so extreme as to dismantle the grounds of *Erlebnis*, but the very effort to keep oneself together, or alternatively, the exhilarating pleasure of schizoid self-division, produces a semblance of *Erlebnis*—a subjective experience without the subject, as it were. Unlike the English novelists, Joyce had to cope with the unappealing task of writing on the "Hibernian metropolis," many degrees removed from the imperial capital London, and with the ambivalence towards a language which to an Irish Catholic is both familiar and foreign. This leads to a series of unique configurations in Joyce that address the vicissitudes of *Erfahrung*, especially in those episodes employing third-person narration in self-deprecating and self-destructive modes.

In all these steps of our inquiry, *Erlebnis* or *Erfahrung* or any other terms or categories never hold sway as dominant master concepts subduing the concrete particulars of the texts. These terms are guides leading us to the works rather than guards restricting our passage. Despotism of "theory" (whether of Simmelian or Benjaminian or Marxian provenance) we avoid by what may at times appear to be distracting digressions on stray themes or myopic attention to textual details. Under whatever name in whatever language, experience means nothing without that openness towards the minute, the minor, and the marginal. Besides, the art of wandering the alleys and boulevards of the metropolitan novel knows how to protect its right to roam.

PART I:

DEFOE

CHAPTER ONE

FROM THE PRIVATE SPHERE

"Our Dear-self is … the End of Living"

We begin with Pepys, before Defoe, for Pepys comes before Defoe in more senses than one. Defoe was born and bred in Pepys's London. Pepys, like Defoe, was a middle-class Londoner and assiduous scribbler. But above all, Pepys the private diarist stands for the textual realm from which Defoe's novels emerge. The canonical view of Defoe scholarship makes him a direct heir to the Puritan-Dissenter tradition of spiritual autobiography and its Lockean (or Weberian) secularization (Watt 74-78; Starr 105-15; Hunter 71-72; McKeon 336). When Pepys comes under the purview of Defoe criticism, it is generally to assess the veracity of the Great Plague in Defoe's *A Journal of the Plague Year* against Pepys's authentic records (Novak 2001: 606; Richetti 2005: 310; Backscheider 505). Pepys merits greater attention than this. Between Defoe's modernizing world and the Puritan Interregnum comes the Restoration, whose greatest prose writer, in quantity if not in quality, is Pepys. His career as a public servant in the Navy Office coincides with the Restoration itself, and the detailed, honest, and monumental journal he kept for ten years has more bearing on the "rise of the novel" than has been credited so far.

Needless to say, Pepys is no fiction writer. This meticulous and diligent public servant would have been offended to find himself in the company of story-mongers, perhaps. Moreover, it is never clear whether he wanted any other mortal to read his secret diary, posthumously published, and fully decoded only in the later decades of the past century. Yet the peculiar textuality of Pepys's diaries, written in shorthand for his private use or pleasure, reveals a vivid, lucid, and undisguised picture of a metropolitan individuality—a blueprint or x-ray of the psyche of a metropolitan subject. In and between the lines of his diary, rather than in his public duties, Pepys articulates his pure private self. Pepys in his journal constructs a textual realm entirely dedicated to preserving a privacy severed from the public world. This locus we may call the "private sphere," which exists within the "public sphere" but in stark separation from it.

Pepys the civil servant living in Restoration London is not quite a citizen girded with Ciceronian virtue ready to take part in the realm of *civitas*. His is a world deprived of the rights to civic political intervention. As he walks the streets of the capital, he has to pass by the lurid, macabre memento of the death of radical republican politics:

> This afternoon, going through London and calling at Crowes the upholster in Saint Bartholomew.—I saw the limbs of some of our new Traytors set upon Aldersgate, which was a sad sight to see; and a bloody week this and the last have been, there being ten hanged, drawn, and Quarterd. (20 Oct 1660 [1.269-70])[1]

With only five months or so into the Restoration of Stuart Monarchy, Pepys goes about the city on private business to see an upholsterer, but he is interrupted—this interruption is graphically marked in the text by dash—by vivid evidence of sanguine public politics. The execution of regicides (the "new Traytors") launches anew a metropolitan regime in London freed from the freedom of republican politics or any other radicalism. The reinstated Crown and Church would soon create a new category of religious-political minority, the "Dissenters" to which Defoe's family belonged, and in which circle he was educated (Novak 2001: 40-50; Backscheider 7-11; Richetti 2005: 3-9). There would be another round of rebellion and battles later in the century over the issue of Protestant succession (the so-called "Glorious Revolution"), but massive bloodshed took place away from London, in Ireland and Scotland. London remained placid politically, far too busy making money. Mob violence, such as the Gordon Riots that fascinated Dickens, rare as it was, offered no real challenge to the continuity of an urban polity that bound the private to the public with the unbreakable knots of market economy. No revolutionary violence, after Restoration, would taint Aldersgate, Saint Bartholomew, or any other locality of London. In that space cleared of politics, Pepys the public servant pursued his own private experience (*Erlebnis*) under the sign of the executed, proscribed, forbidden collective memory (*Erfahrung*) of insurrection.

Modernity begins with the ascendancy of the "public sphere" over the private spheres of household and family, according to Jürgen Harbermas (Habermas 19). It also entails the disjunction from the public sphere of the realm of individualized privacy, connected to the former in the text above only by a mere thread of a dash. Pepys frequents coffee houses which Habermas regards as the quintessential institution of the "bourgeois public sphere" (Habermas 59). Visits to coffee-houses are occasionally recorded in his journal, as in the following.

> Coming by Temple-bar, I bought Audlys *Way to be rich*, a serious pamphlett and some good things worth my minding. Thence homeward; and meeting Sir W. Batten, turned back again to a Coffee-house and there drunk more, till I was almost sick. And here much discourse, but little to be learned. (23 Jan 1663 [4.22])

But interestingly, he writes to himself how his coffee-house experience failed to yield wisdom or learning. An *Erfahrung* of public knowledge garnered from the debates and discussions at coffee houses is what he or other visitors expect, but Pepys merely leaves the place "almost sick" from drinking coffee, gathering "little to be learned" from the profuse "discourse" there. On this as in other days he recollects his daily deeds and thoughts, yet the private subject collects no meaning from his day spent in part at a coffee house. Instead, the *Erlebnis* of physical reaction, of being "almost sick," is what he finds himself remembering, rather than what he heard there.

Privacy in Pepys exists in a subordinate position vis-à-vis the public realm. The passage quoted above, coming at the end of the day's entry, reads almost like an incidental footnote on his body (feeling sick), appended to the record of what he had done that day in the public space (purchasing books and visiting coffee houses). The very secrecy of Pepys's journal written in coded shorthand speaks of the need to protect it from the pressure of the public social life of the writer as civil servant, head of a family, and aspiring Londoner with extensive connections. Or, if his shorthand's value lies in its facility and speed rather than secrecy, as Harry Berger argues (Berger 575-76), it further attests to the force of his public habit over his most intimate private activity. But apart from the question of the peculiar textuality of his diary, there stands the very fact of his mode of living off his public occupation, which underlines the derivative relationship of the private to the public. The private is that which is left to him after all public duties and works have been deducted from it.[2] If Pepys's journal registers an important stage in "that long, long history of change from the sense of the private world as the scene of privation to that of plenitude" (Pooley 88), it does so by securing the private realm as the remainder, as that which is reserved, financially and otherwise, for private appropriation.

Taking advantage of the good fortune that had placed him at the Navy Office (i.e. of his having been personal secretary to Edward Montague, later created 1st Earl of Sandwich, who was responsible for bringing Charles II back to England), he made good use of his talents and position to serve his private interests, as well as those of his king. "The charm and vivacity of his personality have combined with the immensity of his public service to melt the sternest judicial glare" (Ollard 128), as one modern biographer euphemistically states. That potent combination of self-interest and capability was turned to good account indeed, for only after four years of public career at the Navy Board as the Clerk of the Acts, a minor position yielding a dependable but modest salary of £350 per annum (measured against the Treasurer's £2,000 or the Comptroller's £500 ([Latham 293]), we see him in 1664 giving "great thanks to Almighty God," as he finds himself on the credit side "clearly worth 1,104 *l*"—"the first time that ever I was worth 1000 *l* before—which is the heighth of all that ever I have for a long time pretended to," as he glosses with proud enthusiasm (31 July 1664 [5.227]). Public duty and private reward thus seem happily balanced, yet satisfaction has to come from the preponderance of the latter over the former, since the work itself carries no intrinsic meaning or pleasure:

> Up and close at my office all the morning. To the Change, busy, at noon and so home to dinner; and then I to the afternoon at the office till night; and so late home, quite tired with business and without joy in myself, otherwise then [sic] that I am by God's grace enabled to go through it and one day hope to have benefit by it. So home to supper and to bed. (28 April 1664 [5.135])

Two years earlier, the young official had resolved "to give a good account of my time and to grow rich" (3 Mar 1662 [3.40]). Grow rich he certainly did. At the end of 1660, he discovers he is "worth in money clear 240 *l*—for which God be praised" (10 Dec 1660 [1.315]). In September 1661 his fortune amounted to £600 or so ([2.175]). By 1664 it had almost doubled, and in 1666 his possession is "worth above 4600 *l*" (4 Mar 1666 [7.65]), nearly eight times what he had in 1661 (or nearly 20 times what he had in 1660). The profits he makes from his work at the Navy Office accrues to himself as that which remains after his debts and expenses incurred by his social activity have been cleared, and which he can spend as he sees fit. His public work is "business" for him, which he conducts "without joy" but with a well-founded hope to enrich himself by it. In Pepys, then, we find a typical example of a metropolitan psyche, which Simmel describes as pursuing his own individual interest with an "intellectualistic mentality" (Simmel 1997: 177). This mental attitude prevails over the emotional gloom of joyless labour on the strength of the "money economy" of which the metropolis is the "seat" (176).

Pepys was a metropolitan subject in a simpler sense, as well. His city was turning into a modern metropolis over which money held unchallenged sway. Between the careers of Pepys and Defoe, a span of about thirty years, London went through the process of becoming the most populous city in

Europe, growing "from a middle-ranking European town of about 50,000 or 60,000 people" in the early sixteenth century, "smaller than Paris, Rome, Naples, Venice, Antwerp and several others, into a monster of over 500,000, the greatest city in Christendom" (Inwood 157).[3] Among its advantages over its rivals was the fact that the "polar extremes" of the "Prince's Capital and the Merchant's City" (Reader 124), Westminster and London, lay adjacent side by side, linking the centre of trading with that of "conspicuous consumption" (Jones 61). The economy was brisk and the city bustled with men and goods moving about. Traffic jams caused fierce competition on the public thoroughfares throughout the metropolis. Pepys's London suffered traffic blockage as regularly as London in later times. Congestion was almost chronic on Ludgate-hill, so that on one occasion, when Pepys had to return from his trip to take his wife out to dinner, he was forced to change his plans: "And on Ludgate-hill, there being a stop, I bought two cakes and they were our supper at home; and so to bed" (8 April 1662 [3.62]). It was also during this period that one of the first self-conscious usages of *metropolis* can be found, which W. J. Loftie's *A History of London* (1883) locates in a text contemporary with Pepys's *Diary*. A poem praising one De Laune's *Present State of London*, published after the Great Fire (1666), includes this couplet:

> The Grandeur of this fam'd Metropolis,
> Arts, Laws, and Customs thou hast shewn in this. (Loftie 2.292)

Living and writing for himself in this crowded, busy, "fam'd Metropolis," Pepys the secretive diarist paradoxically exemplifies solitude in its unalloyed form. A kindred spirit of solitude runs through Defoe, who in *Serious Reflections during the Life and Surprising Adventures of Robinson Crusoe* writes,

> The World, I say, is nothing to us, but as it is more or less to our Relish: All Reflection is carry'd home, and our Dear-self is, in one Respect, the End of Living. Hence Man may be properly said to be alone in the Midst of the Crowds and Hurry of Men and Business: All the Reflections which he makes, are to himself; all that is pleasant, he embraces for himself; all that is irksome and grievous, is tasted but by his own Palat. (*Serious Reflections* 58)[4]

"All the Reflections which he makes," indeed, are to Pepys himself, living in the "Midst of the Crowds and Hurry of Men and Business." For this citizen of the "fam'd Metropolis," his "Dear-self" remains ever the supreme "End of Living." What he experiences in his daily life and records in his daily journal are not meant to be shared with others as

Erfahrung: they carry the value of *Erlebnis* reserved for his own exclusive rumination.

"To think that this was all my own"

Pepys the voice of the private sphere prefigures Defoe's Moll, who states her credo with superb succinctness: "As for me, my Business was his Money, and what I could make of him" (*Moll* 227). Likewise, Pepys foreshadows Roxana the savvy financier who regularly gives account of her financial worth—a private subject whose identity and self-esteem must first of all be anchored on her monetary possessions:

> I had fifty Thousand Pounds in my Pocket at least; nay, I had the Income of fifty Thousand Pounds; for I had 2500 *l.* a Year coming in, upon very good Land-Security, besides 3 or 4000 *l.* in Money, which I kept by me for ordinary Occasions, and besides Jewels and Plate, and Goods, which were worth near 5000 *l.* more. (*Roxana* 202)

Roxana's may be a "selfhood beyond public revelation," which "tends to negate the entire category of the public sphere" (Richetti 1999: 77), according to John Richetti. Numerical accountability of the self's possession, however, functions as the bond linking the private sphere to the public realm from which her money comes to her. Arguably, the legitimacy of the Navy Clerk's self-enrichment deserves to be cordoned off from the kept mistress's profit derived from her "six and twenty Years of Wickedness" (*Roxana* 188). However, among Pepys's adventurous contemporaries may be included "Robison Crusoe of York, mariner" (Pepys was born in 1633, Crusoe in 1632 [*Crusoe* 5]), whose untiring dedication to the business of survival on his island offers a comparable portrait of a private subject as an indefatigable *homo œconomicus*. Crusoe's private sphere, extreme and idealized as it is, is heavily and providentially mediated by the shipwreck which bequeaths to him, as the sole heir and executor, the ship's goods and materials. Amply provided, equipped, and armed, Crusoe turns himself into a one-man European civilization set up on a terra nullius. Without those valuable instruments the vessel was loaded with, his life would have been "solitary, poore, nasty, brutish, and short" (Hobbes 89), as Hobbes describes the "condition" of mankind in a natural state. Crusoe is more than aware of how much his private world owes to this initial supply of goods manufactured in advanced societies:

> I spent whole Hours, I may say whole Days, in representing to my self in the most lively Colours, how I must have acted, if I had got nothing out of the

> Ship. How I could not have so much as got any Food, except Fish and Turtles; and that as it was long before I found any of them, I must have perish'd first. That I should have liv'd, if I had not perish'd, like a meer Savage. That if I had kill'd a Goat, or a Fowl, by any Contrivance, I had no way to flea or open them, or part the Flesh from the Skin, and the Bowels, or to cut it up; but must gnaw it with my Teeth, and pull it with my Claws like a Beast. (*Crusoe* 111)

His solitary life is one that is fortified by society's goods. Without the well-packed ship, he would have had to lead the life of a "mere Savage." But the beauty of it all is that there are no competitors. His successful survival on the island owes itself to the absence of any Hobbesian war of rivalry in which the animosity of one individual against another is inevitably triggered by the passions of "Competition" and "Diffidence" (Hobbes 88) inherent in human nature. Crusoe enjoys, according to Ian Watt, "the absolute freedom from social restrictions for which Rousseau yearned" (Watt 86), which would have been inconceivable without a prior elimination of competition.

Armed with excellent means to subdue nature, and unhampered by rivals, in a matter of mere ten months or so, his handsome initial outlay grows into a secure estate development project unmolested by king, kith or kin:

> I descended a little on the Side of that delicious Vale, surveying it with a secret Kind of Pleasure . . . to think that this was all my own, that I was King and Lord of all this Country indefeasibly, and had a Right of Possession; and if I could convey it, I might have it in Inheritance, as compleatly as any Lord of a Mannor in *England*. (*Crusoe* 85)

The legality of his claim to an "indefeasible" right of possession may be a moot point from a strict legal point of view, or it may be a rhetorical ploy conferring legitimacy on himself through "a new order of words" (Braverman 12) matching his new world order. But Crusoe's property rights stand upon a more solid footing than Pepys's extra income over and above his salary, since it squarely fits into John Locke's justification of private property through private labour:

> Though the Earth, and all inferior Creatures be common to all Men, yet every Man has a *Property* in his own *Person*. This no Body has any Right to but himself. The *Labour* of his Body, and the *Work* of his Hands, we may say, are properly his. Whatsoever then he removes out of the State that Nature hath provided and left it in, he hath mixed his *Labour* with, and joyned to it something that is his own, and thereby makes it his *Property*. It being by him

> removed from the common state Nature placed it in, it hath by this *labour* something annexed to it, that excluded the common right of other Men. For this *Labour* being the unquestionable Property of the Labourer, no Man but he can have a right to what that is once joyned to, at least where there is enough, and as good left in common for others. (Locke 287-88)

Crusoe indeed exerts himself to employ his labour to remove turtles, goats, trees, and finally grain, "out of the State that Nature hath provided and left" them in. His labour is unquestionably the "Property of the Labourer" himself, for he is hired by no one, nor does he hire anyone else for most of the period of his sojourn in the island. To that extent he can claim his "Right of Possession" on what he has made and maintained. Nonetheless, the work of his hands is crucially dependant on the tools and goods from the ship, produced by other hands than his own.

If social mediation thus intrudes even into the snug privacy of Crusoe in the pastoral seclusion of his delectable island, all the more socially engendered must be the property Pepys makes his own from his busy work in a busy metropolis hemmed in by potential rivals everywhere, all of them as keen as Pepys to advance their private interests. The steadily increasing income Pepys delights to count as his own is inextricably implicated in public (sector) economy. The means of this increase could not be further removed from those acorns picked with no other mortals offering competition that Locke envisions as the perfect example of private property. Pepys in his diary registers the derivative, if not parasitical, relationship of the private to the public, one that illustrates the kind of "Machiavellian" crisis of public virtue, which in J. G. A. Pocock's analysis, entails the inevitable coupling of corruption with prosperity (Pocock 97-98). Pepys was no doubt serious about his work at the office, even as he was sincerely committed to maximizing personal gain. But all that dedication still left him with a sense of alienation from his work. In the expression, "quite tired with business and without joy in myself," quoted above, business in the abstract is opposed to his private self, as he cannot derive joy from his official work. Can life be fulfilling at all for a private subject dedicated to pursuing his economic benefit? This is a question with which both Pepys and Defoe were preoccupied in comparable ways.

"My stomach grew sick"

To measure the monetary wealth Pepys can put down as his own, he has to go through, like Roxana, the process of accounting and calculation. This mental procedure implies that what he owns cannot be grasped or felt as an immediate physical entity. It is an "ideal" or conceptual property, unlike Crusoe's goat meat. Pepys's monetary assets become tangible substance only when exchanged for concrete goods and service. Wealth as money, moreover, is insecure precisely due to its "liquidity," in contrast to Crusoe's island whose watery surrounding secures its "illiquid" existential status.[5] Pepys can take money home; others can take it away from him. In 1665, when he was enriching himself at a rapid rate, he hears one night some strange sounds coming from the ceiling of his house, which give him anxious shivers: "[K]nowing that I have a great sum of money in my house, this puts me into a most mighty affright, that for more then two hours I could not almost tell what to do or say, but feared this and that" (30 Jan 1665 [6.25]). His "great sum of money" can anytime cease to be his own, when some other hands take possession of them. One's body, however, is an inalienable private property which no one can rob. This idea furnishes Locke with a solid premise for his vindication of private property. "The *Labour* of his Body, and the *Work* of his Hands, we may say, are properly his," because his body is indubitably his. In the paragraph following the passage on acorn gathering quoted above, Locke asks a series of rhetorical questions intending to bring home his point:

> He that is nourished by the Acorns he pickt up under an Oak, or the Apples he gathered from the Trees in the Wood, has certainly appropriated them to himself. No Body can deny but the nourishment is his. I ask then, When did they begin to be his? When he digested? Or when he eat? Or when he boiled? Or when he brought them home? Or when he pickt them up? And 'tis plain, if the first gathering made them not his, nothing else could. (Locke 288)[6]

The unintended irony of this example is that you can make something your own, *pace* Locke, by the mere physical act of eating and digestion. The body, rather than the labour of gathering acorns from nature, can become the locus and basis of private appropriation. Let other bodies sweat to produce food from nature. The person who eats it enjoys it. Pepys's *Diary* is remarkable also for the faithful recording his bodily activity, which he can surely claim, like anyone else who is no slave, as his own indefeasibly.

Pepys's unique personal experience of bodily needs, forming the purest level of his private sphere, constitutes a genuine *Erlebnis* which no other body, by definition, can share. In 1660, when his body was relatively younger and fitter, Pepys retreats home after having gone up to Westminster Hall three times, worn out and bruised by fatigue: "I went home and got some Allum to my mouth, where I have the beginnings of a Cancre, and have also a plaster to my boyle underneath my chin" (9 Feb 1660 [1.48]). On the memorable occasion of the coronation day of Charles

II, he bears historic witness to posterity, having been present at Westminster Hall where the ceremony was taking place. Yet his private body pulls him away, charging him with a compelling call of nature that has to be obeyed instantly. "But I had so great a list to pisse," writes the diarist, "that I went out a little while before the King had done all his ceremonies and went round the abby to Westminster-hall, all the way within rayles, and 10000 people, with the ground covered with blue cloth—and Scaffolds all the way" (23 April 1661 [2.84-85]). Such naked somatic experience punctuates and punctures the private subject's relationship to the public world. Inserted in the middle of another entry full of public matters is his observation on the tolls his body paid that day to his sundry social duties, and how his farting served as a self-cure. By allowing himself "plenty of breaking of wind," his body is "now pretty well again, having had a constant akeing" in his back "these five or six days" (4 June 1664 [5.169]).

Novelists would shy away from mentioning such lowly physical activity which offers no erotic or sensational value, except for Joyce who reports Bloom's anal action and sound. During his long career of absolute privacy, Defoe's Crusoe never mentions his bowel activity. Page after page he relates his cooking and dietary regimen but never once his toilet problem, almost as if his body can miraculously dispense with excretory functions altogether. Something does come out of his body, however, at the sight of the leftover human flesh and bones on his island:

> I turn'd away my Face from the horrid Spectacle, my Stomach grew sick, and I was just at the Point of Fainting, when Nature discharg'd the Disorder from my Stomach; and having vomited with an uncommon Violence, I was a little reliev'd. (*Crusoe* 140)

The direction and the organ of discharge are important here: his vomiting does not involve his intestines and anus.[7] In Defoe's novel, the *Erlebnis* of Crusoe's unusual physical reaction contains an implicit *Erfahrung* of how cannibalism is physiologically repulsive. Pepys, writing for his own pleasure, gives voice to his body with no instructive covering, even going as far as to confer religious significance on his excrement: "Late to supper home; and to my great joy, I have by my wife's good advice almost brought myself, by going often and leisurely to the stool, that I am come almost to have my natural course of stool as well as ever, which I pray God continue to me" (11 Dec 1663 [4.414]). Scatology meets theology in this instance, but as a whole, "business" seems the resident genius that rules his intestines, as well as his brain. While on duty as a Navy clerk examining a Thames shipyard, he finds himself "much troubled with a sudden looseness," which gave him no quarter. "I went into a little alehouse at the end of Ratcliffe," he writes, "and did give a groat for a pot of ale and there I did shit" (8 Nov 1660 [1.287]). The timely discharge of bodily matter enables him to resume his activity as a Navy bureaucrat doing business at the shipyard in Ratcliff. In another entry, to the smooth flow of his urine is juxtaposed the influx of liquidity into his private coffers:

> All yesterday and today I have a great deal of pain in making water and in my back, which made me afeared. But it proved nothing but cold which I took yesterday night. All this morning making up my accounts, in which I counted that I have made myself now worth about 80*l*, at which my heart was glad and blessed God. (30 May 1660 [1.164])

The God blessed here seems a deity looking after the smooth circulation of private bodily fluids as well as cash. Theology, accounting, and physiology happily collaborate for the sake of the money-making private body, which is also a body that has to make water.

"I did make myself to do la cosa"

If my body is mine indefeasibly, my bodily activity should be so, too. Ideally, my money ought to be mine in such a naturalized, intimate, inalienable form. Yet for both my money and my body, alienation and discharge cannot be avoided, since mere accumulation or hoarding would by definition destroy the health of the owner. Moreover, just as my money obeys its impersonal logic of circulation, my body acts according to its own needs. "Troubled with sudden looseness," Pepys has to relieve himself; sensing "a great deal of pain in making water," he is beset by fear. The private self is patently not in full control of his body. Your body is yours but it also eludes your will. Such alterity inscribed on the body lies at the heart of La Mettrie's notion of "machine-man" (*l'homme machine*):

> When all the sphincters of the bladder, the rectum, etc. work; when the heart contracts more strongly than any other muscle; when the erector muscles make man's penis stand upright, like that of an animal, where it beats against its stomach, and even of a child, who is capable of an erection whenever that part is stimulated, surely all this happens mechanically? (La Mettrie 28)

Pepys the bureaucratic working machine has a body-machine that asserts its might through its organ of erection as well as its rectum. It makes its own distinct, disjunctive, and disturbing demand for sexual gratification, which cannot but depend on another body, even in autoeroticism in the form of a visual image of a stimulating object. Into the realm of the innermost privacy of the private subject, of its intimate erotic *Erlebnis*, public society makes its insidious intrusion as the cause and force of seduction.

Most scandalously, in the sacred premises of a church during Sunday afternoon service, Pepys worships not so much the Christian God as the pagan goddess of personified sexual drive. He had been enticed into the church building by spotting one "Mrs. Martin," one of his many sexual partners. As he enters the church, Mrs. Martin leaves it, but he is detained when he runs into an acquaintance of his, at whose pew he had to stay through the service, "much against my will." But his pursuit of pleasure continues despite the detention:

> I did entertain myself with my perspective glass up and down the church, by which I had the great pleasure of seeing and gazing a great many very fine women; and what with that and sleeping, I passed away the time till sermon was done; and then to Mrs. Martin and there stayed with her an hour or two, and there did what jo would with her. (26 May 1667 [8.236])

As the substitution of the English first-person pronoun with the Spanish "jo" indicates, the subject of sexual drive is a foreigner. The decent English-speaking subject wants to distance himself from the other lewd agent. This convergence of psychology with international politics becomes more protruding and shocking in an episode at the Queen's chapel, which he visits out of curiosity to see Charles II's (Portuguese) Catholic queen, Catherine of Braganza, attending Christmas-Eve mass there:

> The Queen was there and some ladies. But Lord, what an odde thing it was for me to be in a crowd of people, here a footman, there a beggar, here a fine lady, there a zealous poor papist, and here a Protestant, two or three together, come to see the show. I was afeared of my pocket being picked very much. But here I did make myself to do la cosa by mere imagination, mirando a jolie mosa and with my eyes open, which I never did before—and God forgive me for it, it being in the chapel. (24 Dec 1667 [8.588])

On this most memorable public site and moment of the Queen of England's public appearance, he avidly seeks to cater to his own private pleasure of sexual titillation and its successful culmination in ejaculation. The act itself is denoted in a random combination of Romance languages—Spanish and French—of the two great Catholic powers and antagonists of Protestant England. No less remarkable is the fluent transition from English to "Franglais or Spinglés" (Pooley 83), as in "to do la cosa by mere imagination," which at once mimics and blurs the political enmity at the level of official public sphere. This is achieved thanks to a handy self-division of the subject. In the formula, "I did make myself to do," the grammatical subject is bifurcated into the initiating and the reacting agencies, "I" against "myself." The wonderfully vivacious voyeur's "imagination" is his own, no doubt, as well as his ejaculating body machine. As such, the subject uses them to extract pleasure from his visual perception. Yet they serve the heretical interest of Eros, during Christian service, who commands the lower organ of his sexual body.

"Surely all this happens mechanically?" La Mettrie urges. Pepys, however, still wishes to preserve his "self" in the subject position, naughty and lascivious as that other self may be. But who or what is the subject of the verb "to do" in "I did make myself to do"? It cannot be exclusively the rational subject of perception attracted to the beautiful ladies but clearly aware of the public meaning of the time and place. If that were the case, the penitent reflection of "God forgive me for it" would be an instance of blatant cynicism, which goes against the impression the reader gathers from the diarist's reverential references to God, however lukewarm, as Claire Tomalin estimates (Tomalin 370), his faith may have been. Nor can it be attributed to some devil tormenting him regularly, for he writes that he himself made himself do the unmentionable thing. The divide, if any, between the respectable and the repressed selves seems easily sutured by "God forgive me for it," thanks to the ambiguities attendant on the "privatization of spirituality," which both Anglicanism and Puritanism "left unanswered" (Jagodzinski 43). Your right to commune with God in your privacy entails extracting handy pardon from Him. Pepys wears his faith lightly, indeed: he is no John Bunyan assaulted by the blasphemous Tempter nagging him to betray Christ.[8]

Pepys writes of his *Erlebnis* in a realm or domain derived but severed from the public sphere, yet he cannot share his experience as an *Erfahrung* with other subjects of his society. The masturbation at the chapel, being something experienced by him and no one else, and lacking any moral meaning, cannot be communicated to anyone else, except to himself through the act of writing. By means of keeping his journal, Roger Sharrock argues, Pepys "the double man recognizes his own doubleness," and gives to "the fleeting feelings left by momentary joys" a textual "substance that in life they could never have acquired." In this sense, he becomes "a writer without knowing it" (Sharrock 15). But this writing was never meant to be shared, for Pepys the diarist cares not—unlike John Evelyn, for instance—to write proper and presentable prose.[9] Evelyn writes a public obituary in his diary upon the death of his friend Pepys:

"This day died Mr. Sam. Pepys . . . none in England exceeding him in knowledge of the navy, in wch he had passed thro' all the most considerable offices. . . . He was universally belov'd, hospitable, generous, learned in many things, skill'd in music, a very great cherisher of learned men of whom he had the conversation" (Evelyn 165). During Pepys's lifetime not even his closest acquaintances knew that he had also been a "very great cherisher" of his secret diary.

If a private subject's first-person recounting (in a private journal) of his own errant deeds raises the question of the social, ethical, or religious significance of his personal experience, then such an accounting must do so all the more in the case of a self-conscious professional writer such as Defoe. "What's the point of writing it?" is a question that constantly haunts Defoe's fictional autobiographies of aberrant lives. His "garrulous autobiographers," as Richetti observes, "in effect silence other possible voices" (Richetti 1975: 56). In Defoe's narratives, that ceaseless private voice speaks from a private realm in a common, plain, and decodable language, though laden with moral ambiguity. Defoe, writing in long-hand for the world at large, has to assume *utile* as well as *dulce*, or simply, entertainment value, if *dulce* hardly pertains to his demotic narrators. Yet the status, nature, and character of *utile* are by no means clear, even in the relatively secure case of *Robinson Crusoe*. What knowledge does his adventure offer to the readers, who certainly can never be forced into similar conditions? As a manual for survival on a desert island, it is somewhat irresponsible, to say the least, for one has to have the good luck of being stranded offshore with a ship loaded with expensive cargo. The miraculously perennial sexiness of Roxana defies common sense, as does the invariably successful crimes of Moll. In these ladies' stories, it is never quite clear whether the implicit message is "do likewise" or "be warned by my example." Crusoe's case seems less dubious, as the reader can extract spiritual *Erfahrung* from the providential plot, aided by the narrator's regular religious musings garnished with Biblical references. Yet his is such an absolutely exceptional story that its allegorical value as a Christian homily cannot be large, even for the credulous first readers who accepted it as a true story. Spiritual autobiography, as G. A. Starr defines it, has to be "potentially edifying" to third parties "as a pattern to others" (Starr 33). To do so, a degree of applicability of the narrated event to the reader's life ought to be assumed. But in the case of *Robinson Crusoe*, the *Erfahrung* of counsel the book promises stumbles on the insuperable gap cutting off Crusoe's extraordinary *Erlebnis* from the rest of humanity. "When I came to *England*, I was as perfect a Stranger to all the World, as if I had never been known there" (*Crusoe* 234), remarks this man of extraordinary adventure upon his return to England. Reading *Robinson Crusoe*, like reading Pepys's *Diary*, is to share the *Erlebnis* of privacy, whose strangeness fascinates and estranges.

This brave new world of private sphere at the heart of a crowded commercial metropolis, of Pepys recording his daily life behind the locked doors of his study, is what Defoe sought to dramatize in his fiction. The chilling summary of Crusoe's married life after his repatriation strikes the keynote:

> In the mean time, I in Part settled my self here; for first of all I marry'd, and that not either to my Disadvantage or Dissatisfaction, and had three Children, two Sons and one Daughter: But my Wife dying, and my Nephew coming Home with good Success from a Voyage to *Spain*, my Inclination to go Abroad, and his Importunity prevailed and engag'd me to go in his Ship, as a private Trader to the *East Indies*. (*Crusoe* 256-57)

Inserted as a conditional phrase in a paragraph justifying his peculiar "Inclination to go Abroad," his unnamed wife is fetched off the moment she is introduced, almost in the same breath. We find a sharp rupture wedged into this conjugal conjunction, something the narrator hardly seems to regret. How far can the experience of the first-person narrator step beyond that self-same enclosure of private sphere in those narratives dealing with more complex social relationship? This question Defoe addresses in those subsequent "histories" of individuals following the suit of this striking tale of radical privacy.

CHAPTER TWO

PARATACTIC PROSAICS

"He which hath businesse"

Pepys's life as recorded in his journal is marked by a rapid pace of movement from action to action, from incident to incident, day after day. As the sentences inhabit the same paragraph and the paragraphs share the same entry, some common cord may be assumed to bind them together. Even so, they appear separate, disconnected, cumulative, and even outright disjunctive, adding up to a "paratactic parade of discrete items" (Berger 576). Such peculiar combination of congruence and incongruence, which the quotations in the previous chapter from his *Diary* amply demonstrate, attests to a supremely prosaic reaction to and representation of the modern metropolis, whose spirit is captured in the blunt, unmodified, un-articled noun "business," a word used most extensively by Pepys. Samuel Johnson's *Dictionary* takes the first example of *business* in the sense of "employment" from John Donne's verse, "Must business thee from hence remove?" (Johnson 94). The stanza in full from Donne's "Breake of Day," voicing the complaint of a lover unfortunate enough to be paired with a man of business, goes,

> Must businesse thee from hence remove?
> Oh, that's the worst disease of love,
> The poore, the foule, the false, love can
> Admit, but not the busied man.
> He which hath businesse, makes love, doth doe
> Such wrong, as when a maryed man doth wooe. (13-18)

Pepys fits snugly into this category of "busied man" making love while making money. Eros and business spirit, essentially incompatible in Donne's poem, also converge neatly in Defoe's *Moll Flanders* and *Roxana*. But before we enter into their world, let us first draft, with Simmel, a conceptual blueprint of a busy metropolis in terms of its velocity and temporality. Simmel states how the "dominance of the intellect" in a metropolitan psyche and "money economy" are inseparable as the two interrelated features of "a purely matter-of-fact attitude in dealing with men and with things" (Simmel 1997: 176). In *Philosophy of Money*, he deduces from this premise the change in the "pace" of life incurred by "money economy":

> The basic human trait of interpreting what is relative as an absolute conceals the transitory character of the relationship between an object and a specific amount of money and makes it appear as an objective and permanent relationship. This brings about disturbance and disorientation as soon as one link of the relationship changes. The alteration in what is active and passive is in no way immediately balanced by its psychological effects. When such changes occur the awareness of the economic processes in their previous stability is interrupted from every side and the difference between present and previous circumstances makes itself felt on every side. As long as the new adjustment does not occur, the increase in the quantity of money will cause a constant sense of disorder and psychic shocks, and will thus deepen the differences and the comparative disparity between current conceptions and thereby accelerate the pace of life. (Simmel 2004: 499)

Money creates literally the "busy-ness" of money-earners and money-spenders, by destabilizing previous order and value system, as the supremely relative value of money replaces absolute qualitative values, and as earlier equations are disrupted ceaselessly, creating "a constant sense of disorder" which "accelerate[s] the pace of life." Under the metropolitan condition dominated by such money economy, business for and in itself constitutes life activity, including the daily act of journal writing, written in a "busy" style of adding facts and items, without seeking to maintain "stability." One cannot stop writing a diary, just as one cannot stop earning and spending money. It is a symptom of and reaction to the "constant sense of disorder" and the ever accelerating pace of life. Pepys typically feels he ought to clear any arrears in his diary writing, because it forms part of his regular routine. "At night set myself to write down these three days' diary," he confesses to his journal, even as he hears "the noise of the chambers and other things of the Fireworkes, which are now playing upon the Thames before the King" (24 April 1661 [2.88]). Despite the public festivity taking place at the moment, he cannot see his journal being marred with unrecorded days.

The same spirit and style of business-like regularity dictates Crusoe in his tropical island to keep his journal, part of which repeats what has already been narrated:

> *Nov. 23.* My other Work having now stood still, because of my making

> these Tools; when they were finish'd, I went on, and working every Day, as my Strength and Time allow'd, I spent eighteen Days entirely in widening and deepening my Cave, that it might hold my Goods commodiously. . . .
>
> *Dec.* 11. This Day I went to Work with it ["my Cave"] accordingly, and got two Shores or Posts pitch'd upright to the Top, with two Pieces of Boards a-cross over each Post, this I finish'd the next Day; and setting more Posts up with Boards, in about a Week more I had the Roof secur'd; and the Posts standing in Rows, serv'd me for Partitions to part of my House. (*Crusoe* 64-65)

In this edited, fictional expression of diligent business ethos, made fit for publication, accretion of details linked by paratactic conjunction and parallel punctuations points to Crusoe's natural right of self-preservation, so that their lack of finesses matters less than their referential validity. More conspicuous in this lean format of journal is the largely factual "business" tone of Defoe's narrative, a tone which it shares with Pepys's *Diary*.

Crusoe records strictly the facts of his labour and of its laboriousness. Pepys records the facts of his labour and pleasure, but both decline to explore in depth the emotional or affective by-products of their busy activity. Such tight-lipped "matter-of-fact attitude" which asserts itself even on a desert island not only derives from the Protestant work ethic but belongs specifically to a busy city burgher's restless mentality. Pepys the self-made man pursues both business and pleasure with singular diligence, mingling one with the other whenever he can, even without leaving London, taking full advantage in one instance of the anonymity offered by city traffic:

> [A]bout 3 a-clock up and to dinner, and thence to the office, where Mrs. Burroughs my pretty widow was; and so I did her business and sent her away by agreement; and presently I by coach after her and took her up in Fanchurch-street—and away through the City, hiding my face as much as I could. But she being mighty pretty and well enough clad, I was not afeared; but only lest somebody shall see me and think me idle. I quite through with her, and so into the fields Uxbridge way, a mile or two beyond Tyburne, and then back, and then to Paddington, and then back to Lyssengreen, a place the coachman led me to . . . and there we eat and drank; and so back to Charing Cross and there I set her down—all the way most excellent pretty company. I had her lips as much as I would; and mighty pretty woman she is and very modest, and yet kind in all fair way. (12 July 1666 [7.204-5])

In the drowsy hours of afternoon, his energy is diverted and replenished by the "pretty widow" of a captain whose suit he takes care of, exacting a physical-erotic payment from her for his official service. The sentence merely states, "and sent her away by agreement," having no wish to specify how the widow reacted to his proposition. The prose moves on, after a hasty semicolon, "and presently I by coach after her," followed by another "and." A dash intervenes, with yet another "and," indicating perhaps the excitement of having the woman board the hired coach. Anxious he is to preserve his incognito, but his fears tellingly are of being considered "idle" by anyone who identifies him. After a brief tour around the outskirts of the City, reported with further simple sequential conjunction linked by "and then," another dash breaks the continuum to sum up the experience. Yet the next sentence reverts to the paratactic conjunction of "and," which begs the question of why a "mighty pretty woman and very modest" should not be "kind in all fair way," as the "and yet" connecting the final phrase seems to posit. Such "paratactic parade" is what Defoe's fictional prose profusely puts on show.

In the quotation above from Pepys's *Diary*, the journal writer's need for diversion is appeased and enhanced by the distraction offered by the city travel—from Fenchurch Street through the City to Tyburn through Paddington to Charing Cross—as well as by the yielding lips of his female companion. The unadorned addition of clauses and phrases in Pepys's account may carry whatever psychological reward he may be extracting in writing down what he did that day. Interestingly, however, even when writing for general readership, and for a purpose that lies at the furthest remove from the hedonistic private writing of Pepys, description of the city tends to be disjunctive, paratactic, and additive. Bunyan's *Pilgrim's Progress* surely is a work written with a solid wish to instruct, warn, and edify the reader. "Neither did I but vacant seasons spend / In this my Scribble; Nor did I intend / But to divert my self in doing this," professes the author in his verse "Apology for His Book" (Bunyan 2003: 3). In the main narrative, the most lethally dangerous stop for the pilgrims is the town of Vanity, where Christian's companion Faithful is martyred. Vanity is built around and dominated by its permanent Fair, whose scale and breath of business Bunyan suggests through a parataxis of enumeration, with nouns linked to one another by short-breathed commas:

> … [A]t *this Fair* are all such Merchandise sold, as Houses, Lands, Trades, Places, Honours, Preferments, Titles, Countreys, Kingdoms, Lusts, Pleasures, and Delights of all sorts, as Whores, Bauds, Wives, Husbands, Children, Masters, Servants, Lives, Blood, Bodies, Souls, Silver, Gold, Pearls, Precious Stones, and what not.
>
> And moreover, at this Fair there is at all times to be seen Juglings, Cheats, Games, Plays, Fools, Apes, Knaves, and Rogues, and that of all sorts.
>
> Here are to be seen too, and that for nothing, Thefts, Murders, Adultries,

False-swearers, and that of a blood-red colour.

And as in other Fairs of less moment, there are the several Rows and Streets under their proper names, where such and such Wares are vended: So here likewise, you have the proper Places, Rows, Streets, (*viz.* Countreys, and Kingdoms) where the Wares of this Fair are soonest to be found: Here is the *Britain* Row, the *French* Row, the *Italian* Row, the *Spanish* Row, the *German* Row, where several sorts of Vanities are to be sold. (Bunyan 2003: 86)

Vanity Fair presents to the pilgrims a baffling, daunting, overwhelming list of all that is conceivable in our earthly life, the intangible (e.g. "Delights") as well as the tangible (e.g. "Lands"), personal relationship (e.g. "Husbands") as well as impersonal objects (e.g. "Pearls"), all vended as merchandise to be had for money. Through its globalized collection of imported wares the Fair stands as an epitome of commercial civilization as such. The prose of *Pilgrim's Progress* comes to grips with the absolute manifold of the world in miniature displayed in Vanity Fair by employing a paratactic syntax of simple addition. Although an allegorical assessment of the town and its dangers attempts to pin down its meaning by giving morally transparent names such as "Vanity" and "Lusts," the imperfect closure of the paragraph with "and what not," followed by further list in the next paragraph ushered in by "And moreover," admits the impossibility of distilling the town's "essence" into a single unifying meaning. Even the overriding abstraction "Vanity" is transformed by this enumeration into a general countable noun of "Vanities" at the end of the final paragraph. Despite the firm religious conviction of the author and his devout pilgrims, the language of the text succumbs to the force of the overpowering list Vanity Fair boasts, in that it adopts a paratactic style affected and tainted by the town's distractions.

Can the pilgrims walking through a busy market town such as Vanity preserve spiritual integrity at all? Yes, if they direct their gaze upward away from the alluring objects. A major charge filed against the pilgrims by the town of Vanity has to do with their not making eye contacts with the attractive goods. Having "set very light by all their Wares," the pilgrims "cared not so much as to look upon them; and if they called upon them to buy, they would put their fingers in their ears . . . and look upwards, signifying that their Trade and Traffick was in Heaven" (Bunyan 2003: 87). The heavenly traffic of sacrificing your worldly desires to earn citizenship at the "Cœlestial City" (119) prescribes to the pilgrims a strict ban on sensory perceptions of hearing and seeing, which for most mundane subjects constitute the core of their lived experience (*Erlebnis*). For Bunyan, it is the religious experience of the spiritual subject that occupies the domain of *Erlebnis*, contained and controlled by the

Erfahrung of their spiritual pilgrimage as a whole. Yet for average humanity, unable and unwilling to forgo the pleasures of sight, the fascinating views a thriving city offers numb them into embracing its charm. Back in the first century of the first millennium, when the history of Christian struggle with worldly Vanity was being launched, we find a description of an eloquent surrender to the power of a Vanity Fair, in this instance that of Alexandria, to which the male protagonist-narrator of Achilles Tatius' *Leucippe and Clitophon* travels:

> . . . When I had advanced a few stades into the city, I reached the place named after Alexander, where I saw another city altogether. Its beauty was dissected as follows: a row of columns ran in a straight line, traversed by another of equal length. I divided my eyes between all the streets, an insatiable spectator incapable of taking in such beauty in its entirety. There were sights I saw, sights I aimed to see, sights I ached to see, sights I could not bear to miss . . . my gaze was overpowered by what I could see before me, but dragged away by what I anticipated. As I was guiding my own tour around all these streets, love-sick with the sight of it, I said to myself wearily: "We are beaten, my eyes!" (Achilles Tatius 77)

The eyes of the observer have been overpowered decisively. His prose loses its ground as it lets itself be carried off by the disorienting architecture of this city, by the wonders of this showcase city of Hellenistic era so striking and bold in comparison with the older cities such as Athens (Saïd 231). The paragraph is as "dissected" and "crisscrossed" as this pagan city devoted to worldly trade and traffic. Yet as the prose is focalized on the "insatiable spectator," the subject experiences a mixture of pain and pleasure, "love-sick with the sight of it," which is described as something similar to an *Erlebnis* of erotic shock produced by "sights I ached to see." If such was the dreaded potency of the earthly city's fascinating sights in late antiquity, then surely Bunyan's pilgrims passing through the modern town of Vanity did the wise thing to avert their eyes and look up to heaven.

Coming a generation after Bunyan, Defoe writes a prose which embodies the very dynamism and dangers of Vanity Fair, with little allegorical distance inserted to safeguard the subject's spiritual and bodily purity. "We are beaten, my eyes!" exclaims Achilles Tatius. "We avert our eyes to save our souls," proclaims Bunyan. "We are beaten, my eyes and my soul!" admits Defoe's fiction. But that defeat is transmuted into winning points for his prose. The city becomes an organic part of the narrative at its syntactic and thematic levels. The fatally captivating commercial city is what Defoe's prose, instead of evading or embellishing, vigorously inhabits, inspirits, and embodies, as we shall argue below. The absorbing first-person paratactic vitality of Defoe's style is closer to that of *Leucippe and Clitophon*, yet he also inherits the Puritan ethos of Bunyan which seeks to prevail over "the brilliant beauty" of Vanity Fair. The overwhelmed soul has not completely relinquished its defences against the city's sensual onslaught, which it counters through a breathless iteration of diffuse, distraught, decentered paratactic moves.

"And then took to my Heels, and run"

Not only the plot but the prose style itself of Defoe's fiction, apart from any consideration of its connection to the characteristics of the modern metropolis which London began to manifest in his times, adheres to the principle of what we propose to call "disjunctive conjunction."[1] Words, phrases, and clauses share the space of the same paragraph, which formally holds them together as a sequence or succession. Yet no logical order binds or places them in a hierarchy of significance or develops into an argument. The prose of Defoe's novels is supremely paratactic in principle, in contrast to his journalistic writing, whose persuasive power has to come from a hypotactic distribution of premise and corollary. Here we have a typical passage taken almost randomly from the huge world of Defoe's journalism:

> If there is a necessity for a War with the Dutch, I am sorry for that unhappy Circumstance; but without entring into a Dispute of the Fact, my Draught of the Consequences lies as a Caution to all Parties to consider, with the utmost Seriousness, what that Necessity is, and if possible to remove those Causes, which bring that Necessity on; for if the Effects of a Dutch War are as before, we ought to be very well satisfy'd, that our Reasons for it are of sufficient Weight to balance all the Evils that follow. (*The Danger and Consequences of a War with the Dutch*, *Political and Economic Writings of Daniel Defoe* [hereafter *PEW*] 5.264)

Sentences here are held together by the logical conjunctions of "if" and "for," with the concessionary participle of "without entering" and modifying insertions such as "with the utmost Seriousness" defending the thesis against anticipated objections. The prose appeals to our rational reflective faculty, without seeking to stir up our fear of war's carnage with graphic descriptions. But the reader of the following account of Crusoe's miraculous survival receives no encouragement to take part in a sober debate about the sagacity of the man's action or the plausibility of his account:

> The Wave that came upon me again, buried me at once 20 or 30 Foot deep in its own Body; and I could feel my self carried with a mighty Force and Swiftness towards the Shore a very great Way; but I held my Breath, and assisted my self to swim still forward with all my Might. I was ready to burst with holding my Breath, when, as I felt my self rising up, so to my immediate Relief, I found my Head and Hands shoot out above the Surface of the Water; and tho' it was not two Seconds of Time that I could keep my self so, yet it reliev'd me greatly, gave me Breath and new Courage. I was covered again with Water a good while, but not so long but I held it out; and finding the Water had spent it self, and began to return, I strook forward against the Return of the Waves, and felt Ground again with my Feet. I stood still a few Moments to recover Breath, and till the Water went from me, and then took to my Heels, and run with what Strength I had farther towards the Shore. But neither would this deliver me from the Fury of the Sea, which came pouring in after me again, and twice more I was lifted up by the Waves, and carried forwards as before, the Shore being very flat. (*Crusoe* 40)

The breathless pace of the prose's forward movement captures the danger, uncertainty, and hazard of Crusoe's condition. The "moment" of the occurrence is conveyed in the "median past tense" invented by early journalism to combine "continuity with recentness," as Lennard J. Davis argues (Davis 73). But unlike Defoe's journalist prose, the rushing tide of "recentness" erupts almost breathlessly into a paratactic conjunction of clauses succeeding one another. The only notably hypotactic connection would be, "I was ready to burst . . . when, as I felt my self rising up," but even here, the temporal order of linear movement flows on uninterrupted, leaving no breathing space for reflection or contemplation. What we see here is a quiet, unnoticed revolution in English prose liberating it from the classical model of hypotactic period in depicting dynamic or violent action: a stylistic counterpart to the Glorious Revolution, as it were, in fiction writing,[2] bearing the seeds of the action-filled parataxis which proliferated in the later centuries, particularly in twentieth-century American literature.

If comparing fiction with non-fiction (even though this is a distinction that held no stable authority in Defoe's age) is not the most felicitous way to contrast parataxis with hypotaxis, then we can place the above passage from *Robinson Crusoe* next to a narration of a similar dramatic change of fortune in Aphra Behn's *Oroonoko*. Oroonoko, the African warrior and prince, is enticed by an English captain to come to his ship on a courtesy visit. Having boarded the ship with his followers, unawares of the trap set up to catch him, Oroonoko loses his glorious independence for good:

> The prince, having drunk hard of punch, and several sorts of wine, as did all

> the rest . . . was very merry and in great admiration of the ship, for he had never been in one before, so that he was curious of beholding every place where he decently might descend. The rest, no less curious, who were not quite overcome with drinking, rambled at their pleasure fore and aft, as their fancies guided 'em. So that the captain, who had well laid his design before, gave the word and seized on all his guests, they clapping great irons suddenly on the prince, when he was leaped down in the hold to view that part of the vessel, and locking him fast down, secured him. (Behn 1994: 33-34)

The rhythm of prose in this account moves at a rapid pace from Oroonoko's drunkenness to his being captured. The predominance of comma, the paratactic punctuation par excellence, is also noticeable. Behn's commas, however, arrest the narration to insert explanatory remarks in subordinate positions ("The rest, no less curious, who were"). Along with the frequent appearance of relative pronouns and relative adverbs, the explanatory mission of Behn's commas bespeaks a hypotactic style designed to construct a vertical hierarchy of significance rather than placing the clauses on the same plane of parallelism as in "and till the Water went from me, and then took to me Heels, and run with what Strength I had" in the passage from Defoe.

The paratactic style of Defoe's fiction as first deployed in *Robinson Crusoe* lends itself wonderfully to a representation of experience as a momentary shock (*Erlebnis*), whose immediacy is charted in a factual language disjoined from contemplation. Reflection does come later, as Crusoe ponders on God's providential benevolence of having preserved his life thus. But the main strength of *Robinson Crusoe* as a narrative, the secret of its phenomenal success as a publishing venture which allured the readers to willingly suspend their disbelief, owes a great deal to the paratactic force of the passages such as the one quoted above. That its forte lies in the flow of conjunction, and not simply in a matter-of-fact attitude implicit in the style, can be illustrated by juxtaposing it with a "real" travelogue of seafaring adventures, such as William Dampier's *A New Voyage Round the World* (1697). Dampier describes his crew's coping with rough winds somewhere around the coast of Panama and Guatemala:

> In this extremity we put right before the Wind, every Canoe's Crew making what shift they could to avoid the threatening Danger. The small Canoes, being mostly light and buoyant, mounted nimbly over the Surges, but the great heavy Canoes lay like Logs in the Sea, ready to be swallowed by very foaming Billow. Some of our Canoes were half full of Water, yet kept two Men constantly heaving it out. The fierceness of the Wind continued about half an hour and abated by degrees, and as the Wind died away, so the fury of the Sea abated. For in all hot Countries, as I have observed, the Sea is soon

> raised by the Wind and as soon down again when the Wind is gone. Therefore there is a Proverb among Seamen: Up Wind, Up Sea, Down Wind, Down Sea. (Dampier 115)

The difference between the parataxis of the two texts—for the latter is even more laconic and terse in supplementing the main clauses of the sentences (the "small Canoes, being mostly light and buoyant" is a typical example) than Defoe's narration of Crusoe's plight—has to do with the temporality or rhythm of punctuation. Whereas Defoe's clauses tend to run on and over, jumping over and overriding closure with semicolons, Dampier cuts off one sentence from another with full stops. This allows him to size up the significance of the incident for nautical scientific wisdom. Dampier's adventure, in sum, is packaged as *Erfahrung* of a seasoned mariner's expertise. Crusoe's desperate plight, however, can yield no practical maxim for the reader's benefit, otherwise than the spiritual lessons extracted retrospectively. Defoe's main intention is not to offer a manual for survival under such circumstances. Instead, he captures experience in its immediacy of *Erlebnis*, in all its striking, singular, inexplicable uniqueness. Its moral significance slips past clauses and sentences, to be gathered many pages after, if at all, but not available in the flow of the prose depicting the critical moment and marching onwards with its parallel conjunctions. Similarly, in Defoe's *Captain Singleton*, which is more professionally nautical than *Robinson Crusoe*, fearful weather in the open seas is described in a run-on prose to highlight the fear itself, rather than to offer counsel on how to cope with the danger:

> [T]he Shock of the Air which the Fracture in the Clouds made, was such, that our Ship shook as when a Broadside is fired, and her Motion being check'd as it were at once by a Repulse superior to the Force that gave her Way before, the Sails all flew back in a Moment, and the Ship lay, as we might truly say, Thunder-struck. As the Blast from the Clouds was so very near us, it was but a few Moments after the Flash, that the terriblest Clap of Thunder followed that was ever heard by Mortals. I firmly believe a Blast of a Hundred Thousand Barrels of gunpower could not have been greater to our Hearing; nay indeed, to some of our Men it took away their Hearing. (*Singleton* 162)

The counterpart in the Dampier passage to this detailed, vivid account would be the single clause, "we had a Tornado from the shore, with much Thunder, Lightning, Rain and such a gust of Wind that we were all likely to be foundered," which in Defoe's hand is inflated into an abundance of sensory comparisons accentuating its effect ("as when a Broadside is fired"). The emphasis falls on the eyewitness experience of the narrator ("I firmly believe"), on the authority of *Erlebnis* rather than that of a seafarer's *Erfahrung*.

Crusoe's adventure belongs to an absolutely exceptional category, even measured by the standards of easily inflatable sailors' yarns, whether fictional (*Captain Singleton*) or "real" (Dampier). Few mortals can go through what happened to him. For the rest of humanity living in crammed society, the sheer complexity of human relationship demands a minimal coupling of reflection with action in whatever they do. Such is the circumstance of Moll, as yet called "Betty," and living as a resident companion of the daughters of a well-to-do Colchester family. The first tribulation of her life assumes the curious yet painful form of being torn between two infatuated brothers. To the elder she has already yielded her virginity, but the younger, not knowing this, wishes to marry her.

> I was now in dreadful Condition indeed, and now I repented heartily my easiness with the eldest Brother, not from any Reflection of Conscience, but from a View of the Happiness I might have enjoy'd, and had now made impossible; for tho' I had no great Scruples of Conscience . . . yet I could not think of being a Whore to one Brother, and a Wife to the other; but then it came into my Thoughts, that the first Brother had promis'd to make me his Wife, when he came to his Estate; but I presently remember'd what I had often thought of, that he had never spoken a Word of having me for a Wife, after he had Conquer'd me for a Mistress; and indeed till now, tho' I said I thought of it often, yet it gave me no Disturbance at all, for as he did not seem in the least to lessen his Affection to me, so neither did he lessen his Bounty, tho' he had the Discretion himself to desire me not to lay out a Penny of what he gave me in Cloaths, or to make the least show Extraordinary. (*Moll* 31)

This is surely an artificially concocted situation, almost theatrical in having two brothers love her simultaneously, with one knowing not that the other has taken her chastity clandestinely. Yet it sounds convincing thanks to the force of its presentation, which imitates her own confused wavering state of mind, whetted by the first brother's sugary words and his "Bounty." It displays a good example of psychological realism through the excessively repeated usage of "but" and "yet" demonstrating the dizzy oscillation of her mind between impossible options. The parallel, paratactic juxtaposition of competing considerations are held together by these adverse conjunctions, as well as by the conceding conjunction of "tho' I said," with the semicolon doing duty as the separating link between clauses. As Watt suggests, "such complete disregard of normal stylistic considerations—repetitions and parentheses, the unpremeditated and sometimes stumbling rhythm, the long and involved sequences of coordinated clauses"—keeps us "very close to the consciousness of Moll" (Watt 101). The artless non-decorous prose style of the passage illustrates her consciousness burdened by the "Scruples of Conscience," whose inability to close off and finalize this long sentence, however, dramatizes the urgency of *Erlebnis* prevailing over moralizing voices of *Erfahrung*.

Yet Moll-Betty's diffuse reflection maintains a balance of sorts, precarious as it is, since neither the logic of passionate "Affection" nor of sober "Discretion" holds unchallenged sway over her desire. If rational calculation of her "Happiness," not to speak of Christian morality, has no clear dominion over her mind, nor does pagan Eros retain full control. The relatively lukewarm tone of Moll-Betty's description of her infatuation, as well as its distinctive paratactic disjunction, can be contrasted to that of Aphra Behn's Sylvia in *Love-Letters between a Nobleman and His Sister* (1684-87). In this longest epistolary novel in English before *Pamela*, Sylvia the female protagonist is keen to lose her virginity to her brother-in-law Philander, for the torment of desire has reached such an intolerable pitch as to subdue all other sensible considerations:

> To wish was such a fault, as is a crime unpardonable to own; to shew desire is such a sin in virtue as much to deserve reproach from all the world; but I, unlucky I, have not only betrayed all these, but with a transport void of sense and shame, I yield to thy arms—I'll not endure the thought—by heaven! I cannot; there is something more than rage that animates that thought: some magic spell, that in the midst of all my sense of shame keeps me from true repentance. (Behn 1987: 60)

Erotic entanglement here is as incestuous and scandalous as in the case of the Colchester brothers lusting after Moll-Betty, yet it is given a more blatantly comic twist, for what she refers to is Philander's impotence, his failure to consummate intercourse in his first attempt. The dash after "I yield to thy arms" and before "by heaven" marks literally the failure of his virility. Philander would make ample amends for his first breach of conduct later, yet his female author chooses to humiliate him first, before awarding him his beautiful sister-in-law. The additive style matches the tantalizing incident, creating a parataxis linked by semicolons. The syntax, however, retains its balance, with parallels balancing each other ("To wish" by "to shew," "something more" by "some magic spell"). The oratorical tone of Sylvia's letter, as a whole, registers a different melody from that factual and grating prose of *Moll Flanders*. Moll-Betty is preoccupied, even in the throes of love torment, with the mundane problem of fancy clothes the elder brother bought her and how to use them without being suspected, a far cry indeed from the formulaic outburst of "unknown shameful flame" and "transport void of sense" of Sylvia's letter.

"More pleas'd with the Moral, than the Fable"

Defoe's parataxis, low-temperature and low-key compared with Behn's, is loaded with concerns over material (rather than purely erotic) interests. It subscribes to an economic realism that recognizes the claims of sensation but also discounts its autonomous value by measuring sensual *Erlebnis* against the tangible, durable, convertible profit it yields. Defoe rarely depicts sexual experience in detail, even when it resides at the heart of the plot's action. Moll-Betty's account of her first crucial intercourse with the elder brother suggests she was influenced as much by the material charms of the man's cash as by his "person":

> My Colour came, and went, at the Sight of the Purse, and with the fire of his Proposal together; so that I could not say a Word, and he easily perceiv'd it; so putting the Purse into my Bosom, I made no more Resistance to him, but let him do just what he pleas'd; and as often as he pleas'd; and thus I finish'd my own Destruction at once, for form this Day, being forsaken of my Vertue, and my Modesty, I had nothing of Value left to recommend me, either to God's Blessing, or Man's Assistance. (*Moll* 28-29)

The seducer's purse, thrust into her maiden bosom, rather than his physical organ, seems the main agent of ravishment, according to the syntactic sequence of clauses. Moreover, the owner of the ravished body seems strangely detached from herself, as she "let[s] him do just what he pleas'd." Such self-alienation gives lie to her later protest that her "Affection" cannot be traded for money, which we shall discuss in the next chapter. The dull impersonality of the "Sight of the Purse" already harbors the possibility of ceaseless substitution of human agency, whose potency is anchored on the power of purse. Similarly, sexual service plays an absolutely essential role in Roxana's rise in fortune, but she has little to say about the act itself, as in the following report of how she came to be the kept mistress of a German prince in Paris:

> It is only a loose Habit, My Lord, *said I*, that I may the better wait on *your Highness*; he pulls me to him; You are perfectly obliging, *says he*, and sitting on the Bed-side, *says he*, Now you shall be a Princess, and know what it is to oblige the gratefullest Man alive; and with that, he took me in his Arms,—I can go farther in the Particulars of what pass'd at the time, but it ended in this, that, in short, I lay with him all Night. (*Roxana* 64)

Defoe is an anti-pornographer in that he obdurately refrains from conveying the excitement of sexual *Erlebnis* to the reader.[3] This silence the narrator compensates for by elaborating on how she was treated indeed like a princess in terms of the material "Bounty" from the prince. "As he lov'd like a Prince, so he rewarded like a Prince" (*Roxana* 70), she states. Such transvaluation of the immediate physical experience eschews the conventional requirement to draw worthy moral lessons from it. Keeping distance from sensuous *Erlebnis* does not automatically serve the interest of *Erfahrung*, because the intermediary realm of economic exchange, which speaks an amoral language of numbers, proffers ready answer to the complexities of personal decisions. That the prince's "Bounty" was princely silences all potentially disquieting questions.

Before we reach that destination, we have to deal with the noticeable use of moralizing remarks in Defoe's novels, which gestures towards an *Erfarhung* that purports to frame the illicit deeds of the protagonists into a casuistic religious order of signification. Stories had been told to illustrate moral dictum even before the "rise of the novel," of course. But then there is no guarantee that the intended meaning will be transparent or unambiguous, however short and succinct they may be, as Aesop's Fables or the Biblical stories would readily corroborate. In a longer extensive narrative depicting contemporary life, the danger of the author's intention being elided by the tale becomes almost chronic. Bunyan's *Pilgrim's Progress*, protected as it is by its allegorical framework, fares relatively well in controlling the "lessons" its episodes are meant to communicate. Even here, however, the dramatic interest of the narrative threatens to exceed the discursive interest of the narrator-dreamer's homily, particularly in the Second Part, where a victorious and violent campaign against the foes of Christian pilgrims is conducted by the muscular guides of Christiana and her group. Mr. Great-heart, as "Women and Children stood trembling" on the sideline, fights "Maull a Gyant" in a mortal battle, after a brief parley stating his complaints against the villain who "did use to spoyl young Pilgrims with Sophistry" (Bunyan 2003: 229):

> When they had rested them, and taken breath, they both fell to it again, and Mr. *Great-heart* with a full blow fetch'd the *Giant* down to the ground. Nay hold, and let me recover, quoth he. So Mr. *Great-heart* fairly let him get up; So to it they went again; and the *Giant* mist but little of all-to-breaking Mr. *Great-heart*'s Scull with his Club.
>
> Mr. *Great-heart* seeing that, runs to him in the full heat of his Spirit, and pierceth him under the fifth rib; with that the *Giant* began to faint, and could hold up his Club no longer. Then Mr. *Great-heart* seconded his blow, and smit the head of the *Giant* from his shoulders. Then the Women and Children rejoiced, and Mr. *Great-heart* also praised God, for the deliverance he had wrought. (Bunyan 2003: 229-30)

The details of the scuffle, almost gratuitous, are released from their allegorical mission, as no marginal notes refer them back to relevant passages in the Bible. Great-heart's aiming at the Giant's "fifth rib" carries no numerological significance. Nor does the brute violence of his "blow" belong to a realm superior to his opponent's brandishing of "his Club." Great-heart surely finishes by praising God, but the syntax of "and Mr. *Great-heart* also praised God" seems to hint that it is almost a retroactive act following the relieved onlookers' reaction. The scene no doubt assures the readers of the inevitable triumph of the righteous over God's foes, yet the thrill of the depicted action eludes such theological overdrive.

The rupture between narrative and narrator becomes all the more glaring when the protagonist happens to be an outright reprobate. Bunyan's *The Life and Death of Mr Badman* intends to warn through a negative example. But the problem is that on this side of the grave, no divine justice seems to punish his heinous deeds. Badman entices into marriage a "godly" and well-endowed maiden by dissembling piety. The moment he secures her property through wedlock, he instantly ignores her and goes back to his life of debauchery with impunity, even to the point of inviting his girlfriends home. Bunyan seeks to contain the unruly narrative of Badman's profanity by an ongoing dialogue between the narrator "Wiseman" and "Attentive," the model reader-auditor. Inevitably, questions are raised by the latter, not all of which are met with satisfactory answers. "Attentive" asks whether Badman was subjected to "the wonderfull Judgment of God" at all. "Wiseman" can only give a roundabout response:

> You may be sure that they shall have Judgment to the full for all these things, when the day of Judgment is come. But as for Judgment upon them in this life, it doth not always come, no not upon those that are worthy thereof. *They that tempt God are delivered, and they that work wickedness are set up*: But they are reserved to the day of wrath, and then for their wickedness, God will repay them to their faces. (Bunyan 1988: 452)

Unaffected by such faith in God's ultimate retribution, the narrative of Badman follows his life all the way to his deathbed. With no notable punishment visited on him, he remains unrepentant to the very end and dies a natural death. Defoe's "Badman," or rather Badwomen, raises a stronger doubt as to the dispensation of justice, divine or secular, for they prosper excessively and often implausibly. "Roxana is more or less caught between the positions of Moll Flanders and Mr. Badman," observes Starr. "Roxana is in fact more like Mr. Badman, for she really does harden into final impenitency" and "the force of her moralizing is seriously impaired by her essential similarity to Mr. Badman" (Starr 164). We may add, in agreeing with him, that the difference between Moll and Roxana is rather negligible.

Moral ambiguity is what novels cannot be immune from. Of those fiction writers coming after Defoe, no one was more firmly committed than Samuel Richardson to preach as well as to entertain. Whatever the motives may have been that led this prudish, prudent, and proud printer-businessman to impersonate a young maiden voice and indulge in literary transvestitism in writing *Pamela*, he professes a clear confidence about the narrative's moral value, as in this final note of the "Editor":

> Let the *desponding Heart* be comforted by the happy Issue which the Troubles and Trials of the lovely PAMELA met with, when they see, in her Case, that no Danger nor Distress, however inevitable or deep to their Apprehensions, can be out of the Power of Providence to obviate or relieve; and which, as in various Instances in her Story, can turn the most seemingly grievous Things to its own Glory, and the Reward of suffering Innocence. (Richardson 501)

Yet the reader cannot help being titillated by the author's vivid descriptions of Pamela's "Danger" and "Distress," which may enhance our sense of the "Power of Providence" that overturns them into blessing, but which also ignites the reader's sensory, if not sensual, curiosity. The force of *Pamela* as a narrative fiction has as much to do with a sense of immediacy of *Erlebnis*, as with the secondary spiritual significance of *Erfahrung* the sensational details are meant to yield. The former exceeds the latter, as in the episode of Pamela's contriving the best means to escape from Mr. B's Lincolnshire country house. In dramatizing her desperation, the narrative peeps into the more intimate items of the young girl's clothing:

> So what will I do, but strip off my upper Petticoat, and throw it into the Pond, with my Neck-handkerchief; for, to be sure, when they miss me, they will go to the Pond first, thinking I have drowned myself; and so, when they see some of my Cloaths floating there, they will be all employ'd in dragging the Pond, which is a very large one; and as I shall not, perhaps be miss'd till the Morning, this will give me Opportunity to get a great way off; and I am sure I will run for it when I am out. And so, I trust, that God will direct my Steps to some good Place of Safety. (Richardson 169)

Petticoat and neck-handkerchief correspond to panties and bra in current sartorial language. They are not just "some of my Cloaths" but intimate clothing representing her female sexuality itself. Yet Richardson the author seems blissfully (or self-deceptively?) unaware of the erotic tension these details create, as the prose moves unperturbed into mentioning God's protection, after a paratactic "And so." The narrative glides seamlessly from petticoat to God. Such belief in the possibility of instant transference from the mundane to the transcendental forms a major component of the Puritan tradition which Richardson inherits. Dean Swift, coming from the opposite camp, with a full view of the latent conflict between a narrative and its putative "moral," has his Gulliver, after reporting how he dealt with his toilet problem in Brobdingnag, make an apology for his tale. He begs the reader's indulgence in the name of science rather than religion:

> I hope, the gentle Reader will excuse me for dwelling on these and the like Particulars; which however insignificant they may appear to groveling vulgar Minds, yet all certainly help a Philosopher to enlarge his Thoughts and Imagination, and apply them to the Benefit of publick as well as private Life. (Swift 2005: 85)

Richardson certainly is more self-assured and earnest than Swift, but the burden of having to "excuse" himself "for dwelling" on vulgar "Particulars" cannot be exempted, unless mere entertainment for its own sake is what *Pamela; or, Virtue Rewarded* is content to purvey, which surely is not the case as the very subtitle of the work proclaims.

This brief excursion to works before and after Defoe's fictional autobiographies prepares us to ask the same question of what "excuse" the narratives can submit to justify the morally reprehensible "Troubles and Trials" of Moll or Roxana, who can hardly claim to have exemplified "virtue rewarded." Not surprisingly, *Moll Flanders* comes with a relatively long five-page preface (compared with the single-page, five-paragraph preface to *Robinson Crusoe*), which takes pains to exonerate the work from the possible charge of promoting vice through a sensational memoir of a morally dubious character:

> But as this Work is chiefly recommended to those who know how to Read it, and how to make the good Uses of it, which the Story all along recommends to them; so it is to be hop'd that such Readers will be much more pleas'd with the Moral, than the Fable; with the Application, than with the Relation, and with the End of the Writer, than with the Life of the Person written of. (*Moll* 2)

The responsibility of making the right sense of the tale is passed on to the reader, who is supposed to have mastered the art of making "good Uses of it," i.e. withstanding the diversion and seduction of the "Fable" or the "Relation" to distill the "Moral" or "Application" from it. In this formulation, such proper use entails an interpretive reconstruction of the

"End of the Writer" from the "Life of the Person written of." The last point is further complicated by the fact that the "Writer" and the "Person written of" are nominally identical in this first-person narrative. Of course, the retrospective mode of the writer's looking back on her life in her advanced age gives her ample space to append penitent reflections, which indeed are not absent in the narrative. Yet the main thrust of the "Relation" consists in the sheer force of psychological immediacy, of its *Erlebnis* conveyed in a prose style of disjunctive conjunction, rather than the mediated lesson of moral sense derived from its putative *Erfahrung* neatly encased in sonorous but trite adages. Take, for example, what ought to be the most dramatic moment of her life, when she is given a last-minute reprieve at Newgate. She watches her less fortunate fellow inmates carried off to their last stop in this life:

> [A]ll this while I was seiz'd with a fit of trembling, as much as I cou'd have been, if I had been in the same Condition, as to be sure the Day before I expected to be; I was so violently agitated by this Surprising Fit, that I shook as if it had been in the cold Fit of an Ague; so that I could not speak or look, but like one Distracted: As soon as they were all put into the Carts and gone, which however I had not Courage enough to see, *I say*, as soon as they were gone, I fell into a fit of crying involuntarily, and without Design, but as a meer Distemper, and yet so violent, and it held me so long, that I knew not what Course to take, nor could I stop, or put a Checque to it, no not with all the Strength and Courage I had. (*Moll* 292)

The "I" that relates her experience appeals to the reader's sensation, so that the value of her conversion for the reader is vouchsafed by the vividness of *Erlebnis*, with all the shock and inexplicable momentary spasm besetting Moll, whose turbulence is captured and represented by parataxis glued together by semicolons and the conjunctions "and" or "so that." Whether the sagacious reader would make "good Uses" of this narration can never be ascertained, whereas readers of all qualifications can share or at least sympathize with her "fit of trembling" and her melting tears. In this almost clinical terrain of "Distemper" besetting her body, little is left for legal assessment of her pardon, much less for theological examination of divine dispensation which chose to save her neck. The narrative nudges the reader to greet her with imaginative sympathy, instead of questioning the justice of the incident.

Moll the character regularly appeals to the reader's common sense, in explaining how she came to be a pickpocket preying on the London crowd: "I was reducing my Living so I sold off most of my Goods, which put a little Money in my Pocket, and I liv'd near a Year upon that, spending very sparingly, and eeking things out to the utmost; but still when I look'd before me, my very Heart would sink within me at the inevitable approach of Misery and Want." Yet the dubious plea (for crime is not the inevitable answer to poverty), presented in a typically additive paratactic syntax, is instantly supplemented by an invocation of desperate mental state induced by "Misery and Want":

> O let none read this part without seriously reflecting on the Circumstances of a desolate State, and how they would grapple with meer want of Friends and want of Bread; it will certainly make them think not of sparing what they have only, but of looking up to Heaven for support, and of the wise Man's Prayer, *Give me not Poverty least I Steal.* (*Moll* 191)

A generalizing dictum comes to round off the passage, whose moral message is heavily ambiguous to the point of being almost cynical. But unaffected by ambiguity is the reader's imagination of the "desolate State" Moll was placed in, which can be summoned as a sympathetic witness defending her against moral censure. An emotional community may be secured on the basis of shared sensation of misery, yet the lesson to be drawn from it remains problematic, for poverty rather than stealing becomes the real offender tempting humanity to fall from heavenly grace. What can be shared as common experience (*Erfahrung*) depends on the acceptance of Moll's individual fear of poverty of which she had vivid experience (*Erlebnis*), rather than on a shared sense of morality or justice.

Poverty surely is an ogre fearful enough to turn the readers to side not only with Moll, but with Roxana as well, at least in the earlier phase of the latter's being left to her own devices after the sudden disappearance of her spendthrift husband. "I might appeal to any that has had any Experience of the World, whether one so entirely destitute as I was, of all manner of all Helps, or Friends, either to support me, or to assist me to support myself, could withstand the Proposal." Thus explains Roxana how she came to take the first step into her career as kept mistress. Yet knowing clearly how the "Experience of the World" in itself can by no means serve as solid premise supporting her decision, she goes on to add, "not that I plead this as a Justification of my Conduct, but that it may move the Pity, even of those that abhor the Crime" (*Roxana* 39). Can pity come to her defence, however? Pity being a reflective moral sentiment, one needs better proof of her having had no other choice than to prostitute her body. A second excuse, in the next paragraph, is drawn from a realm relatively free from moral estimation of conducts:

> Besides this, I was young, handsome, and with all the Mortifications I had

> met with, was vain, and that not a little; and as it was a new thing, so it was a pleasant thing, to be courted, caress'd, embrac'd, and high Professions of Affection made to me by a Man so agreeable, and so able to do me good. (*Roxana* 39)

When all other arguments fail, the pleasing sensation of being "courted, caress'd, embrac'd" and flattered can still hold ground as a probable rationale of her succumbing to temptation. Once again, it is the logic of *Erlebnis* rather than the "Experience of the World" shared by the public at large, the *Erfahrung* of the many who lack the special charm and attraction Roxana is endowed with.

Roxana as a narrative, by giving up trying to attach moral values to each of the protagonist's actions, maximizes literary-artistic profit of engrossing the reader's sensation and suspending his moral scruple. However, as we have seen earlier, offering erotic titillation is far from the objective of the novel. The immediacy of the first-person narrator's lived experience needs to be offset, therefore, by a more mediated reflective discourse that gives sense to the "whoredom" of the protagonist. Most interestingly, or almost scandalously, Defoe activates a numerical valuation in lieu of ethical validation. Whatever the moral or religious implications of her deeds may be, the main bulk of Roxana's story is taken up by the growth economy of her "prosperous Wickedness" (*Roxana* 106). She thrives financially and her wealth increases at a marvelous rate. She tells the reader after her relationship with the German prince is terminated that she "was grown not only well supply'd, but Rich, and not only Rich, but was very Rich; in a word, richer than I knew how to think of" (110). The economy of Roxana's expanding wealth will be examined in greater detail in the next chapter, but the peculiar rhetorical strategy in her narrative of mixing monetary accounting into verbal narration can be underlined here. For instance, back in London, and after a brilliant career at Pall Mall as an expensive demimondaine (serving even the King, at one point), she sizes up her possession in a prose daubed all over with numerals and sums:

> I had at the End of the eight Years, two Thousand eight Hundred Pounds coming Yearly in, of which I did not spend one Penny, being maintain'd by my Allowance from my Lord—, and more than maintain'd, by above 200 *l. per Annum*; for tho' he did not contract for 500 *l.* a Year . . . yet he gave me Money so often, and that in such large Parcels, that I had seldom so little as seven to eight Hundred Pounds a Year of him, one Year with another. (*Roxana* 188)

The persuasive force "two Thousand eight Hundred Pounds" or "seven to eight Hundred Pounds a Year" stands tall, towering over the legality or morality of her relationship with "my Lord—." Money talks a language of its own; awesome figures of big money induce the reader to gape in admiration and envy.

Money communicates a similar message towards the end of *Robinson Crusoe*, which has better moral credentials since it can flaunt the honest labour of the pious protagonist, securely different from the illicit and outrageously high-priced sexual service Roxana specializes in. Thanks to the meticulous management of his partner in Brazil, Crusoe's old plantation has been growing handsomely during his long absence. "I was now Master, all on a Sudden," writes Crusoe, "of above 5000 *l. Sterling* in Money, and had an Estate, as I might well call it, in the *Brasils*, of above a thousand Pounds a Year, as sure as an Estate of Lands in *England*" (*Crusoe* 240). Apart from the fact that Crusoe has done little on his island to earn this large profit from his share of the plantation in Brazil, the problem with the language money speaks here is that it lacks any sensation, that it cannot be felt or imagined in itself. The thrill of Moll's picking pockets or Crusoe's eating goat stew can easily command emotional purchasing power to any reader regardless of his or her financial standing. Expressions such as "5000 *l. Sterling* in Money," however, do little more than mutely refer to itself in a dumb gesture. They cannot be converted into coin for shared wisdom, either, simply because such huge windfall is an exclusive and exceptional private experience which others cannot take part in. They tread a territory removed from both sensation (*Erlebnis*) and reflection (*Erfahrung*), in other words. This problem we shall investigate in the next chapter.

CHAPTER THREE

THE IDEAL OF CALCULABILITY

"A frightful Number!"

In the age of Pepys, Bunyan, and Defoe, time was beginning to be measured and experienced as a regular succession of moments. This new species of time was different from its predecessors in that it knew no organic continuity between units. Time inscribed on timepieces moved onward steadily but out of joint, as a self-contained automaton yielding no possibility of synthesis, moral or otherwise. Discourse about mechanical timekeeping in Defoe's days steadily moved away from the Puritan apocalyptic trope of God's "Watch-Bell" tolling the imminence of divine retribution, to seeing it as a wonderful new means of precise measurement.[1] The mechanical or scientific interest in timepieces was growing, as indicated by such works as *The Artificial Clock-Maker, A Treatise of Watch and Clock-Work, Wherein the Art of Calculating Numbers for Most Sorts of Movements is Explained to the Capacity of the Unlearned* (1700), which comes quite close to a full-fledged treatise on mechanical engineering. E. P. Thompson tells us that there was a "great advance in the accuracy of household clocks" through various improvements in clock-making technology from 1660s to 1680s, so that 1680 could possibly be taken "as the date at which English clock- and watch-making took precedence . . . over European competitors" (Thompson 64). Modern time awareness created by vastly improved mechanical timepieces struck root as Defoe grew up. In fact, it is one of the major Western technologies Crusoe is equipped with. Crusoe rigorously drills himself to a busy work schedule, whose intensity he assesses in terms of time expended. "I was very seldom idle," he tells us, "but having regularly divided my Time, according to the several daily Employments that were before me" (*Crusoe* 97). In addition to his daily household chores, he reserves "about four Hours in the Evening" for outdoor work, thus avoiding the "Violence of the Heat" of mid-day:

> To this short Time allow'd for Labour, I desire may be added the exceeding

> Laboriousness of my Work; the many Hours which for want of Tools, want of Help, and want of Skill, every Thing I did, took up out of my Time: For Example, I was full two and forty Days in making a Board for a long Shelf, which I wanted in my Cave; whereas, two Sawyers, with their Tools, and a Saw-Pit, would have cut six of them out of the same Tree in half a Day. (*Crusoe* 98)

Crusoe's labour, in fact, is measured by a mental watch, as it were, since timepiece is not found in the list of the items he took from the stranded ship. He says he only had "about four Hours in the Evening" to do serious work, but that calculation comes with no objective corroboration, unlike his calculating the difficulty of work by days ("two and forty Days" or "half a Day"). Moreover, the division of "my Time" is regulated by his simplified material needs, as he has no occasion to spend time idly on socializing. In this transparent form, his time economy has a utopian quality which those living in crowded society cannot replicate.

The mentality of privileging time over space, of doing things according to schedule instead of remaining "idle" and doing nothing, even on a tropical island, is a habit Crusoe shares with many of his fellow countrymen, such as Pepys. While Crusoe was busy hacking down trees to make himself a canoe, Pepys in London was falling in love with his new "Wach" he had recently purchased: "I cannot forbear carrying my watch in my hand in the coach all this afternoon, and seeing what a-clock it is 100 times. And am apt to think with myself: how could I be so long without one" (13 May 1665 [6.101]). From that initial stage of naturalizing technology into an indispensable part of one's personal existence, Pepys moves on to that of creatively applying his watch to novel usage, such as measuring space in terms of minutes spent: "Up, and walked to Greenwich, taking pleasure to walk with my minute wach in my hand, by which I am now come to see the distances of my way from Woolwich to Greenwich. And do find myself to come within two minutes constantly to the same place at the end of each quarter of an hour" (13 Sep 1665 [6.221-22]). The conjunction of time with space, or what David Harvey calls "time-space compression"—a conjunction bound to be inherently disjunctive due to its mutually opposed attributes—is traceable in Pepys as a condition of modernity rather than of postmodernity.[2] Just as Crusoe's pristine island is transformed by his constant labour measured by his sense of hours, a new type of abstract space conceived and construed at the level of minutes emerges in the formula, "two minutes constantly to the same place."

A corollary to the numerical measurement of space through time Pepys experiments with is the gradual ascendency of numerals as a rival to verbal language, in which precise measurement and accurate calculation become more important than conferring moral or spiritual meaning to one's actions and objects. This is what Simmel calls the "ideal of numerical calculability" (Simmel 2004: 445), enforced by a "money economy" (a term virtually synonymous with the "metropolitan condition" in Simmel's thinking) that hopes to "conceive events and the qualitative distinction of things as a system of numbers" (444). Defoe's *Journal of the Plague Year* presents itself as a real account largely on the strength of its precise calculation of the progressive increase of the plague's victims, Moll and Roxana mark the stages of their lives by submitting to the reader punctual accounting of their current income. For the former, the connubial bliss she enjoys towards the end of her life story—transported, but married and well-off in Virginia—is corroborated by her husband's "telling" her wealth:

> HE was amaz'd, and stood a while telling upon his Fingers, but said nothing, at last he began thus, Hold lets see, *says he*, *telling upon his Fingers still*; and first on this Thumb, there's 246 *l.* in Money at first, then two gold Watches, Diamond Rings, and Plate, *says he*, upon the fore Finger, then upon the next Finger, here's a Plantation on *York* River, a 100 *l.* a Year, then 150 in Money; then a Sloop load of Horses, Cows, Hogs and Stores, and so on to the Thumb again; and now, *says he*, a Cargo cost 250 *l.* in *England*, and worth here twice the Money, well, *says I*, What do you make of all that? make of it, *says he*, why who says I was deceiv'd, when I married a Wife in *Lancashire*? I think I have married a Fortune, a very good Fortune too, *says he*. (*Moll* 341)

As the italicized "*telling upon his Fingers still*" implies, the excitement lies more in telling as counting than in telling as narrating; it is a story told in the language of numerals. Yet numbers in themselves do not necessarily speak of happiness or misery. They have no intrinsic relationship to the human subject using it to count one's blessing. Quantity knows no impediment to relation, yet as this relation lacks meaningful relationship, which has to be a connection of different qualities, it is a "self-relationship," according to Hegel.[3] How then can the self-relationship of calculability contribute to fictions of human gratification or disappointment, of life, love, and death? Ominously, a narrative of death in the city, and no end of deaths at that, contains vital clues to this question.

Defoe's *Journal of the Plague Year* speaks a fluent language of figures in a most interesting, as well as disturbing, context of counting and accounting for the plague's massacre. The horror of Londoners dying in droves from plague is represented through a series of episodes containing varying degrees of lurid detail. Between the requirement to maintain the readers' emotional or sensory involvement in the *Erlebnis* of the victims and the need to size up the anecdotes for reflective generalization

(*Erfahrung*), this strange narrative straddling the borderline between fiction and non-fiction calls itself paradoxically a "Journal," marked by the immediacy and urgency of a first-hand observation by a private subject, of the "Plague Year," a historic event affecting the community of London dwellers as a whole. The account of the 1665 incident may surely have instructive value for municipal hygiene policy of Defoe's times, yet the narrative easily exceeds any such exemplary mission of illustrating how things may go wrong, as there are simply far too many, more or less similar, stories of people infected, infecting, and dying. The "fact-or-fiction dilemma" the work raises can be answered historically, as does Robert Mayer, by pointing to its generic features as a derivation of Baconian historiography (Mayer 208-10). But even by this measure, the realistic effect of the narrative overreaches itself. The narrative which calls itself "a journal" is interested above all in purveying an incessant succession of reports, a kind of "live" coverage of the calamity, with statistical tables corroborating the stupendous scale of the disaster.

The single-minded first-person narrator of *A Journal of the Plague Year* allows himself no leisure for digression from the official duty he assumes of reporting the plague's progress. A comparison with Pepys's journal during the months of the "Plague Year" of 1665 shows to what extent privacy in Defoe's text is strictly controlled and censored for the ostensible purpose of describing the public tragedy. Statistics of body count matter to Pepys as well, but they occupy only an incidental place in his daily record:

> Up by 5 of the clock, mighty full of fear of an Ague, but was obliged to go; and so by water, wrapping myself up warm, to the Tower; and there sent for the Weekly Bill and find 8252 dead in all, and of them, 6978 of the plague—which is a most dreadfull Number—and shows reason to fear that the plague hath got that hold that it will yet continue among us. Thence to Brainford, reading *The Villaine* (a pretty good play) all the way. There a coach of Mr. Povy's stood ready for me, and he at his house ready to come in; and so we together merrily to Swakely, Sir R. Viner's—a very pleasant place, bought by him of Sir James Harringtons lady. (6 Sep 1665 [6.214-15])

Thus the entry goes on to dilate on what other pleasant things Pepys enjoyed that day, despite the "most dreadful Number" of the weekly Bill of Mortality he feels obliged to make note of. Numbers are dreadful in themselves, as both Pepys and the narrator of Defoe's fictive journal would agree. "The next Bill was from the 23d of May to the 30th, when the Number of the Plague was 17: but the Burials in St. Giles's were 53, a frightful Number!" (*Plague Year* 6) exclaims the latter during the relatively milder early stage of devastation. Yet Pepys is busy going about "merrily" to offset this deadly arithmetic. A few days before, we see Pepys typically making best use of his position and body to extract maximum sexual profit, despite the plague which has come quite close to his own circle by then:

> This morning I wrote letters to Mr. Hill and Andrews to come dine with me tomorrow, and then I to the office, where busy, and thence to dine with Sir J. Mennes, where merry—but only that Sir J. Mennes, who hath lately lost two coach-horses, dead in the stable, hath a third now a-dying. After dinner I to Deptford and there took occasion to andar a la casa de la gunaica de mi Minusier and did what I had a mind a hazer con ella, and volvió. To Greenwich, where wrote some letters; and home in pretty good time. (2 Sep 1665 [6.210])

The deviant foreign-looking signifiers, protecting the delectable core of Pepys' private sphere, as we have discussed earlier, register a striking contrast to the dying horses of Sir J. Mennes. Undeterred by possible dangers of the infectious disease, Pepys goes down river to have what he wishes to have from his mistress there.

Defoe's narrator, however, writes only of the plague and what relates to it. Defoe allows him no indulgence either in the lawful cultural diversions of play-going and convivial dining, or in the naughty delights of adulterous intercourse. Unlike Pepys, the private life of "H. F.", as he signs himself at the termination of his narration, is bleak, bare, and sullenly pious:

> Terrified by those frightful Objects, I would retire Home sometimes, and resolve to go out no more, and perhaps, I would keep those Resolutions for three or four Days, which Time I spent in the most serious Thankfulness for my Preservation, and the Preservation of my Family, and the constant Confession of my Sins, giving my self up to God every Day, and applying to him with Fasting, Humiliation, and Meditation. (*Plague Year* 76)

Retire from society he has to, inevitably due to the plague, but his isolation is unmitigated by diversion or communion. A bachelor whose "family" consists of his hired servants, he has among his equals only his "self" to converse with. But about this "self" of his he remains largely reticent. The immediate *Erlebnis* the text transmits is yoked to its mediated preoccupation with the plague as a collective *Erfahrung*. He speaks of himself only when it concerns his self-assigned role of relating the public disaster. He speaks of the public disaster, furthermore, with little regard for the individual "selves" suffering death. In keeping with such tight-lipped reticence, the numerical language of statistics he employs speaks of the "prodigious Numbers that fell" but remains silent about the human question of the dying individuals, whose existential particularity is completely erased as each death is added to produce prodigious sums.

However, the success of the narrative depends on its capacity to turn the disaster into a series of vivid *Erlebnis*, many of which the narrator himself had gone through. Defoe seems to share in this regard Dilthey's privileging of lived experience over history's grand narrative:

> [W]hat moves us especially in these reports is something inaccessible to the senses, something found only in lived experience, which is implicit in the outer processes that arise from it and which in turn react back on it. And this tendency does not rest upon a perspective that approaches life from without. It is grounded in life itself. For every value of life is contained in this experienceable aspect; all the outer noise of history resolves around it. (Dilthey 2002: 104)

Defoe, however, shows little respect for "life itself" and gives full voice to the "outer noise of history." The crucial difference between Defoe's historical narrative and Dilthey's philosophy of history concerns the question of senses: for the former, everything has to be accessible to senses to which the "experiencable aspect" of life is directly tied. "I was indeed shock'd with this Sight" (*Plague Year* 63) is a representative formula, and indeed shocking tableaus of distress make up the main bulk of the narrative. Yet the difficulty of communicating that shock is admitted, as in the following:

> This may serve a little to describe the dreadful Condition of that Day, tho' it is impossible to say any Thing that is able to give a true Idea of it to those who did not see it, other than this; that is way indeed *very, very, very* dreadful, and such as no Tongue can express. (*Plague Year* 60)

The rather lame repetition of "very" properly dramatizes the difficulty of verbalizing the horror of the events, but it also hints that communicating the sensation of dread, rather than forming a "true Idea" conceptually, is what the narrative aims at. The dictates of rational thinking can remain unheeded, as long a feeling of "that Day" being "very dreadful" is passed on. In one among many examples describing the distress of the victims, we see how the details steer towards an appeal to the reader's auditory imagination:

> It was indeed a lamentable Thing to hear the miserable Lamentations of poor dying Creatures, calling out for Ministers to Comfort them, and pray with them, to Counsel them, and to direct them, calling out to God for Pardon and Mercy, and confessing aloud their past Sins. It would make the stoutest Heart

> bleed to hear how many Warnings were then given by dying Penitents, to others not to put off and delay their Repentance to the Day of Distress, that such a Time of Calamity as this, was no Time for Repentance; was no Time to call upon God. I wish I could repeat the very Sound of those Groans, and of those Exclamations that I heard from some poor dying Creatures, when in the Hight of their Agonies and Distress; and that I could make him that read this hear, as I imagine I now hear them, for the Sound seems still to Ring in my Ears. (*Plague Year* 104)

The passage encourages the reader to share the narrator's hallucination, to revive the piercing cries of the dying as a sensory presence. It strategically begins with the articulate sounds of "miserable Lamentations," designed to incite religious anxiety of "him that read this," for die we all must, not knowing what to expect after death. Yet the narrator is preoccupied more with acoustics than catechism: he is worried lest the reader may not share that same degree of horror and dread he himself had experienced in listening to those "Groans." The "Sound seems still to Ring" in his ears, perhaps, but "it is such as no Tongue can express." The "experiencable aspect" of the scene he witnesses is an *Erlebnis* that defies verbal mediation. Shared Christian frame of reference, therefore, has to be erected to provide moral contours to the pitiful sounds. The nature of this gesture towards religious *Erfahrung* is what we now shall examine.

"An almost invisible Hand"

Repentance of sin and fear of divine retribution do provide indispensable building blocks in constructing a broader "moral" to H. F.'s accounts. In fact, *A Journal of the Plague Year* presents some early usage of the trope of "invisible hand" made famous by Adam Smith, yet in a sense opposed to the rational, beneficial, progressive intent Smith bestows on it, for this is a hand of arbitrary intervention, meting out vengeance and salvation that transcend human reasoning. Towards the end of his narrative, H. F. attempts a concluding assessment of the significance of the disaster:

> In the Middle of their Distress, when the Condition of the City of *London* was so truly calamitous, just then it pleased God, as it were, by his immediate Hand to disarm this Enemy . . . so that in a few Days, every Body was recovering, whole Families that were infected and down, that had Ministers praying with them, and expected Death every Hour, were revived and healed, and none died at all out of them.
>
> Nor was this by any new Medicine found out, or new Method of Cure discovered, or by any Experience in the Operation, which the Physicians or Surgeons had attain'd to; but it was evidently from the secret invisible Hand

of him, that had at first sent this Disease as a Judgment upon us; and let the Atheistic part of Mankind call my Saying this what they please, it is no Enthusiasm; it was acknowledg'd at that time by all Mankind; the Disease was enervated, and its Malignity spent. (*Plague Year* 246)

The passage makes a case for a religious interpretation of the outbreak and the end of the epidemic, rejecting a mere scientific (or "Atheistic") trust in "Experience in the Operation" or empirical "Method of Cure." The "immediate Hand" of God, which had allowed the plague to suddenly smite the sinful city of London, also chose to put an end to it as abruptly after having wrecked so much havoc, so that its dispensation appears to be that of "a secret invisible Hand." The invisible hand here does not gradually harmonize pursuits of private interest for the purpose of public benefit, as Smith would later have it. Instead, it suddenly assaults the collective body to chastise, as well as to heal. Similarly, in *Moll Flanders*, divine intervention makes itself felt as a violent interruption of life: "We liv'd in an uninterrupted course of Ease and Content for Five Years, when a sudden Blow from an almost invisible Hand, blasted all my Happiness, and turn'd me out into the World in a Condition the reverse of all that had been before it" (*Moll* 189). The "sudden Blow" coming from the "almost invisible Hand" forces the human subject to acknowledge its authority. However unappealing it may be to human reason, it does explain life's unexpected woes.

Much more so than in *Moll Flanders*, *A Journal of the Plague Year* can claim to have illustrated the absolute sovereignty of God, as Jean Calvin preached. Calvin's theology embraces a rigorous rationality built upon what for him is a rational premise of God's absolute will, streamlining the complex and mutually conflicting elements of Christian doctrine into a legalistic code not distracted by universal love. His deduction of God's predestination demonstrates how rational the apparently irrational dispensation of God's grace and punishment really is:

When we attribute foreknowledge to God, we mean that all things always were, and perpetually remain, under his eyes, so that to his knowledge there is nothing future or past, but all things are present. . . . And this foreknowledge is extended throughout the universe to every creature. We call predestination God's eternal decree, by which he compacted with himself what he willed to become of each man. For all are not created in equal condition: rather, eternal life is foreordained for some, eternal damnation for others. Therefore, as any man has been created to one or the other of these ends, we speak of him as predestined to life or to death. (Calvin 926)

Those who die during the plague were bound to die, those who survived, likewise. What happens to their soul after their death has all been willed, foreknown, and predestined by God who compacts with himself his "eternal decree." Redemption and ruin in this world may appear arbitrary or irrational, but not so from the divine point of view, in the eternal present tense of God that knows neither past nor future. Human life and fictional narrative, however, can only unfold through time, in ever receding past tense, so that God's decree can be known and inferred only retrospectively as an "invisible Hand."

The "invisible Hand," however, is also a visible hand, for it manifests its power visibly through the concrete tangible outcomes that can be accounted for in words, or counted in numbers. Accumulation of lurid episodes is insufficient for this purpose of interpreting Providence, since the sensory and sensational details of affliction do not in themselves yield general propositions. Statistical figures cannot visualize the deformed figures of plagued bodies, but they have the advantage of bolstering the objectivity of description. Any doubt as to the veracity of the account can be dispelled by what the numbers themselves luminously state. The force of its non-human non-language consists in its capacity to represent the collective distress in its totality, which can then be construed as visible clues to God's "invisible Hand."

The Great Plague, erupting only five years after the Restoration and the defeat of Puritan republicanism, occasioned a resurgence of Dissenter preaching, in part because the ministers of the Established Church quickly fled, but also because the enormity of the disaster called for a more impassioned, vindictive apocalyptic theology, so much so that, according to Walter George Bell, the Great Plague almost "established English Nonconformity" (Bell 227). Contemporary religious pamphlets, such as Rev. Thomas Vincent's *God's Terrible Voice* (1665), readily captured the scene with sonorous Biblical eloquence:

> Now death rides triumphantly on his pale horse through our streets, and breaks into every house almost where any inhabitants are to be found. Now people fall as thick as leaves from the trees in autumn, when they are shaked by a mighty wind. Now there is a dismal solitude in the London streets: every day looks with the face of a Sabbath Day, observed with greater solemnity than it used to be in the city. (quoted in Bell 230)

Defoe's narrator, while admitting the supreme authority of God's "invisible Hand," writes in a far more detached and prosaic tone than this. Whereas Vincent employs figures of speech (such as "death rides triumphantly" or "people fall as thick as leaves"), H. F. resorts to figures of numbers to fortify his tale. Mathematics and Puritan theology, the language of figures that tabulates death in sanitized numbers and the "figural language" identified by Everett Zimmerman as that which "places his account within the biblical master narrative" (Zimmerman 90), converge happily in passages such as the following, which combines statistics with Godly phrases:

From the 12th of *September* to the 19th.
St. *Giles's Cripplegate* 456
St. *Giles* in the Fields 140
Clarkenwell 77
....
White-Chapel 532
In the 97 Parishes within the Walls ... 1496
In the 8 Parishes on *Southwalk* Side ... 1636
6060

Here is a strange change of Things indeed, and a sad change it was, and had it held for two Months more than it did, very few People would have been left alive: But then such, I say, was the merciful Disposition of God, that when it was thus the West and North part which had been so dreadfully visited at first, grew *as you see*, much better; and as the People disappear'd here, they began to look abroad again there; and the next Week or two altered it still more, that is, more to the Encouragement of the other Part of the Town. *For Example*:

From the 19th of *September* to the 26th;
St. *Giles's Cripplegate* 277
St. *Giles* in the Fields 119
Clarkenwell 76
....
In the 97 Parishes within the Walls 1268
In the 8 Parishes on *Southwalk* Side 1390
4900 (*Plague Year* 188-89)

The "merciful Disposition of God" manifests itself mathematically in the scale, extent, and composition of the death toll of London parishes. The significant decrease in the numbers, horribly large as they still may be, in the two parishes using the name of St. Giles's (St. Giles's at Cripplegate had seen 554 dead between 25th July to 1st August [*Plague Year* 187]), stands as compelling evidence of God's wish to stem the tide of destruction there. A tone of grateful relief is mixed with the fearful numerals running into hundreds and thousands. Yet even so, the figures stand apart, resisting any colouring of human emotion or religious interpretation. There is no mourning for the dead in the sums cleared of the stench of rotting corpses and shorn of human feelings: calculation of the victims "deterritorializes the plague" (Ellison 97). But it is also countered simultaneously by a reterritorializing reference to the "Disposition of God." But which God? The God behind the figures does not seem to be the God of Love who aches after each stray lamb and weeps for each lost soul. Nor does he seem to be a mere deistic "guiding force of a system," as Novak claims (Novak 1983: 13). The theology employed here hoists the calculating subject onto a transcendental perspective of God who wrecks havoc, as well as dispatch succour.

Statistics is no theology, however. For every instance in *A Journal of the Plague Year* of the two overlapping, we can come up with scores of passages where numbers have no inkling of God above or Hell below. Far more obvious is their psychological utility. The inherently detached, transcendental viewpoint predicated on the mutely eloquent numerals helps to move the subject away from the shock of *Erlebnis*, assisting his psychological self-protection (Birdsall 117). Such "structure of feeling for early modernity" (Albanese 258) articulated in mathematics indeed betrays a spirit of triumphant abstraction similar to the body count of the dead cannibals in *Robinson Crusoe*. Supported by Friday—who is by now baptized, civilized, and armed by his master—Crusoe takes by storm a group of cannibals preparing to regale themselves with human flesh, yielding the multicultural allied force a neat victory with no casualty on their side, but with a variety of casualties on the enemy's side thus charted:

> 3 Kill'd at our first Shot from the Tree.
> 2 Kill'd at the next Shot.
> 2 Kill'd by *Friday* in the Boat.
> 2 Kill'd by *Ditto*, of those at first wounded.
> 1 Kill'd by *Ditto*, in the Wood.
> 3 Kill'd by the *Spaniard*.
> 4 Kill'd, being found dropp'd here and there of their Wounds, or kill'd by *Friday* in his Chase of them.
> 4 Escap'd in the Boat, whereof one wounded if not dead.
>
> ——
>
> 21 In all (*Crusoe* 199)

The dead in London are certainly not as culpable or sub-human as the Caribbean cannibals decimated by Crusoe and Friday, but the role numerals play in both samples are strikingly similar. They serve the interest of a removed, secure, superior, and self-assured intelligence that thinks in terms of quantification rather than of qualified inter-personal sympathy for fellow mortals, which helps the narrator to brush off not only his fear of corpses contaminating the "urban body" (Flynn 1990: 21), but of the emotional infection of pitying the dead.[4] In both instances, God is on the narrator's side, though all but relieved of duty by a modern scientific ethos armed with the emotion-proof technology of mathematics, or more specifically, with "political arithmetic," as statistics was first named by Sir William Petty, a contemporary of Crusoe and H. F. The political arithmetic employed in Defoe's *A Journal of the Plague Year* partakes in the rise of numerals as a new technology of conversion, control, and containment of objectified items, be it the victims of the plague or the hapless cannibals destroyed by a rifled European.

"A Table ... of the Encrease"

Petty's political arithmetic was called so in the literal sense of the Greek etymology of "political": it was a tool of mathematically conceiving and representing *polis*, the city of London above all. It was a localized, municipal arithmetic, rather than a comprehensive calculation of a nation's state and wealth, which it developed into in later centuries. In Petty's *Five Essays in Political Arithmmetick* (1687), for example, he compares London and its Continental rivals, above all Paris, in a bi-lingual parallel text, by computing the populations of both capitals. The method he adopts and blithely explains to the reader relies very much on his calculation of the rate of death ("one dies out of 30 at London") based on the Bills of Mortality:

> I found that the year 1684 and 1685, being next each other, and both healthfull, did wonderfully agree in their Burials, viz. 1684 they were 23202, and Anno 1685 13222, the Medium whereof is 13212; Moreover that the Christnings 1684 were 14702, and those Anno 1685 were 14730, therefore I multiplied the Medium of Burials 23212 by 30, supposing that one dies out of 30 at London, which made the number of People 696360 Souls. (Petty 26-27)

In this tabulation of the city's "Souls," no regard is given to their individual souls, whether in their christening or in their burial. Sums, "Medium" (i.e. average) and multiplication are all that matter for this new soulless soul of numerical rationality, which presumes to grasp, know, and control the city by submitting them to the transparent order of calculability. Similarly, the table cited above from Defoe's *Journal of the Plague Year* captures not only a moment in that eventful year but also the city space as such, whose sprawling, hideous, and crowded devastation is overcome by a lucid tabulation that marks off one parish from another, as well as from one group of parishes ("within the Walls") against another ("on *Southwalk* Side").

Already in the late sixteenth century, the genre of "Survey of London" was born with the first book to use that title written by John Stow. But the work betrays an antiquarian, nostalgic love for things past and gone, despite the mathematical connotation the term "survey" has come to acquire. In charting the city according to the topographical division of its parishes, Stow pays heed to the minute local history interred with the dead, as in the following account of a parish church in Cripplegate Ward:

> Then is the parrish church of S. Mary Aldermanbury a fayre Church with a churchyeard, and cloyster adioyning, in the which cloyster is hanged and fastned a shanke bone of a man (as is said) very great and larger by three inches and a halfe then that which hangeth in S. Lawrence church in the Iury, for it is in length 28. inches and a halfe of assisse, but not so hard and steely like as the other, for the same is light and somewhat Porie and spongie. This bone is said to bee found amongst the bones of men remoued from the charnel house of Powles, or rather from the cloyster of Powls church, of both which reportes I doubt, for that the late Reyne Wolfe Stationer (who paid for the carriage of those bones from the charnell to the Morefieldes) tolde mee of some thousandes of Carrie loades and more to be conueighed, whereof hee wondred, but neuer told of any such bone in eyther place to bee found, neyther would the same haue beene easily gotten from him, if hee had heard thereof, except he had reserued the like for himselfe, being the greatest preseruer of antiquities in those partes for his time. (Stow 1.292-93)

A scientific disposition to examine the veracity of sources and to measure the bones of the past with precision looks forward to the future. The contrast, however, to H. F.'s reference to the same ward is equally notable. For Stow, a peculiar piece of bone of an individual interred in the church merits a paragraph-long discussion, whereas the freshly dead bodies in the latter's Cripplegate are just so many items lumped together for body count expressed in the simplified formula of "St. *Giles's Cripplegate* .... 456." As the plague victims of Cripplegate are reduced into mute Arabic numerals, the quaint and discrete history of the parish remembered and recounted in English are banished without a trace.

Interestingly, in the updated version of Stow's *Survey of London* by Defoe's contemporary John Strype, *A Survey of the Cities of London and Westminster* (1720), published two years before Defoe's *Journal of the Plague Year*, one distinctive contribution of the later complier is "An Account of the dreadful Fire of London, Ann. 1666, the Damage done by it; Computed." In Strype's *Survey*, statistics supplements the verbal account of this momentous disaster:

A Table of Estimates	
In Houses burnt as aforesaid	3 900 000
In Churches and other Publick Edifices as follow:	
The 87 Parish Churches, at 3000 *l.* each, 69	6 000
Six Chappels, at 2000 *l.* each	12 000
The Royal Exchange, at	50 000
The King's Custom-House, at	10 000
The 52 Halls of Companies, 1500 *l.*	73 000
Three of the City Gates, at 3000 *l.* each	9 000
The Gaol of *Newgate*	15 000
Four Stone Bridges, ...	6 000
The *Sessions House*	7 000
The *Guild Hall*, and Courts and Offices .... Belonging to it	40 000
Blackwell Hall	3 000
Bridewell	5 000
Poultry Counter	5 000
Woodstreet Counter	3 000
	939 000 (Strype 226)

A new language heralding the advent of a new system of value is registered in this table, attesting to the ascendency of computational rationality. It is an economic as well as political arithmetic, for not only does it transform reality into numeral tabulation but it does so according to a financial criterion of valuation, the monetary estimate of losses due to the fire. Churches, chapels, and other public buildings have suffered damages each in qualitatively different ways, but financial statistics jumps the queue of detailed attention to their individual stories to allocate numerical assessment to each item. Figures speak what words cannot state with precision. "The whole Damage sustained by this Fire is almost incredible. Yet to make some Computation, that which follows is the Method that hath been taken," thus Strype prefaces his mathematical demonstration shown above. Accounting as computation in terms of money's worth, rather than accounting as verbal elaboration of vanished stories, imposes itself on the city's distinctive cultural, religious, social complexity, whose unique historical and architectural features, in addition to being burnt down by the Great Fire, are now erased by this language of financial estimation. The city meets finance to be subsumed by the latter. From Defoe's and Strype's days onward London's and the nation's history would move in such a direction as to bestow on the City, its financial district, the honour of representing the capital. While numerous factors both local and global contributed to this remarkable career of finance in London, the intimate role mathematics has played in finance hardly needs emphasis. In Defoe's fictional world, we can also trace the hegemony of finance as a trajectory of numerical language, rising from the margins to the centre in *Roxana* and, to a lesser extent, in *Moll Flanders.*

After a successful career overseas of accumulating a sumptuous fortune, Roxana returns to London, where she is greeted not only by the adoring high society of West End but the financial sector of the City, proud, thriving and savvy like its resident financier Sir Robert Clayton,[5] a character who in addition to being the only "real" figure in the narrative is the only person allowed to use a full-name identity by the author:

> I had now all my Effects secur'd; but my Money being my great Concern at that time, I found it a Difficulty how to dispose of it, so as to bring me in an annual Interest; however, in some time I got a substantial safe Mortgage for 14000 Pound, by the Assistance of the famous Sir *Robert Clayton*, for which, I had an Estate of 1800 Pounds a Year bound to me; and had 700 Pounds *per Annum* Interest for it. (*Roxana* 164)

Sir Robert, being "a Man thorowly vers'd in the Arts of improving Money, but thorowly honest" (169), proposes to his client his "Scheme of Frugality" (168): "I might prudently lay-by 1000 *l.* every Year, to add to the Capital; and by adding every Year the additional Interest, or Income of the Money to the Capital, he prov'd to me, that in ten Year I shou'd double the 1000 *l. per Annum*, that I laid by; and he drew me out a Table, as he call'd it, of the Encrease, for me to judge by" (167). How she has amassed her fortune, what her personal background is, and what her character is, such questions the banker finds no reason to ask. Accumulated capital sands self-sufficient as legitimate premise and objective for Sir Robert, well versed in mathematics, and carrying a ready "Table . . . of the Encrease" to persuade moneyed humans. Money talks indeed as never before, and it talks in figures cleansed of human experience.

How then can a fictional narrative, whose business it is to offer interesting experience of plausible individual lives to the reader-customer, make such numerical language of finance sound appealing? In *A Journal of the Plague Year*, the ominous calculation of the dead could be taken at times as signs of the divine invisible Hand working behind it. Can one say the same about the ever "improving" private fortune of this morally reprehensible and profane protagonist? That her pursuit of monetary wealth was utterly free from moral qualms she puts down as a sworn statement:

> I may venture to say, that no Woman ever liv'd a Life like me, of six and twenty Years of Wickedness, without the least Signals of Remorse; without

> any Signs of Repentance; or without so much as a Wish to put an End to it; I had so long habituated myself to a Life of Vice, that really it appear'd to be no Vice to me; I went on smooth and pleasant; I wallow'd in Wealth, and it flow'd in upon me at such a Rate, having taken the frugal Measures that the good Knight directed; so that I had at the End of the eight Years, two Thousand eight Hundred Pounds coming Yearly in. (*Roxana* 188)

Leaving aside morality, then, the fabricator of the tale is still left with the problem of making money-making an appealing topic of his fictional biography. Criminals are safer game, for crimes, such as Moll's picking pockets and shoplifting carry sensational value. But Roxana's whoredom is far less eventful, as it predictably profits from a succession of unappealing follies of her partners, each enslaved to the "vicious Appetite" (75) of profligate expenditure, both erotic and monetary:

> Thus far I am a standing Mark of the Weakness of Great Men, in their Vice; that value not squandering away immense Wealth, upon the most worthless Creatures; or to sum it up in a Word, they raise the Value of the Object which they pretend to pitch upon, by their Fancy; I say, raise the Value of it, at their own Expence; give vast Presents for a ruinous Favour, which is so far from being equal to the Price, that nothing will, at last, prove more absurd, than the cost Men are at to purchase their own Destruction. (*Roxana* 74)

Yet the novel is not primarily interested in targeting the weakness of Roxana's clients, for their "Vice," as in Bernard Mandeville's *The Fable of the Bees* comes as economic virtue.[6] The "Weakness of Great Men" is transformed into "immense Wealth" for Roxana, which in turn circulates in other purchased goods and service, including the excellent assistance of Amy her "indefatigable Girl" (87).

Even so, the long narrative of *Roxana* cannot be reduced to its implicit or explicit business lessons, which Defoe never ceased to offer in his pamphlets and treatises such as *The Compleat English Tradesman.*[7] Can we consider the two Defoes, the fiction writer and the journalist, as interchangeable? Defoe's fame or notoriety as a pamphleteer owed to his daring impersonation of an anti-Dissenter bigot, but one cannot deny that there is a decisive break between the two Defoes, that "Defoe's leap from dramatized propaganda and polemic to extended autobiographical impersonation," as Richetti admits, "is hugely transformative" (Richetti 2005: 185).[8] After his departure from fiction writing after *Roxana* (1724), he adopted the fictive persona, among others, of "Andrew Moreton," from *Every-Body's Business is No-Body's Business* of 1725 to 1728 (Owens 20-21). But this is a mode of impersonation belonging to his pre-novel days. The five years' span of creativity from 1719 to 1724 remains a strange interlude in the writer's career. Stranger still is the singular preoccupation with money economy of his last novel *Roxana*, dedicated to portraying the protagonist's "prosperous Wickedness" (106). How should one make sense of this? Unlike some critics who avidly hold on to this aspect of *Roxana* as a casuistry on money management, seeing a ready echo here of Defoe's pamphlet on "Lady Credit," we seek to trace a deeper implication of the narrative with the world of finance than can be drawn from the pronouncements on money matters scattered throughout the book.[9] This we shall explore by focusing on a key problem of finance in Defoe's time: the question of liquidity.

"Possess'd of almost ten Thousand Pounds"

Liquidity, referring to the convertibility of a given asset into ready cash,[10] is a technical term in finance that seemingly has little to do with fictional narratives of women making the best of their sexual attraction to fend off their economic hardships, a tale which Defoe tells twice, first in *Moll Flanders* and then in *Roxana*. But liquidity matters indeed for them, since they convert their capacity to offer "love," whether genuinely committed to their partner or not, in return for material compensation in the form of money, rather than for legalized marriage settlements. Most impressive, particularly from a feminist perspective, would be Roxana's pursuit of economic independence and her supreme contempt for patriarchal marriage, which she declares to her Dutch Merchant:

> [M]y Heart was bent upon an Independency of Fortune; and I told him, I knew no State of Matrimony, but what was, at best, a State of Inferiority, if not of Bondage; that I had no Notion of it; that I liv'd a Life of absolute Liberty now; was free as I was born, and having a plentiful Fortune, I did not understand what Coherence the Words *Honour* and *Obey* had with the Liberty of a *Free Woman*; that I knew no Reason the Men had to engross the whole Liberty of the Race, and make the Women, notwithstanding any desparity of Fortune, be subject to the Laws of Marriage, of their own making; that it was my Misfortune to be a Woman, but I was resolv'd it shou'd not be made worse by the Sex; and seeing Liberty seem'd to be the Men's Property, I wou'd be a *Man-Woman*; for as I was born free, I wou'd die so. (*Roxana* 170-1)

This remarkably forward-looking vindication of women's economic rights articulates "absolute Liberty" in terms of "an Independency of Fortune," which in turn sets itself apart from "Men's Property." The latter, according to the laws of the realm, are the real properties that remain in the hands of the male heir or husband. The former, by contrast, is the liquid financial fortune which opposes itself to the real property of landed estate by its freedom from the gender constraints welded to the latter.

Peter Earl reminds us that in Defoe's times independent women with "liquid assets" were "actively sought after as marriage partners," especially those widows left with her dead husband's "accumulation of business capital" (Earl 174). Roxana's "Independency" underpinned by her "having a plentiful Fortune" assumes a more radical form, as it is coupled with her vending her feminine charms as commodities to the highest male bidder outside the matrimonial domain altogether. In an earlier part of the novel, Roxana tells the reader how she weighed her financial independence against the dangers of wedlock:

> I found, that a Wife is treated with Indifference, a Mistress with a strong Passion; a Wife is look'd upon, as but an Upper-Servant, a Mistress is a Sovereign; a Wife must give up all she has; have every Reserve she makes for herself, be thought hard of, and be upbraided with her very *Pin-Money*; whereas a Mistress makes the Saying true, *that what the Man has*, is hers, and *what she has*, is her own; the Wife bears a thousand Insults, and is forc'd to sit still and bear it, or part and be undone; a Mistress insulted, helps herself immediately, and takes another. (*Roxana* 132)

A female possessor of financial property can be a "Free Woman," or even a "Man-Woman," recognizing no obligation to follow the ideology of duty patriarchy seeks to inculcate. Mistress rather than wife—the choice by no means ennobles woman as a moral subject, and Roxana can hardly claim to be a subject of edifying *Erfahrung* that can be shared with the readership at large. Yet Roxana is unperturbed by her exceptional and problematic position in a society that pays at least a lip service to "the Words *Honour* and *Obey*." "What she has" is solely important. Or, as Moll puts it bluntly, "his Money" is her "Business." Infatuation of the male lover converted into liquid cash is all that matters. Moreover, the referent of the possessive pronoun "his" in Moll's formulation, as Roxana makes it clear towards the end of the quotation, can be replaced any time by any other male partner: "a Mistress insulted, helps herself immediately, and takes another," all the while keeping and replenishing "his money" with the next fortunate gentleman purchasing her service. This formula summarizes the plot of both novels: the main female protagonist holds her ground and attitude, while her male partners change guard, returning in some cases (as does Moll's "Lancashire husband" or Roxana's "Dutch merchant"), yet regularly substituted or even literally liquidated.

The plots of *Roxana* and *Moll Flanders* hinge upon a logic of liquidity that struggles against the quintessentially illiquid closure of marriage,[11] not through some moral weighing of balance (as in the works of Jane Austen or George Eliot) but through a vigorous conversion of love into money, coupled with vigilant changing of male partners. One representative example in *Roxana* is the assassination of the English jeweller, who was her first benefactor and lover after she became a free agent. He had at first offered to set up with Roxana a *de facto* marital relationship, which she could not fool herself into accepting: "I started a little at the Word *Wedding*: What do ye mean? to call it by such a Name, *says I*; adding, We will have a Supper, but t'other is impossible, as well on your side as mine; he laugh'd, Well, says he, you shall call it what you will, but it may be the same thing, for I shall satisfie you, it is not so impossible as you make it" (*Roxana* 36). Words rather than things, particularly money as liquid things matter as the real substance of sexual interaction. Fatally for him, he has business to go to Paris, accompanied by his mistress. There he deals in selling jewels to aristocratic clients, converting precious gems into liquidity, gaining a "great Sum of Money in Specie" through these transactions, but also risking robbery and worse, "for it is not so safe a thing in *Paris*, to have a great Sum of Money in keeping, as it might be in *London*" (50). Sure enough, Paris does prove to be a perilous place to carry valuables in, for soon he meets his violent death at the hands of those bent on making off with his money. But not before he hands all the portable wealth he possesses to Roxana. She begs him not to go on that particular day, fearing the worst, but he persists, while reassuring her with words and deeds:

> [H]e takes up the Casket, or Case, Here, *says he*, hold your Hand, there is a good Estate for you, in this Case; if any thing happens to me, 'tis all your own, I give it you for yourself; and with that, he put the Casket, the fine Ring, and his Gold Watch, all into my Hands, and the Key of his Scrutore besides, adding, and in my Scrutore there is some Money, 'tis all your own. (52)

Most disturbingly, however, she already sees him as good as dead. The murder takes place in her imagination upon the conveyance of his portable property and the case storing his "great Sum of Money in Specie": "I thought all his Face look'd like a Death's-Head; and then, immediately, I thought I perceiv'd his Head all Bloody; and then his Cloaths look'd Bloody too . . . and immediately I fell a-crying, and hung about him, My Dear *said I*, I am frighted to Death; you shall not go, depend upon it, some Mischief will befal you" (52-53). Leave he does undeterred by her irrational panic, yet that would be the last leave-taking of his life before he is fetched off by the murderers, leaving the liquidity he had owned in the hands of Roxana, who then passes herself off as his widow in this foreign city.[12] His macabre metamorphosis is depicted in eerie detail, exceptionally vivid by the standards of the generally laconic narration of *Roxana*:

> I saw him as plainly in all those terrible Shapes, as above, *First*, as a Skeleton, not Dead only, but rotten and wasted; *Secondly*, as kill'd, and his Face bloody; and *Thirdly*, his Cloaths bloody; and all within the Space of one Minute, or indeed, of a very few Moments.

The sudden decay of the dead bearer of valuables into a skeleton, along with the bloody erasure of his physiognomic and sartorial identity, "all within the Space of one Minute," underscores the superb velocity of liquidation of the illiquid corpse. This "dreamer-laureate of capitalism" (Flynn 1987: 85) habitually employs the device of severing the animate bearer of money from his goods to enable it to flow into other hands. The passage is supplemented almost immediately in the next paragraph by Roxana's realization of how much liquid cash she has gained thanks to the killing:

> [A]fter some time, I began to recover, and look into my Affairs; I had the Satisfaction not to be left in Distress, or in danger of Poverty; on the contrary, besides what he had put into my Hands fairly, in his Life-time, which amounted to a very considerable Value, I found above seven Hundred Pistoles in Gold, in his Scrutore, of which he had given me the Key; and I found Foreign-Bills accepted, for about 12000 Livres; so that, in a Word, I found myself possess'd of almost ten Thousand Pounds Sterling, in a very few Days after the Disaster. (55)

The language of monetary accounting triumphs over everything else, unhampered by the shocking accident; liquidity represented in both Arabic and alphabet sums replaces the dead jeweller, transmogrified now into so many Pistoles, Livres, and Pounds Sterling. Moreover, after the disappearance of her jeweler, uninterrupted cash flow into her coffers is guaranteed by her next partner the German Prince residing in Paris, who enriches her exponentially, before he in turn is relieved of his mission by the Dutch merchant. The Dutchman soon departs from her when his marriage offer is rebuffed, so that Roxana can return to England to meet more male clients, thus insuring the liquid inflow of sperm and cash, including, as she hints, those of the king himself. All the while, liquidity and security for Roxana are happily wedded to each other, helped by Sir Robert and other financial agents.

"My Blood had no Fire in it"

There is one major stumbling block, however, resisting the liquid language of figures that washes away all sins and sorrows. Surely it cannot be the empty words "Honour" and "the Laws of Marriage," but what about affection, of lived experience, which even an amoral subject is capable of or liable to be addicted to? Moll, the earlier version of "the Liberty of a *Free Woman*" treading the borderline of patriarchal laws (even to the point of committing inadvertent incest by marrying her half-brother), has a softer heart, especially at the inception of her career. "Can you Transfer my Affection?" (*Moll* 39) asks Moll-Betty when the elder brother in the Colchester household persuades her to accept the courtship of his younger brother. Body or "sex" can be transferred, but can affection be alienated at will, or transferred "at Demand" just as a financial bill is accepted and cashed? To ask this is to assume that such a thing as genuine affection does exist at a realm separated from the world of things and thing-like values. This is a relatively plausible (if unstated) premise, since "affection" has a wider circulation than conscience or rational judgement. Moll is quite right to ask, "[I]s it in my Power think you to make such a Change at Demand?" (40) Since her faculty of willed action should be based on sober calculation of benefit, it finds itself powerless at the level of sensory affection and impression, which remains entirely her own, by not being her "own" at the level of reflection and moral action. "Vertue" and "Modesty" she has forfeited in exchange for "Purse" (29), but there is still something left in her of "Value" to recommend her, not obviously to "God's Blessing," but to the reader of the novel, a value that stays undiminished, despite her moral disarray, to purvey a series of sensational *Erlebnis*, including, most scandalously, the thrill of larceny. "I step'd into the Shop, and with my Back to the Wench, as if I had stood up for a Cart that was going by, I put my Hand behind me and took the Bundle, and went off with it, the Maid or the Fellow not perceiving me, or any one else" (*Moll* 192), goes the account of the first of Moll's many successful feats, and the reader, seduced by the quick breath of the short paratactic clauses, cannot but be infected by the excitement of the criminal act.

The case of the stern "Protestant Whore" (*Roxana* 69), who wishes to dispel any suspicion of her wanting to indulge her reader's erotic curiosity, however, is different. "I had nothing of the Vice in my Constitution; my Spirits were far from being high; my Blood had no Fire in it, to kindle the Flame of Desire" (*Roxana* 40), she asserts. Affection stirs her not, nor does erotic sensation tickle her. Indeed, throughout the book, the reader is given virtually no opportunity to share her sensory *Erlebnis* of sleeping with her men. The details of her sexual service she keeps strictly locked away, even when they enter into the chain of events constituting the plot. Her last client, an unnamed elderly nobleman, putatively enjoys unusual sex, of which all we are told is that he "grew worse and wickeder the older he grew, and that to such Degree, as is not fit to write of; and made me so weary of him, that upon one of his capricious Humours, which he often took Occasion to trouble me with, I took Occasion to be much less complaisant to him than I us'd to be" (*Roxana* 199). Fed up with his antics, Roxana breaks up the relationship. "I was sick of him," she explains, "and that on some Accounts, which, if I cou'd suffer myself to publish them, wou'd fully justifie my Conduct; but that Part of the Story will not bear telling, so I must leave it" (207). Why does it not bear telling? Why cannot she suffer herself to give a more specific account of it? Ostensibly it is due to the Puritan disposition of her author, Defoe the inventor of the pious Crusoe. Yet the logic of liquidity has also a role in it, according to which the contents of action, or the identity of agents, matter less than their convertibility into portable asset. The process of setting up their relationship, therefore, merits to be narrated in greater detail than what he did to her in the bedroom:

> He told me, that he wou'd make it evident to me, that he did not seek me by way of Bargain, as such things were often done; that as I had treated him with a generous Confidence, so I shou'd find I was in the Hands of a Man of Honour, and one that knew how to value the Obligation; and upon this, he pull'd out a Goldsmith's Bill for 300 *l.* which, putting it into my Hand, he said he gave me as a Pledge, that I shou'd not be a Loser by my now having made a Bargain with him. (*Roxana* 185)

The aging philanderer's words are reported extensively, but above all the precise sum of what he handed her, "a Goldsmith's Bill for 300 *l.*"[13], endorses the veracity of her account (in both senses of the word), as well as the validity of her decision to accept him. Money talks in figures, once again, but abiding by a secular and transparent grammar of transaction and "Bargain," rather than the half-religious intimation of divine intervention as in *A Journal of the Plague Year*. In contrast to the visual prominence of "300 *l.*", the man who offers it remains faceless and nameless. He is a mere "he," for his money, indeed, is her business.

Roxana, and to a lesser extent *Moll Flanders*, are both what we may call "pronoun novels," in that to the grammatical subject "I" is connected the other (mostly anonymous) characters indicated by third-person pronouns. The "I" that narrates her tales marks the items, goods, and agency offered by these others by the possessive pronouns "my" and "mine." This simplified referential nexus applies perfectly well to Crusoe in his isolation:

> During this Confinement in *my* Cover, by the Rain, I work'd daily two or three Hours at enlarging *my* Cave, and by Degrees work'd it on towards one Side, till I came to the Out-Side of the Hill, and made a Door or Way out, which came beyond *my* Fence or Wall, and so I came in and out this Way; but I was not perfectly easy at lying so open; for as I had manag'd *my* self before, I was in a perfect Enclosure. (*Crusoe* 88, italics added)

Crusoe can with a fair degree of justice claim not only that his "self" is his own ("my self"), but his "Cover," "Cave," and "Fence" are all his, by virtue of their being products of his industrious labour, as we observed in chapter one. When a second individual's existence creates minimal society, however, his calling him "my Man" (185) creates legal ambiguity, since his having saved the savage's life does not indubitably make the latter *his* possession in the same sense that his fence is his. All the more so, then, in the complex society where Moll or Roxana has to fend for herself, the private subject's relationship with the other agents (for they are rarely treated as subjects) betrays its strain. For although what Moll gathers from her criminal career is hers, and Roxana's "plentiful Fortune" is her money, their possessions lack the ethical sanction gracing Crusoe's property rights. Moll, typically, has to be made friendless and isolated, a Crusoe in a crowded urban society rather than on a desert island: "I WAS now a single Person again, *as I may call my self*, I was loos'd from all the Obligations either of Wedlock or Mistressship in the World; except my Husband the Linnen Draper, who I having not now heard from in almost Fifteen year, no Body could blame me for thinking my self entirely freed from" (*Moll* 126). She only has her free "self" to care for, but unlike Crusoe, that "self" which is hers has to be disguised, denoted by a pseudonym or nickname given to her at the apex of her thieving career by her jealous colleagues in the profession carried off to Newgate:

> These were they that gave me the Name of *Moll Flanders*: For it was no more of Affinity with my real Name, or with any of the Names I had ever gone by, than black is of Kin to white, except that once, as before I call'd my self Mrs. *Flanders*, when I sheltered myself in the *Mint*; but that these Rogues never knew, nor could I ever learn how they came to give me the Name, or what the Occasion of it was. (*Moll* 214)

The case of "Roxana" is little different in this regard, for it is what she is called by Society beaus after her Turkish dance performed at her Pall Mall residence: "At the finishing the Dance, the Company clapp'd, and almost shouted; and one of the Gentlemen cry'd out, *Roxana*! *Roxana*! by ___, with an Oath; upon which foolish Accident I had the Name of *Roxana* presently fix'd upon me all over the Court End of Town, as effectually as if I had been Christen'd *Roxana*" (*Roxana* 176). "Roxana" and "Moll Flanders" are slippery signifiers with no essential anchorage in the "truth" of the bearers of these names. The subject as subject is liquefied to ensure the influx of liquidity into their pockets. As subjects cloaked in mystery they confront society as their antagonist, as vigilant as Crusoe, fortifying their "perfect Enclosure" against the "Rogues" or the "Gentlemen" of West End, who "never knew" who the women they call "Moll Flanders" or "Roxana" really were. But the city space is a formidable opponent. It is an arena where the contest between deception and detection unfolds permanently, as we shall see in the next chapter.

CHAPTER FOUR

"I" AGAINST THE CITY

"A Stab that touch'd the Vitals"

Defoe's importance in the tradition of the novel's engagement with the city lies above all in the manner in which a distinctively metropolitan outlook and disposition embedded in modernity, clearly visible in Pepys, informs the conception and composition of his works. From the voices of the private sphere through the textuality of disjunctive conjunction to the "ideal of numerical calculability," we have traced the stages and elements constituting the metropolitan conditions of Defoe's fictional narratives. Now we finally focus on the more specific question of how the city is represented in Defoe's major novels, inevitably excluding *Robinson Crusoe* which takes places in a hypothetical setting removed from European society. We begin first with *Roxana*. Although it apparently shows little of the actual cities where the protagonist stays in, the work presents a dominant metropolitan viewpoint or ideology: the perception of the big city as a locus of international finance.

The logic of liquidity constituting the world of finance has as its motto a slightly altered version of the famous characterization of modern bourgeois world by *The Communist Manifesto*: all that is solid melts into numbers.[1] The numerically represented values and assets of financial capital are emptied of their historical, social, moral, and spatial contents, so that they can circulate with least resistance as liquid wealth between individuals living apart, separated geographically even, with little in common beyond their trust in the value represented by the bank notes or bills passed on from one agent to another. Credit, trust, and speculation, with all their attendant perils, attend the world of finance. In the securities market, the price of shares could soar up steeply or plummet as spectacularly and instantly. This has immediate implications for fiction writing, as the rise and fall of private fortunes can be readily converted into plots for novels. In the case of Defoe, one feels tempted to match his tales to the South Sea Bubble, the first major modern stock market crash that took place as Defoe was producing his masterpieces. One may, for instance, point out how the labour theory of value informing *Robinson Crusoe* (1719), written just before the Bubble (1720), supplemented by the huge financial windfall Crusoe receives from his plantation in Brazil, typifies a pre-Bubble faith in an economy of unswerving growth and unfailing reward. By contrast, Moll's fluctuation in her status and possession—as hinted by the vacillating formula peculiar to this book published in 1722 of affirmation yoked to negation, as in "being now . . . a Woman of Fortune, tho' I was a Woman without a Fortune" (*Moll* 106)—arguably reflects a view of market economy as a realm of insecurity and volatility, as a pattern of arbitrary allotment of loss as well as gain, made poignant by the recent Bubble. *Roxana*, written four years after the financial fiasco when the market was more or less recovering stability, reasserts a sense of trust in the economy of uninterrupted growth, yet without the moral or theological beatitude Crusoe's property enjoyed.[2] Moreover, Roxana's wealth takes on a simplified abstract form of financial liquidity, unencumbered by the hand-made utilities Crusoe spent the good part of his life perfecting. The sturdy vision of labour-based appropriation in the earlier novel appears in *Roxana* sorely weakened and irretrievably dated—drowned, as it were, in the South Seas.

Interesting as such allegorical reading, offered for instance by Christina L. Healey (Healy 496-97) may be, it can only remain itself essentially speculative, not merely because there is no direct reference to the Bubble in any of Defoe's fictions, but more significantly because the financial system presupposed in them betrays no sign of being vulnerable to radical disturbance. On the contrary, Roxana's prosperity is predicated on secure investment as guaranteed by the real-name character Sir Robert Clayton, as we have seen already. The case of Moll does register a certain anxiety about the finance market. First, after being abandoned by her Bath gentleman, she invests what stock she has in the business of a Goldsmith, the forerunners of modern banking in early-modern London, who goes bankrupt: "I had sav'd above 100 *l.* more, but I met with a Disaster with that, which was this; that a Goldsmith in whose Hands I had trusted it, broke, so I lost 70 *l.* of my Money, the Man's Composition not making above 30 *l.* out of his 100 *l*" (*Moll* 127). This instance can be construed, however, as underscoring the need to hoist the financial market up from the relatively primitive stage of relying on private goldsmiths to a more de-personalized and institutionalized stage ushered in by the establishment of National Debt and the Bank of England, which secured London's position as the undisputed centre of national (and later, international) finance. The City became synonymous with London, and the representative Londoners were City financiers such as the voting proprietors of the Bank of England, most of whom lived in London or nearby suburbs (Price 73). The hegemony of City's finance sector emerged in Defoe's age, and this is what his characters learn to accept. Moll realizes that having no individual to put her trust in, only the financial institutions can befriend her. She has her misgivings about entrusting them with her money at first, as she "look'd upon it as unsafe" (*Moll* 130), but she decides to visit a bank, finding the clerk there "very Honest and Just" (131). His fair dealings with her dispel her fears, so much so that a human (and sexual) relationship develops with this representative of finance. Unfortunately, however, this honest clerk, whom Moll marries, dies of disappointment when his investment fails: "[T]he Wound had sunk too deep, it was a Stab that touch'd the Vitals, he grew Melancholy and Disconsolate, and from thence Lethargick, and died." But this part of her life story further demonstrates the twofold danger of personalized financial investment. First, the banker husband's fatal mistake was that he had "trusted one of his Fellow Clarks with a Sum of Money too much for our Fortunes to bear the Loss of" (189). Second, Moll's having converted her business relationship with him into a marital tie courted trouble: her marital venture fails simultaneously with her "disconsolate" husband's death. Unaffected by these personal vicissitudes, the fundamentals of financial system seem stable enough in *Moll Flanders*. Even in the commodity-based economy of the New World where tobacco, as well as specie, circulates as hard currency, Moll and her son have no difficulty calculating the value of the plantation Moll's mother bequeathed to her: "I ask'd him what he thought the Plantation might be worth, *he said*, if I would let it out, he would give me about sixty Pounds a Year for it; but if I would live on it, then it would be worth much more, and he believ'd would bring me in about 150 *l.* a Year" (336). Moreover, the translation of the value of tobacco into pound sterling and vice versa (for Moll brings to Virginia virtually all the cash amassed through her criminal career) affirms the reliability of a trans-Atlantic network of financial circulation, quite apart from any morality or legality involved in accumulating the initial sum. In *Roxana*, the free and secure flow of liquidity across national borders and seas is further elaborated, providing the novel with its basic narrative matrix.

Roxana, as she tells the reader in the opening pages of the novel, comes from an expatriate Huguenot family in London hailing from Poitiers, France. Born in this French town to an ethnic-sectarian minority with a strong sense of their distinct identity,[3] she is earmarked for a deterriorialized mode of existence of migrating from one relationship to another, not fully belonging to any one city or country. The stages of her adult life can be marked in terms of where she lives and how much she is worth. Her father marries her to a brewer with a handsome dowry of £2,000 (*Roxana* 7). The husband, however, squanders away both his and his wife's patrimony. Upon his sudden "Elopement" (13), she is left destitute, but not for long, since her landlord the jewel-trader provides for her as his mistress. The next phase of her life takes place in Paris, where her jeweller is killed, leaving her a handsome fortune amounting to £10,000 (65), which is boosted considerably by the German prince who uses her on princely terms indeed, financially and otherwise, in Paris and also during their "*Grand Tour*" (102) in Italy. When this third partner cuts off the relationship, she makes her way back to London via Rotterdam, now aided by a Dutch merchant, whose marriage offer she adamantly rebuffs even as she grants him sexual favors. In London, she establishes herself as a Society mistress at Pall Mall, where she is baptized "Roxana" by her fans. She then shuttles to and from her Kensington house maintaining her pleasure and profit-seeking liaisons with the rich and powerful, having by then become a lady worth £50,000, or £2,800 per annum (188). When she quits her mercenary career, seeking to conceal her identity as "Roxana," and hence is made vulnerable to her daughter Susan's investigations into her past, she domesticates herself at the Minories in the City, where she runs into her old Dutch merchant, whom she now weds. After the mysterious disappearance of Susan, she leaves England and moves to an unidentified Dutch city, where we are told in the last paragraph that "the Blast of Heaven" struck them both and that she is "brought so low again" (330). But throughout the novel, Roxana's fortune steadily and at some phases spectacularly increases, more than making up for the dowry forfeited due to her foolish first husband. While her financial earnings describe a stable upward curve, her changing addresses yield a crisscross pattern, as she moves from London to Paris, from Paris via Rotterdam to London (West End), from West End via Kensington to City, and from City to Holland. These urban spaces serve as the backdrop of her private pursuit of interests, with some men rich in cash taking her up at each stop. Moreover, the cities assist her accumulation of fortune jointly through a pre-established system of financial clearance, namely, that of international bills of exchange.

"An accepted Bill, payable at *Rotterdam*"

A foreign bill of exchange presupposes a network of credit, which Defoe likened in *An Essay Upon Publick Credit* to the "Sun-shine" beaming from the "Sun" of "Probity" and "Honesty" (*PEW* 6.53), all the more so as it depends on a system of mutual trust built on the bona fide acknowledgment of monetary obligation by geographically segregated traders stationed in their respective cities. This network of undersigned confirmations of trust works as a parallel credit-based transactions in two or more nationally divided cities. Bills of exchange were first devised by Italian merchants in the thirteenth century to clear payments between Italian cities and Burges. Later, it was perfected in the sixteenth-century Antwerp and Amsterdam into a pattern of mediated transaction involving the participation of at least four parties in the circulation and clearance of a monetary obligation denoted by a particular bill (Kindleberger 41; Neal 7). Simply put, merchant X in Florence buys goods from Y in Burges, pays for it by buying a bill drawn by A in Florence who had sold goods to B in Flanders; X sends the bill instead of hard currency to Y, who cashes it from B when the bill matures (Kindleberger 41). Actual clearance of payment in international trade will most likely be far more complex than this, with three or more intermediaries signing and passing the bill from one to another in different directions. But what remains unaltered is the fact that parallelism is mandatory for the bills to function at all.

Fictional application of such parallel transaction activated by bills of exchange similarly assumes the form of a globalized network of traders and cities. *Roxana* constructs between London, the French capital, and the cities of the Low Countries a mutually interdependent "city-system" or "system of cities," which the urbanization in this part of Europe had first exemplified (de Vries 260-1; Pred 13). Roxana moves along this inter-city axis: from London to Paris to Rotterdam and finally back to London. Of special importance is Roxana's return to England after the termination of her services to the German Prince, for she is now burdened with large amounts of cash, bills, and valuables. She first has to remove her possessions from Paris, which the Dutch merchant offers to facilitate through his international business connections:

> [A]s to my Money, he gave me first of all an accepted Bill, payable at *Rotterdam*, for 4000 Pistoles, and drawn from *Genoa* upon a Merchant at *Rotterdam*, payable to a Merchant at *Paris*, and endors'd by him to my Merchant; this he assur'd me wou'd be punctually paid, and so it was, to a Day; the rest I had in other Bills of Exchange, drawn by himself upon other Merchants in *Holland*. (*Roxana* 121)

Next, she has to transfer her considerable wealth to England: "I had in Ready-Money, and in Account in the Bank at *Amsterdam*, above One and twenty Thousand Pistoles, besides Jewels; and how to get this Treasure to *England*, was my next Care" (162-63). Averse, however, to risk entrusting her whole fortune to a single agent, she contacts different merchants in

Rotterdam separately, securing different "Bills of Exchange, payable in *London*" (163). All of these bills are "accepted, and currently paid" (164) upon her return to London. Roxana assesses her "Treasure" by calculating its worth in "Pistoles," but the word's Spanish provenance meaning gold coin matters little in this usage as a shorthand term for numerical evaluation. Heavy precious metals need not cross the seas, for in the world of financial liquidity, national borders are melted away so that the airy papers signifying gold can easily travel back and forth. Cities retain importance as the stops in the journey of bills of exchange enacted in the abstract language of credit which supplements, substitutes, and displaces transactions in specie. Yet Rotterdam, Genoa, Paris, Amsterdam, and London, in the above quotations, indicate not so much places of habitation with distinctive histories and heritages of experience, as mere locations of impersonal financial agencies, severed from both the communal contextualizing of *Erfahrung* and the sensory shocks of *Erlebnis*.

The ending of *Captain Singleton* presents an earlier version of these abstracted city names used as signifiers referring to financial markets. The pirate launders his illicit fortune as he returns to England via Italy: "[W]e verted a large Sum of Money in Bales of Silk, left a large Sum in a Merchant's Hands at *Venice*, and another considerable Sum at *Naples*, and took Bills of Exchange for a great deal too; and yet we came with such a Cargoe to *London*, as few *American* Merchants had done for some Years" (*Singleton* 225). Between *Captain Singleton* (1720) and *Roxana* (1724), the finance sector in Defoe's fiction has grown to such an extent that all cargoes and solid goods, which Singleton was burdened with in addition to his bills of exchange, have been converted into paper wealth or what Defoe in *An Essay upon Projects* defined as "memorandum" for money (*PEW* 8.54),[4] thanks to the international network of credit. The business of finance in *Roxana* appears miraculously immune, furthermore, to the ills of stock market, which Defoe the pamphleteer regularly chastised. "Is not the whole Doctrine of Stock-Jobbing a Science of Fraud? And are not all the Dealers, meer Original Thieves and Pick-Pockets?" asks the author of *The Anatomy of Exchange-Alley* (*PEW* 6.132). Others may fall prey to the "destructive *Hydra*" of "Stock-Jobbing" (*PEW* 6.39), but Roxana's fortune is preserved and increased, unaffected by these "Original Thieves." London has been transformed by the introduction of National Debt into "a Corporation of Usury," according to Defoe's *Essay Upon Loans* (*PEW* 6.69), but Roxana could not care less for she stands to benefit from such institutionalized usury. The devastating potentials of stock market and its dubious agents would become a crucial motif in Dickens's *Little Dorrit*, but Defoe the fiction-writer, unlike Defoe the journalist, declines to confront the fraudulent spectres of stock-jobbing.

Metropolitan financial intermediaries and institutions vitally assist the passage of Roxana and her possessions from one country to another. However, her very success as a most expensive kept mistress owes a great deal to a unique feature of big-city life: preservation of incognito through anonymity (or in Roxana's case, through her "pseudonymity"). A rural community either already knows or easily discovers an individual's identity. Although not as transparent, smaller urban communities and towns can also prevent without too much difficulty their members' anonymity. In a sprawling, densely populated metropolis, the very proximity and concentration of strangers paradoxically favours not only what we called earlier the "private sphere" but a complete protection of one's identity from the scrutiny of others. Quite apart from the scale of human concentration in big cities, the development of finance in these locations also contributes to the anonymity of its clients in their place of residence. The metropolitan centres of international finance erect between themselves an aerial transcendental network with tenuous ties to the concrete social space of the locality they are stationed in. At this level of abstraction germane to the world of finance—worked into such formula in current business journalese as "Wall Street resurged" or "City panicked"—the city is reduced to its finance market, whose language is that of numerical figures spoken as a globalized lingua franca tracking the fickle temperaments of Sir "FTSE" and Mr. "Dow Jones."

Just as the abstraction of numbered quantities disjoins the city's financial function from its historical location, it liberates the individuals involved in finance from all ties to solid, illiquid, social relationships to the large community.[5] If this is freedom, it is also lack of freedom, for in *Roxana*, the individual's urban isolation appears as a locked-up seclusion or even incarceration, due to effort to fend off the intrusion of the city's social fabric weaved by its inhabitants. Roxana the owner of financial fortune interacts with the city as finance market, while Roxana the seller of her sexual charms inevitably depends on the city as habitation. In both capacities, she is cut off from the society of city dwellers who set up a community of neighbourhood and livelihood. Above all, in Paris, where she becomes the exclusive property of the German Prince, she enters into a kind of voluntary house arrest, not known to anyone else besides her lover, in a "gay sort of Retirement almost three Years" (*Roxana* 75). Moreover, the very location of her house ideally suits a secretive liaison, as it takes full advantage of the chaotic layout of the densely developed capital:

> [M]y House was the most convenient that could possibly be found in all *Paris*, for an Amour, especially for him; having a Way out into Three Streets,

> and not overlook'd by any Neighbours, so that he could pass and repass, without Observation; for one of the Back-ways open'd into a narrow dark Alley, which Alley was a Thorow-fare, or Passage, out of one Street into another; and any Person that went in or out by the Door, had no more to do, but to see, that there was no-body following him in the Alley, before he went in at the Door. (*Roxana* 66)

The house occupies one part of Paris, but Paris as a space of habitation is cordoned off from her. Roxana prevents herself from conversing with her neighbours or sharing of her life experience (*Erfahrung*), just as she is spared the unpredictable contingency (*Erlebnis*) of outdoor urban space—a space exploited so profitably by Moll the pickpocket. The city itself exists only in an abstracted, suspended state. This urban labyrinth encloses a complete privacy within a piece of privately-owned real estate in Paris, comparable to the locked-doors of Pepys' study in the way its layered barriers keep the public sphere at bay. Situated at the junction of thoroughfares, it is itself a no-thoroughfare, jealously guarding its doors against outsiders who have no business to know who the person living inside is. Roxana's self-captivity appears a utopia of metropolitan privacy, in which the material benefits of sophisticated society can be easily enjoyed, a clear advantage over the rustic ambience of Crusoe's privacy. "No man is an *Iland*, intire of it self" (Donne 441), meditated the Dean of St. Paul's in the early decades of the seventeenth century. A century or so later, Defoe envisions an insular existence inside a bustling metropolis, a secluded privacy at the heart of a crowded city.

"A large and gay City"

Roxana in her youth, however, was by no means so secretive. She used to be an outgoing girl in love with the wonders and curiosities the city streets abounded with: "*London*, a large and gay City, took with me mighty well, who, from my being a Child, lov'd a Crowd, and to see a great-many fine Folks" (*Roxana* 5). Later when she returns to the city where she grew up, she stops being a privately appropriated and enclosed mistress she was in Paris, to live as a lady renting an expensive Pall Mall town house with her doors open to the rich and powerful of the "gay City." And this time, too, London takes with her might well indeed. She puts on "as gay a Show" (165) as she could devise on the stage of her halls, where her fabulous Turkish dance earns her the sobriquet "Roxana." This controlled publicity meant to appease her desire for social entertainment, as well as her desire for maximum monetary gains from illicit sexual relationship, moves partially away both from the abstract "city systems" finance constructs and the complete urban anonymity her service to the Prince required. Human society, however, proves a formidable match for her. The city as a concrete historical space of dwelling reasserts its force, threatening to resurrect the personal history of the pseudonymous figure called "Roxana." Roxana's socializing with the select society at Pall Mall helps her wash herself clean of her past experience. Things go well for the time being, but that degree of public openness necessary for her social existence sows the seed of later trouble, as one of her menial maids turns out to be a daughter from her first marriage. In this regard, her being tormented by the detective work of Susan, bent on having her mother recognize her blood ties, illustrates something more than the "inevitable moral-psychological laws of nature" (Richetti 1975: 225). In this novel where laws of nature hold little sway, Susan's intrusion into Roxana's privacy signifies the return of the repressed, that is, the irrepressible return not merely of one of its disinherited subjects but of the city as fundamental locus of concrete familial, social, and historical relationships with all the codes, demands, and powers that challenge Roxana's appropriation of the city for private profiteering—the return of the city as a storehouse of *Erfahrung*, in short.

The city that returns now, moreover, has a topography on which class disparity is indelibly inscribed. Driven by compunction, Roxana remembers her two daughters left at "Spittle-Fields" at London's East End, the elder of whom (i.e. Susan) "had liv'd with a great Lady at the other-end of the Town" (*Roxana* 190). The return of the city signaled by the entrance of Susan into the narrative registers a return not only of maternal truth, as critics have readily pointed out (Kibbie 1031; Healey 504), but of the proletarian truth of labour and its exploitation that the numerical language of figures spoken by finance attempts to suppress and erase. The class polarization between the affluent West End of Roxana's High Society and the shabby districts towards the east was firmly established by the seventeenth century, if not earlier, so that those ensconced behind wealth could comfortably forget the city of the poor pushed eastward.[6] As far as the *rentiers* such as Roxana and her clients past and present are concerned, money is a miracle breeding more money thanks to the "technology" of financial mathematics. But its miracle translates into a nightmare for those at the lower end of the social ladder: as the great critic of capitalism put it, money as capital is a vampire that fattens itself by preying on human labour.[7] In the false account fabricated by Amy of what happened to her destitute mistress after her husband disappeared, Roxana is supposed to have become a London seamstress, like Dickens's Amy Dorrit, "very shabby, and poor in Cloaths," leading a miserable existence working "with her Needle, for her Bread" (*Roxana* 89). Compared with the series of remarkably fortunate turns of events that lead to the wealth and fame of "Roxana," this negative scenario has the merit of being far more plausible. This proletarian spectre of menial life the narrative keeps at bay vigilantly, yet the greatness of *Roxana* as a novel lies in its succumbing to another proletarian nemesis, which presents a self-criticism of its aerial mythos of self-perpetuating finance capital, of "directly self-valorizing value" (Marx 1981: 515).

Susan, the former maid of Roxana is a proletarian historian or a Benjaminian storyteller bent on sharing her *Erfahrung* with others, as she seeks to connect the mother who had abandoned her children with her employer who made the fatal but unavoidable error of showing herself to her servants. With the intrusion of Susan into Roxana's life, the "history excluded from her commodity identity" returns to disrupt the "constant present elicited in the pattern of commodity exchanges," as Janet Sorensen argues (Sorensen 87). The language of figures finance speaks can pretend ignorance of the messy world of hired domestic labour allotted to the likes of Susan, as well as the myriad life stories the menial proletarians bear on their humble (and often aching) backs. The grammar of novelistic realism, however, cannot turn a deaf year to their outcries and tearful voices, to the "Passion of crying" (*Roxana* 269) which attends Susan like a leitmotif whenever she interacts with Amy. At stake is the real identity and history of the person known as "Roxana," who wishes to give herself a new respectable identity by erasing her past. It is a spatial issue, too, as the force of the antagonistic socioeconomic topography of London batters the protective barrier of Roxana's realm of private interests. It immediately results in her financial fortune itself turning into a bitter pill of reproach: "They might be said to have gnaw'd a Hole in my Heart before; but now they made a Hole quite thro' it; now they eat into all my pleasant things; made bitter every Sweet, and mix'd my Sighs with every Smile" (*Roxana* 264). Roxana retreats helter-skelter from Society to the neutral territory of urban burghers between the "other-end of the Town" and East End. Susan's mother thinks she has found in the rooms of a Quaker lady in the "little narrow Passage in the *Minories*" just what she needs to launder her identity and preserve her incognito: "I was now in perfect Retreat indeed; remote from the Eyes of all that ever had seen me, and as much out of the way of being ever seen or heard-of by any of the Gang that us'd to follow me, as if I had been among the Mountains in *Lancashire*" (211). Minories, located at the eastern border of the City, may be distant enough from West End but dangerously close to "Spittle-Fields." Sniffed out by the indefatigable Susan, Roxana has to flee the City further down river to Redriff, only to find she is followed by the girl who "spar'd no Pains"

(316) and who desperately pursues her mother, "as if, *like a Hound*, she had had a hot Scent" (317). Run down breathless by this female Inspector Hound, Roxana seethes with impotent rage when Amy dispatches the pursuer mysteriously, relieving her of her worries but adding new torments of conscience that will plague her remaining days. The city, and all its formidable reality of social relationships, returns with vengeance, destroying the dream of perfect privacy at a perfect retreat. No man or woman is an island, indeed, in a city pregnant with *historia* (history and/as narrative), grand or small.

"Dropt down Dead in the very Markets"

Defoe, nevertheless, sought to contain the communal history of his city within the purview of an individual subject. He took immense pains to reconstruct a private subject's experience of coping with the collective tragedy of the Great Plague, giving it an authenticating objective name of "A Journal of the Plague Year." This first-person narrative occupies a major post in the author's exploration of the possibilities and limitations of the private sphere which permeates his lasting fictional monuments named after each protagonist from *Robinson Crusoe* to *Roxana*. The disjunctive conjunction embedded in the title of the work yokes together the public ethos of reporting on the plague and the presumption of the private individual who arrogates to himself such right of representation. But the narrator's public role paradoxically hinges upon his maintenance of rigid distance from his fellow inhabitants. Interaction with the city's crowd becomes a taboo due to his fear of contamination, compelling the narrator to preserve his incognito, actual and emotional. As he roams around the devastated city streets, he defends himself from the dangers of contact as unfailingly as if he were a Roxana secluded behind the doors of her Parisian apartments. The premise of this fiction is that "there was no such Thing as Communication with one another" (*Plague Year* 69). The city is turned into a veritable state of nature where "self Preservation indeed appear'd here to be the first Law," and where "every one's private Safety lay so near them," so that "they had no Room to pity the Distresses of others" (115). Or better still, since it takes place not in a savage wilderness but in an advanced commercial city, the situation belongs to a state of exception, of "anomie" (*a-nomos*, "no-law") induced by the epidemic, to draw on Agamben's analysis (Agamben 2005: 70). Here the a-nonymous and exceptional "I" who observes and narrates the plague assumes supreme sovereignty unbound by any law or moral imperative otherwise than that of protecting one's own life. Thanks to his armory of anonymity (he signs himself "H. F." only towards the very end of the narrative) and the psychological *cordon sanitaire* protecting his emotions from excessive pity, as well as guarding his natural right to "self Preservation," the writer of the "Journal" can make close observation of the disaster, supplemented by other people's reports. The immediacy of the account is such that it almost turns him, as it were, into a live camera eye capturing the spectacle of death and destruction at close quarters, alert to the danger he risks and hostile to the potential threat of contamination fellow citizens pose.

The peril of interacting with other humans living or dying in the city is real enough. The city in *A Journal of the Plague Year* is a nightmare version of the commercial city, the city as marketplace (*Stadt-Markt*), which for Max Weber is the major archetype of Western cities (Weber 1213-14). The minimum interaction in the marketplace requisite for daily subsistence has become itself a prime cause of mutual contamination. As he writes, "this Necessity of going out of our Houses to buy Provisions, was in a great Measure the Ruin of the whole City, for the People catch'd the Distemper, on those Occasions, one of another, and even the Provisions themselves were often tainted" (78). The lethal effect of exchanging cash with commodities among the "tainted" individuals is shockingly instantaneous:

> Innumerable dismal Stories we heard every Day on this very Account: Sometimes a Man or Woman dropt down Dead in the very Markets; for many People that had the Plague upon them, knew nothing of it; till the inward Gangreen had affected their Vitals and they dy'd in a few Moments; this caus'd, that many died frequently in that Manner in the Streets suddainly, without any warning: Others perhaps had Time to go to the next Bulk or Stall; or to any Door, Porch, and just sit down and die. (*Plague Year* 78-79)

This amounts to a "market failure" indeed, in the literal sense of the term. Neither the numeral language of figures spoken in the world of finance, nor the strategic network of cities enabling the bills of exchange to circulate freely, can rescue the city's retail market from this horrifying destruction. That Defoe was not entirely exaggerating the danger and anxiety of infected goods can be corroborated by Pepys' diary during the plague months. Pepys purchased a new wig but is afraid to use it, because

> the plague was in Westminster when I bought it. And it is a wonder what will be the fashion after the plague is done as to periwigs, for nobody will dare to buy any haire for fear of the infection—that it had been cut off of the heads of people dead of the plague. (3 Sept 1665 [6.210])

Pepys' explanation of his reservations about wearing his periwig refers to three related but separate circuits of transformation involved in the production of the item. The normal extraction of the raw material from human body and the processing of human hair into vendible wigs are preceded by what he fears is the macabre conversion of living body of humans into "the heads of people dead of the plague." Pepys' disquiet reflects what Defoe's H. F. attributes to the "Power of Avarice" which led some to "run any Hazard to steal and to plunder, and particularly in Houses where all the Families, or Inhabitants have been dead" (*Plague Year* 83). Apart from the alienated surplus labour that goes into commodity production in general, the literal death of the original owners of the hair haunts this particular metamorphosis of nature into merchandise. Moreover, thrust by the undying "Power of Avarice" to enter circulation, the hairs of the dead menace to be undead, since in its afterlife its lethal power lives on to taint the purchaser and user.

The "Power of Avarice," however, also had provided for the segregation of the city's dwellings of the well-to-do from those assigned to the destitute. Those who have to go out to purchase their daily bread are mostly the poor tenants of the city, unable to turn their houses into well-provisioned barracks, like the Dutch merchants "who kept their Houses like little Garrisons besieged, suffering none to go in or out, or come near them" (*Plague Year* 55). The rich and the fashionable, including the king, had already fled the dangerous city:

> It is true, a vast many People fled . . . yet they were chiefly from the *West* End of the Town; and from what we call the Heart of the City, that is to say, among the wealthiest of the People; and such People as were unencumbered with Trades and Business: But of the rest, the Generality stay'd and seem'd to abide the worth. (18)

A clear class divide separates those who are tied to their business and trade from those with comfortable income, supporting and supported by the city's finance sector as its agents or clients, which is the realm of society Roxana moves in. The latter can afford to transcend the physical constraints of daily money-making or bread-earning, but those at the other extreme are bound for life to the city as labour and provisions market. The proletarian conditions of the poor dictate their having to sell their labour power on a daily, weekly, or monthly basis, and the purchase of their daily needs follows the same rhythm of repetition:

> [T]he poor People cou'd not lay up Provisions, and there was a necessity, that they must go to Market to buy, and others to send Servants or their Children; and as this was a Necessity which renew'd it self daily; it brought abundance

of unsound People to the Markets, and a great many that went thither Sound, brought Death Home with them. (78)

One may say that the labour market (and not just during the early stage of industrial revolution!) has always been this death-inducing mechanism, which depletes human labour power and often rewards the workers with occupational diseases that accelerate their early death. Yet such critique of capitalism is only dimly intimated by this tableau of the city as market revealing its murderous features. The epidemic wrecks havoc mostly on the poor, which, furthermore, is credited by H. F. as having a beneficial side effect of culling excess population. The plague's killing of "thirty or forty Thousand" of the poor unemployed he deems a "Deliverance in its Kind," for "had they been left, would certainly have been an unsufferable Burden," since "the whole City could not have supported the Expence of them, or have provided Food for them" (98). The language of political arithmetic injects a proto-Malthusian sanitation into human casualties, which is explicitly understood as a class-bound calamity affecting the jobless masses of the poor. The rich, or the half-rich such as Pepys, could carry on their habitual routine elsewhere or with less exposure to the dangers of infection.[8]

As for the narrator himself, being a wholesale saddler, his "Business and Shop" detain him, for his stock has the misfortune of existing as bulky cumbersome substance: "I was a single Man 'tis true, but I had a Family of Servants, who I kept at my Business, had a House, Shop, and Ware-houses fill'd with Goods; and in short, to leave them all as things in such a Case must be left . . . without any Overseer of Person fit to be trusted with them, had been to hazard the Loss not only of my Trade, but of my Goods, and indeed of all I had in the World" (*Plague Year* 8-9). To this prudent business consideration is added "some Accident or other" (10), which worked towards his abandoning the idea of evacuation, obliging him to leave everything in the hands of God, who, according to orthodox Calvinist doctrine, "had an undisputed Right of Soveraignity in disposing of me" (11). Submit to divine Providence one may, yet lead one's daily life one has to, as well. Like others remaining in London, he has to grapple with the breakup of smooth circulation of goods and service the thriving capital was famed for. His solution is to turn his house into a self-sufficient island, having provided himself with everything he needs for bare survival; he becomes, in other words, an urban Robinson Crusoe:

[F]irst, as I had Convenience both for Brewing and Baking, I went and bought two Sacks of Meal, and for several Weeks, having an Oven, we baked all our own Bread; also I bought Malt, and brew'd as much Beer as all the

> Casks I had would hold, and which seem'd enough to serve my House for five or six Weeks; also I laid in a Quantity of Salt-butter and *Cheshire* Cheese; but I had no Flesh-meat, and the Plague raged so violently among the Butchers, and Slaughter-Houses, on the other Side of our Street, where they are known to dwell in great Numbers, that it was not advisable, so much as to go over the Street among them. (77-78)

Both H. F. and Crusoe pursue self-sufficiency, but H. F.'s dietary regime appears even more frugal than that of Crusoe, as he has to forego the pleasure of eating red meat, supplied by the flock of goats in the latter's case, although the former's beer is what Crusoe might certainly envy.

The comparison cannot be taken too far, of course. H. F. lives in a crowded city, full of humans, alive, afflicted, or dying. He has more to be preoccupied with or interested in than securing his daily bread. He appears a quintessential metropolitan subject addicted to appeasing his visual appetite for the fascinating spectacle the city offers. Tolerably prepared to weather the storm behind locked doors of his house, he nevertheless repeatedly makes sally into the streets, unable to contain his "unsatisfy'd Curiosity" (80) which "led, or rather drove" him "to go and see" (60) the sights of hellish torments again and again:

> [T]he swellings which were generally in the Neck, or Groin, when they grew hard, and would not break, grew so painful, that it was equal to the most exquisite Torture; and some not able to bear the Torment, threw themselves out at Windows, or shot themselves, or otherwise made themselves away, and I saw several dismal Objects of that Kind. (*Plague Year* 76)

The almost placid tone of describing this "most exquisite Torture" shows little signs of commiseration for the poor victims. Most improbably, and more so even than the timely replenishment of Roxana's income by willing male partners, he survives his peregrinations in the infected city unscathed, in part no doubt owing to the healthy diet he maintained, but above all, by keeping a safe distance between himself as the observing subject and the "dismal" human "Objects" he encounters. As such, the narrative as a whole enacts a fantasy of assertive privacy, in contrast to the largely reserved defensive privacy of Roxana. Moreover, he is spared, armed by "the sustaining power of reflective isolation" (Bender 82), the torment of conscience which besets Roxana towards the end of her tale, or the depressions the lonesome Crusoe has to cope with. "*A dreadful Plague in* London *was, / In the Year Sixty Five, / Which swept an Hundred Thousand Souls / Away; yet I alive!*" (*Plague Year* 248), goes the closing "Stanza" of the book. The final emphasis of *A Journal of the Plague Year* falls on the very first word of the title, *a* journal kept by *an* anonymous private subject (concealed behind his last-minute signature of "H. F") describing the devastating public calamity but also prevailing over the universal havoc which decimated the overpopulated metropolis.

The victory of "I" over the "Hundred Thousand" dead is a distinction indeed, but its glory appears somewhat tarnished when we recall how among those who fell, a disproportionate number belongs to the poor, both in the tale and in actual history. The poor, in Defoe's fiction, however, react at times to the situation rather robustly. For instance, they transform the disruption of market economy into a utopian economy of free taking and common sharing. Private property itself, the foundation stone of market economy and capitalism, is what they instantly assault. The narrator in one episode stops by at his brother's warehouse. His brother, a wholesale merchant like himself, had fled the city earlier, leaving his stocks vulnerable to prying hands. In his brother's warehouse storing "several Packs of Womens high-Crown'd Hats" (*Plague Year* 86), he finds a group of women making free with his brother's wares "fitting themselves with Hats, as unconcerned and quiet, as if they had been at a Hatters Shop, buying for their Money." Moreover, these looters eloquently defend their actions: "They all told me, they were Neighbours, that they had heard any one might take them, that they were no Bodies Goods, and the like" (87). He tries at first to lock them up and have them suffer legal consequences for their crime, but since "at this Time the Plague was so high, as that there dy'd 4000 a Week," he realizes he may be risking his own life in prolonging the interaction with the offenders. Upon second thoughts, he just takes down the "Names and Place where some of them liv'd" (88), and lets them go. In this struggle of the private subject to safeguard property against the members of the public transgressing the sanctity of ownership, the former has to give in. The individual wishing to protect private property risks antagonizing a crowd of property-less citizens and potential transmitters of the epidemic. This warehouse episode sheds light, inadvertently perhaps, on the city's concealed or derided reality of being one vast human warehouse of indigent masses.

The plague is a sworn enemy to human life, no doubt, but it soon gets embroiled in other conflicts that have always plagued the city. With the rapid spread of the epidemic, a major concern for the narrator and other owners of property shifts from the purely medical aspect of the case to its sociological implications, particularly the likelihood of the starving proletarians rioting en masse:

> Let any one who is acquainted with what Multitudes of People get their daily Bread in this City by their Labour, whether Artificers or meer Workmen; I say, let any Man consider, what must be the miserable Condition

> of this town, if on a sudden, they should be all turned out of Employment, that Labour should cease, and Wages for Work be no more.
>
> This was the Case with us at that Time . . . nor were they [Lord Mayor and Sheriffs] without Apprehensions as it was, that Desperation should push the People upon Tumults, and cause them to rifle the Houses of rich Men, and plunder the Markets of Provisions. (*Plague Year* 96-97)

Fortunately for those who have more than their lives to lose, "the Mob" was prevented from "doing any Mischief," thanks to the fact that "the Rich" had wisely "lock'd themselves entirely up" along with their provisions. H. F. credits the "Vigilance of the Lord Mayor" for preventing looting by relieving the "most desperate with Money" and employing others in public work such as "watching Houses that were infected and shut up" (97). As the fortified gates of the rich and the shrewd strategy of the city government evince, a defensive war is waged on the part of the propertied classes to preempt the rebellion of the "Multitudes of People" who "get their daily Bread" by selling their labour. The miraculous survival of H. F., then, has to be reassessed in the context of a group victory of those who stand on the winning side of the property divide. The social antagonism tainting the disaster is also unmistakably revealed in a passage from Pepys's journal: "Called up by break of day by Captain Cocke by agreement, and he and I in his coach through Kent Streete (a sad place through the plague, people sitting sick and with plasters about them in the street, begging) to Vines and Colvills about money business" (14 Oct 1665 [6.297]). Those lining Kent Street are literally bracketed in the long parenthesis separating the infected masses from those inside the coach bent on pursuing their "money business." Dispirited and vanquished, the poor entreat the mercy of the victors. The sick and the dying of the Plague Year have already been defeated by a class society where some ride coaches for business or pleasure, while others squat begging.

Yet the plague in Defoe's account does come close to bringing about "the Ruin of the whole City" (*Plague Year* 97). At first, the sudden clearance of bustling human presence from the streets strikes the narrator with its ominous calm: "[I]t was a most surprising thing, to see those Streets, which were usually so thronged, now grown desolate, and so few People to be seen in them, that if I had been a Stranger, and at a Loss for my Way, I might sometimes have gone the Length of a whole Street, I mean of the by-Streets, and see no Body to direct me" (17). At a more advanced stage, the same streets are occupied by the dead, turning the city into one vast open tomb with a host of unburied corpses scattered about promiscuously. Pedestrians walking through any of the plague-stricken part of London would be greeted by "several dead Bodies . . . lying here and there upon the Ground" (79). These are memorable, fearful, haunting pictures, for sure, but the unique combination this uncanny masterpiece accomplishes of appealing to sensation (*Erlebnis*) while portraying the collective experience of the city community (*Erfahrung*) is perhaps best exemplified by the mad wretches running up and down the empty streets:

> This running of distemper'd People about the Streets was very dismal, and the Magistrates did their utmost to prevent it, but as it was generally in the Night and always sudden, when such attempts were made, the Officers cou'd not be at hand to prevent it, and even when any got out in the Day, the Officers appointed did not care to meddle with them, because, as they were all grievously infected to *be sure* when they were come to that Height, so they were more than ordinarily infectious, and it was one of the most dangerous Things that cou'd be to touch them; on the other Hand, they generally ran on, not knowing what they did, till they dropp'd down stark Dead, or till they had exhausted their Spirits so, as that they wou'd fall and then die in perhaps half an Hour or an Hour, and which was most piteous to hear, they were sure to come to themselves intirely in that half Hour or Hour, and then to make most grievous and piercing Cries and Lamentations in the deep afflicting Sense of the Condition they were in. (163)

This macabre madness is remarkable for its abnormality. Yet in a sense the running victims expire in a gesture that imitates the typical life rhythm of the busy capital, measuring time nervously for "half an Hour or an Hour"; even under the normal circumstances of a metropolis, everyone runs, literally or figuratively, against the clock to and fro to make money or to make ends meet, until "they had exhausted their Spirits" and "wou'd fall and then die." This eerie busy-ness of those meeting their final moment in the city streets, and the "laissez faire" policy of the officers who just let them be and let them die, all add up to a picture of a "London peculiar," which other offshoots around the world in later times would reproduce and magnify.[9]

"Mingling myself with the Crowd"

Death haunts the streets of busy cities, paradoxically, charged with life as they are. Moreover, according to Moll Flanders, speaking as an expert on street larceny, it is where the Devil himself holds sway, whose "Business" it is, according to Defoe's *Political History of the Devil* (1726), to encourage "Thieving and Robbing, Trick and Cheat" (*History of the Devil* 265-66). Whereas a relatively innocuous curiosity drove H. F. to go out to the dangerous streets of London under the Great Plague, "the diligent Devil," writes Moll, was the instigator who "continually prompted" her to "go out and take a Walk, that is to say, to see if any thing would offer in the old Way" (*Moll* 199). The last third of *Moll Flanders*, depicting her criminal career in the streets of London, is a portrait of the thief, serving the "diligent Devil," as a "woman of the crowd." In Poe's story "The Man of the Crowd," which holds a strategically crucial place in Benjamin's analysis of the metropolis as the "X-ray picture of a detective story" (Benjamin 2003: 27), an unidentified old man keeps close to the crowd all day and all night. The narrator, upon giving up the idea of following the old man, exclaims how he is "the type and the genius of deep crime" (Poe 481). In Defoe's *Moll Flanders*, we already have a (wo)man of the crowd who is properly a "type and genius of crime," preying on and hiding among the crowd, as she takes full advantage of the precarious, chaotic conditions of the late seventeenth-century London streets.[10] Her criminal campaign unfolds in an urban maze, which if not patrolled by Old Nick himself, favours evil over good, greed over compassion. Spotting at Aldersgate Street "a pretty little Child" going home alone from her "Dancing-School," she decides to fall prey on her, or in Moll's phrasing, "my Prompter, like a true Devil, set me upon this innocent Creature" enticing her through the meandering streets of the City to steal the child's necklace. The Devil, true to his "Strategem, and soft still Methods," in the analysis offered by Defoe's later pamphlet, "such as Persuasion, Allurement, feeding the Appetite, prompting, and then gratifying corrupt Desires" (*History of the Devil* 253), goads her on relentlessly:

> Here, I say, the Devil put me upon killing the Child in the dark Alley, that it might not Cry; but the very thought frighted me so that I was ready to drop down, but I turn'd the Child about and bad it go back again, for that was not its way home; the Child said so she would, and I went thro' into *Bartholomew Close*, and then turn'd round to another Passage that goes into *Long-lane*, so away into *Charterhouse-Yard* and out into *St. John's-street*, then crossing into *Smithfield*, went down *Chick-lane* and into *Field-lane* to *Holbourn-bridge*, when mixing with the Crowd of People usually passing there, it was not possible to have been found out. (*Moll* 194)

Satanic urban setting, as much as her own innate depravity, instigates Moll to become a thief, then. Yet the rhetoric of the passage barely conceals a clear rupture between the theological interpretation the narrator attempts at the level of *Erfahrung* (in the manner of Bunyan's description of Vanity Fair) and the sheer excitement she conveys of the *Erlebnis* of meandering through the streets. The italicized names of London streets and landmarks succeed one another at a rapid pace, dragging the reader along from one lane to another, diffusing and dispelling any sense of religious fear the reference to the Devil might have aroused. The "I," the subject of narration, is lost in the "Crowd of People," but so is the reader's sense of moral orientation.

Furthermore, the city space in the passage above is evoked as a labyrinthine series of place names, juxtaposed to one another in a parallel move, through a disjunctive conjunction that connects and separates at the same time. Another typical example depicting Moll's robbery in a crowded urban setting further illustrates the force of this rhetoric of distraction. This time Moll decoys away a maid looking after her mistress' child to make off with the parcel they brought to be dispatched via a stage coach to Barnet:

> As soon as I had got the Bundle, and the Maid was out of Sight, I goes on towards the Ale-house, where the Porter's Wife was, so that if I had met her, I had then only been going to give her the Bundle, and to call her to her Business, as if I was going away, and cou'd stay no longer; but as I did not meet her I walk'd away, and turning into *Charter-house-Lane*, made off thro' *Charter-house-Yard*, into *Long-Lane*, then cross'd into *Bartholomew-Close*, so into *Little Britain*, and thro' the *Blue-Coat-Hospital* into *Newgate-Street*. (*Moll* 239)

The very shape of the paragraph is disjunctive: the first half explains the precise method of her theft, but the latter half rushes off away from the scene through a maze of topographical names, in a gesture flaunting the authority of factual information, whose comic potentials Joyce would amplify in "Ithaca." The ethical and legal questions raised by the fairly impassive (if not enthusiastic) detailing of the process of the criminal act is dispelled by the clause following "but as I did not meet her" at the middle. The prose hastens away and hides behind the proper names jammed into the narrow space of the paragraph. Not only is Moll an expert woman of the crowd; the prose style likewise is a prose of the crowd, both serving to conceal and protect the private subject's incognito.

In the second sample above, the names of the streets and other landmarks can be construed as inviting an allegorical reading to some extent. "Little Britain" can be one candidate, but the fact that the list ends with Newgate Street particularly favours such reading. Successful as she is now, she will inevitably end up at Newgate Prison, as her direction here intimates. Indeed, when she is finally caught and imprisoned there, Moll herself readily interprets the incident as something that was bound to happen:

> [T]hat horrid Place! my very Blood chills at the mention of its Name; the

> Place, where so many of my Comrades had been lock'd up, and from whence they went to the fatal Tree; the Place where my Mother suffered so deeply, where I was brought into the World, and from whence I expected no Redemption, but by an infamous Death: To conclude, the Place that had so long expected me, and which with so much Art and Success I had so long avoided. (*Moll* 273)

Her returning to her birthplace completes her destiny, according to this view which elevates her life into an *Erfahrung* of divine retribution. Yet the plot reserves a further stage beyond Newgate, rescuing her from Newgate and "Little Britain" to the vast lands of British colony in North America. Moreover, before being captured Moll is allowed to enjoy the full extent of her expertise of manipulating the crowd, from which she emerges with valuable trophy unscathed, often aided by the urban throng. The crowd is no mere background but a vivid presence in *Moll Flanders*. As Carl Fisher observes, Defoe stands out as "an anomaly in eighteenth-century fiction" in the way the crowd is "factually constructed rather than rhetorically condemned or tacitly ignored" (Fisher 76-77). At one point, the crowd becomes even eloquently vocal, as it acts as a makeshift jury vindicating Moll's innocence. She is all but caught in her act at a mercer's shop, but a throng of people intercedes on her behalf:

> [A]t length we went all very quietly before the Justice, with a Mob of about 500 People at our Heels; and all the way I went I could hear the People ask what was the matter? and others reply and say, a Mercer had stop'd a Gentlewoman instead of a Thief, and had afterwards taken the Thief, and now the Gentlewoman had taken the Mercer, and was carrying him before the Justice; this pleas'd the People strangely, and made the Crowd encrease, and they cry'd out as they went, which is the Rogue? which is the Mercer? and especially the Women, then when they saw him they cryed out, *that's he, that's he*; and every now and then came a good dab of Dirt at him; and thus we march'd a good while. (*Moll* 246)

The crux of this felicitous intercourse with the crowd lies in her successful concealment of her real identity behind her sartorial guise as a respectable gentlewoman. The only evidence of her innocence is her being "a Gentlewoman," or to be more exact, her having dressed herself like a gentlewoman. This and other tricks work so well for so long. The terms of her relationship with the crowd give her an unequal advantage over the rest of urban humanity, whom she exploits unperturbed, undetected, and unchallenged. Just as H. F.'s uninfected peregrination among the plagued streets of London puts him above the other less fortunate inhabitants of the city, Moll's unfailing victory over her potential foes—"marvelously in and out of circumstances, above (or besides) the mad flow of urban violence," as Richetti puts it (Richetti 1975: 127)—such as the poor mercer in the above quotation, fortifies the fantasy of the private sphere, of the private subject's successful manipulation of the public space.

Without a perfect preservation of incognito, however, Moll's sartorial tactics can never bear fruit. As she assures the reader, "on these Adventures we always went very well Dress'd, and I had very good Cloaths on, and a Gold Watch by my Side, as like a Lady as other Folks" (211). This woman of the crowd is a female dandy, who in Baudelaire's essay on Constantin Guy has the "proud satisfaction of never oneself being astonished" and of maintaining that "haughty exclusiveness, provocative in its very coldness" (Baudelaire 1964: 28). Though Moll's dandyism has nothing to do with the blasé idleness Baudelaire picks as the first characteristic of a dandy (Baudelaire 1964: 26), and even though hers is a fake dandyism camouflaging her business-like pursuit of utility, dressing up helps her conceal her real character. Interestingly, when London first becomes a concrete spatial presence in the novel (other localities such as Colchester or Virginia never does), Moll immediately resolves to disguise her identity as she goes about the town, trying to gather information about her ex-partner the "Bath gentleman": "One Night I had the Curiosity to disguise my self like a Servant Maid in a Round Cap and Straw Hat, and went to the Door, as sent by a Lady of his Neighbourhood" (*Moll* 121). Thus begins her undercover adventure in the city streets, before she became a criminal, which would remain a hallmark device of her lucrative criminal career. Moll's incognito, moreover, makes her a mysterious anti-social predator confronting the city as her opponent. "They all knew me by the Name of *Moll Flanders* . . . but how to find me out they knew not, nor so much as how to guess at my Quarters, whether they were at the East-End of the Town, or the West; and this wariness was my safety upon all these Occasions" (222). Not content to merely preserve her incognito behind a false identity to manipulate the crowd and to prey on the victims of her criminal design, Moll assumes new identities on each occasion, taking up "new Figures" and appearing "in new Shapes" (262). The constant transformation of her appearance leads her even to reverse, like a true virtuoso that she is, her gender: "I WAS Tall and Personable, but a little too smooth Fac'd for a Man; however as I seldom went Abroad but in the Night, it did well enough; but it was a long time before I could behave in my new Cloths" (214-15). In her own way, she is another "Man-Woman" like Roxana, proudly independent and economically free. Moreover, this particular transvestitism saves her neck, for she narrowly escapes being caught in her male disguise, which she discards after fleeing into her rooms at the house managed by her "Governess" and receiver. She tries also shifting her status appearance into that of a poor woman: "I HAD dress'd myself up in a very mean Habit, for as I had several Shapes to appear in I was now in an ordinary Stuff-Gown, a blue Apron and a Straw-Hat" (238). Once she even turns herself into a female beggar, which she finds a bad business idea, as well as bad taste, for she "naturally abhorr'd Dirt and Rags," having been brought up "Tite and Cleanly, and could be no other, whatever Condition I was in; so that this was the most uneasie Disguise to me that ever I put on" (253). Dandy by nature, she is unwilling and unable to play pauper.

Having acted her part to perfection among the City crowd, she takes on the stage of West End streets:

> [T]he next Day I dress'd myself up fine, and took a Walk to the other End of the Town, I pass'd thro' the *Exchange* in the *Strand*, but had no Notion of finding any thing to do there, when on a sudden I saw a great Clutter in the Place, and all the People, Shop-keepers as well as others, standing up, and staring, and what should it be? but some great Dutchess come into the *Exchange*; and they said the Queen was coming; I set myself close up to a Shop-side with my back to the Compter, as if to let the Crowd pass by, when keeping my Eye upon a parcel of Lace, which the Shop-keeper was showing to some Ladies that stood by me; the Shop-keeper and her Maid were so taken up with looking to see who was a coming, and what Shop they would go to, that I found means to slip a Paper of Lace into my Pocket, and come clear off with it, so the Lady Millener paid dear enough for her gaping after the Queen. (*Moll* 256)

As the setting of the episode indicates, to her character as a woman of the crowd and dandy can be added that of the flâneur, who, according to Baudelaire, is the "passionate spectator" whose life activity is "to see the world, to be at the centre of the world, and yet to remain hidden from the world" even when placed at the "heart of the multitude" (Baudelaire 1964: 9). This early-modern *flâneuse avant la lettre* haunting the luxury boutiques in and around the New Exchange, a prototype of later shopping arcades,[11] and hence a precursor of Parisian *passages*, is gifted with most sensitive eyes, herself hidden but standing at the centre of the bustle. But she is there with a clear purpose, and by no means simply to enjoy the spectacle of the nobles or royals showing off their glamour. Her soul is glued to the commodity on display, as she has her "Eye upon a parcel of Lace" which she intends to rifle. She has to keep her visual organs on alert for more reasons that one. As she writes, "my Business was of a kind that requir'd me to have my Eyes every way" (*Moll* 271). This circuit of "my Eyes" serving "my business" of lining "my Pocket" with valuables closes off Moll into a secluded self-enclosed universe, a moving island as it were among the crowd. Like H. F. she belongs and does not belong to the crowd, in a mode comparable to Roxana's residing and not residing in the different cities where she pursues her interests. In sharp opposition to "all the People, Shop-keepers as well as others" who act in concert, Moll has a different objective and a different direction, even as she mingles with the mob: "I WENT off from the Shop, as if driven along by the Throng, and mingling myself with the Crowd, went out at the other Door of the *Exchange*, and so got away before they miss'd their Lace" (256-57).

According to Baudelaire, the crowd offers to the "solitary and thoughtful stroller" the *jouissance* of a "divine prostitution of the soul giving itself entire . . . to the unexpected as it comes along, to the stranger as he passes" (Baudelaire 1970: 20). Indeed, Baudelaire's lyric "À une passante," which we shall discuss later, depicts such "prostitution of the soul" among a crowd of "deafening" city streets ("la rue assourdissante"), as the poet encounters and loses sight of a female passer-by, who vanishes into the crowd. Moll's passerby disappears, too, but not before he has bequeathed material goods to her. Moll approaches an elderly gentleman at a gambling house at Bartholomew Fair, lets him use her body, but also makes him sorely drunk, and leaves him after loading herself with his goods:

> I TOOK this opportunity to search him to a Nicety; I took a gold Watch, with a silk Purse of Gold, his fine full bottom Perrewig, and silver fring'd Gloves, his Sword, and fine Snuff-box, and gently opening the Coach-door, stood ready to jump out while the Coach was going on; but the Coach stopping in the narrow Street beyond *Temple-Bar* to let another Coach pass, I got softly out, fasten'd the Door again, and gave my Gentleman and the Coach the slip both together, and never heard more of them. (*Moll* 225-26)

There is surely nothing mysterious or holy about this prostitution of body for tangible remuneration, which the "fugitive beauty" awards herself. "As for me, my Business was his Money, and what I could make of him"—this credo of Moll, once again, bluntly reveals the bleak reality of the modern metropolis as seen, charted, and imagined from the point of view of an isolated anti-social private subject, cut off from her society even during her intimate intercourse with it. Moll's narrative assumes the form of an *Erfahrung*, of reflecting on an unfortunate sinful life, yet it appeals to the solitary readers of the novels more as an *Erlebnis* of thrilling transgressions.

However, parallels with Benjamin's charting of the nineteenth-century Paris should not elide a crucial difference between the leisurely loafer of Parisian arcade and Defoe's Moll. The flâneur disdains the bourgeoisie's business concerns:

> In the year of Baudelaire's death, an entrepreneur could still cater to the comfort of the well-to-do with a fleet of five hundred sedan chairs circulating about the city. . . . There was the pedestrian who wedged himself into the crowd, but there was also the flâneur who demanded elbow room and was unwilling to forgo the life of a gentleman of leisure. He goes his leisurely ways as a personality; in this manner he protests against the division of labor which makes people into specialists. (Benjamin 2003: 30-31)

Baudelaire fits this description neatly, with his contemptuous attitude to the bourgeoisie and their carriages, cultivating leisure and "personality" while resisting business discipline and demands. Defoe's fictional universe, not to mention his pamphlets on commerce and business, could not be farther removed from such lax, pointless, inefficient disposition. Moll Flanders diligently moves around to increase her income, through fair means or foul. Considering the hectic pace of life in the grand capitals such as London or Paris, the actual history of modernity shares more with the untiring busy seekers of profit Defoe's first-person narrators represent. Defoe's city leaves no shade or corner for poetic musing or loitering. The heartless soul of the metropolis, which Simmel sought to anatomize, saturates Defoe's narrative. The distance between Baudelaire and Defoe measures the triumph of a self-interested metropolitan outlook over both the classical ideal of civic urbanity and the Romantic fantasy of individual transcendence of the city's economic reality. Defoe's London is a no-nonsense arena where the private subject soberly and meticulously battles to maximize its gains at the expense of, or in spite of, society. The metropolis in Defoe is nothing else than the mode of existence of the private sphere.

PART II:

DICKENS

CHAPTER FIVE

THE "BOZ" STYLE

"We are fourteen strong"

In part reflecting the publishing conventions of his times, and in part abiding by his own reserved ethos, Defoe took pains to conceal his authorial identity by presenting his fictional narratives as fabricated autobiographies of "real" individuals other than himself. The language used for this purpose likewise unfolds in a prose style marked with studied artlessness, whose disjunctive, additive, and paratactic flow is designed to capture the level of literacy and mentality of a Crusoe, Moll, or Roxana. They also embody the digressive, distracting, divisive conditions of an urbanized world, where the subject seeks to advance the interests of her privacy while manipulating the social space under maximum secrecy. Dickens presents a sharp contrast to this mode of self-centered, self-concealing prose. He built for himself an uncontested publishing platform in an already densely populated literary market supplying various genres of printed matters, including those narratives of dubious veracity fathered by Defoe more than a century earlier. Defoe hid behind his first-person narrators, certainly not pairing his fingernails nonchalantly, as Stephen Dedalus believes an ideal artist ought to be doing, but energetically working to preserve his (and also his character's) incognito. Dickens, by contrast, presented himself to the public as "Boz," a knowing, likeable, congenial public persona with "inimitable" stylistic signature. He sought maximum recognition of his literary identity by committing himself to a combination of certain trade-mark features, both technical and thematic. "Boz" offered, above all, delightful depictions of the city's manifold curiosities. Whereas the city in Defoe's fictions was something implied, embedded, or incorporated in the narrative's perspective and the narrator's persona, in Dickens the metropolis received full exposure to be visualized, framed, and characterized as an object. As Boz the stylist unearthed oddities from the nooks of the bustling city of London, Dickens the storyteller weaved episodes into plots that satisfied the common sense of common readers.

Dickens comes almost a century after Defoe and obviously Dickens's

London was by no means the same city. Any difference between them has first to be attributed to objective historical factors. The London Defoe lived and wrote in was already the largest city in the Western world at the time, but none of his contemporaries could have predicted the magnitude of the city's expansion in the next century. Already in 1801, the population of Greater London reached almost a million, and every decade after that added another fifth, to bring up the figure by 1901 to approximately 6.5 million, with a growth in its spatial extent to match it. London in Defoe's age was "a mere 4 miles from east to west," but London at the end of Dickens's century was "almost 18 miles across, and covering nearly 70 square miles" (Inwood 411). Such rapid and momentous change entailed corresponding alterations in the rhythm of the inhabitants' and visitors' physical mobility. Already in the early decades of the nineteenth century, short-stage coaches, hackney coaches, and omnibuses made their busy round through the city's streets clogging them chronically, obstructing one another as they tried to transport humans and goods to their destination on time. Soon congestion reached such an impasse that railways had to be introduced in the 1830s to cater to the commuter needs of the ever growing population (Inwood 546-47; Sheppard 264-65). It was also in the 1820s and '30s that the term "metropolis" gained wide circulation to refer to this new spatial entity, unprecedented in its menacing enormity and sprawling formlessness, as evidenced by the name of London's new police force, "Metropolitan Police" (Sheppard 279).

Policing crime and preventing riots seemed the urgent issues for this "metropolis," yet a far more formidable disruption was driven by ostensibly innocuous forces of transportation business. To make way for railway tracks, train stations, and underground railways (from the 1850s), vast stretches of cheaper and therefore expendable neighbourhoods were demolished (Ball and Sunderland 215; Rasmussen 134-35). Dickens makes a nostalgic indictment of the destruction of these suburbs in his description of (what used to be) Staggs's Gardens in *Dombey and Son*:

> There was no such place as Stagg's Gardens. It had vanished from the earth. Where the old rotten summer-houses once had stood, palaces now reared their heads, and granite columns of gigantic girth opened a vista to the railway world beyond. The miserable waste ground, where the refuse-matter had been heaped of yore, was swallowed up and gone; and in its frowsy stead were tiers of warehouses, crammed with rich goods and costly merchandise. (*Dombey* 217-18 [chap. 15])

The same passage, however, also acknowledges the intrepid forces of industrialism, of the "conquering engines" and their "secret knowledge of great powers yet unsuspected in them, and strong purposes not yet achieved" (*Dombey* 219). These "great powers" had already achieved their purpose, however, not only in the industrial North but in London as well. The capital became a major manufacturing centre in the nineteenth century, as the 1851 Census revealed; it turned out to be the largest manufacturing town in the nation employing a third of the nation's male labour force (Schwarz 23), and a third of London population was classified as working in the manufacturing sector (Inwood 444). This fact was half-concealed by the extensive sub-contract system which dispersed workplaces to households and other smaller units (Ball and Sunderland 294-95). The demographic composition of London also went through constant changes caused by steady influxes of migrants. In the mid-century 38 per cent of Londoners were born elsewhere (Inwood 412), including those born overseas such as the Irish Catholics who provided cheap labour as bricklayers and casual workers (Dorothy George 120-21).

The vast straggling metropolis of the nineteenth century, so different from the relatively snug city of Pepys or Defoe, overshadowed the private individual's efforts to construct a private sphere for herself, whose personal life experience would be quickly drowned in the surging sea of London crowds. The sheer scale and complexity of London undergoing industrialization and massive expansion, however, offered new challenges to writers. Defoe took London for granted, embodying its callous, calculating, individualist spirit in his first-person narratives. For Dickens and his readers, the identity of London could no longer be assumed as something understood implicitly. For those bemused, appalled, or fascinated by London—those in the provinces curious about the metropolis, but above all those living there as resident strangers born or bred elsewhere—the city needed to be defined, characterized, "sketched." Moreover, objective conditions of the capital's publishing industry could not be more auspicious. London boasted the highest literacy in the nation (Ball and Sunderland 165), and London's publishing market had grown rapidly during the 1830s thanks to the debates on the First Reform Bill (Drew 5). Seizing the moment, Dickens invented himself as "Boz" to capture the spirit of the place and the age. A typical passage from *Sketches by Boz*, his first set of published prose, can be taken from "Hackney-Coach Stands," which deals with a topic drawn from London's commuter traffic:

> We maintain that hackney-coaches, properly so called, belong solely to the metropolis. We may be told, that there are hackney-coach stands in Edinburgh; and not to go quite so far for a contradiction to our position, we may be reminded that Liverpool, Manchester, "and other large towns" (as the

> Parliamentary phrase goes), have *their* hackney-coach stands. We readily concede to these places the possession of certain vehicles, which may look almost as dirty, and even go almost as slowly, as London hackney-coaches; but that they have the slightest claim to compete with the metropolis, either in point of stands, drivers, or cattle, we indignantly deny. (*Sketches* 81)

Boz extends a friendly hand to the community of readership of those who identify with the "metropolis." An almost proprietary claim is carried by the pronoun "we," setting up a dichotomy of Us vs. Them, which also amounts to a patronizing assertion of civic pride in the absolute superiority of London over other second-rate cities of the United Kingdom. That the distinction London enjoys is soiled with dirt and inefficiency only serves to highlight Boz's sense of possessive pride in the incomparable eccentricities of London hackney-coaches, which its hapless satellites can never rival. The half-polemic tone adopted by Boz here makes him an advocate and defender of a metropolitan identity, yet such public posture is coupled with his desire to please his clients, as the humour conveyed by "and other large towns" or "almost as dirty, and even go almost as slowly" unmistakably gesticulates. A community of sense, prejudice, and experience (*Erfahrung*) can be formed upon such basis of shared position and disposition, which the main text of the sketch fortifies by offering sensory (and regularly entertaining) details from the writer's own first-hand experience (*Erlebnis*).

Boz's representation of London, then, has to be both general and particular, both communal and individual. One handy device of achieving this objective would be to capture the typical features of the city from the point of view of a stranger, novice, or outsider. The following example from "Seven Dials," by borrowing the dazzled eyes of a provincial visitor to London, at once asserts the civic communal identity of Londoners and achieves an aesthetic balance between familiarity and strangeness:

> The peculiar character of these streets, and the close resemblance each one bears to its neighbour, by no means tends to decrease the bewilderment in which the unexperienced wayfarer through "the Dials" finds himself involved. . . . Here and there, a little dark chandler's shop, with a cracked bell hung up behind the door to announce the entrance of a customer, or betray the presence of some young gentleman in whom a passion for shop tills has developed itself at an early age: others, as if for support, against some handsome lofty building, which usurps the place of a low dingy public-house; long rows of broken and patched windows expose plants that may have flourished when "the Dials" were built, in vessels as dirty as "the Dials" themselves; and shops for the purchase of rags, bones, old iron, and kitchen-stuff, vie in cleanliness with the bird-fanciers' and rabbit-dealers', which one

> might fancy so many arks, but for the irresistible conviction that no bird in its proper senses, who was permitted to leave one of them, would ever come back again. (*Sketches* 71)

The forte of this description rests largely on the details of the locality, such as the "cracked bell" of the chandler's shop, the plants exhibited on the "rows of broken and patched windows," dashed off with a touch of humour spicing the closing remark about bird-fanciers. Such sumptuous and inoffensively vivified facts of this dirty, shabby and no doubt malodorous corner of London could be consumed by both Londoners and outsiders, by those who know them well as well as by those akin to the "unexperienced wayfarer." The community of readership thus gains a national footing, as everyone can join in to laugh with Boz.

Dickens in his mature career, when he became infinitely more affluent and secure than when he wrote his first sketches, never entirely left off playing the Boz of his early years. His expertise remained that of blending peculiarities with generalities, of adding humour to seriousness. In the 1850s and '60s, now under a different sobriquet of the "Uncommercial Traveller," and presenting himself in the first-person singular rather than plural, Dickens was yet reluctant to relinquish his public persona as one who speaks to and of the communal. In the most memorable instances of his "Uncommercial" travels, he likes to haunt the deserted city centres either during nighttime or times of rest. In "City of London Churches," he stops by different churches and chapels of the City. Many of them were built in the age of Pepys and Defoe, but with the depopulation of the City and its conversion to office blocks, they are now left nearly empty and hollow. His choice is "a church oddly put away in a corner among a number of lanes . . . of about the date of Queen Anne":

> As a congregation, we are fourteen strong: not counting an exhausted charity school in a gallery, which has dwindled away to four boys, and two girls. In the porch, is a benefaction of loaves of bread, which there would seem to be nobody left in the exhausted congregation to claim. . . . There is also an exhausted clerk in a brown wig, and two or three exhausted doors and windows have been bricked up, and the service books are musty, and the pulpit cushions are threadbare, and the whole of the church furniture is in a very advanced stage of exhaustion. We are three old women (habitual), two young lovers (accidental), two tradesmen, one with a wife and one alone, an aunt and nephew, again two girls . . . and three sniggering boys. The clergyman is, perhaps, the chaplain of a civic company; he has the moist and vinous look, and eke the bulbous boots, of one acquainted with 'Twenty port, and comet vintages. (*Uncommercial* 87)

Despite the bleak and vacant state of the premise, the Uncommercial Traveller nevertheless seeks to construct a community of "us," even though "we" consist of a diminished company of "three old women," "two young lovers," "two tradesmen," "an aunt and nephew, again two girls," and "three sniggering boys." Such unpromising roll-call notwithstanding, the singular first-person subject of "I saw" has managed to lift itself onto a communal formula of "*we* are fourteen strong." Boz returns not only in this grammatical orientation towards civic communality, but also in the rich comic details protruding from them, such as the parenthetical characterization of the members of the congregation, or in the tropes pulling down the spiritual authority of the minister to the endearing human scale of his odd "vinous" physiognomy. Yet a new tone can be heard in this later example, one that displays the expertise of the mature prose writer. A musical principle of repetition and variation is activated to create an overriding image of the place's being "exhausted," which embraces different characters and objects inside the church, leading to the closing coda of "the whole of the church furniture is in a very advanced stage of exhaustion." All in all, it yields a superb prose rhythm that dances to a music of its own, which compares favorably with that of metrical language. To justify this claim and to measure the full gamut of Dickens's prose rhythm, we shall digress briefly on classical poetic devices used to depict urban experience from antiquity to Dickens's century.

"O ye associate Walkers, O my friends"

Of all the stylized representations of the urban world, satire enjoyed a more respectable and continuous tradition than any other genre, thanks to the canonical status granted to classical Latin verse. In Juvenal's *Satire* III, the great metropolis of the Roman empire is taken to task for its blatant flaunting of wealth, the appalling conditions of its poor, and its culture of lavish consumption—in short, for being a Vanity Fair writ large. "*Virtu*" (virtue, innate strength, manliness) is obstructed by the sheer cost of maintaining appearance (166-67), of living "in a state of pretentious poverty" (183-84). To those without enough money to squander away, the public thoroughfares of Rome are rife with lethal danger:

> si vocat officium, turba cedente vehetur
> dives et ingenti curret super ora Liburna
> atque obiter leget aut scribet vel dormiet intus;
> namque facit somnum clausa lectica fenestra.
> ante tament veniet; nobis properantibus opstat
> unda prior, magno populus permit agmine lumbos

qui sequitur; ferit hic cubito, ferit assere duro
alter, at hic tignum captit incutit, ille metretam.

(When the rich man has a call of social duty, the mob makes way for him as he is borne swiftly over their heads in a huge Liburnian car. He writes or reads or sleeps inside as he goes along, for the closed window of the litter induces slumber. Yet he will arrive before us; hurry as we may, we are blocked by a surging crowd in front, and by a dense mass of people pressing in on us from behind: one man digs an elbow into me, another a hard sedan-pole; one bangs a beam, another a wine-cask, against my head.) (238-46 [Loeb edition])

Juvenal's hexameter imposes a sense of order on the social and moral disorder, but his verse appears affected by the disjunction of what it depicts, as lines are pushed on to override each six-foot unit. The rupture between the rich man inside his sedan chair marked by the relative security of lines 240 and 241 (closed respectively by "intus" and "fenestra") and those shoved out of the way by his attendants is dramatized by unstable enjambment from line 242 on ("opstat / unda prior," "lumbos / qui sequitur," "duro / alter"), which imitate the very peril and hazard of walking. A wedge is drawn, as it were, between the first four lines inhabited by the drowsy rich citizen, and the rest depicting the woes of pedestrians. At night the city streets become even more perilous, and the verse gestures in kind to augment a sense of insecurity, by pushing the last foot of each line onto the next:

quod spatium tectis sublimibus unde cerebrum
testa ferit, quotiens rimosa et curta fenestris
vasa cadant, quanto percussum pondere signent
et laedant silicem. possis ignavus haberi
et subiti casus inprovidus, ad cenam si
intestates eas: adeo tot fata, quot illa
nocte patent vigiles te praetereunte fenestrae.

(See what a height it is to that towering roof from which a potsherd comes crack upon my head every time that some broken or leaky vessel is pitched out of the window! See with what a smash it strikes and dints the pavement! There's death in every open window as you pass along at night: you may well be deemed a fool, improvident of sudden accident, if you go out to dinner without having made your will.) (269-75)

The first four lines come from a sentence finished at the middle of line 272, cutting it into two. Conjunction and disjunction thus become intricately yoked to each other, as an emblem of the dangerous condition of nocturnal

Rome, which the Loeb translator sought to convey by exclamation marks. Juvenal's poetry encounters the bustling, mean, dirty streets of Rome, wrenching from his engagement a prosodic mimesis that marvellously captures the city's rickety and rowdy character.

Like other Latin classics, Juvenal became one of the curriculum authors in the West read and imitated throughout the subsequent ages by generations of later poets. John Gay's *Trivia, Or the Art of Walking the Streets of London* (1716), published a few years before Defoe the pamphleteer invented his pseudo autobiographies, presents itself as an informative didactic poem, an urban adaptation of Virgil's *Georgics* dilating on the art of walking the streets of London. Yet the inspiration and invention of the work comes clearly from Juvenal's *Satire* III. As the title of the poem promises, it contains useful advice to pedestrians having to use the streets of London:

> Careful Observers, studious of the Town,
> Shun the Misfortunes that disgrace the Clown.
> Untempted, they contemn the Jugler's Feats,
> Pass by the *Meuse*, or try the Thimble's Cheats
> When Drays bound high, they never cross behind,
> Where bubbling Yest is blown by Gusts of Wind:
> And when up *Ludgate-hill* huge Carts move slow,
> Far from the straining Steeds, securely go,
> Whose dashing Hoofs, behind them, fling the Mire,
> And mark, with muddy Blots, the gazing 'Squire. (2.285-94)

Who needs to be thus instructed? Surely not those who have set up their residence or tenancy in London, for they know already all too well the "art" the poem means to teach them. Yet their familiarity with their city's oddities may not hamper their enjoying the work for its *dulce* rather than *utile*: in fact, it can enhance their pleasure to see those un-poetic place names of Meuse and Ludgate-hill transformed into building blocks of poetic artifice. Moreover, they can chuckle in delight at how Ludgate-hill has an ugly welcome gift in store for the "gazing 'Squire" stunned by the city's heavy traffic. Since the dirt-bespattered country squire—being a potential consumer of the poem—is too respectable a personage to be turned into a laughing stock, the poet picks a "Peasant, with enquiring Face / Bewilder'd" (2.77-78) by the intricacies of the "fam'd Saint *Giles's* ancient Limits" (2.73):

> He dwells on ev'ry Sign, with stupid Gaze,
> Enters the narrow Alley's doubtful Maze,
> Trys ev'ry winding Court and Street in vain,

And doubles o'er his weary Steps again. (2.79-82)

Thus run the couplets allotted to the poor rustic, in contrast to whose doubtful and "weary Steps," the poem's meter strides firm, clever, and wily, bundling the peasant's "Gaze" with "Maze," as "Mire" is paired with "'Squire" in the first sample. This disjunctive conjunction of poetic music superimposed on the diffuse manifold of the metropolis lacks "coordinated moral insight," as John H. Johnston complains (Johnston 48). But formal coordination, as well as the poet's dependable knowledge of his city, supplements this weakness by holding the details together within the unifying musical framework of heroic couplets.

Marching on armed with urban expertise, Gay's *Trivia* yet stumbles on the question of the social standing of the knowing subject. The poet-persona is himself a pedestrian by necessity rather than choice; he cannot have friendly feelings towards the rushing carriages. He evokes London's mythical past before coaches and wheels colonized it:

O happy Streets to rumbling Wheels unknown,
No Carts, no Coaches shake the floating Town!
Thus was of old *Britannia*'s City bless'd,
E'er Pride and Luxury her Sons possess'd;
Coaches and Chariots yet unfashion'd lay,
Nor late invented Chairs perplex'd the Way. (1.99-104)

Gay's posture here echoes Juvenal's denunciation of "pretentious poverty," but it replaces the bitterness of the endangered pedestrian in Juvenal with an impersonal tone of genteel castigation. Furthermore, the sociological problem of potential antagonism between owners of coaches and coach-less walkers slips into a physiological question of individual health:

O ye associate Walkers, O my friends,
Upon your State what Happiness attends!
What, though no Coach to frequent Visit rolls,
Nor for your Shilling Chairmen sling their Poles;
Yet still your Nerves rheumatic Pains defye,
Nor lazy Jaundice dulls your Saffron Eye. (2.501-6)

The "associate Walkers" need form no political alliance, then, for their having no business with the world of "Coach" or "Shilling Chairmen" is conducive to the salutary absence of "rheumatic Pains" and "lazy Jaundice." In Juvenal's Rome, to go out to the streets at night was to risk your life. In Gay's London, walking the streets is supremely life-enhancing.

Not only in its message but in its form does Gay's *Trivia* register a modern urban rhythm marked by security and punctuality. The unperturbed pace of heroic couplets, which Gay employs to survey the streets and lives of outdoor London, imitates the sturdy footwork of the walker-poet, as the second line never fails to catch up with the first with a consorting rhyme each time. Beyond the unit of each couplet, however, the orderliness of the meter verges on sheer monotony of uniform movement. The fact that the consonance of each couplet has no relationship to the preceding or following rhymes makes the connection between the couplets merely additive. When compared, retrospectively, with the rhyme scheme of Dante's *terza rima*, the absence of resonance between the rhymed units sounds incurably drab, and not merely because of the difference in language. Here is Dante describing Malebolge in *Inferno* Canto 18, where he likens the sinners swarming at the bottom of the pit to a crowd in Rome:

> Nel fondo erano ignudi i peccatori;
> dal mezzo in qua ci venien verso 'l volto,
> di là con noi, ma con passi maggiori
>
> come i Roman per l'essercito molto,
> l'anno del guibileo, su per lo ponte
> hanno a passar la gente modo colto,
>
> che da l'un lato tutti hanno la fronte
> verso 'l castello e vanno a Santo Pietro,
> da l'altra sponda vanno verso 'l monte. (25-33)

(At the bottom were the sinners, naked; on this side of the midpoint they came with their faces toward us, on the other side they were with us, but with longer steps: as the Romans, the year of the Jubilee, because of the great throng, found a way to move people across the bridge, for on one side they are all turned toward the Castle and are going towards Saint Peter, and on the other they are going toward the mountain.) (Durling translation)

The *-olto* rhyme that rounds off the second *terzina* is drawn from the second line of the first, "volto" (face), which chimes with "molto" (many), and "colto" (cooked, jammed-packed), to yield a poetic statement across the lines among themselves (i.e. "the faces of the many are jammed together"). Similarly, the *-onte* rhyme linking "ponte" (bridge), "fronte" (fronting, facing), and "monte" (mountain), hints at the sinners' yearning to fly away from the stifling congregation. The temporality of Dante's rhyme scheme has an architectonic or polyphonic level, as melodies echo vertically as well as flow horizontally. In comparison, Gay's couplets are monophonic and two-dimensional. Their effect is to amplify the predictable regular repetition of coupled lines, reminding us of the "tick-tock" sound of a timepiece. Considering all the dirt, danger, and dreariness of London, only a few degrees removed from Dante's Hell, Gay's steady pace appears improbably serene and mechanical.

The Romantics, rebelling above all against the kind of poetic complacency exemplified by Gay's *Trivia*, had their own antinomy to cope with, particularly when faced with the vast metropolis, a world apart, for William Wordsworth, from the placidity of his home country the Lake District. Wordsworth allows himself to relish the beautiful sights of London, significantly, when the city is surveyed at the early hours of the morning. No humans intrude upon the poetic subject's perception of the cityscape, in his "Composed upon Westminster Bridge, September 3, 1803" (Bloom and Trilling 173):

> This City now doth, like a garment, wear
> The beauty of the morning; silent, bare,
> Ships, towers, domes, theatres, and temples lie
> Open unto the fields, and to the sky. (4-7)

Distance is crucial here, for the privileged view from Westminster Bridge enables the poet to extol the "beauty" of London's City, which a closer view of that bustling business district would instantly shatter. The idyllic mood, however, rides a rather jolting vehicle, for prosaic enumeration ("Ships, towers, domes, theatres, and temples") infringes on the trope of "like a garment." The metropolis, even in this rare moment and spot, leaves its marks on the short poetic space of the sonnet. But the paratactic discord is brushed off by rhyming couplets which these four lines constitute. This equanimity can be maintained thanks to the vanishing point of perspective, which passes over the sundry particulars of the city space, flying above the "towers, domes, theatres, and temples" to the "fields," and thus reducing London to a component of the larger landscape beyond. A closer view of the metropolis in *Prelude 1805* (Book Seventh, "Residence in London" [Wordsworth 1979: 256]) disrupts such composure of contemplation. The sheer abundance of the city's objects offers a serious challenge to the subject's mimetic faculty of representation:

> I glance but at a few conspicuous marks,
> Leaving ten thousand others that do each—
> In hall or court, conventicle, or shop,
> In public room or private, park or street—

With fondness reared on his own pedestal,
Look out for admiration. Folly, vice,
Extravagance in gesture, mien and dress,
And all the strife of singularity—
Lies to the ear, and lies to every sense—
Of these and of the living shapes they wear
There is no end. (567-77)

The overwhelming succession of discrete "singularity," of "marks" embroiled in "strife," assails the poem to disperse it into paratactic lists, pushing the lines to catch their breath with the repeated assistance of dash. Such distraught shape of the verse dramatizes a genuine crisis of poetic intelligence:

How often in the overflowing streets
Have I gone forwards with the crowd, and said
Unto myself, "The face of every one
That passes by me is a mystery." (595-98)

In this thoroughly anonymous realm of humans living adjacent to each other physically but without entering into any meaningful human relationship, the other is a problem, a "mystery," for the subject. Confounded by the mystifying crowd, the subject can at best speak to himself, unheeded, unnoticed. Or he could adopt the antagonistic perspective of the "private sphere," a view of an exclusive, hostile, self-seeking subject bent on using others for her profit, the perspective of Defoe's Moll, in short.

Cracking the mystery of the strange faces of the city can take two forms: allegory and "character," of which the former has a more illustrious place in literary history. Treading the visionary steps of Bunyan's pilgrims to whom the city was a sinful Vanity Fair, William Blake in "London" (Bloom and Trilling 26-27) reads sinister signs of oppression and exploitation inscribed on the city and its denizens:

I wander thro' each charter'd street,
Near where the charter'd Thames does flow.
And mark in every face I meet
Marks of weakness, marks of woe.

In every cry of every Man,
In every Infants cry of fear,
In every voice: in every ban,
The mind-forg'd manacles I hear. (1-8)

Sonorous as these lines are, they do little justice to the individual distinctness of each and "every face," all speaking of different degrees and kinds of "weakness" and "woe." Percy Shelley, likewise, in *Peter Bell the Third* (Shelley 350-51) adopts an allegorical device. Hell is structured like a densely inhabited medieval city in Dante; in Shelley, it has caught up with the changing trends of big cities on this side of the grave.

> Hell is a city much like London—
> A populous and smoky city;
> There are all sorts of people undone,
> And there is little or no fun done;
> Small justice shown, and still less pity.
>
> ………………..……………..
>
> Thrusting, toiling, wailing, moiling,
> Frowning, preaching—such a riot!
> Each with never-ceasing labour,
> Whilst he thinks he cheats his neighbor,
> Cheating his own heart of quiet. (147-51, 197-201)

The rhymes are ingenious ("riot" contrasted to "quiet") and funny ("London" echoed by "done" and "undone"), yet the individual acts and agents of "thrusting, toiling, wailing, moiling" are given no right to stand on their own. Allegory in Blake or Shelley purports to epitomize the city's significance, but does so only by shunning its "strife of singularity."

Can lyric poetry confront the city and emerge victorious from the scuffle? This is what Baudelaire, Dickens's contemporary on the other side of the English Channel, wrestled with in his "Tableaux Parisiens," where he sought to wrench lyrical transcendence from the dirt, noise, and injustice of Paris. Just to look at the famous example "À une passante" again, canonized by Benjamin as the representative urban lyric of the nineteenth century, we find that the poem's episode of erotic excitement is triggered by the "deafening" city street itself:

> La rue assourdissante / autour de moi hurlait.
> Longue, mince, en grand deuil, / douleur majesteuse,
> Une femme passa, / d'une main fastueuse
> Soulevant, balançant / le festoon et l'ourlet. (1-3 [Baudelaire 1975: 1.92-93])

(Around me roared the nearly deafening street. / Tall, slim, in mourning, in majestic grief, / A woman passed me, with a splendid hand / Lifting and swinging her festoon and hem) (Baudelaire 1993: 189)

The metonymic logic of the first three lines makes the appearance of "une femme" an attribute, if not the consequence, of the "rue assourdissante" that assaults "moi" with its clamor. The conjunction is disjunctive, for the city's hostile din in itself promises no meaningful erotic encounter, as it indeed turns out to be the case after another stanza. But the logical ambiguity does not disturb the classicism of Baudelaire's alexandrine. With controlled caesura inserted into the middle of each line (indicated by slash above) and its ABBA rhyme scheme, the sonnet sets up the quatrain as an autonomous order of its own. This semblance of security will be rudely destroyed, however, after another quatrain, as the shock of the poet's eye contact with the woman strikes him numb. "Un éclair . . . puis la nuit!—Fugitive beauté" (9), exclaims the poet: a flash of light, followed by the darkness of night, as the woman vanishes. Benjamin points to the "profound gulf" (Benjamin 2003: 25) between the first two stanzas and the remainder heralded by this memorable outburst, but the line itself depicts a striking rupture in its very shape. The passing time sweeps away the *passante*, leaving only bleak, dumb, empty dots in its wake. From this devastation the poem attempts to recuperate with a rhyme matching "beauté," but in this duel with the rhyming fencer,[1] the clamorous street departs with an easy victory. The city is surely hostile to rhyme; to prose, however, it can be more hospitable.

"The miracle of a poetic prose"

In his dedication to Arsène Houssaye, prefatory to *Le Spleen de Paris*, Baudelaire states that "poetic prose" is something germane to the literary ethos of city strollers:

> Which one of us, in his moments of ambition, has not dreamed of the miracle of a poetic prose, musical, without rhythm and without rhyme, supple enough and rugged enough to adapt itself to the lyrical impulses of the soul, the undulations of reverie, the jibes of conscience?
>
> It was, above all, out of my exploration of huge cities, out of the medley of their innumerable interrelations, that this haunting ideal was born. (Baudelaire 1970: ix-x)

The poetic prose, or the "short poems in prose" (*petits poèmes en prose*), as the subtitle of the collection goes, though without rhythm or rhyme, is "supple enough and rugged enough" to serve the needs of the lyrical soul. The key expression here is "rugged," which in French is *heurté* (Baudelaire 1975: 1.275-76), meaning "abrupt, jerky, knocked against," i.e. a textual attribute attuned to the hazards of city streets. The "haunting" or obsessive (*obsédant*) ideal of a metropolitan prose at once flexible and sturdy, expressive and mimetic, subjective and objective, emerges from Baudelaire's "exploration" of the metropolis. Whether Baudelaire's prose poems approximate this ideal is a complex question which we cannot investigate here properly, but some obvious facts can be stated. Most works gathered in *Le Spleen de Paris* belong to familiar, pre-existing prose genres (meditation, fable, anecdote, essay etc.).[2] Their most original feature concerns not so much their prose style itself as the moral conundrum of the message: the poet beats an old mendicant for the sake of philanthropy ("Beat Up the Poor," [Baudelaire 1970: 102-3]) or breaks the window glasses of a glazier to make "life beautiful" ("The Bad Glazier," [Baudelaire 1970: 14]).

Dickens's prose, by comparison, combines description and argument, without depicting violent body language, in its unique prose rhythm, at once supple and rugged. In the typical Boz style, whether influenced by the "undulations of reverie" or dictated by some "jibes of conscience," subjective musing never disrupts the self-appointed posture of a voice speaking of and for the public. Since the objective world rather than his subjective realm is what Boz commits himself to portraying, his sentences offer themselves as vessels conveying factual particularities in their discrete contingency. To carry on this commission, while aspiring to rhythmic language in so doing, is a daunting task, as any sample from his first novel *Pickwick Papers* illustrates. Here we choose a description of one wet morning at White Horse Cellar, to which Sam Weller is dispatched by his employer to make preparations for a coach trip to Bath:

> The next was a very unpropitious morning for a journey—muggy, damp, and drizzly. The horses in the stages that were going out, and had come through the city, were smoking so, that the outside passengers were invisible. The newspaper-sellers looked moist, and smelled mouldy; the wet ran off the hats of the orange-vendors as they thrust their heads into the coach windows, and diluted the insides in a refreshing manner. The Jews with the fifty-bladed penknives shut them up in despair; the men with the pocket-books made pocket-books of them. Watch-guards and toasting-forks were alike at a discount, and pencil-cases and sponges were a drug in the market. (*Pickwick* 490 [chap. 35])

The transformation of the cityscape brought about by rain, which was a set topic of Augustan satire as in Swift's "A Description of a City Shower," is presented in two pairs of parallel clauses allocated to the scene's detail—the newspaper-sellers placed next to the orange-vendors, and the Jewish knife-sellers paired with pocket-books vendors—with the final sentence doubling the pairing. The paragraph brings order to the rambling objects, yet the technique is rudimentary and contrived, due to its excessive reliance on paratactic parallelism. The awkwardness of "smoking so, that" also seems glaringly obvious, and "muggy, damp, and drizzly" in the first sentence seems a failed attempt at consonance. The mature Dickens style, however, employs in a more prosaic mode a richer arsenal of rhetorical devices without drawing attention to their presence. A relatively less noted example would be the view of Barnard's Inn as seen by the freshly gentrified Pip, as he is led by Wemmick to his assigned chambers there:

> . . . My depression was not alleviated by the announcement, for, I had supposed that establishment to be an hotel kept by Mr Barnard, to which the Blue Boar in our town was a mere public-house. Whereas I now found Barnard to be a disembodied spirit, or a fiction, and his inn the dingiest collection of shabby buildings ever squeezed together in a rank corner as a club for Tom-cats.
>
> We entered this haven through a wicket-gate, and were disgorged by an introductory passage into a melancholy little square that looked to me like a flat burying-ground. I thought it had the most dismal trees in it, and the most dismal sparrows, and the most dismal cats, and the most dismal houses (in number half a dozen or so), that I had ever seen. I thought the windows of the sets of chambers into which those houses were divided, were in every stage of dilapidated blind and curtain, crippled flower-pot, cracked glass, dusty decay, and miserable makeshift; while To Let, To Let, To Let, glared at me from empty rooms, as if no new wretches ever came there, and the vengeance of the soul of Barnard were being slowly appeased by the gradual suicide of the present occupants and their unholy interment under the gravel. (*Expectations* 162 [chap. 21])

The passage begins on a comic note as it relates the ignorance of Pip who took Barnard's Inn literally as "an hotel kept by Mr. Barnard." To the humour of this remark is added the evocative force of the trope that equates Barnard's ghastly presence with "a disembodied spirit," which in turn is tempered by the closing joke of likening the establishment to "a club for Tom-cats." The next paragraph builds on another trope, that of the place appearing to him "like a flat burying-ground," which then leads to a repetition-cum-variation of "the most dismal" applied to trees, sparrows, cats, and houses. The broad brushstroke of this adjectival characterization is supplemented immediately by factual information about the place, "crippled flower-pot, cracked glass, dusty decay," which, however, prepares for a sudden leap into the staccato of "To Let, To Let, To Let." Commercial language thus meets the sensitive soul of the prose poet, which outstretches itself into the image of Barnard's vengeful and macabre soul presiding over "the gradual suicide of the present occupants"—a striking expression in itself and one that completes the mortuary trope employed at the beginning of the paragraph.

The poetic force of Dickens's prose can be measured against another hallowed name in poetry, T. S. Eliot. Both "Prufrock" and *The Waste Land* add fog to the picture of dejection and desolation, although "the brown fog of a winter dawn" (*The Waste Land* 1.61 [T. S. Eliot 62]), developing the idea of an "Unreal city" (1.60), is terse and (intentionally?) trite compared with the feline fog in the former: "The yellow fog that rubs its back upon the window-panes . . . / Licked its tongue into the corners of the evening . . . / Slipped by the terrace, made a sudden leap . . . / Curled once about the house, and fell asleep," ("The Love Song of J. Alfred Prufrock" 5-11 [T. S. Eliot 13]). The fog in Dickens's *Our Mutual Friend*, his last finished novel, is similarly animated and coloured, but its pervasive persistence defies the simpler approach of transmuting the fog into a single recognizable animal:

> It was a foggy day in London, and the fog was heavy and dark. Animate London, with smarting eyes and irritated lungs, was blinking, wheezing, and choking; inanimate London was a sooty spectre, divided in purpose between being visible and invisible, and so being wholly neither. Gaslights flared in the shops with a haggard and unblest air, as knowing themselves to be night-creatures that had no business abroad under the sun; while the sun itself when it was for a few moments dimly indicated through circling eddies of fog, showed as if it had gone out and were collapsing flat and cold. . . . From any point of the high ridge of land northward, it might have been discerned that the loftiest buildings made an occasional struggle to get their heads above the foggy sea, and especially that the great dome of Saint Paul's seemed to die hard; but this was not perceivable in the streets at their feet, where the whole metropolis was a heap of vapour charged with muffled sound of wheels, and enfolding a gigantic catarrh.
>
> At nine o'clock on such a morning, the place of business of Pubsey and Co. was not the liveliest object even in Saint Mary Axe—which is not a very lively spot—with a sobbing gaslight in the counting-house window, and a burglarious stream of fog creeping in to strangle it through the keyhole of the main door. (*Mutual Friend* 420 [book 3, chap.1])

While the comic touch of "animate London" paralleling "inanimate London" in this last finished novel attests to the continuity of the "Boz" style, the passage activates a more complex figurative strategy when compared not only with his earlier city sketches but with Eliot's "brown fog." It is a "foggy day" and the "fog was heavy and dark." This fog, then, seizes London dwellers, the "animate London," literally by the throat, as they go "wheezing, and choking," which thus diminishes the living humans into helpless victims of London's unnatural climate (the sun is squeezed out "flat and cold" as soon as it rises). Gaslights, by contrast, are personified into "night-creatures" with "a haggard and unblest" countenance. In the meantime, inanimate London takes up the centre stage, as animate London becomes completely blurred by the fog. The buildings wrestle against the fog to secure breathing space for themselves, led by the dome of Saint Paul's Cathedral desperate to save itself from being choked. The "whole metropolis," all the while, suffers from a "gigantic catarrh," and the "muffled sound" of traffic hiccups like so many compulsive coughs of a sickly patient. With such overview of the city, close-up views of the business streets can hardly be cheerful. At Pubsey and Co. "a sobbing gaslight" and a "burglarious stream of fog" signal the beginning of a most inauspicious new day in this particular portion of animate London called "Saint Mary Axe."[3] Conversant with the unreal force of things and their demonic vitality, Dickens's prose in this and other great cityscapes orchestrates a supple language of trope that more than rivals any landmark urban poetry in the Western tradition.[4] The city as object comes alive in the musically poetic prose of Boz, which superbly balances sensation and sense, impression and reflection, information and implication.

"On account of his complexion"

A metropolis, however, is not simply a scene but a crowded, stirring object populated by a vast number of people embroiled in the "strife of singularity." If a metropolis is like Hell, it shares the features of Dante's Hell, where the sinners aggressively retain their individual passion and animus, despite their eternal torments and anguish. As each seeks to "appear 'to the point,' to appear concentrated and strikingly characteristic" under the conditions of "brief metropolitan contacts," in Simmel's analysis (Simmel 1997: 183), the subject captures and categorizes the others in terms of their salient traits. Dickens exhibits his mastery of this visual technology of the metropolitan subject by packing each of his novels with scores of funny, bizarre, odd, pathetic figures, each and every one of them endowed with distinct features marking them off from the others. The chapters of Dickens's first novel swarm with a greater number of characters than will be accommodated in any of his subsequent works, but their presence is justified by the entertainment value of their individual quaintness, each captured in a single dominant detail, as the first appearance of Sam Weller's father demonstrates:

> The stout man was smoking with great vehemence, but between every half-dozen puffs, he took his pipe from his mouth, and looked first at Mr. Weller and then at Mr. Pickwick. Then, he would bury in a quart pot, as much of his countenance as the dimensions of the quart pot admitted of its receiving, and take another look at Sam and Mr. Pickwick. Then he would take another half-dozen puffs with an air of profound meditation and look at them again. At last the stout man, putting up his legs on the seat, and leaning his back against the wall, began to puff at his pipe without leaving off at all, and to stare through the smoke at the new-comers, as if he had made up his mind to see the most he could of them. (*Pickwick* 270 [chap. 20])

Added to the static physical characteristic of Weller senior's stoutness is the dynamic characteristic of his action, his smoking and puffing "with great vehemence." Whenever he is summoned to the stage of the novel's action, his puffing and/or stoutness will attend him as signs of his individuality.

The instantaneous and visual quality of Dickens's method of introducing a new character becomes noticeable when put beside earlier precedents in English fiction, such as Fielding's introduction of Parson Adams, as he emerges on the scene of *Joseph Andrews*:

> Mr *Abraham Adams* was. . . . a perfect Master of the *Greek* and *Latin* Languages; to which he added a great Share of Knowledge in the Oriental Tongues, and could read and translate *French, Italian* and *Spanish*. He had applied many Years to the most severe Study, and had treasured up a Fund of Learning rarely to be met with in a University. He was besides a Man of good Sense, good Parts, and good Nature; but was at the same time as entirely ignorant of the Ways of this World, as an Infant just entered into it could possibly be. As he had never any Intention to deceive, so he never suspected such a Design in others. He was generous, friendly and brave to an Excess; but Simplicity was his Characteristic. (Fielding 19)

Whereas Fielding defines Adam's individuality in terms of his intellectual and moral worth, no mention is made of Weller senior's mental or moral qualities. The narrator shows no interest in whether Mr. Weller is "a Man of good Sense," but focuses instead on the shape of his stout "Parts," so that his "Nature" remains as much a mystery as the faces of the crowd rushing past Wordsworth. For Adams, one dominant element of his personality, his "Simplicity," is what represents him; for Weller, his physical appearance and action represent him at the level of external sensory perception. That this description of Weller senior is a product of the metropolitan condition of fast, fugitive, fragile human encounter seems obvious. Those living in a big city size up each other in silence on the spot as they interpret the other's external appearance. Amusement and diversion, rather than sympathy and admiration, form the basis of the community of experience enacted by such extrinsic perception. Adams' "simplicity" is funny but he also commands respect; Weller's puffing is morally neutral but comic. The moral indifference of the humour which Boz skillfully concocts here reflects the conditions of metropolis, where each moment of seeing leaves no room for sustained moral contemplation, due to the sheer abundance of visual stimuli and the velocity of their succession.

Dickens's technique of bringing out traits of individuality can be compared with another predecessor in the field, Sir Walter Scott. Following the description of the physical appearance of Mr. Weller quoted above comes a report of his words, whose linguistic peculiarity immediately reveals his social and topographical identity:

> "I took a good deal o' pains with his eddication, sir; let him run in the streets when he was wery young, and shift for his-self." (*Pickwick* 271)

Dickens employs thus a typographical convention of transcribing Cockney speech (replacing "w" for "v," for example), following the model set by the transcription of Lowland Scots in Scott's Waverley novels, as in the following example from *The Heart of Mid-Lothian*:

> "And had just cruppen to the gallows' foot to see the hanging, as was natural for a wean; and what for might na she hae been shot as weel as the rest o' them, and where wad we a' hae been then? I wonder how Queen Carline (if her name be Carline), wad hae liked to hae had ane o' her ain bairns in sic a venture?" (Scott 1994: 47 [chap. 4])

Mrs. Howden, the character speaking these words, voices the popular political sentiments of average Edinburgh townsfolk in their shared accent and idiom. The peculiarity of the lexical ("wean" and "bairn," both meaning "child") and phonetic ("hae" for "have") markers puts distance between English readers and the Scottish characters who speak this way, but this is a linguistic distance that can be bridged at least in part, for it sounds strange but familiar to the English ear. The same thing can be said about the thematic orientation of Scott's novelistic project, which is to assert the autonomy of Scottish culture against the backdrop of a shared "Britishness." Similarly, the Cockney accent exploited with great relish by Boz whenever Sam Weller and his father make appearance has the effect of making their social and topographical identity outlandish but endearing, as they remain largely innocuous. No social animosity colours their accents, which merely create a diverting dissonance among the relatively well-off associates of Sam Weller's employer.

Original and distinctive as Dickens's technique of characterization may be, it inherits the legacy not only of the established predecessors such as Fielding or Scott, but that of an older tradition of urban prose writing, a tradition which remains largely ignored and relegated to the obscure margins of literary history. A heritage of seventeenth-century "character," or characteristic writing, certainly lends force to Dickens's project of individualizing the city dwellers in terms of their physical and social peculiarities. The very term "character," however, is burdened with ambiguity, for in most usages in literary criticism, it either refers to an element in fiction in general or to the fictional individual's moral attribute. It is rarely used as a historical and generic term referring to a distinct group of prose pamphlets which emerged in the print market of seventeenth-century London, a neglect that is evident even when the "rise" of the novel is the topic discussed. McKeon, following Watt, is preoccupied with the early novel's standing in intellectual history. For him "character" is an abstract theological category of one's spiritual state (McKeon 95). The *True Story of the Novel* by Doody, bent on highlighting the attractions of early Greek novels, is interested only in the "idea" of "character" rather than telling the true story of the texts bearing the name of "character" (Doody 270-71). Characters as a genre seemed to have been silently forgotten in what William Warner calls the "nationalization of the novel" (W. Warner 21), as the ancestry of the great "English novels" was being tidied up or suppressed to form a self-enclosed canon. In the populous field of Dickens criticism, Dickens's lineage is traced to earlier English (and Scottish) novelists such as Fielding, Smollett and Scott, and that is where it usually stops. One rarely hears of the heritage of seventeenth-century characters that predates these sanctified names.[5] Character also tends to be snubbed in what ought to be its proper slot in literary history. In *Cambridge Companion to English Literature 1650-1740*, for example, both the chapter discussing the birth of the modern novel and the chapter devoted to satire (reserved for satirical poetry mostly, with Swift's prose added to his verse) remain silent on the character pamphlets of the period. Instead, the names of the prominent authors are presented as self-sufficient cause and effect of new narrative forms (as in chapter 12, "Swift, Defoe, and Narrative Forms"), with little attention paid to any earlier history of prose publication.[6] However important the key innovators of English prose narrative may be as ancestors to many other illustrious descendants including Dickens, the largely anonymous genre of "character" merits better acknowledgment, at least as a precursor of prose sketches of human figures in a metropolitan context, which form a major layer of Dickens's artistry.

We state the premise again: "The face of every one / That passes by me is a mystery," as Wordsworth mused. Or, in Friedrich Schiller's analysis of modernity's antinomies, the fragmentation of human beings into individuals frustrates the subject's efforts to maintain a comprehensive view of humanity as a "species" [*Gattung*]. Unlike the ancients, the moderns can only perceive "the image of the human species" as "fragments [*Bruchstücken*]," so that "one has to go to the rounds from one individual to another in order to be able to piece together a complete image of the species" (Schiller 33). This indeed is what the inhabitants of populous modern cities do routinely, who go to the rounds from one individual to another clustered into crowds, all appearing as so many ruptured splinters (in the literal meaning of "Bruchstück") of the obfuscated whole. One sees countless number of faces each day, forgetting many of them in the very act of observing, and guarding oneself against unwelcome human contact. Knowledge is the key issue here, for to know the others for what they are while remaining unknown yourself (like Moll or H. F.) ensures superiority as well as safety. But this knowledge, for the busy and largely un-philosophical city dwellers, cannot possibly approach the level of a Baconian scientific observation induced from "the repetition of the singular" (Maxwell 127). It more often assumes the format of a simple, often illogical, classification of the strangers peopling the city into clearly marked categories. Such capacity to define and classify human objects was already considered a most desirable faculty to possess in seventeenth-century London, as can be seen in the flourishing popularity in that century of pamphlets bearing the title of "Character of X," which also asserted the potency of the print medium, as the character or essence of human figure was spelled out in printed characters (Lynch 35).

The character pamphlets published in seventeenth-century London thrived under the factious atmosphere of the Interregnum, as the "character" of a political enemy was vividly (as well as viciously) laid bare by a series of statements verging on invectives. The following extract from *An Agitator Anotomised: Or, The Character of an Agitator* (1648) attacking Puritan radicals graphically illustrates the pugnacious spirit of the genre:

> Hee is of the same parentage with good lawes, both lim-becked out of corruptions; and hath great affinity with Rats, especially those that are bred in an old Ship; for as they are engendred out of the cresset-fallen man of War, so is he a beast created of the corruption of a land-man of War, an iddle and unrigged army; you cannot distinguish him in any thing from a Rat, but he fears man; and hee neither feares God nor man, nor any thing else but

> disbanding. (*An Agitator Anotomised* n.p.)

How to tell a dangerous "agitator" roaming the streets of London and Westminster from a loyal law-abiding citizen? As the times are dangerous and urgent, one has no leisure to stop him and investigate his political views; instead, look for the "great affinity with Rats" in his appearance and deeds, for he is such infectious "beast" concocted by the "land-man of War," i.e. by the Civil War. The truth of the "agitator" unfolds in the vivid, sensuous specificity of the rhetorical figure that first compares and then identifies him with a rat.

Not all character pamphlets in the seventeenth century brimmed over with political animus, however. *Whimzies: Or, A New Cast of Characters* (1631), for instance, offers a sociological typology of different occupational groups, but it adopts the same strategy of translating the identity of each type into a set of distinct physical traits and facts about his circumstances, as in this description of a typical "Almanack-maker":

> Hee ha's the true situation and just proportion of the principall Angles or houses of the Heaven or Firmament: yet can hardly pay house rent for his owne. Forty shillings is his yeerely pension upon every impression: but his vailes are meaner, unlesse he have the Art for stolen goods to cast a figure: wherein, trust me, hee ha's a prety smattering. He walks in the Clouds, and prates as familiarly of the influence of the Moone, as if hee had beene the man that was in her. (*Whimzies* 3-4)

The inherently fraudulent pretensions of the almanac-maker, as a pseudo-intellectual trader offering knowledge of the heavens, stars, and one's annual fortune, is evidenced by how poorly he lives and dresses. An attitude of snobbish contempt pervades this characterization, which taxes the targeted person for his poverty itself (living on "forty shillings" per annum, he "can hardly pay house rent for his owne"), rather than for any proven fact of his reprehensible or fraudulent deeds. Further down the scale of social hierarchy, an indigent sailor's shabby circumstances are gloatingly detailed as dirty, ugly, and safely risible:

> Hee must feede his valour with the liquid spirit of some piercing Elixir: and thus hee ducks and dives out his time like a true Didapper. Hee makes small or no choice of his pallet; he can sleepe as well on a Sacke of Pumice as a pillow of downe. . . . He is most constant to his shirt, and other his seldome-wash'd linnen. He ha's been so long acquainted with the surges of the Sea, as too long a calme distempers him. He cannot speake low, the Sea talkes so loud. (*Whimzies* 140-41)

At all the levels of visible appearance and audible sounds, from what he wears to how he speaks, there is a remarkable consistency in his "sailor-ness," which, on terra firma, has nothing to recommend itself to the gentle urban society. Admittedly, his drinking strong spirits should be condemned, and his speaking too loud is bad manners. But his sleeping on rough bed, his strong digestive capacity, and his wearing the same dirty linen by no means prove his moral depravity. Such fault in syllogism does not deter the readers of *Whimzies* from enjoying this character description, for all that matters is their sense of superiority to these marginal figures they could run into in the busy streets and shops of London. A sense of control may be drawn from reading such characters, which strengthens their sense of security in the vast and fast urban world.

Offending items of clothing represent metonymically the offensive human figure wearing them, according to the logic of characters. In the *Character of a Diurnal-Maker* (1654), an obvious offshoot of *Whimzies*, the entire apparel of the human figure is dissected, one item at a time, as so many signs of his shabbiness and awkwardness from head to foot:

> I begin with his head, which is ever in the Clouts, as if the night-cap should make Affidavit, that the brain was pregnant. . . . His collar is wedged with a peece of peeping linnen, by which he meanes a band, 'tis the forlorne of his shirt, crawling out of his neck, indeed it were time that his shirt were jogging, for it has serv'd an apprenticeship, and (as prentices use) it hath learned his trade too, to which effect 'tis marching to the Paper Mill, and the next week sets up for it self in the shape of a Pamphlet. . . . His Bootes are the Legacyes of two black Jacks, and till he pawn'd the silver that the Jacks were tipp'd with, it was a pretty mode of boot-hose-tops. (*The Character of a Diurnal-Maker* 8-10)

The cardinal sin of the human object thus lampooned lies in his wearing shabby headgear and ill-matched boots. Details come alive, such as "a peece of peeping linnen, by which he meanes a band, 'tis the forlorne of his shirt, crawling out of his neck," which approaches a "Boz"-like humour. Yet not much sympathy is extended to the model of this portraiture, painted to accentuate the decrepit signs all around his body indicating his shabby profession. As with the Almanac-Maker, the Diurnal-Maker is represented and "known" as an item in a world of second nature, of a universe constructed of manufactured goods and documents, of the modern metropolis where things substitute humans as the more reliable witnesses to their "truth."

Character pamphlets create the effect of distancing and objectifying the other with whom the subject shares physical proximity in a bustling city space. To do so, they employ a paradoxical textual strategy of close observation coupled with emotional severance from the object described. That Dickens inherits, without their callous sarcasm, the textual expertise of these character pamphlets, whether consciously or not, can be illustrated by the passage from *Pickwick Papers* quoted above, but those works that came after pose a more complex question. The Wellers, father and son, could be both laughable and lovable. But laughter may not always be mollified by affection in an urban environment. Baudelaire's remarks in "On the Essence of Laughter" about the complete lack of commiseration in city streets seem to present a convincing view of metropolitan humanity. The "delight" of laughing at the "sight of a man falling on the ice or in the street, or stumbling at the end of a pavement," he points out, arises from the "unconscious pride" of saying to oneself, "Look at me! *I* am not falling . . . Look at me! *I* am walking upright. *I* would never be so silly as to fail to see a gap in the pavement or a cobblestone blocking the way" (Baudelaire 1964: 152). The description of the poor diurnal-maker or the sailor unfortunate enough to wear the wrong clothes and boots incites the readers' scornful laughter, mixed with their assurance that they would never wear such shabby outfits or would lead such precarious lives. In Dickens the diversion offered by character sketches is never as explicit and remorseless as in these early-modern character pamphlets, but that they do inspire a sense of indifferent detachment, or even superiority, cannot be denied.

A telling instance can be found in those chapters depicting the economic tribulation of young David Copperfield, forced to earn his own living in London. In this first-person narrative, the narrator chooses not to objectify his own appearance through any significant detail, but is merely content to state what an odd figure he might have appeared, as when he rewards himself with a handsome dinner at a "famous alamode beef-house near Drury Lane": "What the waiter thought of such a strange little apparition coming in all alone, I don't know; but I can see him now, staring at me as I ate my dinner, and bringing up the other waiter to look" (*Copperfield* 160 [chap. 11]). His fellow workers at Murdstone and Grinby's warehouse, however, are given summary "characters," as the narrator assigns to each a salient sensory attribute:

> His name was Mick Walker, and he wore a ragged apron and a paper cap. He informed me that his father was a bargeman, and walked, in a black velvet head-dress, in the Lord Mayor's Show. He also informed me that our principal associate would be another boy whom he introduced by the—to me—extraordinary name of Mealy Potatoes. I discovered, however, that this youth had not been christened by that name, but that it had been bestowed

> upon him in the warehouse, on account of his complexion, which was pale or mealy. (*Copperfield* 155 [chap. 11])

Mick Walker's human worth is welded to his "ragged apron and a paper cap," whereas the crux of Mealy Potatoes' individuality lies in his "mealy" complexion evidently caused by his having worked long hours indoors from an early age. In both instances the description grants David a marginal superiority over them, for his complexion is not pale from lack of contact with wholesome air, while his clothing, as yet, has not reached that "mealy" stage of proletarian raggedness. The distancing effect of delineating a character's face in *David Copperfield* is nowhere more pronounced than in the introductory description attached to Uriah Heep's first appearance:

> The low arched door then opened, and the face came out. It was quite as cadaverous as it had looked in the window, though in the grain of it there was that tinge of red which is sometimes to be observed in the skins of red-haired people. It belonged to a red-haired person—a youth of fifteen, as I take it now, but looking much older—whose hair was cropped as close as the closest stubble; who had hardly any eyebrows, and no eyelashes, and eyes of a red-brown, so unsheltered and unshaded, that I remember wondering how he went to sleep. He was high-shouldered and bony; dressed in decent black, with a white wisp of a neckcloth; buttoned up to the throat. (*Copperfield* 218-19 [chap. 15])

Having escaped from his socioeconomic Hades, David starts a new stage of life when he is adopted and funded by his aunt. His rivals, therefore, now need to have some other defect than that of economic deprivation. With signs of "cadaverous" malignity marked all over his body and clothes, Uriah Heep steps in as the timely candidate to play the part. A self-made hypocrite clad in deceptively "decent black, with a white wisp of a neckcloth," always muttering "I am much too umble for that!"(235 [chap. 16]), must be distinguished as an essentially loathsome figure visually, before anything else has been proven about his ill character.

Evading the extremes of Blake's visionary allegorization of the city from distance and the mystified bewilderment Wordsworth experienced amidst the crowd, Dickens overcomes the "mystery" of passing faces by individualizing their characters according to their visual appearance. This is what the early-modern characters had already established as a strategy of objectifying human figures in terms of graphic specificity, which, however, is neither objective nor impartial. Moving all the way to his very last finished novel, *Our Mutual Friend*, we have the following characterization of Bradley Headstone, whose awkward looks, apart from his personality, have much to do with what Pierre Bourdieu calls the "concern for appearances" (Bourdieu 253) of someone who had to struggle hard to escape from the working-class background to which he was born:

> Bradley Headstone, in his decent black coat and waistcoat, and decent white shirt, and decent formal black tie, and decent pantaloons of pepper and salt, with his decent silver watch in his pocket and its decent hair-guard round his neck, looked a thoroughly decent young man of six-and-twenty. He was never seen in any other dress, and yet there was a certain stiffness in his manner of wearing this, as if there were a want of adaptation between him and it, recalling some mechanics in their holiday clothes. He had acquired mechanically a great store of teacher's knowledge. He could do mental arithmetic mechanically, sing at sight mechanically, blow various wind instruments mechanically, even play the great church organ mechanically. From his early childhood up, his mind had been a place of mechanical stowage. . . . There was a kind of settled trouble in the face. It was the face belonging to a naturally slow or inattentive intellect that had toiled hard to get what it had won, and that had to hold it now that it was gotten. (*Mutual Friend* 217 [book 2, chap. 1])

Like the writer of *The Character of a Diurnal-Maker*, Dickens magnifies the details of Headstone's overly "decent" sartorial appearance. That such characteristics have an essential connection to his modest means—he is "never seen in any other dress," simply because he cannot afford another set of outfit—forms an item of the charges pressed against him. Moreover, his strenuous effort to improve himself is used as evidence of his unappealing personality. Not only is he guilty of appearing, despite his effort to conceal his humble origin, like one of the "mechanics in their holiday clothes," but what he has acquired all partake of mechanical features, as "mechanically" is repeatedly added to all of his professional skills. As the story unfolds, incidents and dialogues will corroborate what this character's appearance intimates. Yet whether he truly deserves the novel's meager and hostile treatment remains a moot point, for he is driven to desperation by circumstances as well as his own innate character. Character determines fate in Dickens, often on the basis of the prejudices the novelist chooses to share with his readers. A community of *Erfahrung* is enabled through the sensory *Erlebni*s of reading the close observation presented by Dickens's character sketches—one that connects but also severs, excludes as it includes.

CHAPTER SIX

THE MAN OF THE CROWD

"Made stories for myself, out of the streets"

In Poe's "The Man of the Crowd" (1850), a work contemporary with Dickens's *David Copperfield* (1849-50) and set in London rather than the American cities Poe was familiar with, after twenty-four hours of relentless pursuit of an unknown old man, the narrator finally abandons his hope of penetrating the man's mystery. "He is the man of the crowd," admits the exhausted narrator, "It will be in vain to follow, for I shall learn no more of him, nor of his deeds" (Poe 481). The narrator, a convalescent barely recovering from illness, had been lured into chasing the stranger by his striking countenance "which at once arrested and absorbed" his senses, and which, moreover, seemed to promise some narrative attached to it:

> As I endeavored, during the brief minute of my original survey, to form some analysis of the meaning conveyed, there arose confusedly and paradoxically within my mind, the ideas of vast mental power, of caution, of penuriousness, of avarice, of coolness, of malice, of blood-thirstiness, of triumph, of merriment, of excessive terror, of intense—of supreme despair. I felt singularly aroused, startled, fascinated. "How wild a history," I said to myself, "is written within that bosom!" Then came a craving desire to keep the man in view—to know more of him. (Poe 478)

This craving to know, to read the face, to destroy the incognito of the other is, in this story, a desire unrequited and utterly defeated. An option for Poe's narrator would have been to turn the object into a character, giving him moral and social significance on the basis of inferences made from the material details of his appearance. This he fails to do, resorting at the last moment of the narrative to allegory, a move reminiscent of Blake's "London," except that neither "marks of woe" nor "mind-forg'd manacles" are the issue, but simply the tautological conclusion that he is "a man of the crowd." Dickens's narrators clearly have better training than Poe's narrator in this regard. His autobiographical novel *David Copperfield* explains how the now successful novelist David Copperfield had learned his craft as a storyteller in the streets of London: the "boy of the crowd" exercises the art of inventing narratives crowded with characters. Speaking of his recollection of Micawber, Copperfield offers this vital clue to Dickens's creativity: "I set down this remembrance here, because it is an instance to myself of the manner in which I fitted my old books to my altered life, and made stories for myself, out of the streets, and out of men and women" (*Copperfield* 168 [chap. 11]). He fashioned stories out of the faces in the throng he encountered, giving to them characters of "penuriousness, of avarice, of coolness, of malice, of blood-thirstiness, of triumph, of merriment, of excessive terror, of intense—of supreme despair." These are passions peopling Dickens's novels, but their embryonic forms can be traced in his short city sketches, as well.

An early example from among his *Uncommercial Traveller* articles, "Night Walks," reveals an illuminating pattern of how the wanderings of Dickens the man of the crowd, who ambles all night long around London, and indulges in "a fair amateur experience of houselessness" (*Uncommercial* 127), tends constantly to fashion narratives out of the figures he runs into. As "the last veritable sparks of waking life trailed from some late pieman or hot-potato man," like Poe's man of the crowd he seeks what stray leftover humanity the city's space still accommodates at those late hours. "And then the yearning of the houseless mind," writes the "houselessness" incarnate, "would be for any sign of company, any lighted place, any movement, anything suggestive of any one being up—nay, even so much as awake, for the houseless eye looked out for lights in windows" (128). As night verges on the brink of dawn, he enters Covent Garden, which is already packed with the day's grocery supply:

> Covent-garden Market, when it was market morning, was wonderful company. The great waggons of cabbages, with growers' men and boys lying asleep under them, and with sharp dogs from market-garden neighbourhoods looking after the whole, were as good as a party. But one of the worst night sights I know in London, is to be found in the children who prowl about this place; who sleep in the baskets, fight for the offal, dart at any object they think they can lay their thieving hands on, dive under the carts and barrows, dodge the constables, and are perpetually making a blunt pattering on the pavement of the Piazza with the rain of their naked feet. A painful and unnatural result comes of the comparison one is forced to institute between the growth of corruption as displayed in the so much improved and cared for fruits of the earth, and the growth of corruption as displayed in these all uncared for (except inasmuch as ever-hunted) savages. (*Uncommercial* 133-34)

A budding story of these youthful "savages" scattered around the place seems to be bubbling out of this description. These youthful beggars "sleep in the baskets, fight for the offal, dart at any object they think they can lay their thieving hands on, dive under the carts and barrows, dodge the constables" and fend for themselves as best as they can. No Covent Garden street urchin made his way into Dickens's novels, but he has his cousins in Jo the crossing sweep of *Bleak House* or the Artful Dodger the expert pickpocket in *Oliver Twist*. David tramping his way out of London to his aunt's house in Dover barely conceals his resemblance to this tribe, as he indeed is taken to be one by his aunt construing his appearance: "'Go away!' said Miss Betsey, shaking her head, and making a distant chop in the air with her knife. 'Go along! No boys here!'" (*Copperfield* 191 [chap. 13]).

Dickens's concern for the young unfortunates at Covent Garden does not prevent him from having his breakfast there. As he enjoys his coffee and toast, he entertains himself with a character sketch of the person serving it:

> [T]he towzled-headed man who made it, in an inner chamber within the coffee-room, hadn't got his coat on yet, and was so heavy with sleep that in every interval of toast and coffee he went off anew behind the partition into complicated cross-roads of choke and snore, and lost his way directly. (*Uncommercial* 134)

This "towzled-headed man," without his coat on, poised at the "complicated cross-roads" of choking and snoring, seems to promise a comic episode. But this mildly humorous sketch is interrupted by another, more gruesome encounter with an ill-favored stranger, who takes out from "his hat a large cold meat pudding." His manner of eating his pudding is no less bizarre. He stabs the pudding "like a mortal enemy" and tears the pudding "asunder with his fingers" before devouring it. Dickens attempts to apply his physiognomic acumen to the stranger's "excessive face" which "promised cadaverousness," but the man himself preempts it by blurting out his own short narrative about his countenance:

> [H]e said huskily to the man of sleep, "Am I red to-night?" "You are," he uncompromisingly answered. "My mother," said the spectre, "was a red-faced woman that liked drink, and I looked at her hard when she laid in her coffin, and I took the complexion." Somehow, the pudding seemed an unwholesome pudding after that, and I put myself in its way no more. (*Uncommercial* 134-35)

A story is half-born around the "mysterious man" carrying pudding in his hat, presented with instant character traits and the idiosyncratic habit of stabbing his meal. The man, however, stifles the birth of a possible narrative with his own vocal relation explaining his complexion. In the novels matters will be better stage-managed. This scene reminds one of the sudden re-appearance of Magwitch in *Great Expectations*. Pip is in his London chambers on a windy, rainy night that makes him feel as though he were "in a storm-beaten light-house." As he looks outside he finds the lamps "shuddering" due to the bitter weather (*Expectations* 298-99 [chap. 39]). Out of this windswept, cold, watery atmosphere emerges a figure, calling out Pip's name as he walks up the stairs:

> Moving the lamp as the man moved, I made out that he was substantially dressed, but roughly; like a voyager by sea. That he had long iron-grey hair. That his age was about sixty. That he was a muscular man, strong on his legs, and that he was browned and hardened by exposure to weather. As he ascended the last stair or two, and the light of my lamp included us both, I saw, with a stupid kind of amazement, that he was holding out both his hands to me. (299-300)

Unlike the pudding-stabbing stranger in "Night Walks," a human relationship gradually blossoms between Pip and this person who holds out his hands with affection. In the non-fiction sketch, the words of the man leave behind an intriguing echo of a truncated personal narrative. "My mother . . . was a red-faced woman that liked drink, and I looked at her hard when she laid in her coffin, and I took the complexion"—this promising self-introduction may be good enough to give him at least a minor role in any full-length Dickens novel. Had we known more about the mysterious pudding-eater's background, his sinister looks may very well change their tenor, as is the case with Magwitch in the latter half of *Great Expectations*.

The figures emerging from the crowd that Dickens the novelist makes stories out of are not simply men and women "of the crowd." They are individuals with personal histories carrying seeds of *Erfahrung* to be shared with others. In this sense, the "becoming-narrative"[1] of descriptive sketches can neutralize or even reverse the distancing and stereotyping aspects of characterization discussed in the previous chapter. Becoming-narrative and character sketch constitute the two poles of Dickens's fictional textuality. His narratives move back and forth between one to the other, adding new episodes, characters, and connections between them as the plot unfolds. One can say that this polarity also alters the balance of *Erfahrung* and *Erlebnis* in Dickens, for the community of experience built through narration about the characters bridges the distance character sketches set up, which latter, as we have suggested, is a restricted (if not spurious) *Erfahrung* involving exclusion as well as inclusion. The shock of encounter, which in Benjamin constitutes the essential form of *Erlebnis*, Dickens's narrations overcome by the *Erfahrung* of the characters' life stories.

A minor but representative example can be taken from *David Copperfield*, where the mature David, a secure, successful, and married professional author living in London, volunteers to help out one of his old friends from the province, Mr. Peggotty, who desperately searches for his niece Little Emily. While wandering the streets of London together, they spot Martha, a girl of dubious moral character but one who holds the key to the whereabouts of Emily. The two men follow her, believing "she might be more disposed to feel a woman's interest in the lost girl" hoping to accost her "in a quieter place, aloof from the crowd, and where we should be less observed" (*Copperfield* 677 [chap. 46]). Thus they follow her at a safe distance, and the woman walks on unawares of her being chased. Copperfield reveals how there is more to his action than solicitude about his friend's loved-one:

> She went on a long way. Still we went on. It was evident, from the manner in which she held her course, that she was going to some fixed destination; and this, and her keeping in the busy streets, and I suppose the strange fascination in the secrecy and mystery of so following any one, made me adhere to my first purpose. (*Copperfield* 678)

Apart from the charitable intention of helping Mr. Peggotty, David confesses how chasing Martha turned into a captivating *Erlebnis* in its own right, "the strange fascination in the secrecy and mystery of so following any one" incognito. The sheer excitement of pursuit and detection, however, is challenged once they draw closer to her, in an ambience gruesome and funereal, as there "was a story that one of the pits dug for the dead in the time of the Great Plague was hereabout" (*Copperfield* 680 [chap. 47]). Unlike Defoe's H. F., impassively walking about the sites of infection and devastation, David is beset by vague fears of the buried dead: "I did not approach her solitary figure without trembling; for this gloomy end to her determined walk . . . inspired a dread within me" (680). He subdues his trepidation, as he and Peggoty identify her and themselves. As she begins to tell her story to her followers and former acquaintances, the mood turns into an *Erfahrung* of human tribulation, which replaces their sense of brooding uneasiness with that of pity and commiseration.

When following another human in the crowd fails to evolve into any human relationship, the result can be quite devastating. This is the case with Eugene Wrayburn enticing Bradley Headstone to chase him around all over London, as he tells his friend Mortimer:

> "Having made sure of his watching me, I tempt him on, all over London. One night I go east, another night north, in a few nights I go all round the compass. Sometimes, I walk; sometimes, I proceed in cabs, draining the pocket of the schoolmaster who then follows in cabs. I study and get up abstruse No Thoroughfares in the course of the day. With Venetian mystery I seek those No Thoroughfares at night, glide into them by means of dark courts, tempt the schoolmaster to follow, turn suddenly, and catch him before he can retreat. Then we face one another, and I pass him as unaware of his existence, and he undergoes grinding torments. . . . Night after night his disappointment is acute, but hope springs eternal in the scholastic breast, and he follows me again to-morrow." (*Mutual Friend* 542-43 [book 3, chap.10])

In these inhospitable "night walks," the two strollers who know each other act like completely indifferent strangers. The disdainful posture is Eugene's pleasure, in particular, for he enjoys pretending utter unawareness of the other's existence, like Poe's "man of the crowd" refusing to recognize his pursuer. "I grew wearied unto death, and, stopping fully in front of the wayfarer, gazed at him steadfastly in the face. He noticed me not, but resumed his solemn walk" (Poe 481), writes Poe's narrator. The rejection and disregard of the other person's humanity surge into a murderous encounter at a later point in Dickens's novel. Eugene pays for his haughtiness by a near death at the hands of the desperate, irate, and jealous schoolmaster. The "abstruse No Thoroughfares" Eugene cultivates hints at the darker, dangerous side of mingling with the crowd while eschewing human relationship.

Community, then, is what matters in Dickens's metropolitan experience, in contrast to the urban narratives of Defoe or Poe. If Dickens shows no symptom from his first to his last novel of any "skepticism about the principle of mere aggregation in literature as well as politics," which beset George Eliot in the 1860s (Gallagher 224), it is so because he always writes inside the "aggregation" of the metropolitan crowd as one of them. Moll, Roxana, and H. F. stand apart and alone, retaining their incognito, even to their readers, for they reserve a large part of their feelings to themselves. In Poe's case, the city's anonymity paves the perfect ground for icy ratiocination of detecting crime, with no sympathy extended whatsoever to the mangled victims.[2] Despite the emphasis on inspection and policing in Dickens promoted by D. A. Miller (see Miller 93-95), the narrative logic of Dickens's novels fundamentally differs from detective plots, in that building a human relationship—as the episode of David and Peggotty tailing Martha illustrates—between the pursuer and the pursued is what matters, rather than mere discovery of concealed crime. The urban aggregation for Dickens is not something to be controlled as an object; rather, it is a living environment of human habitation to be joined, however precarious doing so may be. Most typically, Arthur Clennam in *Little Dorrit* is saved the knowledge about his birth, even to the very end, whereas to the self-appointed detective Rigaud-Blandois is meted out the punishment of violent death, when Clennam's parental roof crushes on his head. Arthur never quite manages to penetrate the family mystery shrouding his parents and Amy Dorrit. In fact, his not fully knowing his own birth secret, his state of "suspension between mystery and revelation" (Maxwell 271), is the price he has to pay for his membership in the small community built around him in the novel. In Dickens, unlike in Poe, the value of relationship overrides the interest or fascination of pursuit or discovery.

"A hideous little street of dead wall"

Communities, however, are as much the outcomes of objective socioeconomic convergence, as of interpersonal goodwill. One lives where one can afford to, not always where one wants to. One's address, in the past centuries as well as now and most likely in any foreseeable future, is subjected to a minute gradation in prestige and social status inscribed on the map of a vast metropolis with a long continuous history such as London. The broad contours of London's spatial division into West End, City, East End, the Docks, Southwark, and so forth reflect objective forces of political, economic, or natural advantage, such as the seat of government, facility of water traffic, concentration of business function, provision of cheap labour and even the direction of wind.[3] But not everything can be explained in terms of these objective conditions, for what makes London distinctive, like other historical cities, is the way the broad categories of socioeconomic distribution are elided and overlapped by checkered modes of marginal, borderline topographical articulation. These intermediary cases fascinated Dickens very much, for their literary value exceeds that of the more predictable patterns of class topography. They can sit for intriguing portraits as it were: the unlikely communities of humans gathered together in the interstices of the city's social regimentation can pose as objects or even characters to be sketched.

We can trace the technical evolution of Dickens's character of city neighborhood from the earliest novels, as in the following passages, the first from *Pickwick Papers* and the second from *Nicholas Nickleby*:

> There is a repose about Lant Street, in the Borough, which sheds a gentle

melancholy upon the soul. There are always a good many houses to let in the street: it is a bye-street too, and its dulness is soothing. A house in Lant Street would not come within the denomination of a first-rate residence, in the strict acceptation of the term; but it is a most desirable spot nevertheless. If a man wished to abstract himself from the world—to remove himself from within the reach of temptation—to place himself beyond the possibility of any inducement to look out of the window—we should recommend him by all means go to Lant Street. (*Pickwick* 433 [chap.32])

Cadogan Place is . . . the connecting link between the aristocratic pavements of Belgrave Square, and the barbarism of Chelsea. It is in Sloane Street, but not of it. The people in Cadogan Place look down upon Sloane Street, and think Brompton low. They affect fashion too, and wonder where the New Road is. Not that they claim to be on precisely the same footing as the high folks of Belgrave Square and Grosvenor Place, but that they stand, with reference to them, rather in the light of those illegitimate children of the great who are content to boast of their connections, although their connections disavow them. Wearing as much as they can of the airs and semblances of loftiest rank, the people of Cadogan Place have the realities of middle station. It is the conductor which communicates to the inhabitants of regions beyond its limit, the shock of pride of birth and rank, which it has not within itself, but derives from a fountain-head beyond; or, like the ligament which unites the Siamese twins, it contains something of the life and essence of two distinct bodies, and yet belongs to neither.
(*Nickleby* 264-65 [chap. 21])

In the first passage, the "repose about Lant Street" is developed into a "gentle melancholy" and "dullness," yet the characterization runs into a dead-end in the final sentence, which, witty as it may be, fails to sharpen the sensory attribute of the street, as the windows are shut upon it, literally. The second passage, however, succeeds in connecting the social identity of Cadogan Place as a cross between the properly fashionable Belgrave Square and the less glamorous Chelsea. To those who live there, their pretentious posture, however ludicrous it may be, is essential to maintaining their sense of worth. This the writer sums up in the simple but sonorous formula of being "in Sloane Street, but not of it." The physical location of Sloane Street, in other words, serves as the intangible social space of "symbolic struggles" of distinction incited by the "relative indeterminacy represented by the petite bourgeoisie" (Bourdieu 244) erected above (and in part independently from) the former. The hallmark Boz touch of likening Cadogan Place to the "illegitimate children of the great" fortifies the depiction with the rather brutal simile of Siamese twins. Given the spurious, hybrid, tenuous, but nonetheless entertainingly peculiar character of the place, the Witterlies, who represent the location in the novel, naturally partake of its snobbish sense of superiority. The two go hand in hand according to the literary grammar of Dickens. Humans and their space of habitation are intertwined like Siamese twins indeed—they retain their separateness without being separated.

The effect of these character sketches of neighbourhoods, however, exceeds the interests of social satire. The folly and vain pretentiousness of Cadogan Place and its human embodiment in Mrs. Witterly deserve to be turned into laughing stocks. Yet they also succeed in being memorable as marked manifestations of particularity composed of more than one sociological element. Cadogan Place derives its identity from both Belgrave Square and Brompton, both equally essential to its positioning, but its precarious location on the corner of Sloane Street provides a crucial ingredient to the peculiar flavor of its posture. What the postcode implies the humans living there explicitly embody—whether as tenants or owner-occupiers matters little here—as they actively assert and sustain the "character" of the place. The human dwellers of the city space, as Henri Lefebvre emphasizes (Lefebvre 109), transform a location into a space of habitation, so that it becomes something more complex than an abstract space of property value. This point can be further illustrated by comparing the description of Cadogan Place in *Nicholas Nickleby* with that of Mews Street in *Little Dorrit*, another address stationed on the ambiguous circumference of West End:

> Mews Street, Grosvenor Square, was not absolutely Grosvenor Square itself, but it was very near it. It was a hideous little street of dead wall, stables, and dung-hills, with lofts over coach-houses inhabited by coachmen's families, who had a passion for drying clothes and decorating their window-sills with miniature turnpike–gates. The principal chimney-sweep of that fashionable quarter lived at the blind end of Mews Street; and the same corner contained an establishment much frequented about early morning and twilight for the purchase of wine-bottles and kitchen-stuff. Punch's shows used to lean against the dead wall in Mews Street, while their proprietors were dining elsewhere; and the dogs of the neighbourhood made appointments to meet in the same locality. Yet there were two or three small airless houses at the entrance end of Mews Street, which went at enormous rents on account of their being abject hangers-on to a fashionable situation; and whenever one of these fearful little coops was to be let . . . the house agent advertised it as a gentlemanly residence in the most aristocratic part of town, inhabited solely by the elite of the beau monde. (*Dorrit* 109 [book 1, chap. 10])

The first sentence informs the reader of the physical location of Mews Street, which the second elaborates in terms of various social indicators of active habitation of the resident group, the coachmen's families. To them is added another socially marginal personage, the "principal chimney-sweep of that fashionable quarter," whose side of the street bustles with vibrant popular cultural life. Punch and Judy shows are regularly put on there, with the canine members also choosing that spot for their socializing occasions.[4] The other end of the street, adjacent to the unambiguously patrician Grosvenor Square, is colonized by the "abject hangers-on to a fashionable situation," housing a leading member of the Barnacle clan, who is dedicated to living off the sinecure and privileges of Circumlocution Office. The satirical edge is sharpened by the unmentionable neighbours further up Mews Streets—from the dogs to the resident chimney sweep—whom the "two or three small airless houses at the entrance end" would be anxious to disown. Yet the overall image of diversity, of mixed, irregular, disjunctive, jumbled, and therefore less monochrome social ambience of the place conveyed by the description lingers on, intimating vibrant vivacity of the place as a whole. Abstract quantitative evaluation of property value, the "enormous rents" those houses at the end of Mews Street yield, are not so much an economic base supporting a social superstructure as an economic superstructure deriving its bubbly worth from the world of minute social distinctions built into the city space.

An implication of this relative autonomy of residential space from real estate economics is that those who in legal terms do not own the place can nonetheless assert their right to inhabit the space according to their life style, to turn it into a social space of their own making. Even if it is a cramped, destitute living, the poor will be literally alive and kicking, not quite dejected or defeated. The lodgers of Seven Dials, for instance, celebrated in one of the first published sketches of Boz, strikes the note unmistakably of what Lefebvre calls the "right to the city" (Lefebvre 158) of these poor lodgers of the area. Boz the sketch writer joins a "little crowd" in Seven Dials, gathered around two drunken wives brawling with each other over allegations of extramarital flirting. They are about to settle their "quarrel satisfactorily, by an appeal to blows, greatly to the interest of other ladies who live in the same house, and tenements adjoining, and who are all partisans on one side or other."

> "Vy don't you pitch into her, Sarah?" exclaims one half-dressed matron, by way of encouragement. "Vy don't you? if *my* 'usband had treated her with a drain last night, unbeknown to me, I'd tear her precious eyes out—a wixen!"
>
> "What's the matter, ma'am?" inquires another old woman, who has just bustled up to the spot.
>
> "Matter!" replies the first speaker, talking *at* the obnoxious combatant, "matter! Here's poor dear Mrs. Sulliwin, as has five blessed children of her own, can't go out a-charing for one arternoon, but what hussies must be a

> comin', and 'ticing avay her oun' 'usband, as she's been married to twelve year come next Easter Monday, for I see the certificate ven I vas a drinkin' a cup o' tea vith her, only the werry last blessed Ven'sday as ever was sent. I 'appen'd to say promiscuously, 'Mrs. Sulliwin,' says I —"
>
> "What do you mean by hussies?" interrupts a champion of the other party, who has evinced a strong inclination throughout to get up a branch fight on her own account ("Hooroar," ejaculates a pot-boy in parenthesis, "put the kye-bosk on her, Mary!"), "What do you mean by hussies?" reiterates the champion. ("Seven Dials," *Sketches* 70)

In these four paragraphs appear some four characters ("half-dressed matron," "another old woman," "a champion of the other party," "a pot-boy"), in addition to the principal warriors, Susan and Mary. A collective voice soars up among them, dissonant and discordant, but also unified by its strong colloquialism presented with relish by the young writer with bold typographical aberrations. Aided by the present tense of the narrating sentences, the passage conveys a vivid sense of being there among them: a communal *Erfahrung* conveyed as an *Erlebnis* of auditory and visual effects evoking the immediacy of the scene. Even the poorest, the least respectable members of the city's humanity thus assert their right to be known or at least heard by the larger community of readers, however mean their lodgings and however poor their daily fare. Indeed, however far down in social scale, people improbably set up residence in the most unlikely manner, with a strong sense of their belonging to their neighbourhood, as we find in the description of Jacob's Island in *Oliver Twist*.

> [A] stranger, looking from one of the wooden bridges thrown across it at Mill Lane, will see the inhabitants of the houses on either side lowering from their back doors and windows, buckets, pails, domestic utensils of all kinds, in which to haul the water up; and when his eye is turned from these operations to the houses themselves, his utmost astonishment will be excited by the scene before him. Crazy wooden galleries common to the backs of half-a-dozen houses, with holes from which to look upon the slime beneath; windows, broken and patched, with poles thrust out, on which to dry the linen that is never there; rooms so small, so filthy, so confined, that the air would seem too tainted even for the dirt and squalor which they shelter; wooden chambers thrusting themselves out above the mud, and threatening to fall into it—as some have done; dirt-besmeared walls and decaying foundations; every repulsive lineament of poverty, every loathsome indication of filth, rot, and garbage; all these ornament the banks of Folly Ditch. (*Oliver* 381-82 [chap. 50])

The "inhabitants" of these "crazy wooden galleries" present to the eyes of a stranger an unwholesome, dirty, muddy, precarious life. The description is ostensibly designed to horrify the genteel reader, but one sniffs nonetheless some pungent evidence of persistent life vegetating on this improbable soil. The details inevitably evoke the tenacity of these dwellers "lowering from their back doors and windows, buckets, pails, domestic utensils of all kinds to haul the water up," along with a sense of their abject poverty.

The obviously dismissive attitude encouraged by the last phrases of the passage above from *Oliver Twist*, "every repulsive lineament of poverty, every loathsome indication of filth, rot, and garbage," downplay the vitality of those living there, for sure. It does so to serve the interest of the novel's plot, for here Sykes is soon going to be hunted down and punished with death. In his most skillfully worked-out mature works, *Bleak House* and *Little Dorrit*, Dickens' description of the less affluent neighbourhoods strikes a fine balance between destitution and habitation. A "series of bleak and corrupt houses" runs through *Bleak House*, as F. S. Schwarzbach suggests (Schwarzbach 135), yet people lead their everyday lives in these bleak places, even in those cramped and marginal premises, such as the rooms above Krook's shop which Miss Flite has made her home or Rouncewell's shooting gallery where George and Phil Squod make a happy pair. Tom-all-Alone's is surely a national shame, but it does provide "ruined shelters" to "ruined human wretches" (220 [chap. 16]). Close by, the Cook's Court in *Bleak House*, on "the eastern borders of Chancery Lane" (127 [chap. 10]), socially and topographically many steps below the fashionable squares of West End or even of Mews Street, is depicted, above all, as an inhabited communal space. It is a neighbourhood colonized by law-related occupation, such as Snagby's stationary shop "Peffer and Snagsby," and Coavinse the sheriff's officer's residence. The novel's third-person narrator delineates a community of livelihood, experience, and values, conveying a sense of closeness through its hallmark present-tense mode:

> Mr Snagsby refers everything not in the practical mysteries of the business to Mrs Snagsby. She manages the money, reproaches the tax-gatherers, appoints the times and places of devotion on Sundays, licenses Mr Snagsby's entertainments, and acknowledges no responsibility as to what she thinks fit to provide for dinner; insomuch that she is the high standard of comparison among the neighbouring wives, a long way down Chancery Lane on both sides, and even out in Holborn, who, in any domestic passages of arms, habitually call upon their husbands to look at the difference between their (the wives') position and Mrs Snagsby's, and their (the husbands') behaviour and Mr Snagsby's. Rumour, always flying bat-like about Cook's Court, and skimming in and out at everybody's windows, does say that Mrs Snagsby is

> jealous and inquisitive; and that Mr Snagsby is sometimes worried out of house and home, and that if he had the spirit of a mouse he wouldn't stand it. (*Bleak House* 129-30 [chap. 10])

Mr. and Mrs. Snagsby, admired for their ideal matrimonial relationship, lead a thoroughly communal existence as members of Cook's Court, with their worth assessed by the "neighbouring wives a long way down Chancery Lane on both sides," and with anything that happens in their domestic setting "always flying bat-like about Cook's Court and skimming in and out at everybody's windows." Unlike the brawling wives of Seven Dials, these would-be respectable housewives prize domestic peace obtained by female supremacy. But like their poorer counterparts, they express their own idiomatic, autonomous views on connubial behaviour as they assess the instructive example of Mr. Snagsby's docile temper.

Whereas domestic arrangement is the preferred topic of the public debate among those living at Cook's Court, those coping with more biting economic hardships have other woes to worry about, including having to pay extortionate rents each month. Bleeding Heart Yard, the representative working-class address in the London of *Little Dorrit*, bled raw by the hypocritical landlord Casby through his amiably quaint agent Pancks, is "inhabited by poor people, who set up their rest among its faded glories, as Arabs of the desert pitch their tents among the fallen stones of the Pyramids." Yet "there was a family sentimental feeling prevalent in the Yard, that it had a character" (*Dorrit* 135 [book 1, chap. 12]). This "character" is ascertained by the representative tenant of the Yard, Plornish the plasterer, who waxes quite eloquent in his criticism of social inequality:

> What was they a doing in the Yard? Why, take a look at 'em and see. There was the girls and their mothers a working at their sewing, or their shoe-binding, or their trimming, or their waistcoat making, day and night and night and day, and not more than able to keep body and soul together after all—often not so much. There was people of pretty well all sorts of trades you could name, all wanting to work, and yet not able to get it. There was old people, after working all their lives, going and being shut up in the workhouse, much worse fed and lodged and treated altogether, than—Mr Plornish said manufacturers, but appeared to mean malefactors. Why, a man didn't know where to turn himself for a crumb of comfort. As to who was to blame for it, Mr Plornish didn't know who was to blame for it. He could tell you who suffered, but he couldn't tell you whose fault it was. (*Dorrit* 143 [book 1, chap. 12])

His malapropism notwithstanding, Mr. Plornish gives voice to the shared

Erfahrung of the Yard's residents, a confused but angry protest against the contradictions of a free-market economy that leaves the industrial reserve army to wait indefinitely on the pleasure of employing capital, while they do whatever it takes to feed and house themselves. At this level, the communal complaint of Bleeding Heart Yard verges on a class discontent not only of London proletarians but of workers of the world who, however, have yet to unite to fight their enemies, not being sure "whose fault it was." In the novel it is Pancks who assaults his employer on their behalf, cutting off the latter's benevolent hair and exposing his true nature to the amused audience of the Yard. They cheer with their "murmur of 'Shame!' and 'Shabby!'" in response to Panck's indictment (*Dorrit* 801 [book. 2, chap. 32]), which certainly seems to belong to a different category from that of a concerted political action. Casby's tenants at Bleeding Heart Yard remain mere spectators as Pancks metes out rough justice on their landlord. Moreover, they would remain tenants of the Yard, having to work "day and night and night and day" to pay their rents. But what if the Plornishes of London (and elsewhere) decided they knew who was to blame, and whose fault it was? The merit of Dickens's two historical novels, although generally not counted among his best works, is to have broached the sensitive question of the crowd turning rebellious, of their becoming a revolutionary mob, under the protection offered by distance in time and space.

"A creature of very mysterious existence"

Those living near one another in a city form a knowable community among themselves, sharing certain articulate or inarticulate values and views, based on the specific social, economic, and topographical conditions of their habitation. The crowd as mob, which drowns all distinctions of individuality or social belongings, and which acts on a will and impulse of its own, poses problems at different levels to the subject attempting to know it. Is there a "head" or some driving centre of the mob, or does it elude any conscious control whatsoever? When, how and why does the otherwise quiet and quiescent metropolitan throng transform itself into a destructive mob defying law and order? Can justice be served through mob action, or is it bound to be inherently demonic, defeating any noble intentions? Dickens had no clear answers to these political questions, nor should we perhaps expect them from him. Yet interestingly, he does offer a quasi expert view on mob behaviour in *Barnaby Rudge*. "A mob," the narrator asserts,

> is usually a creature of very mysterious existence, particularly in a large city. Where it comes from or whither it goes, few men can tell. Assembling and dispersing with equal suddenness, it is as difficult to follow to its various sources as the sea itself; nor does the parallel stop here, for the ocean is not more fickle and uncertain, more terrible when roused, more unreasonable, or more cruel. (*Barnaby* 396 [chap. 52])

In this formulation, then, the dominant attribute of a mob is its inscrutable, mystical unpredictability, comparable to that of the sea; its determinant factor is its being indeterminable. But as in other cases of epistemological production of meaning, it depends on where you position the knowing subject. To describe the mob in a stable unperturbed prose, your physical and psychological distance from it is crucial. If you are at the mercy of its force, like Crusoe running for his life, you have no leisure to observe its action but instead can only describe what you are going through. Similarly, when the writing subject has immersed itself in the action of the wild mob, the perspective and language of prose reflect the perilous condition and excitement of the crowd.

In *Oliver Twist*, we have a rare example of a narrator writing in the midst of an excited mob. The scene is where poor Oliver, forced to join his fellow pickpockets, has to run for his life, singled out by the mob as a member of the gang. The perspective of the narrator is adjusted to the eye-level of a participating member of the chasing crowd:

> "Stop thief! Stop thief!" There is a magic in the sound. . . . Away they run, pell-mell, helter-skelter, slap-dash: tearing, yelling, screaming, knocking down the passengers as they turn the corners, rousing up the dogs, and astonishing the fowls: and streets, squares, and courts, re-echo with the sound.
>
> "Stop thief! Stop thief!" The cry is taken up by a hundred voices, and the crowd accumulate at every turning. Away they fly, splashing through the mud, and rattling along the pavements: up go the windows, out run the people, onward bear the mob, a whole audience desert Punch in the very thickest of the plot, and, joining the rushing throng, swell the shout, and lend fresh vigour to the cry, "Stop thief! Stop thief!"
>
> ....
>
> Stopped at last! A clever blow. He is down upon the pavement; and the crowd eagerly gather round him: each new comer, jostling and struggling with the others to catch a glimpse. "Stand aside!" "Give him a little air!" "Nonsense! he don't deserve it." "Where's the gentleman?" "Here he is, coming down the street." "Make room there for the gentleman!" "Is this the boy, sir!" "Yes." (*Oliver* 66-67 [chap. 10])

The present tense of description is mobilized here for the narrative purpose of depicting action, and the enumerative clauses fall on one another, at once imitating the phalanx of pursuers and transmitting the sensation of excited crowd as an *Erlebnis* to the reader. The rhythmic percussion effect of "Stop thief! Stop thief!" and the succession of present participles ("tearing, yelling, screaming, knocking etc.") beat the drum, as it were, goading on the mob to hunt down the boy. Finally, when Oliver is caught, the quotation mark encasing "Stop thief!" is taken off. The distinction between the mob's voice and the narrator's language has now been blurred. "A clever blow"—the sentence fragment makes no distinction of subject and object in order to gesticulate the condition of being engulfed by the sea-like crowd. The last paragraph of the passage closes with a group speech that reminds us of the scene from "Seven Dials" cited earlier, yet unlike the ladies choosing sides there, the community here is both unanimous and anonymous. The quoted words, except for the last "Yes" coming from Mr. Brownlow, float about as unassigned impersonal voice of the mob.

Judged by the achievement of the creative anomaly of the *Oliver Twist* passage above, the mob scene in *Barnaby Rudge* seems devoid of any real commotion, in large part because of the explicit moral police line that separates the reader from the mob. The rioters are led by dubious criminal characters, "Simon Tappertit (assisted by a few subalterns, selected from the Brotherhood of United Bulldogs), Dennis the hangman, Hugh, and some others" (*Barnaby* 371 [chap. 49]), as well as the half-wit Barnaby—a line-up that precludes any sympathy or respect from the outset. The cause and the occasion also lack any real human or political appeal. The Gordon Riots depicted in the novel, which agitated to repel Poppery in 1780 was an anachronistic paranoid fiasco, despite its distinguished position in London's history as an exceptional and atypical outburst of mob violence and destruction.[5] The narrator dons a historian's mantle to report on the incident:

> Through this vast throng, sprinkled doubtless here and there with honest zealots, but composed for the most part of the very scum and refuse of London, whose growth was fostered by bad criminal laws, bad prison regulations, and the worst conceivable police, such of the members of both Houses of Parliament as had not taken the precaution to be already at their posts, were compelled to fight and force their way. Their carriages were stopped and broken; the wheels wrenched off; the glasses shivered to atoms; the panels beaten in; drivers, footmen, and masters, pulled from their seats and rolled in the mud. Lords, commoners, and reverend bishops, with little distinction of person or party, were kicked and pinched and hustled; passed from hand to hand through various stages of ill-usage; and sent to their fellow-senators at last with their clothes hanging in ribands about them, their bagwigs torn off, themselves speechless and breathless, and their persons

> covered with the powder which had been cuffed and beaten out of their hair. (*Barnaby* 374)

The clichéd phrase "the very scum and refuse of London" neutralizes the passage's paratactic addition through semicolon of clauses depicting the mob action, whose urgency is further dissipated by the fairly full-bodied clauses of the last sentence. The historian's voice assumed by the narrator appears undecided as to how the scene's sensory *Erlebnis* will be transferred to a reflective *Erfahrung*, due in large part to the weak logic of its analysis. Is the violence to be imputed to "bad criminal laws, bad prison regulations, and the worst conceivable police," or is sectarian religious politics the prime culprit?

The contemporary events taking place when *Barnaby Rudge* (1841) was conceived, written, and published had a clearer political profile, as well as better ideology than the Gordon Riots. Chartist agitation of the late 1830s and the brooding sense of danger due to the widening gap between the rich and the poor must have dictated the creation of this historical novel. Dickens expressed his active interest in the plight of the underprivileged in his (anonymous) letter sent on 25 July 1842 to the *Morning Chronicle*, concerning the political wrangle over a legislation proposing to prohibit the employment of women and children at collieries. The law faced formidable opposition since it affected the hereditary peers at the House of Lords who owned the mining fields. "The mining labourers, with no complaint or hope of change," he contended, "are bound to work, from year to year, and from age to age, their fingers to the bone; to turn their women into men, and children into devils; and do all this to live. These are the 'rights of labour' with your collier lords!" (*Letters* 3.282). The righteous ire against the "collier lords" is unmistakable, but the reassuring phrase of "with no complaint or hope of change" implicitly stifles the legitimacy of collective action on the part of the labourers. Dickens could expose the stark reality of the enraged uprising of the poor and their clamorous "complaint" and demand for change, only after transposing the time frame to another century and the place to another country across the Channel. About two decades later (1859), *A Tale of Two Cities*, which revive the spectres of revolution in its pages, goes back to the more engaged narrative voice of *Oliver Twist*, as in the following depiction of the storming of the Bastille.

> With a roar that sounded as if all the breath in France had been shaped into the detested word, the living sea rose, wave on wave, depth on depth, and overflowed the city to that point. Alarm-bells ringing, drums beating, the sea raging and thundering on its new beach, the attack began.

....

> Cannon, muskets, fire and smoke; but, still the deep ditch, the single drawbridge, the massive stone walls, and the eight great towers. Slight displacements of the raging sea, made by the falling wounded. Flashing weapons, blazing torches, smoking waggonloads of wet straw, hard work at neighbouring barricades in all directions, shrieks, volleys, execrations, bravery without stint, boom, smash and rattle, and the furious sounding of the living sea; but, still the deep ditch, and the single drawbridge, and the massive stone walls, and the eight great towers, and still Defarge of the wine-shop at his gun, grown doubly hot by the service of Four fierce hours.
>
> A white flag from within the fortress, and a parley—this dimly perceptible through the raging storm, nothing audible in it—suddenly the sea rose immeasurably wider and higher, and swept Defarge of the wine-shop over the lowered drawbridge, past the massive stone outer walls, in among the eight great towers surrendered! (*Two Cities* 205-6 [book 2, chap. 21])

What catches our attention first is the trope of sea chosen by Dickens in *Barnaby Rudge* to define the formless mob. Here it has become a central metaphor orchestrating the tumult, as in "the living sea rose, wave on wave" or "suddenly the sea rose." The violence of the action, as in the pursuit of criminal suspects in *Oliver Twist*, is processed to be shared by the reader, not only in the use of paratactic parallels, but in the sentence fragments which dominate the second paragraph in the passage (beginning with "Cannon, muskets, fire and smoke"). "The dynamics of the revolutionary crowd are rendered as terrible and frightening" (Willis 102) remarks Mark Willis, but the mode of rendering encourages the reader to share the excitement. The style, by eliding the subject-object divide, obfuscates individual agency and thus exonerates the violent actions of the participants. Of course, "Defarge of the wine-shop" and his frightful wife represent the vengeful, inhuman, sanguine face of the revolutionary mob, but their representative status is metonymic—more of a contiguous connection to the oppressed and exasperated working-class Faubourg de Saint Antoine than a logical cause of the tumult. It is not their fault that things have reached this pass. Moreover, the picture of the husband's part in this mob action is given a heroic touch: "Defarge of the wine-shop worked like a manful soldier, Two fierce hours" (205), reports the narrator-historian. Apart from what the novelist outside his work or the narrator inside it has to say about revolutions in general and French Revolution in particular, the stylistic gestures of this passage imply a sense of communal alliance with the revolutionary mob, at this early stage at least. Later, as the mob becomes more vengeful and bloodthirsty, the plot of the novel veers towards an unconvincing sacrificial romance, at which stage the narrator's enthusiasm becomes more tempered. In this scene, too, just after the quoted paragraphs, the narrator remarks that the whole chaos amounted to a "deafening and maniacal bewilderment, astounding noise, yet furious dumb-show" (206). In revisiting the historic moment of the storming of the Bastille, Dickens seeks to maintain a balance between emotional empathy and mental distancing vis-à-vis the angry crowd, for the rage of the mob cannot be presented as an unalloyed *Erlebnis* without trimming its disturbing political implications.

Even so, most astonishingly, towards the very end of the novel the lively sensation of beheading victims at the Guillotine is thrust at the reader in engrossing present tense peppered with exclamation marks, as an *Erlebnis* in and for itself:

> . . . The ministers of Sainte Guillotine are robed and ready. Crash!—A head is held up, and the knitting-women who scarcely lifted their eyes to look at it a moment ago when it could think and speak, count One.
>
> The second tumbrel empties and moves on; the third comes up. Crash!—And the knitting-women, never faltering or pausing in their work, count Two. (*Two Cities* 355 [book 3, chap. 15])

More extraordinary still is the "real-time" broadcast of Sydney Carton's state of mind as his head is chopped off:

> The murmuring of many voices, the upturning of many faces, the pressing on of many footsteps in the outskirts of the crowd, so that it swells forward in a mass, like one great heave of water, all flashes away. Twenty-Three. (357)

The novel terminates with a "lived experience" (*Erlebnis*), paradoxically, of death, rather than gathering itself into a political *Erfahrung* advising the readers to be warned by history. Dickens's project of enlarging communal *Erfahrung* through enhanced *Erlebnis* runs into an impasse, when he allows himself to contemplate the possibility of collective uprising of urban community. What further complicates this vicissitude of Dickens's communal novelistic project is that *A Tale of Two Cities* was born as a weekly serial novel in Dickens's own journal *Household Words*. Dickens the novelist's relationship to Dickens the journalist-editor has to be examined next, for into the mutually supplementary relationship of *Erlebnis* and *Erfahrung* intrudes the potent prose of journalism, whose "absolutely . . . plausible" information, as Benjamin analyzes, is so much "shot through with explanations" that it undermines the storyteller's capacity to impart experience (Benjamin 2002: 147). The case with Dickens is more complex than this, as we shall see in the following chapter.

Chapter Seven

Journalist and Novelist

"Conducted by Charles Dickens"

Knowledge of the crowd and assuming the prerogative of writing on its behaviour exceed the province of novelists in general, as most of them deal with private individual lives. Journalists, in contrast, write of and to the public, representing the actions of the public to the public.[1] The inherent antagonism between the two professions affects *A Tale of Two Cities*, serialized in a weekly popular magazine edited by the author himself. The public dimension of the narrative, which sustains it as a historical novel proper as standardized by Scott, stands in an awkward relationship to the story of private fortunes, particularly of Sydney Carton, whose self-sacrifice—reported "live" to the reader as we have seen above—does little to confer conclusive significance on either the political history or his personal life-story. In a sense, Dickens had attempted to write a "Journal of the Revolutionary Years," converting the known facts of the historical event into a vivid *Erlebnis* in order to captivate the reader. Maintaining an organic balance between public events and private perspective, however, remains only a partially accomplished task. In *A Journal of the Plague Year*, the observations of the first-person narrator and the reported collective calamities coexist with no serious dissonance thanks to the minimization of the narrator's private history. What little glimpse at his personal life the reader is allowed only marginally infringes upon his self-assigned mission of bearing witness to the disaster. In *A Tale of Two Cities*, the resilience of Boz's prose holds together with a fair degree of success the personal and the public, the sensational and the informative. Moreover, this internal fissure could remain less visible when the novel first appeared as a serial amid the heterogeneous world of juxtaposed miscellaneous articles of *All the Year Round*.

Journalism and periodical culture have been inseparable from the modern metropolis, thanks to its concentration of personnel, information, and interests, to such an extent that in the case of London, "Fleet Street" in the City came to stand for "the Press" as such. This close relationship between the two reflects something more than mere extrinsic convenience. Journalism takes up a major portion of the metropolitan lifestyle, since it is a means of making sense of the rapid, dizzy, hectic life of modern society, at a pace commensurate with it of daily, weekly, or monthly succession which supersedes previous news regularly and relentlessly. Journalism's neurotic temporality and imbedded amnesia (one constantly forgets the "news" that have ceased to be new) militate against sustained recollection essential to *Erfahrung*, while its stylized representation of shocks numbs one's capacity for *Erlebnis*. Ever ready to stand in for both features of experience, periodical reportage colonizes the psyche of individuals seeking to cope with the astounding or enervating conditions of metropolitan living. That the more leisurely rhythm of the smaller capital of Scotland housed the headquarters of the pioneer quarterly of the century *Edinburgh Review*, can be taken as an obvious indication of the different urban birthmarks different periodical genres bear. In London, news could rarely survive a day or a week or at most a month's shelf-life. The slower pace of life in the Scottish capital, many degrees removed from London in terms of size, posed less threat to a quarterly magazine. London was the undisputed capital of information business. Printing and publishing could claim to be a major industry in London's manufacturing sector. Printers, engravers, bookbinders, and publishers collectively took up a substantial portion of London's manufacture (8 to 10%) in the 1820s (Barnett 48-49), a trend which later decades further accelerated, with the workforce in the industry doubling at the latter half of the century to employ some hundred thousand workers by 1911 (Ball and Sunderland 165).

At once a product and producer of this thriving publishing business, Dickens offered his novels to his customers on a periodical basis of monthly or weekly serialization, which was a mode of production attuned to the very pulse and rhythm of the metropolitan heartbeat. In this particular case at least, one can accept Sommerville's assertion that the "pace of the novel was the pace of the news, which had come to seem the pace of life itself" (Sommerville 114), to the urban humanity, above all. In its very format, as in its style, ethos, and topic, Dickens's novels embodied the conditions of the metropolis through and through. Dickens, whose works were avidly anticipated by tantalized readers each month or each week, was not content to be the city's best known periodical novel producer. Indeed he sought to expand his public influence by setting up and managing his own periodical organ. Quite unique among the major Victorian novelists, Dickens not only combined his career as journalist with that of novelist simultaneously, but he owned and controlled his own journals, *Household Words* (1850-59) succeeded by *All the Year Round*

(1859-93), which together occupy a fairly long stretch of time coinciding with his mature career.[2] In the previous century, the industrious hands of Defoe had produced both fictional works and journalistic pamphlets, but as we have emphasized, the former were not properly acknowledged as legitimate brainchildren of the writer of *The True-born Englishman* or *A Review of the Affairs of France*. The partition separating the two roles had all but crumbled down after a century. While professional journalists such William Russell of *The Times* "resembled" Dickens in style and attitude (Peck 31), Dickens and his major rivals in the mid- to late nineteenth century, Thackeray and George Eliot, were all involved in the periodical press. The popular but respectable author Thackeray was the founding editor of the new *Cornhill Magazine*. But since his position was that of one employed by the magazine's rich owners, Smith and Elder, his responsibilities and rights were relatively limited. George Eliot the learned novelist stood aloof from Mary Ann Evans the sub-editor of *Westminster Review*, fashioning a new identity for herself under a new name, supported by the arch-conservative *Blackwood's Edinburgh Magazine*, whose proprietors published her novels. Unlike them, Dickens the novelist could leave an uncontested signature, "Conducted by Charles Dickens," on the title page (as well as in the header of each even page) of his *Household Words* and *All the Year Round*. These journals, which he edited and managed himself (aided by like-minded but subordinate young writers), displayed all the distinctive marks of the famous writer-editor.[3]

Dickens the "conductor" and proprietor of *Household Words* at first kept his novel writing and his journal editing separate. Commercial pressure, however, soon dictated the confluence of his two careers. As the circulation of *Household Words* (sold aggressively at a down-market price of mere two pence) lagged behind his expectations, he began to serialize *Hard Times* from 1 April 1854 (no. 210). Its appearance was heralded by an advertisement in the previous number:

> New Tale by Mr. Charles Dickens to be published Weekly in *Household Words*. On Wednesday, the 29th of March will be published, in Household Words, the First Portion of a New Work of Fiction called
>
> Hard Times.
>
> By Charles Dickens. (*Household Words* 209 [25 March 1854])

The next number, which came out a few days later on Saturday 1 April, offered the following fare, along with the first installment of *Hard Times* (the first three chapters):

(1) Hard Times. By Charles Dickens 141-45

Conspicuous almost to an unseemly degree is the name "Charles Dickens" appended to the first entry, with all other articles shrouded in anonymity, following the convention of the time (Shattock 15-16). It gives one an impression of "Charles Dickens" acting not simply as its "conductor" but its despotic overlord. But like other dictators, he cannot do without loyal subjects. Of the seven submissions that meekly follow the leader, the second, "Orange and Lemons," is an informative article on "the many interests involved, the many energies brought into action, in the production and transport of these fruits from the south to our cold, dull countries of the north" ("Orange and Lemons" 145), and the third, "Sharpening the Scythe," is a non-fiction anecdote of a scythe-stone cutter in Devonshire. The relatively serious tone—although seasoned with humour such as the insertion of "cold, dull countries" in the first page of "Orange and Lemons"—of the first three is dissipated by a light comic verse, "Our Coachman" (the last two entries are similar to this in spirit and content) reminiscent of the titles given to *Sketches by Boz* (such as "Our Next-Door Neighbour"). The fifth entry, "Where Are They," is a review of newspaper advertisements and other topical incidents of the past years. Mildly satirical of food counterfeiting, the article inquires,

> I should like to be informed, if you have no objection, where are the rogues who put red lead into my cayenne pepper, Venetian red, fuller's earth, and bad starch into my cocoa; chicory, burnt beans, and chopped hay into my coffee; Prussian blue, gummed and varnished sloe-leaves, emerald green, and bits of birch brooms in my tea; chalk, water, calves' and horses' brains into my milk; alum, gypsum, and dead men's bones into my bread; sand and clay into my sugar; cabbage leaves, lettuce leaves, hay, and brown paper into my tobacco and cigars . . . dogs, cats, and horses into my sausages; and drowned puppies and kittens into my mutton pies. ("Where Are They" 156)

Its comic edge, sharpened with lively enumeration, matches the distinctive topical and satirical ethos of *Hard Times* leading the number.

Satire, however, in *Household Words*, can at times run rather rampant, both in the politically progressive and regressive directions, in both socially alerting and distracting modes. Lashing out at the adulterators of food in "Where Are They" may help society to overcome its barbarism, but this is precisely what utilitarianism, ridiculed in the first chapters of *Hard Times*, pursues. More puzzling still is "Rights and Wrongs of Women," which objects to the professions being open to women, as in the following rejection of "doctoresses":

> The care and the cure of the sick belong to women, as do all things gentle and loving. And though we can scarcely reconcile it with our present notions of the fitness of things, that a gentlewoman of refinement and delicacy should frequent dissecting-rooms among the crowd of young students, and cut up dead bodies and living ones as her mother cut out baby-clothes, yet the care of the sick is so holy a duty, that if these terrible means are necessary, they are sanctified by the end, and God prosper those who undertake them! But they are not necessary. Women are better as medical assistants than as independent practitioners; their services are more valuable when obeying than when originating orders; and as nurses they do more good than as doctors. ("Rights and Wrongs of Women" 159)

The stance of the passage, which, contrary to what John Lucas claims, evinces no sign of joining the "radical journals of the time" (Lucas 146), accords with the hardly innovative portrayal of women in the novel by the magazine's "conductor" serialized with it. *Hard Times* demonstrates Dickens's stilted view of women as naturally less fitted to "originating orders" than to "obeying" them. Despite the obvious divide in intellectual and social capital between the writer of this article and Stephen Blackpool, what the latter suffers at home due to his truant wife, over and above the ills of radical working-class movement and long working hours, chimes in with the overall anxiety against women's assertiveness voiced in the article. Stephen shares his family troubles with, of all people, the bugbear of a factory-owner Bounderby:

> "From bad to worse, from worse to worsen. She left me. She disgraced herseln everyways, bitter and bad. She coom back, she coom back, she coom back. What could I do t' hinder her? I ha' walked the streets nights long, ere ever I'd go home. I ha' gone t' th' brigg, minded to fling myseln ower, and ha' no more on't. I ha' bore that much, that I were owd when I were young." (*Hard Times* 72 [book 1, chap. 11])

Upon which rightful complaint, Stephen asks his employer (and his housekeeper Mrs. Sparsit) whether he could not divorce her. He can, but it costs a truckload of money, he is told. The factory worker accepts this as another blatant confirmation of how everything is "just a muddle a'toogether" (75), at which his employer turns aghast, sniffing in it insubordination and sedition, or, in his own words, "traces of the turtle soup, and venison, and gold spoon in" (76). The novelist remembers to address class injustice in this scene but he does so in a most skewered manner which holds that restricting divorce as a luxury for the super rich is a sign of society's unfairness. Industrial action should be proscribed, but divorcing a bullying wife who scorns her "gentle and loving" duties should be a common right for all, "Hard Times / By Charles Dickens" suggests.

Being a pronouncedly topical fiction dealing with a factory town up north, *Hard Times* enjoyed a felicitous relationship with the articles sharing the numbers of *Household Words* where it made its weekly appearance. *A Tale of Two Cities*, which presents nothing new at the level of factual account, or *Great Expectations* whose first chapters regale the reader with the *Erlebnis* of young Pip, has dubious kinship ties to the other texts making up the weekly number of *Household Words*' successor. *All the Year Round*, the second "Weekly Journal / Conducted by Charles Dickens," and offered at the same competitive price of two pence, placed the first number of *Great Expectations* (Chapter 1) in its 1 December 1860 issue (no. 84) in the company of the following submissions:

(1) Great Expectations. By Charles Dickens	169-74
(2) A Roman Cook's Oracle	174-77
(3) The Wolf at the Church Door	177-80
(4) A Day's Ride: A Life's Romance	180-85
(5) Five Hundred Years Ago. Dress and Food ...	185-88
(6) Inconveniences of Being a Cornishman	188-92

Coming right after Dickens's fiction is "A Roman Cook's Oracle," a humorous travelogue containing culinary adventures set in Italy, followed by "The Wolf at the Church Door." This third entry, after chastising the mismanagement of the Established Church, closes on an indignant note asking, "Did that dignitary with the high sense of decorum in others, and the small sense of decorum in himself, inhabit one of the eight palaces, on the replenishing of which the Ecclesiastical Commissioners had bestowed its charity of one hundred and forty thousand pounds?" ("The Wolf at the Church Door" 18). The fourth article, "A Day's Ride: A Life's Romance," which is another serial narrative of travel offering generous dosage of anecdotes humorous and sentimental, recuperates the bonhomie of the journal's tone—which is what readers would expect of a weekly "conducted by Charles Dickens." The last two pieces are both informative and light-spirited in an innocuous fashion: the former on medieval gastronomy, the latter a comic sketch of a typical Cornishman's character.

As a whole, these articles make up a strange company to keep for young Pip, "brought up by hands" by a belligerent older sister and her meek blacksmith husband at a Kentish village. Pip's narrative shares with them an undertone of humour, but being a personal life story marked by exceptional coincidence, above all, of Pip's encountering a runaway convict with a heart of gold, it contains little of informative value, unlike the other texts constituting the number.

"A masquerade-like jumble of ranks and degrees"

The peculiarity of Dickens's journals becomes perspicuous when placed against the more established, expensive, and conservative magazines of the mid-century, such as *Blackwood's Edinburgh Magazine*, which chose to patronize George Eliot. The tenor of their editorial ethos can be fathomed by browsing the following contents of its May 1860 number (no. 85):

(1) War and Progress in China 525-42
(2) Munich, and its School of Christian Art 543-60
(3) Captain Speke's Adventures in Somali Land 561-80
(4) Judicial Puzzle—Elizabeth Canning 581-90
(5) Wellington's Career—Part II 591
(6) The Mill on the Floss 611-23
(7) Narcissus 624-27
(8) The Snowdrops 628
(9) A Feuilleton 629-34
(10) Switzerland and French Annexation 635

Instead of queuing behind a leading serial fiction written as a first-person narrative by a popular author-cum-editor, *Blackwood's* opens with a grave discussion of a serious issue of the British Empire, "War and Progress in China," whose author emphasizes the merits of accelerating in China "the introduction, of a better civilisation and a purer creed among the many millions who long for our coming, but who are forbidden to hold intercourse with us by the edicts of the Brother of the Moon" ("War and Progress in China" 525-26). Criticism rather than narrative (whether fictional or not) is what the monthly assumes as its appointed task. The second entry, "Munich, and its School of Christian Art," is a travelogue combining art criticism, and the sixth, "The Mill on the Floss," is (predictably enough) a favorable review of the George Eliot novel published by the owners of *Blackwood's*. The review finds the plot of the novel particularly attractive in that "the story, which in Adam Bede was subordinate to the other attractions of the book, is here one of its greatest charms" ("The Mill on the Floss" 611). When narrative does make its appearance as the main mode of an article, it concerns itself with serious real issues related to Britain's imperial interests and global politics, as the relevant titles, "Wellington's Career—Part II" and "Switzerland and French Annexation," loudly announce. The tone is in keeping with the matter dealt with, as in the following passage from "Captain Speke's Adventures in Somali Land," written as an open letter by J. H. Speke introducing a first-person journal account of his own adventures there:

> I then engaged two other men, a Hindustani butler named Imam, and a Seedi called Farhan: this latter man was a perfect Hercules in stature, with huge arms and limbs, knit together with largely developed ropy-looking muscles. He had a large head, with small eyes, flabby squat nose, and prominent muzzle filled with sharp-pointed teeth, in imitation of a crocodile. He had been tried in warfare, and was proved valorous and cunning in the art, and promised to be a very efficient guard for me. ("Captain Speke's Adventures in Somali Land" 569)

The magazine regularly printed stories of such imperial adventurers armed with a lucid system of ethnic stereotypes, bolstered by readily recognizable physiognomic traits in this instance. Any lighter touch *Blackwood's* stoops to admit perhaps to ease its earnest tone maintains a degree of dignity and status shared by "Judicial Puzzle—Elizabeth Canning," dealing with a curious legal case from the previous century, and the two verse contributions, "Narcissus" and "The Snowdrops."

In its content, form, and posture, *Blackwood's* self-consciously occupies a position in the literary field set above Dickens's weeklies, which were heavily dependent on the celebrity status of their "conductor," supplemented when necessary by the appearance of a new serial novel in their pages. The distance between the two can be measured not merely by the topics covered, but by the predominance of literary criticism in *Blackwood's* and its virtual non-existence in *Household Words* or *All the Year Round*. Criticism, particularly pertaining to the inchoate and intangible realm of art and culture, presupposes prior acquisition by the critic of superior cultural capital which authorizes his right to pass judgment on creative outputs. Both Dickens the novelist and Dickens the journalist-editor never shied away from propounding strong views on the more tangible issues of society and politics, yet his literary and cultural frame of reference could not accommodate informed, persuasive, learned opinions on delicate matters of educated taste. At the opposite end of the cultural spectrum stands *Blackwood's* favorite author George Eliot. Behind her mature, self-confident narrative persona, she never ceased to display her intellectual distinction through intrusive analysis of her characters' actions and worth. Her learned commentaries assume the possibility of uplifting the narrative incidents onto a general *Erfahrung* deduced from universal premises. The following vindication of Casaubon's lack of social glitter in *Middlemarch* is a good example:

> I am not sure that the greatest man of his age, if ever that solitary superlative existed, could escape these unfavorable reflections of himself in various small mirrors; and even Milton, looking for his portrait in a spoon, must submit to have the facial angle of a bumpkin. Moreover, if Mr. Casaubon, speaking for himself, has rather a chilling rhetoric, it is not therefore certain that there is no good work or fine feeling in him. Did not an immortal physicist and interpreter of hieroglyphs write detestable verses? Has the theory of the solar system been advanced by graceful manners and conversational tact? Suppose we turn from outside estimates of a man, to wonder, with keener interest, what is the report of his own consciousness about his doings or capacity. . . . Doubtless his lot is important in his own eyes; and the chief reason that we think he asks too large a place in our consideration must be our want of room for him, since we refer him to the Divine regard with perfect confidence; nay, it is even held sublime for our neighbour to expect the utmost there, however little he may have got from us. Mr. Casaubon, too, was the centre of his own world; if he was liable to think that others were providentially made for him, and especially to consider them in the light of their fitness for the author of a Key to all Mythologies, this trait is not quite alien to us, and, like the other mendicant hopes of mortals, claims some of our pity. (Eliot 1997: 77-78)

No reader can fail to notice the narrator's adoption of an overtly argumentative tone as she tests the soundness of logic, brandishes conclusions ("it is not therefore") and rejects the fallaciousness of unthinking common opinion. Her judgement on the character in question draws strength from the citation of venerable cases and learned minds, who have little to commend themselves besides a reputation for intellectual merit, a prestige which the narrator is happy to applaud. The narrator-critic's induction is supplemented by deduction from the premise that all humanity suffers from a forgivable degree of vanity, which is bound to be more poignantly the case for "the author of a Key to all Mythologies." The kind of readership expected to welcome this sophisticated reasoning of the narrator (who boldly asserts her views in the first-person singular) cannot be further removed from the democratic reading public Dickens addresses.

George Eliot's cumbersome plea on Casaubon's behalf speaks with the

In the first paragraph, the present-tense of the third-person narrator, eager to bring forth the vividness of the incident and convert it into *Erlebnis*, seeks to transfer its shock ("Oh, horror, he IS here!") onto a socio-political terrain where it can be linked to the collective *Erfahrung* of the real Lord Chancellor's oppression. Krook's nickname is Lord Chancellor, yet that hardly suffices to use him as a symbolic representative of "all lord chancellors in all courts and of all authorities in all places." Relieved of the duty to advance the narrative's action, the third paragraph aims to attack "the corrupted humours of the vicious body" politic, yet its journalistic force has feeble organic link to the fiction in *Bleak House*. This death is an "impossible course of action" not primarily because it goes against (our contemporary) scientific common sense. Such charge Dickens rebuffed in his preface to the novel, asserting he had done his homework studying the phenomenon, which indeed was "one of the great physiological debates of the first half of the nineteenth century" (West 128). The greater offense of the passage comes with its jumpstarting the action of the plot in the unfolding scramble for the papers of Captain Hawdon (Nemo), which will become crucially important for subsequent arts of the novel. Even so, the force of its sensory appeal, matched with atirical extravaganza, overwhelms any strictures of common sense robability.

These two passages taken from *Bleak House* by no means do justice to complexity of the novel and its variegated features. To further examine m, we shall refer them back to the journalistic realm proper from which novel's satirical animus is patently drawn—the anti-Chancery ourse which preceded, and which in turn was strengthened by, kens's novel.

"It was all up with it at last!"

House repeats public criticism of Chancery's problems. This in itself be no particular blemish to its novelistic artistry. The novel is a in which repetition and originality are inseparable. Prose, the n of the novel, can never be free from repetition of certain words, ions, and ideas, when it deploys the sheer force of its expansiveness trast to the regulated language of lyric where unwelcome repetition ds can be minimized, if not completely avoided). The mode in character is registered in the reader's mind as a distinct entity also avily on the repeated appearance of the character's name (whereas production, to each character is allotted a separate human body), s a certain stock expression reserved for him, a device skillfully

authority of accumulated learning and wisdom, but this *Erfahrung* does not entail communicability in itself. It is one thing to sound wise, quite another to impart it to the reader. The typical sensation-based characterizations of Dickens are geared to inducing an instantaneous sensory response in readers. Notwithstanding the strengths and limits we have explored in the preceding chapters, they belong to the realm of immediacy and *Erlebnis*. Yet the unique strength of Dickens lies in his ability to make *Erlebnis* communicable to the readers as an *Erfahrung*. The lawyer Jaggers, for example, of *Great Expectations*, is an embodiment of the popular dread of the secretive power of legal professionals, particularly those thriving on criminal justice. The biting statements Jaggers spits out attest to his clever and quick mind, one that can rarely command our admiration, much less "our pity." Pip is summoned to Jaggers' office to receive cash relieving him from debts, but Pip, still the naïve country boy, cannot refrain from inquiring into the source of the money earmarked for his use. Jaggers, visualized to the reader by his "dark deep-set eyes" and made audible by his snappish speech, gives him the predictable answer:

> "Now, here," replied Mr Jaggers, fixing me for the first time with his dark deep-set eyes, "we must revert to the evening when we first encountered one another in your village. What did I tell you then, Pip?"
>
> "You told me, Mr Jaggers, that it might be years hence when that person appeared."
>
> "Just so," said Mr Jaggers, "that's my answer."
>
> As we looked full at one another, I felt my breath come quicker in my strong desire to get something out of him. And as I felt that it came quicker, and as I felt that he saw that it came quicker, I felt that I had less chance than ever of getting anything out of him.
>
> "Do you suppose it will still be years hence, Mr Jaggers?"
>
> Mr Jaggers shook his head,—not in negativing the question, but in altogether negativing the notion that he could anyhow be got to answer it. (*Expectations* 275 [chap. 36])

One may accept George Eliot's defence of Casaubon at the conceptual level, but one can share the antipathy for this "negativing" lawyer's unappealing character conveyed in his "chilling rhetoric" without grasping any allusion to "an immortal physicist and interpreter of hieroglyphs."

Blackwood's, however, because it represented those who, being in the possession of a certain degree of educational capital, would thus feel obliged to admire someone seeking to excavate the "Key to all Mythologies," disdained the populist and popular realm of Dickens's fictions, never granting him the kind of respectful attention it lavished on its own "house" author George Eliot.[4] Instead, a mere passing remark, caustic and cursory, is Dickens's share in the monthly. For instance, in a review of the American author Miss Wetherall's *The Old Helmet*, chosen as ready evidence of the barbarous popularity of low quality books, the anonymous critic uses the occasion to voice his consternation at Dickens's and other popular novelists' gross misrepresentation of "English social life":

> [H]ow grotesque, distorted, and absolutely and ridiculously improbable one and all are! What a masquerade-like jumble of ranks and degrees—what impossible combinations in some, what impossible courses of action in others! ("A Religious Novel" 275-76).[5]

Biased and careless as this dismissive verdict is, one finds it does not lack truth entirely insofar as it points to the bold liberty Dickens takes to stretch and shock the sedate, smug common sense of bourgeois readers. The plot of the relatively well-plotted *Great Expectations* may still be found guilty in the court of *Blackwood's* of having relied on "impossible combinations" and "impossible courses of action" of having a convict in New South Wales endow lavishly a young stranger who did not exactly volunteer to help when the said convict was in dire needs. But above all, Krook's Spontaneous Combustion would be a particularly notorious case, in a novel full of topical pretensions and political posturing.

Two passages from *Bleak House* can be representative of the work's "grotesque, distorted, and . . . improbable" originality, the first lampooning the high statesmen of the realm from Lord Boodle to Lord Noodle, and the second, nonchalantly reporting a curious case of a human body's self-destruction. We begin with the first of the two:

> Then there is my Lord Boodle, of considerable reputation with his party, who has known what office is and who tells Sir Leicester Dedlock with much gravity, after dinner, that he really does not see to what the present age is tending. . . . He perceives with astonishment, that supposing the present government to be overthrown, the limited choice of the Crown, in the formation of a new Ministry, would lie between Lord Coodle and Sir Thomas Doodle—supposing it to be impossible for the Duke of Foodle to act with Goodle, which may be assumed to be the case in consequence of the breach arising out of that affair with Hoodle. Then, giving the Home Department and the leadership of the House of Commons to Joodle, the Exchequer to Koodle, the Colonies to Loodle, and the Foreign Office to Moodle, what are you to do with Noodle? You can't offer him the Presidency of the Council; that is reserved for Poodle. You can't put him in the Woods and Forests; that is hardly good enough for Quoodle. What follows? That the country is

> shipwrecked, lost, and gone to pieces (as is made manifest to the patriotism of Sir Leicester Dedlock) because you can't provide for Noodle! (*Bleak House* 160-61 [chap. 12])

Boisterously satirical as it is, the prose adopts a newspaper style reporting what Lord Boodle said to Sir Leicester Dedlock, which tu more literary as signaled by free indirect speech in the latter half (a "Then . . . what are you to do with Noodle?") and the final exclam mark. The politics of the satire takes aim at the kind of conserv *Blackwood's* professes and upholds, by revealing the mercenary serving underside of its pretentious concern for the welfare of th Dickens's satire reveals how "absolutely and ridiculously" p prejudices belonging to the power elite can be, who would r grotesque and ridiculous any criticism of their privileges by the or their favorite writers. Political journalism of populist radical p is thus accommodated in this serial novel exposing the foibles o venerable institutions and their activities, from the ineffecti Equity to "telescopic philanthropy." Dickens's novels, as r weekly journals, behave like a journalist organ addressing issues of the times, as daring and bold as any radical pamp genres or realms of realistic prose combine their force to "Boz" platform.

The second example from *Bleak House*, however, stret to its extreme. Matter-of-fact tone and figurative hyperbol at social wrongs and gratuitous indulgence in sensatio together to concoct a most unusual incident:

> Here is a small burnt patch of flooring; here is the t bundle of burnt paper, but not so light as usual, seemi something; and here is—is it the cinder of a small charr wood sprinkled with white ashes, or is it coal? Oh Ho this from which we run away, striking out the light another into the street, is all that represents him.
>
> Help, help, help! come into this house for Heaven's
>
> Plenty will come in, but none can help. The Lord C true to his title in his last act, has died the death of a Courts, and of all authorities in all places under all pretences are made, and where injustice is done. C Your Highness will, attribute it to whom you will prevented how you will, it is the same death engendered in the corrupted humours of the only—Spontaneous Combustion, and none othe died. (*Bleak House* 455-56 [chap. 32])

authority of accumulated learning and wisdom, but this *Erfahrung* does not entail communicability in itself. It is one thing to sound wise, quite another to impart it to the reader. The typical sensation-based characterizations of Dickens are geared to inducing an instantaneous sensory response in readers. Notwithstanding the strengths and limits we have explored in the preceding chapters, they belong to the realm of immediacy and *Erlebnis*. Yet the unique strength of Dickens lies in his ability to make *Erlebnis* communicable to the readers as an *Erfahrung*. The lawyer Jaggers, for example, of *Great Expectations*, is an embodiment of the popular dread of the secretive power of legal professionals, particularly those thriving on criminal justice. The biting statements Jaggers spits out attest to his clever and quick mind, one that can rarely command our admiration, much less "our pity." Pip is summoned to Jaggers' office to receive cash relieving him from debts, but Pip, still the naïve country boy, cannot refrain from inquiring into the source of the money earmarked for his use. Jaggers, visualized to the reader by his "dark deep-set eyes" and made audible by his snappish speech, gives him the predictable answer:

> "Now, here," replied Mr Jaggers, fixing me for the first time with his dark deep-set eyes, "we must revert to the evening when we first encountered one another in your village. What did I tell you then, Pip?"
>
> "You told me, Mr Jaggers, that it might be years hence when that person appeared."
>
> "Just so," said Mr Jaggers, "that's my answer."
>
> As we looked full at one another, I felt my breath come quicker in my strong desire to get something out of him. And as I felt that it came quicker, and as I felt that he saw that it came quicker, I felt that I had less chance than ever of getting anything out of him.
>
> "Do you suppose it will still be years hence, Mr Jaggers?"
>
> Mr Jaggers shook his head,—not in negativing the question, but in altogether negativing the notion that he could anyhow be got to answer it. (*Expectations* 275 [chap. 36])

One may accept George Eliot's defence of Casaubon at the conceptual level, but one can share the antipathy for this "negativing" lawyer's unappealing character conveyed in his "chilling rhetoric" without grasping any allusion to "an immortal physicist and interpreter of hieroglyphs."

Blackwood's, however, because it represented those who, being in the possession of a certain degree of educational capital, would thus feel obliged to admire someone seeking to excavate the "Key to all Mythologies," disdained the populist and popular realm of Dickens's fictions, never granting him the kind of respectful attention it lavished on its own "house" author George Eliot.[4] Instead, a mere passing remark, caustic and cursory, is Dickens's share in the monthly. For instance, in a review of the American author Miss Wetherall's *The Old Helmet*, chosen as ready evidence of the barbarous popularity of low quality books, the anonymous critic uses the occasion to voice his consternation at Dickens's and other popular novelists' gross misrepresentation of "English social life":

> [H]ow grotesque, distorted, and absolutely and ridiculously improbable one and all are! What a masquerade-like jumble of ranks and degrees—what impossible combinations in some, what impossible courses of action in others! ("A Religious Novel" 275-76).[5]

Biased and careless as this dismissive verdict is, one finds it does not lack truth entirely insofar as it points to the bold liberty Dickens takes to stretch and shock the sedate, smug common sense of bourgeois readers. The plot of the relatively well-plotted *Great Expectations* may still be found guilty in the court of *Blackwood's* of having relied on "impossible combinations" and "impossible courses of action" of having a convict in New South Wales endow lavishly a young stranger who did not exactly volunteer to help when the said convict was in dire needs. But above all, Krook's Spontaneous Combustion would be a particularly notorious case, in a novel full of topical pretensions and political posturing.

Two passages from *Bleak House* can be representative of the work's "grotesque, distorted, and . . . improbable" originality, the first lampooning the high statesmen of the realm from Lord Boodle to Lord Noodle, and the second, nonchalantly reporting a curious case of a human body's self-destruction. We begin with the first of the two:

> Then there is my Lord Boodle, of considerable reputation with his party, who has known what office is and who tells Sir Leicester Dedlock with much gravity, after dinner, that he really does not see to what the present age is tending. . . . He perceives with astonishment, that supposing the present government to be overthrown, the limited choice of the Crown, in the formation of a new Ministry, would lie between Lord Coodle and Sir Thomas Doodle—supposing it to be impossible for the Duke of Foodle to act with Goodle, which may be assumed to be the case in consequence of the breach arising out of that affair with Hoodle. Then, giving the Home Department and the leadership of the House of Commons to Joodle, the Exchequer to Koodle, the Colonies to Loodle, and the Foreign Office to Moodle, what are you to do with Noodle? You can't offer him the Presidency of the Council; that is reserved for Poodle. You can't put him in the Woods and Forests; that is hardly good enough for Quoodle. What follows? That the country is

> shipwrecked, lost, and gone to pieces (as is made manifest to the patriotism of Sir Leicester Dedlock) because you can't provide for Noodle! (*Bleak House* 160-61 [chap. 12])

Boisterously satirical as it is, the prose adopts a newspaper style in reporting what Lord Boodle said to Sir Leicester Dedlock, which turns more literary as signaled by free indirect speech in the latter half (as in "Then . . . what are you to do with Noodle?") and the final exclamation mark. The politics of the satire takes aim at the kind of conservatism *Blackwood's* professes and upholds, by revealing the mercenary self-serving underside of its pretentious concern for the welfare of the state. Dickens's satire reveals how "absolutely and ridiculously" *probable* prejudices belonging to the power elite can be, who would regard as grotesque and ridiculous any criticism of their privileges by the populace or their favorite writers. Political journalism of populist radical persuasion is thus accommodated in this serial novel exposing the foibles of society's venerable institutions and their activities, from the ineffective Court of Equity to "telescopic philanthropy." Dickens's novels, as much as his weekly journals, behave like a journalist organ addressing the topical issues of the times, as daring and bold as any radical pamphlet. The two genres or realms of realistic prose combine their force to strengthen the "Boz" platform.

The second example from *Bleak House*, however, stretches probability to its extreme. Matter-of-fact tone and figurative hyperbole, moral outrage at social wrongs and gratuitous indulgence in sensation are all brewed together to concoct a most unusual incident:

> Here is a small burnt patch of flooring; here is the tinder from a little bundle of burnt paper, but not so light as usual, seeming to be steeped in something; and here is—is it the cinder of a small charred and broken log of wood sprinkled with white ashes, or is it coal? Oh Horror, he IS here! and this from which we run away, striking out the light and overturning one another into the street, is all that represents him.
>
> Help, help, help! come into this house for Heaven's sake!
>
> Plenty will come in, but none can help. The Lord Chancellor of that Court, true to his title in his last act, has died the death of all Lord Chancellors in all Courts, and of all authorities in all places under all names soever, where false pretences are made, and where injustice is done. Call the death by any name Your Highness will, attribute it to whom you will, or say it might have been prevented how you will, it is the same death eternally—inborn, inbred, engendered in the corrupted humours of the vicious body itself, and that only—Spontaneous Combustion, and none other of all the deaths that can be died. (*Bleak House* 455-56 [chap. 32])

In the first paragraph, the present-tense of the third-person narrator, eager to bring forth the vividness of the incident and convert it into *Erlebnis*, seeks to transfer its shock ("Oh, horror, he IS here!") onto a socio-political terrain where it can be linked to the collective *Erfahrung* of the real Lord Chancellor's oppression. Krook's nickname is Lord Chancellor, yet that hardly suffices to use him as a symbolic representative of "all lord chancellors in all courts and of all authorities in all places." Relieved of the duty to advance the narrative's action, the third paragraph aims to attack "the corrupted humours of the vicious body" politic, yet its journalistic force has feeble organic link to the fiction in *Bleak House*. This death is an "impossible course of action" not primarily because it goes against (our contemporary) scientific common sense. Such charge Dickens rebuffed in his preface to the novel, asserting he had done his homework studying the phenomenon, which indeed was "one of the great physiological debates of the first half of the nineteenth century" (West 128). The greater offense of the passage comes with its jumpstarting the action of the plot in the unfolding scramble for the papers of Captain Hawdon (Nemo), which will become crucially important for subsequent parts of the novel. Even so, the force of its sensory appeal, matched with satirical extravaganza, overwhelms any strictures of common sense probability.

These two passages taken from *Bleak House* by no means do justice to the complexity of the novel and its variegated features. To further examine them, we shall refer them back to the journalistic realm proper from which the novel's satirical animus is patently drawn—the anti-Chancery discourse which preceded, and which in turn was strengthened by, Dickens's novel.

"It was all up with it at last!"

Bleak House repeats public criticism of Chancery's problems. This in itself should be no particular blemish to its novelistic artistry. The novel is a genre in which repetition and originality are inseparable. Prose, the medium of the novel, can never be free from repetition of certain words, expressions, and ideas, when it deploys the sheer force of its expansiveness (in contrast to the regulated language of lyric where unwelcome repetition of words can be minimized, if not completely avoided). The mode in which a character is registered in the reader's mind as a distinct entity also relies heavily on the repeated appearance of the character's name (whereas in drama production, to each character is allotted a separate human body), as well as a certain stock expression reserved for him, a device skillfully adopted, indeed all but created, by Dickens. Moreover, there is the serial form of production initiated and refined by Dickens: each monthly number repeats without repeating the tale, with enough variation to justify its separate existence, but never too much to disrupt its identity as a single novel. On a different dimension, the fictional texts themselves repeat the topographical information about London already known to most contemporary readers, and more crucially, the currently topical issues covered by London journalism, such as urban slum, cholera, civilizing mission in Africa, and above all the costly delay of Chancery suits. To examine the relationship of *Bleak House* to the journalistic sphere of public opinion, the nature and history of the topic itself should be traced, first.

A common feature of the "realistic" novels from the eighteenth to the twentieth century relates to the contrived continuity between the novel and the prose world outside it, in which a "theme," in the musical sense of the term, is taken from the larger world of prose to be subjected to "variations" by each novelist, as is exemplified by Defoe's use of shipwreck adventure stories, criminal biographies, and histories of disaster. Dickens follows this tradition in a far more focused manner, so that each novel sets up an agenda for public debate: Poor Law in *Oliver Twist*, provincial education in *Nicholas Nickleby*, railway development in *Dombey and Son*, stock market craze in *Little Dorrit*, and, most famously, the ills of Chancery in *Bleak House*. In this relationship a main idea, such as the Court of Chancery being a pernicious institution preying on suitors, is tossed backed and forth between the fictional texts and the journalistic world at large, between the novelist's personal vision and the "public sphere." The ideas or "theme," in other words, exist as a *topos* in the sense Ernst Robert Curtius gives to the term, when he writes how rhetoricians of antiquity kept a "stockroom" of set ideas from which practitioners could draw their resources repeatedly (Curtius 79). A *topos* is not so much an immutable formula as freely pirated source material, as each historical and social occasion makes use of the *topos* in its own distinctive, if not original, manner (Curtius 80-82). In the prosaic age of modern publicity novelists join other writers in scooping ideas from the *topoi* of public opinion, to serve their own artistic and commercial interests, no one more so than Dickens and nowhere more so than in *Bleak House*.

The complaints against Chancery, repeated by many, were gathered through decades into a set of widely-held views, within and against which Dickens carried out the labour of fashioning his novel. His interest in the Court of Chancery may very well reflect his own biographical experience of 1844, when he unsuccessfully sought to defend his copyright on *A*

Christmas Carol against piracies, mostly by small-scale publishers and booksellers (Shatto 29) at the Court of Equity. Yet the appearance of the Chancery prisoner already in his first novel *Pickwick Papers* (chap. 41-42) indicates that the Court's inefficiency was a circulating topic on offer in the public realm quite apart from any episode from the author's life. But why attack the Court of Chancery in *Bleak House*, published in 1852? The established answer proposed by John Butt, in his "'Bleak House' in the Context of 1851" credits the Chancery debates of 1851 as the originating "context" in which the Chancery of *Bleak House* were fermented. According to Butt, in 1851 "everyone" was interested in reforming the Court of Chancery, the "everyone" being no other than the readers and contributors of *The Times*, in whose December 1850 and January 1851 columns "most of the charges in Dickens's indictment of chancery" is contained (Butt 5). Lord John Russell's new Liberal government passed the Chancery Reform Act later that year, but "the public was still critical" (7), the public here, once again, solely represented by the "Times" which "was right again" (6). The embryo of *Bleak House*, in Butt's account, was being incubated by the same illustrious public organ's "hammering at the inadequacies of legal education, and at the eminent members of the legal profession." From these newspaper clippings Butt draws the conclusion that "Dickens's indictment of chancery . . . followed in almost every respect the charges already leveled in the columns of the Times" (7). Plausible as this is, we cannot but ask whether there is any reliable evidence that Dickens the popular-radical writer acted as a faithful pupil of the conservative *Times*' sermonizing. Moreover, on what basis can the *Times* claim to be the sole representative of public opinion? As Robert L. Patten conjectures, "many of Dickens's customers would be unlikely to have read *The Times*" (Patten 219). There is also a problem with chronology. If Dickens was going to capitalize on the general public's enthusiasm for Chancery reform, it would have been crucial that his work appear *before* any tangible reform took effect. As a matter of fact, two important laws were already passed in 1850 (the Court of Chancery Acts) for England and Ireland, respectively, which sought to redress the infamous delay and inordinate increase in expense of Chancery suits. While the novel was being serialized in 1852, two more acts were passed, the Chancery Procedure Act and the Suitors in Chancery Relief Act, followed in 1854 by the Common Law Procedure Act. The combined effect of these laws more or less solved the more glaring among the ills of Chancery (Shatto 29). Dickens, if so, was a step too late, and the satirical edge of *Bleak House* as a topical novel was being blunted as quickly as it was scoring points.

What then was left of the value of Chancery for the *Bleak House* monthly numbers? True, its topical value could have survived a few new acts, to the extent that any reform of such an ancient stronghold of vested interests can never be satisfactory enough for those who suffer from it. This is evidenced by *A "Bleak House" Narrative of Real Life* (1856), where the writer extols Dickens in these words:

> In a work some time since published, entitled "Bleak House," and written with a view to illustrate the peculiar mode of litigation for which the Court of Chancery is distinguished, the author has drawn a vivid, and yet true picture, of the wrongs inflicted upon those who have had the misfortune to experience the tender mercies of Chancery law.
>
> I, for one, can bear witness to the truthfulness of his delineations of the misery, and wretchedness resulting from the operation of the system carried on under the Court of Chancery, for, I believe, it would be impossible, even with the power of imagination which he possesses, to convey an exaggerated impression of the bitter reality of suffering produced by it. (*A "Bleak House" Narrative* 5)

Bleak House, of course, was written not simply to "illustrate the peculiar mode of litigation" in the Court of Chancery, but rather, as this writer fully understands, to expose with felt accuracy the "bitter reality of suffering" caused by the Court. Moreover, the actual experience of the contemporary public did not fully square with the neat chronology of Chancery reform. In 1855, "Letters on Chancery Reform to the Times by P. J. Locke King, Esq. M. P.," appended to *A "Bleak House" Narrative*, repeated the by-now standard complaint against Chancery, namely that it is an infernal machinery, "an engine of oppression" (*A "Bleak House" Narrative* 56) responsible for inhuman "cruelties" inflicted on the suitors (63).

The *topos* of Chancery abuse still retained currency, then, both during and after the serialization of *Bleak House*.[6] Yet a popular author such as Dickens cannot afford to confine his clientele to the victims of Chancery, but has to draw larger meanings from the urgency of the topical appeal. The value of the issue for the very first monthly number of the novel consisted in the possibility of magnifying its abuse into something at once larger and less specific than the actual Court of Chancery itself. Critics since Hillis Miller have been almost unanimous on this score, reading philosophic meanings behind Chancery as a "symbol" of human existence itself, in that is something "which is going on at his birth and remains unfinished throughout his life" (J. Miller 196). But symbolic comprehensiveness can be only one of the many elements of any novel, and not perhaps the most central one. The many distractions and diversions of a long prose fiction cannot but dilute its author's figurative intent. The use of Chancery in the thick volume of *Bleak House* seems more topical than symbolic, as the close relationship of the novel with certain *Household Words* articles suggests. First came the "The Martyrs of Chancery" in *Household Words* 37 (7 Dec 1850), written by Alfred Cole, a barrister, according to Susan Shatto (Shatto 29), which identifies the wrongs in a calm, factual tone.

> The Chancery prisoner has no such certainty; he may, and he frequently does, waste a lifetime in the walls of a gaol, whither he was sent in innocence; because, perchance, he had the ill-luck to be one of the next of kin of some testator who made a will which no one could comprehend, or the heir of some intestate who made none. Any other party interested in the estate commences a Chancery suit, which he must defend or be committed to prison for "contempt." A prison is his portion, whatever he does; for, if he answers the bill filed against him, and cannot pay the costs, he is also clapped in gaol for "contempt." Thus, what in ordinary life is but an irrepressible expression of opinion or a small discourtesy, is, "in Equity," a high crime punishable with imprisonment—sometimes perpetual. ("The Martyrs of Chancery" 250)

This passage repeats the depiction of the poor Chancery prisoner in Fleet prison in *Pickwick Papers*. A cobbler who had the misfortune of being a legatee to disputed property languishes in jail for no sin of his own. "My lawyers have had all my thousand pound long ago," he summarizes his misery, "and what between the estate, as they call it, and the costs, I'm here for ten thousand, and shall stop here, till I die, mending shoes" (*Pickwick* 621 [chap. 44]). He dies soon after, fulfilling his own grim prophecy. Dickens uses this motif of the dying victim of Chancery again in *Bleak House*, in the episode of Gridley, wanted for his contempt of court and hunted down by Inspector Bucket. Exhausted and worn out, he dies, despite the latter's cynical cheering: "Give in? Why, I am surprised to hear a man of your energy talk of giving in. You mustn't do that. You're half the fun of the fair, in the Court of Chancery" (*Bleak House* 352-53 [chap. 24]). Gridley gives in, yet Dickens did not leave off targeting inefficient self-serving institutions of the nation, such as the Court of Chancery, a campaign initiated in his very first novel.

Further links between *Household Words* and its conductor's novels can be found in "A December Vision," which surveys the state of society at the end of the year 1850. The "Vision" spots the Court of Equity (i.e. Chancery) among the plagues of that year:

> I saw a portion of the system, called (of all things) EQUITY, which was ruin to suitors, ruin to property, a shield for wrong-doers having money, a rack for right-doers having none: a by-word for delay, slow agony of mind,

> despair, impoverishment, trickery, confusion, insupportable injustice. A main part of it, I saw prisoners wasting in jail; mad people babbling in hospitals; suicides chronicled in the yearly records; orphans robbed of their inheritance; infants rights (perhaps) when they were grey.
>
> Certain lawyers and laymen came together, and said to one another, "In only one of these our Courts of Equity, there are years or this dark perspective before us at the present moment. We must change this."
>
> Uprose, immediately, a throng of others, Secretaries, Petty Bags, Hanapers, Chaff-waxes, and what not, singing (in answer) "Rule Britannia," and "God save the Queen," making flourishing speeches, pronouncing hard names, demanding committees, commissions, commissioners, and other scarecrows, and terrifying the little band of innovators out of their five wits. ("A December Vision" 266)

This is the same kind of critical vision—if somewhat "melodramatic" in its "strong moralizing tendency, and its theatricality" (John 90)—which Dickens later developed into his satire on Circumlocution Office in *Little Dorrit* and on "Podsnappery" in his last finished novel. The vested interests of the ruling block form a tight, impenetrable phalanx effectively thwarting any effort to reform the "system." Chancery (Equity) is in itself symptomatic of this nefarious alliance, which in *Little Dorrit* is seen to be intimately (and dangerously) serviced by big finance represented by Merdle. The "system" is responsible, in these complex social novels, not merely for the misery of those involved in the cases concerned (such as Gridley, Richard, and Ada), but for the overall sickness of the body social as a whole. When Jo the crossing sweep dies in *Bleak House*, the narrator places his corpse on the doors of the powers-that-be: "Dead, your Majesty. Dead, my lords and gentlemen. Dead, Right Reverends and Wrong Reverends of every order. Dead, men and women, born with Heavenly compassion in your hearts. And dying thus around us every day" (*Bleak House* 649 [chap. 47]). In *Little Dorrit*, the burst of Merdle's financial bubble resonates throughout the entire society, affecting everyone, including Arthur Clennam:

> The admirable piratical ship had blown up, in the midst of a vast fleet of ships of all rates, and boats of all sizes; and on the deep was nothing but ruin: nothing but burning hulls, bursting magazines, great guns self-exploded tearing friends and neighbours to pieces, drowning men clinging to unseaworthy spars and going down every minute, spent swimmers floating dead, and sharks. (*Dorrit* 711 [book 2, chap. 26])

Employed here is the same device we see in "December Vision," of picturing British society as a total system infected by a major plague which spares no one in its rampant destruction of savings, hopes, dreams, as well as lives. "A journalism of plague years," is how one may describe the critical battle Dickens waged through both his novels and his weeklies.

Yet unlike in the periodical articles, in these extended novels a justice of sorts is meted out—rough, summary, and violent justice, at that. Tulkinghorn, the resident solicitor catering to Equity clients, is shot dead, somewhat improbably by an irate French woman. Merdle kills himself with his daughter-in-law's penknife, before the truth of his bank failure spreads around, a death with a better motivation in terms of plot development than poor Tulkinghorn's. But executed they both are by the novelist. If the bold and—in the eyes of *Blackwood's*—"impossible" measures taken to punish those implicated in the evil "system" can be credited as Dickens the novelist's singlehanded decision, it draws its persuasive force from the widely held view of Chancery as a monstrous machinery of oppression. For example, in *Chancery Delays, and Their Remedy* (1830), written by a solicitor with an "experience of many years in several hundred suits in equity" (6) specifically characterizes the court as a "machinery" in poor repair, ill suited to handle the ever increasing business of equity. It follows from this premise that expanding the productive force of the machinery will be the logical solution of the problem, not the least since, as *Delays in Chancery Considered with Practical Suggestions for their Prevention or Removal*, a 1843 pamphlet published at Chancery Lane itself, believes, solicitors lose rather than gain from the procrastination of the equity court, in that "the consequence of delay in Chancery to country practitioners is in many instances worse than a total loss" due to "the court fees, counsel's fees, and agency charges, and loss of interest" (4). The machinery of Chancery becomes more monstrous as we move away from those in the legal profession to those outside it. H. W. Weston's *Chancery Infamy; Or, A Plea for an Anti-Chancery League* (1849) presents the institution not simply as a malfunctioning cumbersome tool but as a demonic symbol of evil itself. "[T]he hydra-headed monster still in all its rampant malignity extends itself more and more over the community," Weston writes, as "it lays about its hideous claws, clutching into its insatiate grasp all possible interests of thousands of deluded and defrauded suitors" (Weston 3). This species of apocalyptical, Dissenter-radical rhetoric, reminiscent of Bunyan rather than the watered-down jibes of the *Times* leaders Butt credits as the source of *Bleak House*, surely comes closer to the disposition of the novel and its author. *Chancery Infamy* captures the mercenary nature of the Court's "legalised mode of robbing the community of their hard earnings and savings, for the benefit of keeping up such a monstrous court as this, principally for the sake of patronage, and for the subsistence and fattening of hungry, sordid, and selfish lawyers" (3-4). The economy of this legalized robbery, furthermore, is marked by an utterly non-productive, non-circulating self-absorption, which can only lead to a Spontaneous Combustion of itself:

> Now here comes the pinch. It has been asked what the costs of all parties will be, and the moderate guess is £2,500. The estates are worth about £5,000; so it is estimated, by the time they are sold, and the costs and expenses paid, there will be NOTHING left. Yea, verily, the Court, the twelve counsels, and the ten lawyers have swallowed up the £5,000. Verily they have indeed taken the oyster, and they will not even leave a shell each, in this instance, for the poor suitors that have been thus duped, and robbed, and plundered. (Weston 6-7)

In *Bleak House*, this extraction of cost to the maximum leading to the reduction of the estate to "NOTHING" is precisely the doomed end of the famous case of Jarndyce and Jarndyce:

> [A] break up soon took place in the crowd, and the people came streaming out looking flushed and hot, and bringing a quantity of bad air with them. Still they were all exceedingly amused, and were more like people coming out from a Farce or a Juggler than from a court of Justice. We stood aside, watching for any countenance we knew; and presently great bundles of paper began to be carried out—bundles in bags, bundles too large to be got into any bags, immense masses of papers of all shapes and no shapes, which the bearers staggered under, and threw down for the time being, anyhow, on the Hall pavement, while they went back to bring out more. Even these clerks were laughing. We glanced at the papers, and seeing Jarndyce and Jarndyce everywhere, asked an official-looking person who was standing in the midst of them, whether the cause was over. "Yes," he said; "it was all up with it at last!" and burst out laughing too. (*Bleak House* 865 [chap. 65])

In this memorable crowd scene, a momentary spasm of laughter infects everyone at Westminster Hall, a Satanic laughter at the expense of the victims, old and young, represented early in the novel by Miss Flite whose life withered in expectation of the "Day of Judgment" (33 [chap. 3]). The *Erfahrung* of Chancery's predatory callousness communicated through journalist and fictional organs finds its counterpart in the shock of a personal *Erlebnis* of hollow, helpless, and distraught disappointment.

"A Megalosaurus … up Holborn Hill"

The pamphlets and *Bleak House* join their voice in denouncing Chancery's wrongs; as to the remedy, however, they part company, for the novel refuses to settle with mere technical improvement, or even with institutional reform as such, which can also be traced in the total absence in the novel of a common point these pamphlets make that the state of Chancery was a shame for such an otherwise advanced and advancing society as Britain. The Whiggish notions of national self-improvement and self-importance (at their most flagrant in and following 1851, the year of the Great Exhibition), Dickens flatly snubs by having a primeval dinosaur stroll the capital city of the British Empire in the very first paragraph of the novel:[7]

> London. Michaelmas Term lately over, and the Lord Chancellor sitting in Lincoln's Inn Hall. Implacable November weather. As much mud in the streets, as if the waters had but newly retired from the face of the earth, and it would not be wonderful to meet a Megalosaurus, forty feet long or so, waddling like an elephantine lizard up Holborn Hill. (*Bleak House* 1 [chap. 1])

This is an atavistic vision of London, of a modern metropolis oppressed, stifled, and conquered by an archaic, monstrous system, fed and fattened by the insatiable greed of litigants and their legal agents such as the lawyers Kenge and Vholes. If the city is thus colonized by dinosaurs of extortion, its streets can produce little fresh air of freedom or life. In *Pickwick Papers*, the basic optimism of the buoyant picaresque narrative posits the liveliness of the outside city as a vigorous antithesis to the unfortunate Chancery prisoner's darkened cell:

> The noise of carriages and carts, the rattle of wheels, the cries of men and boys, all the busy sounds of a mighty multitude instinct with life and occupation, blended into one deep murmur, floated into the room. Above the hoarse loud hum, arose from time to time a boisterous laugh; or a scrap of some jingling song, shouted forth by one of the giddy crowd, would strike upon the ear for an instant, and then be lost amidst the roar of voices and the tramp of footsteps; the breaking of the billows of the restless sea of life that rolled heavily on, without. (*Pickwick* 627 [chap. 44])

In *Bleak House*, on the other hand, the outside society at large of the "mighty multitude instinct with life and occupation" is itself tainted with the diseases of Chancery-like injustice, delay, and fleecing. The crowd bursts into a cynical laughter at the demise of the protracted case, and the very "sea of life," in this novel whose stage is strewn with corpses (of Coavinse, Captain Hawdon, Gridley, Krook, Tukinghorn, Jo, Richard, Lady Dedlock, and unnamed bricklayer's baby), seems to be ebbing and receding. *Bleak House* marks one clear limit to Dickens's urbanism, to his trust in the rejuvenating power of the open city streets and its variegated characters. The city in Dickens, as the list of the dead evinces, brings together the lowly and the lofty, the old and the young, all before the court of plaguing death, more equally so than in Defoe's *Journal of the Plague Year*, where mostly the poor suffered. The corpses in *Bleak House* weave the classes, regions, and districts into one large interconnected, mutually contaminating network of relationship or kinship emanating from the ancient premises of London's legal institutions. Chancery may not simply be a "topic" but a "topography," in D. A. Miller's phrase (Miller 61), but if so, it has a concrete topography traceable to specific postcodes. The lawyers' town at the centre of London, supported by Snagsby's stationery shop, is linked spatially to Tom-All-Alone's, the pestilential, lethal spot which nonetheless claims a ghoulish destructive kinship with the affluent circles of Dedlocks and Jarndyce. One further comparison can be made with Defoe's *Journal of the Plague Year*, the first journalism-novel in English. Whereas the "invisible hands" of Providence dealt out destruction and havoc in the case of Defoe's work, in *Bleak House* the *visible* hands of human greed taint one another, setting up a total national system of swindling—not merely of those involved in the legal circle, but of those least expected to exploit others, from the cultured men of sensibility (Skimpole and Turveydrop senior) to the evangelical philanthropists (Mrs. Jellyby and Chadband). The plague does not spare even those with the warmest human heart, such as Esther, whose face bears the scars of the new London plague.

The case of Esther also reminds us that the greatness of Dickens the novelist, in contrast to Dickens the journalist, asserts itself, finally, in his introducing as his second theme (in the musical sense) the anxiety about cholera affecting the respectable Londoners, as well as the city's destitute. By developing and intertwining these two topics taken from the public sphere, of Chancery ills and public sanitation, Dickens creates a polyphonic view of the metropolis and society at large smothered by muddy pestilence of social and moral distemper. Dickens's interest in sanitary reform, vigorously pursued by Edwin Chadwick, is evidenced by his speech given to the Metropolitan Sanitary Association on 10 May 1851, during the incubation period of conceiving *Bleak House*. The speech, brimming over with his characteristic wit and humour, contains the following crucial embryo of the novel:

> "That no one can estimate the amount of mischief which is grown in dirt; that no one can say, here it stops, or there it stops, either in its physical or its moral results, when both begin in the cradle and are not at rest in the obscene grave . . . is now as certain as it is that the air from Gin Lane will be carried, when the wind is Easterly, into May Fair, and that if you once have a vigorous pestilence raging furiously in Saint Giles's, no mortal list of Lady Patronesses can keep it out of Almack's." (*Speeches* 128)

This vision of interconnected uncanny familial link between St. Giles's and Lady Patronesses fits neatly into the conception of the Court of Equity as a family court, where disputes regarding family property are dealt with. Whereas for Chadwick, granting power to the experts, particularly himself, was the answer, Dickens is not merely "ambivalent" about "modern expertise," as Lauren Goodlad suggests (Goodlad 94), but goes further to show in *Bleak House*, and later in *Little Dorrit*, how bureaucratic machinery itself exacerbates society's malaise. In *Bleak House*, society as a whole is enlarged into one vast family connection (around John Jarndyce, Nemo, Smallweed, and so on), hence its title, which does not refer to any individual character (as in most of his novels before it up to *David Copperfield*) but to a "house," a family estate, or family seen as a question of legal property. In an unlikely familial economy of provision (i.e. *œconomia* in the original Aristotelean sense of the word), to which the characters and actions of the novel are more or less connected directly or symbolically, everything is consumed but nothing is produced. Gordon Bigelow states that the "killing principle of static, horizontal circulation that Chancery represents" (Bigelow 598) pervades the novel, but it may perhaps be more accurate to describe it as non-circulation, or arrested circulation of money into goods but never back again to money. Jarndyce himself embodies a typical "Chancery" economy in that his philanthropic consumption appears as a miraculously one-sided, unprincipled (as Skimpole's presence in his company hints at and his "giving" Guster to Esther as a "gift" corroborates), unilateral, arbitrary, and hence potentially dictatorial disposal of wealth that is never clearly accounted for. Thus, overlapping the *topos* of Chancery woes to that great mid-Victorian *topos* of "domesticity," which he had already debunked in *Martin Chuzzlewit, Dombey and Son*, and *David Copperfield*, Dickens points out how no family can be free from the question of death, of living off the dead and the disputed property left behind. The antidote to death, medically and economically, is circulation, of blood and money. Yet the stilted, consumptive economy depicted in the novel—of the costs devastating the asset, of dependence on charity or goodwill, of making money out of dangerous personal secrets—unifies the novel into one vast system of parasitism. Two strong exceptions to this are the Ironmaster Rouncewell and doctor Allan Woodcourt, who represent productive economy in goods and service, respectively, but they can do little to alter the inevitable conclusion that a self-destructive mechanism of non-circulating economy is bound to end up in complete self-consumption, in the "NOTHING" of death.[8]

Moving upwards and out from the family relationship to the city as a whole, one finds that London in Dickens's *Bleak House* and elsewhere is typically a city of consumption and service, with little direct production going on. This goes against the actual historical circumstances of the city, which, as noted earlier, was a major manufacturing centre. The *Erfahrung* of work, craft, and trade is generally treated marginally, if at all. We recall how the skill and labour of Lucien and his friend David occupy the core of the plot in Balzac's *Lost Illusions*. In one full-length Dickens novel where work experience ought to have mattered most, David Copperfield's childhood and adult labour take up just a small portion of the long narrative compared with his dealings with his or other people's personal affairs. In *Little Dorrit* what Doyce the inventor's workshop precisely produces is never specified, and never vigorous enough to resist the anti-productive forces of the Circumlocution Office. This industrious author appears reluctant to incorporate economic activity positively into his novels. The actual location of real industrial work, when visited by George Rouncewell close to the end of *Bleak House*, turns out to be hardly acceptable as a viable counterforce to the stagnation of Chancery-dominated London or even to the arch-reactionary Chesney Wold. The unidentified industrial town is merely glimpsed at by George, as a "busy town, with a clang of iron in it, and more fires and more smoke than he has seen yet" (*Bleak House* 845 [chap. 53]), before he walks into his brother's factory. Once inside the building, a quick transition to a scene of fraternal reconciliation protects the family drama from the smoke and noises of the town. The combination in *Hard Times*, another topical journalism-novel written right after *Bleak House*, of a closer view of industrial town and family economy erodes any trust one might wish to place on the industrial producers and their ideologues as potential candidates to set right a world gone out of joint, as represented by London in *Bleak House*. If moving away from both London and the new factory towns in the North promise no solution, then, crossing the Channel and travelling overseas perhaps offer at least a momentary relief? To answer this question, we examine in the next chapter the role of foreign travel and foreigners in Dickens's mature novels, particularly in *Little Dorrit*.

CHAPTER EIGHT

TRAVELLERS AND STRANGERS

"A flourishing city, too! An architectural city!"

Dickens the journalist-cum-novelist purveyed a vision of society in part by adopting what John Drew describes as "the travelling mode" in which the first-person reporter of *Uncommercial Traveller* or the third-person narrator of *Bleak House* can shift "from an impressively general, powerfully metaphorical critique of society, based on ideological grounds, to focus on minutiae" (Drew 172). The gamut of stylistic registers which he commanded bridged the immediate sensory *Erlebnis* of London life and the need for a generalizing *Erfahrung* of the capital's numerous ills which his readers were more or less familiar with. The communality of "Boz" style, in short, benefitted from the communality of London life. The litmus test assessing the extent of Dickens's narrative strategy of making oddities a shareable experience, then, should involve those other cities besides London, up north and across the seas.

The challenge for a travel narrative consists in its ability to produce, while upholding its informative veracity, a synthesis between "counsel" of the storyteller (a traveller's tale is a prototype of narrating *Erfahrung* in Benjamin's thinking, we recall) on one hand, and impressive moments of *Erlebnis* on the other. On both counts of instructive reflection and memorable incidents, one has small chance of telling a convincing story of a journey which the storyteller did not undertake himself. Dickens comes from a modest and not particularly exceptional milieu of lower-middle-class London. Unlike an author with a rustic background such as Hardy, he had no local lore or tales to draw on. Not having had the benefit of gentlemanly education (of Thackeray, for instance), which included some version of the Grand Tour to France and Italy, in his earlier novels he had no experience or memory of European travel to utilize. Pickwick, after a lifetime of virtual hibernation at his narrow London quarters—"Goswell Street was at his feet, Goswell Street was on his right hand—as far as the eye could reach, Goswell Steet extended on his left; and the opposite side of Goswell Street was over the way"—decides to "penetrate to the hidden countries which on every side surround it" (*Pickwick* 6 [chap. 2]) vigorously enough, yet never too far from London. *Barry Lyndon*, in contrast, the first novel of Thackeray, educated at Charterhouse and Cambridge, has its Irish protagonist spend a good deal of his eventful life in Europe, making excellent use of the author's firsthand knowledge of the Continent. Redmond Barry (also known as Chevalier de Balibari) brags with some fair degree of justice that "there is not a capital in Europe, except the beggarly one of Berlin, where the young Chevalier de Balibari was not known and admired, and where he has not made the brave, the high-born, and the beautiful talk of him" (Thackeray 1984: 178). Similarly, in *Vanity Fair*, a part of the action unfolds in Continental capitals (Brussels and Paris), in those "happy days of 1817-18" when the "great cities of Europe had not been as yet open to the enterprise of our rascals," on which momentous topic the narrator has more to say, as he bemoans the degeneration of modern times:

> And whereas there is now hardly a town of France or Italy in which you shall not see some noble countryman of our own, with that happy swagger and insolence of demeanour which we carry everywhere, swindling inn-landlords, passing fictitious cheques upon credulous bankers, robbing coachmakers of their carriages, goldsmiths of their trinkets, easy travellers of their money at cards—even public libraries of their books: thirty years ago you needed but to be a Milor Anglais, travelling in a private carriage, and credit was at your hand wherever you chose to seek it, and gentlemen, instead of cheating, were cheated. (Thackeray 1968: 433-34)

Neither Pickwick nor his author could be suspected of being related to this breed of upstart swindling "noble countryman" inundating European cities, for their world was set apart from those conspicuously expensive foreign travels.

Not only *Pickwick Papers*, but most of the novels that followed have domestic settings. Martin Chuzzlewit is the first of Dickens's heroes to go abroad, yet it is to a dubious frontier town of Eden in the United States, where the protagonist seeks to mend his fortune. The travel contributes to the novel's satire on American foibles and when that mission has been accomplished, the plot abandons the new republic, with Martin's circumstances hardly improved. He returns home to England, though not to London straight. Martin, along with his "servant" Mark, is delighted by the familiar sights and noises of his home country, unquestionably authentic unlike the spurious American towns:

> Bright as the scene was; fresh, and full of motion; airy, free and sparkling; it was nothing to the life and exultation in the breast of the two travellers, at

> sight of the old churches, roofs, and darkened chimney stacks of Home. The distant roar, that swelled up hoarsely from the busy streets, was music in their ears; the lines of people gazing from the wharves, were friends held dear; the canopy of smoke that overhung the town was brighter and more beautiful to them than if the richest silks of Persia had been waving in the air. (*Chuzzlewit* 548 [chap. 35])

The returned natives would soon run into the hypocrite Pecksniff, who gives lie to the welcoming hospitality of "Home," yet the affection for the historic, old, irregular life of old English cities colouring this passage offers itself as a palliative after a series of vitriolic chapters ridiculing American boorishness. Similarly, David Copperfield, to cure his heart wounded by his bride's death, leaves for the Continent, yet his extended travels in Europe is only vaguely summed up: we know nothing about his itinerary. The point falls on his return home, which confirms the strong pull of the metropolis:

> … As I looked out of the coach-window, and observed that an old house on Fish-street Hill, which had stood untouched by painter, carpenter, or bricklayer, for a century, had been pulled down in my absence; and that a neighbouring street, of time-honoured insalubrity and inconvenience, was being drained and widened; I half expected to find St. Paul's Cathedral looking older.
>
> ………………………………………
>
> They expected me home before Christmas; but had no idea of my returning so soon. I had purposely misled them, that I might have the pleasure of taking them by surprise. And yet, I was perverse enough to feel a chill and disappointment in receiving no welcome, and rattling, alone and silent, through the misty streets.
>
> The well-known shops, however, with their cheerful lights, did something for me; and when I alighted at the door of the Gray's Inn Coffee-house, I had recovered my spirits. (*Copperfield* 820 [chap. 59])

London comes closest to being a hometown for him, although only a portion of his childhood was spent there, and although the vast metropolis is essentially indifferent to whoever professes heart-felt attachment to it. The emphasis falls on the welcoming constancy (and quaintness) of London and on David's clinging to his illusory sense of belonging, anchored on the fragile vessel of the "well-known shops" and expressed in terms of the money economy of "Gray's Inn Coffee-house." Which foreign cities he visited during the interval is not worth mentioning: they can remain anonymous foils to London. Such cultural Cockneyism of not bothering to recognize the existence or worth of any other well-established city besides London permeates the majority of Dickens novels, with only

two exceptions, *A Tale of Two Cities* and *Little Dorrit*, which allots significant proportions of their thematic and narrative assets to foreign cities (Paris, Marseilles, Rome, Calais).

But before we leave English shores, we ought to consider Dickens's attitude to other cities of the United Kingdom. This turns out to be a relatively simple task, for we instantly realize how other regions and cities of the British Isles outside England are rarely visited by his protagonists. The capitals of the constituent nations of the United Kingdom, Edinburgh, Cardiff, and Dublin, are almost nonexistent in Dickens's map. Remaining silent on these ancient cities can perhaps be taken as a sign of Dickens's indirect respect for them. The less prestigious towns, however, are subjected to outright derision. Dickens bestows skewered, stingy, stinted attention on the Northern industrial cities of Lancashire represented by Coketown (modelled after Preston) in *Hard Times*, whose unappealing picture does poor justice to the vibrant, energetic, Dissenter-based civic life of the key centres of Industrial Revolution:

> You saw nothing in Coketown but what was severely workful. If the members of a religious persuasion built a chapel there—as the members of eighteen religious persuasions had done—they made it a pious warehouse of red brick, with sometimes . . . a bell in a birdcage on the top of it. . . . All the public inscriptions in the town were painted alike, in severe characters of black and white. The jail might have been the infirmary, the infirmary might have been the jail, the town-hall might have been either, or both, or anything else, for anything that appeared to the contrary in the graces of their construction. Fact, fact, fact, everywhere in the material aspect of the town; fact, fact, fact, everywhere in the immaterial. (*Hard Times* 22-23 [chap. 5])

The towns of the industrial North, *pace* Dickens, proudly erected stately Gothic town-halls with façades that do not seem "severely workful" in the least. They also set up "fact"-oriented educational institutions that grew into respectable "red-brick" universities in the next century (see Hylton 191-93). This profile of "Coketown" contains a great deal of truth, no doubt, but many factory towns had more to them than this description allows. This "Cockney" bias against the Midlands and the North evident in Dickens's novels leads them to ignore the natural beauty of the neighbouring nation north of the Firth. This is somewhat surprising given the strong influence of Scott on the development of his novelistic artistry and career, not to mention his numerous trips to Scotland for business or pleasure (Slater 455-56; Kaplan 1988: 115-16), many parts of which were being transformed into tourist resorts, thanks no doubt to Scott's promotion of the natural charm of his home country in his novels. In

Waverley, the titular English hero coming from an English family with Jacobite sympathies is lured step by step into the rebellious heartland of the Highlands, where he is enraptured as much by Flora, the sister of the rebel chieftain Fergus, as by the exotic landscape:

> The rocks now receded, but still showed their grey and shaggy crests rising among the copse-wood. Still higher, rose eminences and peaks, some bare, some clothed with wood, some round and purple with heath, and others splintered into rocks and crags. At a short turning, the path, which had for some furlongs lost sight of the brook, suddenly placed Waverley in front of a romantic waterfall. It was not so remarkable either for great height or quantity of water, as for the beautiful accompaniments which made the spot interesting. After a broken cataract of about twenty feet, the stream was received in a large natural basin filled to the brim with water, which, when the bubbles of the fall subsided, was so exquisitely clear, that, although it was of great depth, the eye could discern each pebble at the bottom. (Scott 1972: 176)

Against this backdrop appears Flora, like "one of those lovely forms which decorate the landscapes of Poussin." Although this is a focalized description geared to Waverley's romantic mind, it easily convinces the reader of the idyllic beauty of the retreat. Such charming exotic spots of the British Isles have no place in Dickens's topography, however, which is circumscribed by London or at best forms a network of satellite towns around the metropolis (as in *Pickwick Papers* or *David Copperfield*).

In *Barnaby Rudge*, his historical novel most pronouncedly influenced by Scott, Lord Gordon, a member of a powerful Scottish aristocratic family, makes his (rather unimpressive) appearance. But then the venue has to be London. The kind of fervent Calvinist heritage which Lord Gordon inherits, and which is embedded in the Edinburgh tradition emanating from John Knox, can be identified only in Dickens's antipathetic characterization of his Protestant fanaticism, as when he enlarges on his noble resolution to save his "unhappy country" in a stilted rhetoric to his scheming "secretary" Gashford: "Who says I doubt? If I doubted should I cast away relatives, friends, everything, for this unhappy country's sake . . . forsaken of God and man, delivered over to a dangerous confederacy of Popish powers; the prey of corruption, idolatry, and despotism! Who says I doubt? Am I called, and chosen, and faithful? Tell me. Am I, or am I not?" (*Barnaby* 275 [chap. 36]). Dickens pays little heed to the fact that the anti-Catholic riots in London had lurid and effective precedents in Scottish cities. Violent destruction of Catholic citizens' property had already taken place in Glasgow and Edinburgh one year before, leading to the General Assembly in Edinburgh to vote against the repeal of anti-Catholic laws (Hume Brown 279). Dickens reduces the scale of this nation-wide agitation to an aberration in London's otherwise harmoniously jangling life. As far as the novel is concerned, Gordon is nothing more than a deluded agitator greeted by the rabbles and semi-criminal elements of the metropolis.

London's uncontested supremacy in the world of Dickens's novels over other cities, domestic or foreign, can be almost obtrusive at times, particularly when one sails west to the New World. In *Martin Chuzzlewit*, to maximize the contrast between London and the unlikely towns of the United States, Dickens has Martin consider settling, not in the established East-Coast cities of Boston or New York, but in a fake township somewhere out in the Midwest which calls itself "Eden." The locality with such promising name has as yet not advanced much from the stage of pictorial incubation, as Martin quickly realizes at the "office of the Eden Settlement" (*Chuzzlewit* 353 [chap. 21]), managed by its "agent" Scadder:

> "Heyday!" cried Martin, as his eye rested on a great plan which occupied one whole side of the office. . . .
>
> "That's Eden," said Scadder. . . .
>
> "Why, I had no idea it was a city."
>
> "Hadn't you? Oh, it's a city."
>
> A flourishing city, too! An architectural city! There were banks, churches, cathedrals, market-places, factories, hotels, stores, mansions, wharves; an exchange, a theatre; public buildings of all kinds, down to the office of the Eden Stinger, a daily journal; all faithfully depicted in the view before them. (355)

The jeering exclamation marks of the sentences and the description of the plan invite all those living in proper cities and ancient towns of England with real "banks, churches, cathedrals, market-places, factories, hotels, stores, mansions, wharves; an exchange, a theatre; public buildings of all kinds," particularly those living in London, to laugh Eden to scorn. Had Martin moved to the already well-developed populous cities of the former Thirteen Colonies, where an ambitious but needy young Englishman like him could have found a more welcome opportunity to improve his lot, the novel's action might very well have terminated in America, as does *Moll Flanders*.

Boz the writer specializing in London's proud oddities cannot stoop to admit any rival to London, certainly not in the New World. His *American Notes*, the companion piece to *Martin Chuzzlewit*, both written after his first visit to North America in 1842, frequently betrays a patronizing attitude of a Londoner and Englishman towards the new towns and cities of the young republic, such as Lowell, near Boston, whose being necessarily new earns the amused sneer of the traveller-writer:

> One would swear that every "Bakery," "Grocery," and "Bookbindery," and other kind of store, took its shutters down for the first time, and started in business yesterday. The golden pestles and mortars fixed as signs upon the sun-blind frames outside the Druggists', appear to have been just turned out of the United States' Mint. (*American Notes* 65)

However diverting this apparently harmless description of the "young town," it characterizes the place around its dominant trait of "newness," which becomes something to be ashamed of almost, for no other reason than for being new. Similarly, the planned capital of the young nation fails to impress Boz:

> Take the worst parts of the City Road and Pentonville . . . where the houses are smallest, preserving all their oddities, but especially the small shops and dwellings, occupied in Pentonville (but not in Washington) by furniture-brokers, keepers of poor eating-houses, and fanciers of birds. Burn the whole down; build it up again in wood and plaster; widen it a little; throw in part of St. John's Wood; put green blinds outside all the private houses, with a red curtain and a white one in every window; plough up all the roads; plant a great deal of coarse turf in every place where it ought *not* to be . . . leave a brick-field without the bricks, in all central places where a street may naturally be expected: and that's Washington. (*American Notes* 115)

Washington is compared with London and found wanting, not surprisingly. Its streets, houses, and gardens all disappoint the Londoner's sense of how they ought to have been arranged. But above all, it lacks a distinctive character of its own, approximating at best a gauche combination of City, Pentonville and St. John's Wood. Washington is less new than Lowell and certainly real unlike Eden, but in the final analysis, this "flourishing . . . architectural city," like them, appears somewhat spurious.

"That land of poetry with burning mountains"

Not everything in the description above of Washington has to do with European prejudices, for it does make an important point: a city's cultural identity has to be rooted (and not artificially devised) in culture and history, in the specific climate, custom, and contradictions clustered into sediments over a period of time. American cities in the nineteenth century, compared with those of Europe, inevitably appeared abstract, vapid, and contrived. They were clearly at a disadvantage when this criterion of historicist urbanism was applied. By the same token, European cities with long history such as the fascinating metropolis of England's ancient enemy France, or the very first modern cities of Italy (such as Florence or Genoa), not to mention Rome, could offer formidable challenge to London's pretensions to cultural prestige. This challenge also involved literary competition for Dickens or any other writer seeking to describe them, since these cities had been far too often written about to enable fresh creative approach. The "convention of writing about each city" of Italy became something "handed down from writer to writer, until they turn into virtual *topoi*" (Ross 11). Dickens's approach to the task of refreshing the established *topos* of travellers' adulation of Italian charms is, characteristically, a comic move. Flora Finching, Arthur Clennam's youthful flame now grown plump and prolix, upon hearing about Amy Dorrit's sojourn in Italy, pours out all the typical predicates about Italy to be expected of those who can only envy the lucky visitors to that land:

> "In Italy is she really?" said Flora, "with the grapes and figs growing everywhere and lava necklaces and bracelets too that land of poetry with burning mountains picturesque beyond belief though if the organ-boys come away from the neighbourhood not to be scorched nobody can wonder being so young and bringing their white mice with them most humane, and is she really in that favoured land with nothing but blue about her and dying gladiators and Belvederas." (*Dorrit* 535-36 [part 2, chap. 9])

She speaks, laughable as her speech is, from a venerable tradition of English travel writing on Italy, going back to the times of Pepys, with whom we started this book, such as *The Present State of the Princes and Republicks of Italy with Observations on Them* (1671). As its title indicates, the book mainly discusses the political system of various Italian states, but the culture and the people are given careful attention throughout. The author begins by praising the land:

> That must needs be a Rare Countrey which is pleasant and plentiful, watered with many Rivers; at the season adorned with Corn in the fields, and Grass in the Meddows, with delightful Land-skips, that in most parts hath a wholesome Air, that abounds in strong and stately Cities, where the eye is delighted with most sumptuous buildings, recreated with variety of Pictures and Statues, the ear pleased with as great a variety of harmonious musick as can be upon earth; where the Palate is satisfied with the best fruits, and other delicacies, and the rarest Wines of *Europe*; where in a certain season, the nose enjoyes the sweet smell of *Orange* and *Jasmin* flowers, which lay over head or under feet; and at the same time, and in the same place to behold fine perspectives, and hear the murmur of several fountain waters: in a word, that

> Countrey which produces plenty, and variety to please all the Senses, and which hath the *Alpes* of one side for Walls, and the Sea on the other for bounds, must needs be an excellent Country; such is *Italy*. (Gailhard 1-2)

This land of plenty and delight cannot fail to entice the dwellers of the dark, dull, damp British isles. The description becomes an irresistible invitation to voyage, actual or virtual. Even in this early representation, Italy becomes the obligatory destination of a new kind of secular pilgrimage, not in search of spiritual awakening but of sensory delights of various kinds. But the glorious plenty the land abounds in and its intoxicating pleasures can also be dangerous, for the country is inhabited by volatile people. The Italians, though remarkable for their "sobriety" and "frugality" (Gailhard 189), can be too "fiery" (193) when disputes arise, and quite lethal when vengeance is called for (196), more so since an Italian "dissembles and conceals his desire of revenge, which aims at no less than the death of the offendor, by the means of poison, dagger, or any other way, leaving nothing unattemped to bring his design to pass" (197). Italy is a marvellous land blessed by nature and endowed with wonderful artifacts, but Italians are inflammable and bloodthirsty.

Similarly, the author of *A New Voyage to Italy* (1695) feels incumbent in his preface to caution readers, before regaling them with the wonders of the land, about the Italians having "so much Fire in their Imagination" (Misson n.p) that their words are not to be taken at face value. Extreme both in its attractions and perils, Italy promises but undermines *Erfahrung* due to such preconceptions: one knows all too well in advance what to discover. In the next century when the Grand Tour was properly established as a cultural institution of the English gentry, those who went to Italy carried with them such manuals as Thomas Nugent's *The Grand Tour*, which, as the author himself boastingly puts it, is the first travel book designed not for the "sedentary readers" but tailor-made to be an "instructive companion" for "those who consult them for real use" (Nugent v-vi). This handy guidebook, in addition to practical information for travel, provides helpful analysis of the Italian character:

> Their predominant passions are jealousy and revenge, which are the source of an infinite deal of mischief. They are jealous very often without any reason, and the least suspicion throws them into a fit of rage. They are easily offended and hard to be reconciled, though sometimes they will feign a reconciliation, in order to pursue their revenge with greater security. They are great masters in the art of dissimulation, and are very suspicious, observing the looks and gestures of those with whom they converse, with a view of discovering their minds. In outward appearance they shew a great deal of civility and kindness, but their complaisance is frequently a mixture of

> flattery and design. They are too much addicted to pleasure and idleness, and extravagantly violent in their amours. (Nugent 43-44)

Anne Radcliffe's *The Italian*, coming at the end of the eighteenth century, capitalized on this bifurcation of Italy that set the desirable land with admirable relics against its volatile natives.[1] It proved a potent notion not confined to Gothic fiction, for it flew into most unlikely quarters, such as George Eliot's provincial fiction. Caterina in "Mr Gilfil's Love-Story," the second of her *Scenes of Clerical Life*, is an Italian orphan bred in a Midlands country house, yet sober English manners have failed to tame her fiery Italian tempers. She is at heart "a fierce little thing, though she seems so quiet generally" (Eliot 1984: 132), as one of the characters diagnoses her.

Dickens made his first journey to Italy, somewhat belatedly, after establishing his fame with his first hit novels, from 1844 to 1845. It was the first extensive sojourn abroad in his life, made possible by his financial security. From this experience evolved his travelogue *Pictures from Italy*, and from his return visit to Italy in 1853 the Italian chapters of *Little Dorrit* (1855-57). In the former book, somewhat atypical as an English traveller in Italy is his focus on Genoa, rather than the more illustrious cities of Florence, Venice, or Rome. Genoa was convenient as a port (along with Livorno/Leghorn) for the English sailing to Italy but hardly renowned for its art or monuments. Yet this deviation from the beaten track enabled him also to evade the generally stylized and stinted response of English visitors writing predictable encomiums on the beauty of the landscape or the marvels of relics and artworks. Dickens is interested in the live Italians rather than the eminent dead. He is drawn to the vivacity, as well as the amiable quaintness, of the common inhabitants of Genoa, such as the peasant women washing their linen in public:

> The Peasant Women, with naked feet and legs, are so constantly washing clothes, in the public tanks, and in every stream and ditch, that one cannot help wondering, in the midst of all this dirt, who wears them when they are clean. The custom is to lay the wet linen which is being operated upon, on a smooth stone, and hammer away at it, with a flat wooden mallet. This they do, as furiously as if they were revenging themselves on dress in general for being connected with the Fall of Mankind. (*Pictures* 299)

The hallmark "Boz" touch of light humour inscribed into "as if they were revenging themselves on dress in general" spices up a tableau of vibrant, resilient, popular life, which seems safely removed from predictable admirations of magnificent but dead monuments to past greatness, and even further from Flora's "favoured land with nothing but blue about her and dying gladiators and Belvederas."

Nonetheless, Italy *is* a strange place, for Dickens writes as a stranger neither fluent in the language nor seasoned by intimate experience of the community. The perceptive foreigner, no matter how much sympathy he may have for the locals, really has no qualification to package his observations as an authentic *Erfahrung* to the reader. He manages to avoid the tourist's stereotypical view, at least in his chapter on Genoa, yet his position remains detached from the real life of the inhabitants. A telltale sentence proclaims that he came "to have an attachment for the very stones in the streets of Genoa, and to look back upon the city with affection as connected with many hours of happiness and quiet!" (283). Stones of the streets could make for excellent friendship, but they are inanimate, non-human, non-verbal friends. Conversing with the silent pavement stones is conversing with one's self, as a matter of fact. Dickens's intense dialogue takes place within himself, even when socializing with remarkable material objects, such as Genoa's palazzo:

> The great, heavy, stone balconies, one above another, and tier over tier: with here and there, one larger than the rest, towering high up—a huge marble platform; the doorless vestibules, massively barred lower windows, immense public staircases, thick marble pillars, strong dungeon-like arches, and dreary, dreaming, echoing vaulted chambers: among which the eye wanders again, and again, and again, as every palace is succeeded by another . . . the steep, steep, up-hill streets of small palaces (but very large palaces for all that), with marble terraces looking down into close by-ways—the magnificent and innumerable Churches; and the rapid passage from a street of stately edifices, into a maze of the vilest squalor, steaming with unwholesome stenches, and swarming with half-naked children and whole worlds of dirty people—make up, altogether, such a scene of wonder: so lively, and yet so dead: so noisy, and yet so quiet: so obtrusive, and yet so shy and lowering: so wide awake, and yet so fast asleep: that it is a sort of intoxication to a stranger to walk on, and on, and on, and look about him. A bewildering phantasmagoria, with all the inconsistency of a dream, and all the pain and all the pleasure of an extravagant reality! (*Pictures* 292-93)

What the description speaks of ultimately is the "phantasmagoria" of the subject's self-communion, an *Erlebnis* that blurs the objective details of architecture, whose "dreary, dreaming, echoing" vacancy reflects as much the detached position of the strolling "stranger" as the actual condition of being deserted and empty. The inhabitants assert their right to the city, occupying and using the space for their daily—and destitute—subsistence, as the streets are "steaming with unwholesome stenches, and swarming with half-naked children and whole worlds of dirty people." Yet the life rhythm there strikes one as surreally mute, when contrasted with that of "Seven Dials," whose clamorous vitality Boz captured in a kindred spirit. Genoa is "so lively, and yet so dead: so noisy, and yet so quiet" in the eyes of the alien visitor. The bemused, becalmed, bewildered visitor can use the space of habitation only as a pretext for his subjective musing.

The paradox of an objective account of journeys in foreign lands based on real experience of the traveller is that it can rarely share with the reader the experience of communal living (*Erfahrung*) in those places. That difficulty Dickens admits to in describing the inhabitants as "so lively, and yet so dead": the subject approaches the objects but is also repulsed by them and retreats back to its own "phantasmagoria." Whether such an aspect can be described in terms of "proto-filmic elements" (Bowen 208) may not be the most urgent question. One first has to define the meaning of "filmic," for hyperrealism rather than hallucination could very well be regarded as the essence of cinema. On the other hand, it seems clear that such travel narratives illustrate the predominance of what Gerard Curtis calls the "commodification of observation" (Curtis 218), avidly pursued by the publishing market of the times and its representatives, including Dickens. Even though the text names itself "Pictures from Italy," the postcards sent home from Italy threaten to turn stale and sour, after two centuries or more of stereotyped travel writings on Italy. Rome, the mother of all Western cities, yields the following paragraph, which contains, compared with his description of Genoa, fewer signs of the expert prose writer's stylistic virtuosity:

> What a bright noon it was, as we rode away! The Tiber was no longer yellow, but blue. There was a blush on the old bridges, that made them fresh and hale again. The Pantheon, with its majestic front, all seamed and furrowed like an old face, had summer light upon its battered walls. Every squalid and desolate hut in the Eternal City (bear witness every grim old palace, to the filth and misery of the plebeian neighbour that elbows it, as certain as Time has laid its grip on its patrician head!) was fresh and new with some ray of the sun. (*Pictures* 406)

Otherwise than the parenthetical remarks on "the filth and misery of the plebeian neighbour" of "grim old palace," the passage heavily relies on standard tourist clichés. The exclamation point in the parenthesis looks almost like the writer's anger at seeing his own stylistic ego smothered. Dickens's writing becomes more stylized, vapid, and lackluster as he visits Florence towards the end of his *Pictures from Italy*:

> But, how much beauty of another kind is here, when, on a fair clear morning, we look, from the summit of a hill, on Florence! See where it lies before us in a sun-lighted valley, bright with the winding Arno, and shut in by swelling hills; its domes, and towers, and palaces, rising from the rich country in a glittering heap, and shining in the sun like gold!
>
> Magnificently stern and sombre are the streets of beautiful Florence; and the strong old piles of building make such heaps of shadow, on the ground and in the river, that there is another and a different city of rich forms and fancies, always lying at our feet. Prodigious palaces, constructed for defence, with small distrustful windows heavily barred, and walls of great thickness formed of huge masses of rough stone, frown, in their old sulky state, on every street. (*Pictures* 429-30)

Except perhaps for "in their old sulky state," one finds virtually no trace of Boz's poetic prose; the passage repeats a much-recycled account of the much-visited city, offering neither new information nor interesting personal anecdote. The more impressive parts of the book, then, are framed as pictures not so much of Italy as of the traveller's subjective *Erlebnis*, often momentary and mystifying, such as the second passage from the Genoa chapter quoted earlier. Vivid *Erlebnis* and communal *Erfahrung* could be harmonized when Dickens wrote on his familiar city. Can the balance be maintained even when writing on an alien setting? This question is what *Little Dorrit* addresses. As a way of assessing this novel's rare achievement we shall make a detour to examine a comparable case in George Eliot, who, after having established her position as a novelist specializing in Warwickshire local life and accent, ventured to use her Italian travels in her historical novel *Romola*.

"Altro to you, old chap"

George Eliot, after five published books of fiction, went on a belated Grand Tour to Italy in 1860, thanks to the remarkable commercial success of her novels. The journey yielded, in addition to her historical novel *Romola* set in Renaissance Florence, a mini-travelogue, "Recollections of Italy," a brief and factual text moving fast from one place to another. In this shorter work, Florence, which would soon engross her imagination in her work on *Romola*, is represented as any tourist's quick collation of famous names and predictable epithets:

> There is Brunellschi's mighty dome, and close by it, with its lovely colours not entirely absorbed by distance, Giotto's incomparable Campanile, beautiful as a jewel; farther on, to the right, is the majestic tower of the Palazzo Vecchio, with the flag waving above it, then the elegant Badia and

> the Bargello close by; nearer to us, the grand campanile of Santo Spirito, and that of Santa Croce. (Eliot 1998: 354)[2]

The overall impression one gathers from this passage is that of an obligatory enumeration of mandatory stops and objects, the places one has to visit and the things one has to see. In contrast to such stylized perspective, Dickens felt more interested in the human figures of Genoa, as noted above, not only in *Pictures from Italy*, but also in *Little Dorrit*. The souvenir of the Italian city is embodied in the Genoan character Giambattista Cavaletto (or "John Baptist") and his "altro!" in the novel, whom we shall discuss shortly. George Eliot, however, feels no need to mention living Italians. Florence for her is a city of dead masters—Giotto, Michelangelo, Benvenuto Cellini, and Dante—and their great works. The last particularly appealed to the literati in her, as she stands on the venerable poet's memorial: "I used to feel my heart swell a little at the sight of the inscription on Dante's tomb: '*Onorate l'altissimo poeta*'" (Eliot 1998: 356). Yet unlike her and Lewes' trip to Weimar which was in part a pilgrimage to Goethe's holy relics, the "altissimo poeta" (the highest poet) is given a mere passing tribute in their first visit to his hometown. One can agree with Margaret Harris when she regards George Eliot's 1860 trip to Italy "a version of the Grand Tour" (Harris 10), for contemporary life finds hardly any resonance in the traveller's mind.

Her "Italian novel" (Eliot 1998: 102) *Romola*, likewise, is Italian only in a "touristic" sense. The historical period she chose to revisit in her novel, the so-called "years of crisis" in the hegemony of the Medici ascendancy from 1490s to 1512 was not insignificant. It was the high point of Florentine republicanism, soon to be stifled by the restoration of Medici supremacy by Spanish troops (Holmes 76-79). But George Eliot is particularly interested in the years during which the radical visionary preaching of Savonarola held sway over the people. Put in a larger historical context, the period and the central figure she chose to focus on are both atypical of Renaissance Italy. The spiritualist evangelical reformer Savonarola could have been a revolutionary figure in any city of any other country. George Eliot uses "Renaissance material to advocate just that Puritanical, and anti-Renaissance, ethos of duty and self-sacrifice" (Churchill 144), which the Victorians were ostensibly adopting as their quotidian ideology. Moreover, a major actor of the drama is not even Italian by birth: he is a Greek totally dedicated to his own private and selfish gains. Tito, of course, is no pariah but as a Greek fluent with both Italian and his mother tongue attracts the classics-loving Florentine elite, especially Bardo. But Tito nonetheless is an alien and outsider, a traveller who feels no attachment to Florence. He sells off his father-in-law's cherished library and seeks to flee the volatile Republic to graze at a more placid turf. In all of these qualities, his wife Romola figures as the diametrical opposite. The novel is called "Romola" and the plot, in a nutshell, tests the moral strength of Romola's sense of duty and self-sacrifice, first towards her father before her marriage, then against her fortune-hunting Greek husband, and finally in the context of Savonarola's radical idealism, which she ardently espouses. She gives herself physically to her husband and spiritually to Savonarola, but both of her weddings disappoint her, which may be the most moving dimension of the novel for modern readers. Yet Romola's quest after spiritual dignity, her striving against the matrimonial yokes imposed on her by patriarchy, has a universal value which may well have done without the elaborate Italian scaffolding.

The justification for using Italian background in *Romola* would best be found in its meticulous resurrection of Renaissance Florence. The strength and weakness of the novel have both to do with the fact that the novel takes the reader on a guided historical tour. Sure enough, in the first installment, the reader stands next to Tito, himself a traveller visiting Florence, to be treated with the best possible view of Florence's glories:

> The mercurial barber seized the arm of the stranger, and led him to a point, on the south side of the piazza, from which he could see at once the huge dark shell of the cupola, the slender soaring grace of Giotto's campanile, and the quaint octagon of San Giovanni in front of them, showing its unique gates of storied bronze, which still bore the somewhat dimmed glory of their original gilding. The inlaid marbles were then fresher in their pink and white and purple than they are now, when the winters of four centuries have turned their white to the rich ochre of well-mellowed meerschaum; the façade of the Cathedral did not stand ignominious in faded stucco, but had upon it the magnificent promise of the half-completed marble inlaying and statued niches, which Giotto had devised a hundred and fifty years before. (Eliot 1994: 31)

A rare treat it is indeed. When compared with the passage on the same scene from "Recollections of Italy" quoted above, we have travelled back some "four centuries" in time to see the marbles in their pristine freshness and magnificence. The narrative time-machine is constantly at work throughout the novel. "And Midsummer morning, in this year 1492, was not less bright than usual," we are told. "It was betimes in the morning that the symbolic offerings to be carried in grand procession were all assembled at their starting-point in the Piazza della Signoria—that famous piazza, where stood then, and stand now, the massive turreted Palace of the People, called the Palazzo Vecchio" (81). Lest we forget that this is a most unique and privileged view of old Florence as it really was, the sonorous announcement of "this year 1492" is buttressed by a phrase spanning the distance in time, "stood then, and stand now." Spectacles of history are painted throughout the novel against the backdrop of Florence's landmark monuments. Italy as a locality, however, tends to be congealed into mere spectacle in this process.

People travel to an overseas destination because it promises something new and foreign. Yet in this particular case, the readers of *Cornhill,* where the novel was serialized, could embark on their journey in their familiar English tongue, which comes moreover in a far more standard version than in other George Eliot novels which insert Midlands dialects regularly to boost their stylistic variety. To convey a sense of foreignness, the author scatters small pinches of Italian phrases in italics, particularly in the dialogues of the "chorus" characters, as in the following examples:

> "San Domenico roaring *é vero* in one ear, and San Francisco screaming *é falso* in the other" (Eliot 1994: 20)

> "It seems to me a thousand years till I can be of service to a *bel erudito* like yourself" (30)

> "*Pian piano*—not so fast," said Nello (36)

> "*Addio! bel giovane!* don't forget to come back to me" (42)

This handy device of literally italicizing Italian, with instant English translations when necessary, whets the English reader-traveller's appetite for exotic Italian fare, while easing his anxiety about its strong garlic taste, as it were. The more important speeches, however, are made in prim proper English. Similarly, in Dickens's *Little Dorrit*, the French speech of the "cosmopolitan" villain Rigaud (or Blandois) whose mother tongue is French ("My father was Swiss—Canton de Vaud. My mother was French by blood, English by birth. I myself was born in Belgium" [*Dorrit* 9 {book 1, chap. 1}]), comes with a distinctively foreign profile, as when he inquires for lodging at an inn on the banks of river Saône: "One can lodge here to-night, madame?" (*Dorrit* 125 [book 1, chap. 11]). This is almost a verbatim translation of "On y peut loger ce soir, madame?" Or, when he later asks, "Pardon me again—[Rigaud] has contracted your displeasure, how?" (128), the final "how?" is a rendering in English of French *comment.* Similarly, in Dickens's "half-French" novel *A Tale of Two Cities*, Defarge's speech occasionally is marked by obvious Francophone features, as when he asks his neighbour, "Say, then, my Gaspard, what do you do there?"

(30 [book. 1, chap. 5]), which mimics “Dites donc, mon Gaspard, que faites-vous là?” But in the more thematically important speeches, the English sentences and phrases shed their foreign cloak, even when these characters are supposed to be speaking in their own tongue.

> “How has society respected those qualities in me? I have been shrieked at through the streets. I have been guarded through the streets against men, and especially women, running at me armed with any weapons they could lay their hands on. I have lain in prison for security, with the place of my confinement kept a secret, lest I should be torn out of it and felled by a hundred blows.” (*Dorrit* 132 [book 1, chap. 11])

Thus goes Rigaud’s dilation on society’s cruelty, transcribed into perfect English, although the language he announces this in is French.

Riguad can be excused for sounding eloquent in any language, but the case of Cavalletto is different, for he lacks the background, education, and character of the pan-European Rigaud. The tactic which Dickens employs here is similar to George Eliot’s “*é vero*” but is more economic in that a single word, *altro* is made to stand for all that is foreign, authentic, and peculiar about the man. The word is glossed immediately in the first chapter of the book: “The word being, according to its Genoese emphasis, a confirmation, a contradiction, an assertion, a denial, a taunt, a compliment, a joke, and fifty other things, became in the present instance, with a significance beyond all power of written expression, our familiar English ‘I believe you!’” (*Dorrit* 8 [book 1, chap. 1]). Later, when Cavalletto becomes somewhat improbably a tenant at the Bleeding Heart Yard, the rent-collector picks up the same word as a password opening the gate to human intercourse with the foreigner:

> “What’s Altro?” said Pancks.
>
> “Hem! It’s a sort of a general kind of expression, sir,” said Mrs Plornish.
>
> “Is it?” said Pancks. “Why, then Altro to you, old chap. Good afternoon. Altro!”
>
> Mr Baptist in his vivacious way repeating the word several times, Mr Pancks in his duller way gave it him back once. From that time it became a frequent custom with Pancks the gipsy, as he went home jaded at night, to pass round by Bleeding Heart Yard, go quietly up the stairs, look in at Mr Baptist’s door, and, finding him in his room, to say, “Hallo, old chap! Altro!” To which Mr Baptist would reply with innumerable bright nods and smiles, “Altro, signore, altro, altro, altro!” After this highly condensed conversation, Mr Pancks would go his way; with an appearance of being lightened and refreshed. (305 [book 1, chap. 25])

This single word speaks volumes, literally, but it also highlights the linguistic and social disparity between the Genoese immigrant and the humble Londoners who would never travel to Italy. In all these cases of Defarge, Rigaud and Cavalletto, the linguistic security of English is never seriously challenged. For that to happen systematically, one has to wait until the advent of Joyce's *Ulysses*.

Dickens, nonetheless, shows a heightened sense of his sympathy for a foreigner coping with the daunting task of surviving in monolingual London. The natives believe, however abject their own lives may be, that "it was a sort of Divine visitation upon a foreigner that he was not an Englishman, and that all kinds of calamities happened to his country because it did things that England did not, and did not do things that England did" (302 [book 1, chap. 25]). But since Bleeding Heart Yard is peopled with those with "kind hearts," they decide to "accommodate themselves" to the poor foreigner's level of inferior intelligence, "calling him 'Mr Baptist,' but treating him like a baby, and laughing immoderately at his lively gestures and his childish English" (303):

> They spoke to him in very loud voices as if he were stone deaf. They constructed sentences, by way of teaching him the language in its purity, such as were addressed by the savages to Captain Cook, or by Friday to Robinson Crusoe. Mrs Plornish was particularly ingenious in this art; and attained so much celebrity for saying 'Me ope you leg well soon,' that it was considered in the Yard but a very short remove indeed from speaking Italian. Even Mrs Plornish herself began to think that she had a natural call towards that language. As he became more popular, household objects were brought into requisition for his instruction in a copious vocabulary; and whenever he appeared in the Yard ladies would fly out at their doors crying "Mr Baptist—tea-pot!" "Mr Baptist—dust-pan!" "Mr Baptist—flour-dredger!" "Mr Baptist—coffee-biggin!" At the same time exhibiting those articles, and penetrating him with a sense of the appalling difficulties of the Anglo-Saxon tongue. (303-4 [book 1, chap. 25])

The satire on English jingoism and colonial prejudices, as they reveal their ugly face among these shabby Londoners, hits its target, for sure. Charitably but tyrannically, they thrust on the Italian the civilized tongue of the English. Yet "Mr Baptist" is allowed by the author to retain the speech habits of Cavalletto, as he takes an active part in closing in on Rigaud-Blandois in the second half of the novel:

> "E ope you no fright," said Mrs Plornish then, interpreting Mr Pancks in a new way with her usual fertility of resource. "What appen? Peaka Padrona!"
>
> "I have seen some one," returned Baptist. "I have rincontrato him."

> "Im? Oo him?" asked Mrs Plornish.
> "A bad man. A baddest man. I have hoped that I should never see him again." "Ow you know him bad?" asked Mrs Plornish.
> "It does not matter, Padrona. I know it too well."
> "E see you?" asked Mrs. Plornish.
> "No. I hope not. I believe not." (577 [book. 2, chap. 13])

Ironically, Mrs. Plornish, a resident subject of British Crown, speaks, following her own EFL pedagogy, a Friday-like broken English, while the Genoese speaks passable English with only a word or two of Italian thrown in, such as *rincontrato* or *padrona*. In this and other aspects, *Little Dorrit* seeks to modify the London and England-centered bias of the author. With an amiable (but alert) Italian living among Dickens's beloved plebeian Londoners, London appears a trifle more cosmopolitan. Or one may say it appears almost prophetic of what London would become in the age of European Union, a European metropolis graced with ubiquitous Italian restaurants and Italian visitors.

"Welcome to the Marshalsea!"

Cavalletto is such a lone exception in Dickens's London, however. The virtue and identity of London in *Little Dorrit* have more to do with what it is not than what or who it is or has. The city triumphs in *Little Dorrit* as a negative truth over both its deluded self-confidence and spurious foreign experience. The representative traveller in the novel is Meagles, the retired London banker and full-time tourist, but he lacks the linguistic missionary zeal of Mrs. Plornish, as he "never by any accident acquired any knowledge whatever of the language of any country into which he travelled" (*Dorrit* 22 [book. 1, chap. 2]), and moreover, with a clear sense of how things foreign, particularly French, are inherently inferior and bad. "Allong and marshong, indeed," he complains to Arthur at the quarantine in Marseilles. "It would be more creditable to you, I think, to let other people allong and marshong about their lawful business, instead of shutting 'em up in quarantine!" (15). Foreign tongues have been conveniently bundled up in Meagles' vocabulary into "Allong and marshong," but above all, his overseas travels have been transformed into so many items of purchased souvenir:

> Of articles collected on his various expeditions, there was such a vast miscellany that it was like the dwelling of an amiable Corsair. There were antiquities from Central Italy, made by the best modern houses in that department of industry; bits of mummy from Egypt (and perhaps

> Birmingham); model gondolas from Venice; model villages from Switzerland; morsels of tesselated pavement from Herculaneum and Pompeii, like petrified minced veal; ashes out of tombs, and lava out of Vesuvius; Spanish fans, Spezzian straw hats, Moorish slippers, Tuscan hairpins, Carrara sculpture, Trastaverini scarves, Genoese velvets and filigree, Neapolitan coral, Roman cameos, Geneva jewellery, Arab lanterns, rosaries blest all round by the Pope himself, and an infinite variety of lumber. (192-93 [book 1, chap. 16])

Such is the collection amassed from his adventures abroad stored at his house at Twickenham—a stagnant storehouse pretending to bear witness to the authenticity of his experience but in fact cleared of any trace of either *Erfahrung* or *Erlebnis*.

Woven into the texture of the novel's plot is Little Dorrit's inability to accept the "reality" of the Italian cities she has to visit as a member of the newly enriched Dorrit clan on their belated Grand Tour. The narrative, focalized entirely on her, sees little to excite her mind in the famous cities, such as Venice, which has the honour of being

> the crowning unreality, where all the streets were paved with water, and where the deathlike stillness of the days and nights was broken by no sound but the softened ringing of church-bells, the rippling of the current, and the cry of the gondoliers turning the corners of the flowing streets. (466 [part. 2, chap. 3])

Mrs. General the chaperon's efforts to convert the younger daughter of her employer sees little effect, for the honest genuine heart of Amy cannot let itself be deceived into believing that the "waters of Venice and the ruins of Rome were sunning themselves for the pleasure of the Dorrit family" (514 [part. 2, chap. 8]). Nor can she fail to perceive the comfortable but predictable journey they (and other affluent English visitors) are enjoying has any chance of approaching genuine experience:

> All that she saw was new and wonderful, but it was not real; it seemed to her as if those visions of mountains and picturesque countries might melt away at any moment, and the carriage, turning some abrupt corner, bring up with a jolt at the old Marshalsea gate. (463 [part 2, chap. 3]).

Her bittersweet *Erfahrung* of misery, pain, caring and self-sacrifice, which Marshalsea represents to her, stands as the antithesis to the spurious *Erlebnis* of expensive tourism, which is "all a dream—only the old mean Marshalsea a reality" (464). So it does for her father, who finally succumbs to the triumphant and lethal return of the repressed reality of Marshalsea, as he addresses the dining members of expatriate English high society in Rome.

> "Ladies and gentlemen, the duty—ha—devolves upon me of—hum—welcoming you to the Marshalsea! Welcome to the Marshalsea! The space is—ha—limited—limited—the parade might be wider; but you will find it apparently grow larger after a time—a time, ladies and gentlemen—and the air is, all things considered, very good. It blows over the—ha—Surrey hills. Blows over the Surrey hills. This is the Snuggery. Hum. Supported by a small subscription of the—ha—Collegiate body. In return for which—hot water—general kitchen—and little domestic advantages. Those who are habituated to the—ha—Marshalsea, are pleased to call me its Father. I am accustomed to be complimented by strangers as the—ha—Father of the Marshalsea. Certainly, if years of residence may establish a claim to so—ha—honourable a title, I may accept the—hum—conferred distinction. My child, ladies and gentlemen. My daughter. Born here!" (647-48 [part 2, chap. 19])

This outburst of insanity is a victory of entrenched lifelong *Erfahrung* with its own justification and pride (as evinced in "My child, ladies and gentlemen. My daughter. Born here!") over the precarious elevation of the Dorrits' status, predicated as it is on their complete denial of their past. It is also a victory of London over Rome and other urban landmarks of the illustrious civilization Italy represents—patently not a triumph for the jingoistic, complacent confidence in the superiority of London (and England) over foreign capitals, but of the inhabited, communal, historical *Erfahrung* of living in London over the stilted, stereotyped, secluded usage of foreign cities as a mere prop of vanity and greed.[3] It is in this sense of embodied *Erfahrung* that London matters for Dickens, so much so that in the counterpart to *Romola* in Dickens's works, *A Tale of Two Cities*, where he travels back in time to a foreign city to deal with a revolutionary turmoil, he kept one foot firmly in London to fashion its plot as a shuttling back and forth between the two capitals, rather than presuming to write a historical novel set entirely in a foreign city with an all-foreign cast.

London in *Little Dorrit*, however, is far from being a safe haven from bloody revolutionary history, or from painful personal history. London is represented in the novel by Marshalsea Prison, a ludicrous, run-down debtor's prison implicated in the machinery of Circumlocution Office. Not only does William Dorrit's mind return to Marshalsea before his death, but the debtors' prison is also the final destination of Arthur Clennam's return trip to his native city, when his investments in Merdle's ventures evaporate into thin air. Even before reaching that final stage, when Clennam first returns to his native city, after having been "shipped away to the other end of the world" at a tender age, and "exiled there" (*Dorrit* 20 [book. 1, chap. 2]) to lead a monotonous life he loathed, a depressing sense of incarceration encircles him. No delightful noises greet him as they did Martin Chuzzlewit, nor is there any consolation to be bought at a familiar eatery, as was the case with David Copperfield. London instead rewards him with an *Erlebnis* of bleak melancholy, as he gazes at the city streets which has nothing endearing or alive about it:

> Melancholy streets, in a penitential garb of soot, steeped the souls of the people who were condemned to look at them out of windows, in dire despondency. In every thoroughfare, up almost every alley, and down almost every turning, some doleful bell was throbbing, jerking, tolling, as if the Plague were in the city and the deadcarts were going round. Everything was bolted and barred that could by possibility furnish relief to an overworked people. No pictures, no unfamiliar animals, no rare plants or flowers, no natural or artificial wonders of the ancient world—all *taboo* with that enlightened strictness, that the ugly South Sea gods in the British Museum might have supposed themselves at home again. Nothing to see but streets, streets, streets. Nothing to breathe but streets, streets, streets. Nothing to change the brooding mind, or raise it up. (*Dorrit* 28 [part 1, chap. 3])

This is the London of Blake's "charter'd streets," or more disturbingly, the London of Defoe's *Journal of the Plague Year*, as the narrator (if not Clennam) sees the ghosts of the dead-carts carrying the victims of the Great Plague. "Dickens's London," in Alexander Welsh's analysis, partakes of "an image of classical hell" (Welsh 65), in which the "living" are "already dead," whereas the "dead" are "not dead enough" (64). Indeed the plot of *Little Dorrit* hinges upon the fact that the past of personal and collective history, as in Dante's Hell, is permanently alive, however much you wish to brush it off and bury it. Of course, this is no afterlife, and life moves onward. History has advanced since the Plague Year so that the imperial global power of the British Empire behaves like Meagles, stacking its souvenirs of world travels in the British Museum, including its collection of savage gods. Yet the past lingers and loiters in the spatial fixture of the "melancholy streets." The past is "raised to the intensity of present" in *Little Dorrit*, as Angus Easson suggests, despite its contemporary setting in early nineteenth-century London (Easson 36).

Against this unpromising background garnished with the melancholy relics of early-modern Puritanism and smeared with the "prison taint" (*Dorrit* 3 [book 1, chap. 1]) of Marshalsea, Dickens works out a difficult love story between Clennam and Amy Dorrit, consummated only towards the very end of the novel. Can life and love foster human community in a money-making and money-loving metropolis? Defoe's answer was clearly in the negative: it is only your precious self with whom you share your love and your money. Dickens's reformed Scrooge would readily refute Defoe, pointing to the "Heavenly sky" (*Christmas Books* 72) above and dispatching prize turkeys to fellow mortals. But this short, stirring, and succinct "Christmas Carol in Prose" does not quite represent the sprawling world of prose Dickens erected throughout his long career. Can the impersonal metropolis be ever warmed with human fellowship? This foundational question of Dickens's engagement with the metropolis receives in his mature novels only a tentative and ambiguous answer in the affirmative, as a shade of misgiving resounds with the sonorous monotony of "streets, streets, streets," looming over the stray patches of affectionate human relationships Dickens hopes to celebrate.

PART III:

JOYCE

CHAPTER NINE

TRIESTE-ZURICH-PARIS

"A servant of two masters"

As we arrive at Joyce, our third and final destination, we need first to justify the company forced upon the three novelists, particularly the last. The transition from Defoe to Dickens needed no particular justification, since they both write from and on the same city. Though divided by their different approaches, as well as their respective centuries, the two are related as fellow London novelists brought up and buried there. They also write in a language which is properly theirs: English, including the Cockney dialect appearing in the later writer, is unquestionably and legitimately their mother tongue. Matters stand on a different footing, however, with Joyce. He comes from an Irish Catholic background in the colonial capital of Dublin, whose existence neither Defoe nor Dickens cares to acknowledge in their novels. The historical, political, and ethnic distance between Defoe and Joyce is glaringly denoted by the landmark figure William of Orange, praised by the former as the "True-Born Englishman" but responsible for crushing the last hopes of Catholic Ireland's autonomy at the bloody and tragic Battle of the Boyne, which initiated the era of Protestant Ascendancy bolstered by a series of notorious Penal Laws against the Catholics.[1] Moll's amiable, dashing, and daring "Lancashire Husband" with whom she finally settles down in Virginia has Irish roots, but there is no indication in the novel that he is indigenous to the island rather than a member of the Protestant minority with connections in England or Scotland. Typically, Crusoe in his first phase of adventure, when rescued by a Portuguese ship, is helped by a "*Scots* Sailor" on board (Crusoe 29), as yet when he spoke no Portuguese. A British or Protestant alliance with the Scots or the Dutch is what Defoe's fiction or pamphlets easily accommodate, but the Irish, literally, remain "beyond the pale."

Representation of the Irish or the lack thereof of in Dickens, who is closer to Joyce in time and, as a Londoner bound to have been clearly aware of the sizable Irish presence in the metropolis, is even more puzzling. It stands as a salient contrast to his rival Thackeray who embarked on his novelistic career by capitalizing on the flare and flamboyance of the Irishman Redmond Barry in his first novel *Barry Lyndon*. In the diverse, bustling, and profuse collection of Dickensian characters not one of them has distinctive Irish provenance or traits. The closest one comes to meeting the Irish as distinctive characters in his novels is ironically in the remote American Midwestern bogus town of Eden. The reader arrives there with Martin Chuzzlewit, to find that the place overflows with Republican fervour, which inspirits the "Watertoast Association of United Sympathisers," whose name, as well as its members' hatred of all things British, echoes the United Irishmen. The novel caricatures their politics as damaging evidence of the silliness and lunacy of the place. Their bombast, however, contains a grain of truth. The staunch Republican rebuke that General Choke inveighs against the "British Lion" is not entirely groundless:

> "In Freedom's name, sir, I advert with indignation and disgust to that accursed animal, with gore-stained whiskers, whose rampant cruelty and fiery lust have ever been a scourge, a torment to the world. The naked visitors to Crusoe's Island, sir; the flying wives of Peter Wilkins; the fruit-smeared children of the tangled bush; nay, even the men of large stature, anciently bred in the mining districts of Cornwall; alike bear witness to its savage nature. Where, sir, are the Cormorans, the Blunderbores, the Great Feefofums, named in History? All, all, exterminated by its destroying hand.
>
> "I allude, sir, to the British Lion." (*Chuzzlewit* 360 [chap. 21])

In its own right this is a striking speech almost foreshadowing anti-colonial or even ecological criticism of the British Empire, yet equally striking is the erasure of the rightful place of Ireland as the very first victim of the British Lion's "rampant cruelty and fiery lust." Perhaps the Irish are left out of the list because they have not quite been "exterminated by its destroying hand," but, on the contrary, are alive, kicking, growing, and even menacing the conquerors. London would come to a rude awakening to the gravity of the Irish radical resistance in the Fenian bombing of Clerkenwell prison in December 1867. Earlier that year, Dickens was visiting Belfast and Dublin on his commercial public reading tours. "Tremendous success in Ireland" was what mattered to him, "notwithstanding the Fenian alarms," as he wrote to Frances Elliot (*Letters* 11.338 [20 March 1867]). "Fenian alarms" withstood the business-as-usual complacency of the English writer and celebrity with Fenian arms.

Joyce comes from that troublesome city across the Irish Sea seething with sworn enemies of the British Lion. He also comes later than Dickens, not to mention Defoe. Dublin itself is an old city, but times had changed so that new opportunities for new exploration of metropolitan modernity were opening up, as the Irish capital no longer retained its exclusive colonial character of the eighteenth-century Ascendancy Dublin. The majority of the inhabitants now belonged to another, subordinate racial-sectarian category, the Irish Catholics, including the Joyce clan themselves who originally hailed from Cork. Belatedness has its benefits, too, for it allows one to reflect critically on the predecessors' works. As he was working on his novels in Trieste, Joyce wrote literary criticism either for publication or for lecture (or both), some of which make direct references to Defoe and Dickens. A quick survey of these textual records may serve as a mediating link between the first two parts of this book and the third devoted to Joyce.

In his lectures on "Realism and Idealism in English Literature" delivered to Italian audience in Italian at the Università Popolare di Trieste, Joyce credits Defoe rather than Shakespeare, "an Italianised Englishman" (*un'inglese italianizzato*), as the first properly English author, because Defoe was able, "without copying or adapting foreign works, to create without literary models, to instill a truly national spirit into the creations of his pen" (*Occasional, Critical, and Political Writings* [hereafter *OCPW*] 164/270). Whether his individualist characters stranded on remote foreign lands or shuttling between England and abroad can be considered "national" may be debatable. Less so is their otherwise hardy adherence to the dictates, perspective, and the rights of what we have called the "private sphere," which England, or at least London, fostered. However, what Joyce means by this encomium is revealed towards the end of the lecture. In *Robinson Crusoe*, above all, he sees the embodiment of "the cautious and heroic instinct of the rational being and the prophecy of the empire":

> The true symbol of the British conquest is Robinson Crusoe who, shipwrecked on a lonely island, with a knife and a pipe in his pocket, becomes an architect, carpenter, knife-grinder, astronomer, and cleric. He is the true prototype of the British colonist just as Friday (the faithful savage who arrives one ill-starred day) is the symbol of the subject race. All the Anglo-Saxon soul is in Crusoe; virile independence, unthinking cruelty, persistence, slow yet effective intelligence, sexual apathy, practical and well-balanced religiosity, calculating dourness. (*OCPW* 174)

Joyce speaks as an Irishman of the "British colonist" foreshadowed in the foundational author of British (colonial) modernity. Defoe indeed advocates, with a veritable "calculating dourness," as much colonization of the world's tribes as possible, urging his countrymen to penetrate "all the remote Parts, where it is proper and practicable, to civilize and instruct the Savages and Natives of those Countries" (*PEW* 7.302). Joyce's postcolonial interpretation of *Robinson Crusoe* rings wholesomely true, even without such auxiliary proof drawn from Defoe's statements. Yet what of the "faithful savage" whom the master seeks "to civilize and instruct"? If he is the "symbol of the subject race," does it not make him also a figurative representative of Joyce's own "subject race," the Irish Catholics? The answer, implied in his lecture introducing Irish history, "Ireland: Island of Saints and Sages," tilts towards the affirmative: "A conqueror cannot be amateurish, and what England did in Ireland over the centuries is no different from what the Belgians are doing today in the Congo Fee State, and what the Nipponese dwarfs will be doing tomorrow in some other lands. She inflamed the factions and took possession of the wealth" (*OCPW* 119). Yet "bitter invectives against England" do little to counter the skilled English exploitation of Ireland, as long as one does not come to terms with the "tyranny of Rome" that "still holds the dwelling place of the soul [*occupa il palazzo dell'anima*]" (125/259). Physical master and spiritual dictator each stationed in its palazzo is an image which Stephen Dedalus thrusts at the Englishman Haines in the first episode of *Ulysses*:

> —I am a servant of two masters, Stephen said, an English and an Italian.
> —Italian? Haines said.
>
> ....
>
> —The imperial British state, Stephen answered, his colour rising, and the holy Roman catholic and apostolic church. (1.638-39, 644)[2]

As is readily noticeable, Joyce in *Dubliners* and *A Portrait of the Artist as a Young Man* (hereafter *Portrait*) took on the latter master with particular relish and vehemence, to the point of leading some readers to attribute the famous "paralysis" of Dubliners solely to Catholicism, thus exonerating the first and surely the more formidable master.

Merely fulminating against the English does little to stop them, Joyce remarks. Nor would it do to boast that "ancient Ireland" used to be more civilized than the England, for that dubious past glory is just as "dead" as "ancient Egypt." "Today other bards, inspired by other ideals, have their turn" (*OCPW* 125), asserts the as yet little known aspiring bard himself. Again, in "Telemachus," the supposedly authentically native dairy lady delivering milk to Stephen's Martello Tower has lost complete touch with her ancestor's tongue. Haines the Saxon interested in Celtic Irishness speaks Gaelic to her, to which she responds, "Is it French you are talking, sir?" (1.425). Not only did Joyce pay (some of) his bills teaching English as a "native speaker" and British subject in Trieste, but for all other purposes, too, English had become the only real language available for the

Irish, even for someone as talented, bold, and unusual as Joyce himself. In the more experimental episodes of *Ulysses* such as "Sirens" or "Circe" the linguistic territory of English is stretched to its utmost limits, and in *Finnegans Wake*, which occupied his working hours after *Ulysses*, Joyce speaks both English and anti-English. English becomes something less or more than itself in his last novel, as we can see in the opening sentences of the novel's third chapter:

> Chest Cee! 'Sdens! Corpo di barragio! you spoof of visibility in a freakfrog, of mixed sex cases among goats, hill cat and plain mousey, Bigamy Bob and his old Shanvocht! The Blackfriars treacle plaster outrage be liddled! (*Finnegans* 48)

The language of the other "Italian" master intrudes on the scene, but English holds its ground despite the contortions. To the end of his life, Joyce wrestled with the chronic "language question," summed up succinctly by Stephen in the last chapter of *Portrait*. In front of the English-Catholic Dean of Studies at his university, he becomes pensive, as he reflects on how English is not quite his mother tongue:

> The language in which we are speaking is his before it is mine. How different are the words home, Christ, ale, master, on his lips and on mine! I cannot speak or write these words without unrest of spirit. His language, so familiar and so foreign, will always be for me an acquired speech. (*Portrait* 159)

Using English as a familiar yet foreign tongue was the strategy Joyce chose to counteract its innate claim to superiority over its colonial accents. The presence of the word "master" in the list of sample words in Stephen's thought is in keeping with the parallel assumed to exist between English colonialism in Ireland and that of Belgians in the Congo, and also his lucid detection of the colonial spirit in Defoe's Robinson Crusoe.

It is worth noting, in this context, that Defoe himself first experimented with making English something other than itself in presenting the speech of Crusoe's Moorish "Boy" Xury, and later, the savage-turned-servant Friday. Coming in a book published in 1719, during the hey-day of "Augustan" neoclassicism, Xury's speech—as in "*then we give them the shoot Gun . . . make them run wey*" (*Crusoe* 23)—is a stunning linguistic deviation indeed, reflecting perhaps the fact that broken Creole English could be heard fairly easily in Defoe's London, as spoken "by immigrant, poorer city dwellers, the servants and slaves" (Wright 630). Friday's broken English, furthermore, serves to characterize the peculiar but plausible blending of his indigenous simplicity with a profitably blind devotion to the master. When his "master" bids him go back to his tribe, Friday waxes eloquent in angry and tearful protest:

> *Why, you angry mad with* Friday, *what me done? . . . No angry! No angry! . . . Why send* Friday *home away to my Nation? . . . Yes, yes, . . . wish be both there, no wish* Friday *there, no Master there. . . You take, kill* Friday . . . *take, kill* Friday, *no send* Friday *away.* (*Crusoe* 190-1)

Passionately devoted to his master as Friday may be, he does not care as much about the grammar of his master's language. English is "broken" literally here, yet in that failure to be properly English, a new identity articulates itself, one that cannot simply be laughed off, for it carries a power of persuasion strong enough to convince his "master" to retain him. It would not do, of course, to pull down the elaborate and sophisticated belabouring of English in Joyce, such as the quote from *Finnegans Wake* above, to the bare, naked minimalist English of Friday, yet a precedent is set by Defoe, the first genuinely "English" novelist.[3] This heritage of Friday's free appropriation of English is one that *Ulysses* inherits and subverts. In "Hades," Bloom's thoughts wander off to Crusoe's desert island and his faithful servant: "Say Robinson Crusoe was true to life. Well then Friday buried him. Every Friday buries a Thursday if you come to look at it" (6.810-12). The master becomes "Thursday," not a bit stronger than his "Man Friday," who buries Crusoe-Thursday and, in this scenario, takes possession of the island. Joyce, similarly, absorbs, buries, and embeds Defoe in his novel, not only in such protruding passages as Molly commenting on *Moll Flanders*—"I dont like books with a Molly in them like that one he brought me about the one from Flanders a whore always shoplifting anything she could cloth and stuff and yards of it" (18.657-59)—but in the Friday-like linguistic freedom he takes in using and abusing the "master" language of English.[4]

What Joyce learnt from Dickens can be inferred with a greater degree of certainty. In his unpublished manuscript submitted to the Università degli Studi di Padua, "The Centenary of Charles Dickens," he identifies Dickens's major strength as his attachment to London in the period around the First Reform Bill:

> If Dickens is to move you, you must not allow him to stray out of hearing of the chimes of Bow Bells. There he is on his native hearth and there are his kingdom and his power. The life of London is the breath of his nostrils: he felt it as no writer since or before his time felt it. The colours, the familiar noises, the very odours of the great metropolis unite in his works as in a mighty symphony wherein humour and pathos, life and death, hope and despair, are inextricably interwoven. (*OCPW* 184)

One may, without much distortion, substitute in this passage "Joyce" for "Dickens" and "Dublin" for "London," to underline the peculiarity of a writer who, even in his self-imposed European exile, never strayed out of his native city in his novels. To Joyce, the life of Dublin captured during a specific phase of the first decade of the twentieth century remained indeed "the breath of his nostrils." Both Dickens and Joyce were superbly reluctant to venture out of their cities to the countryside beyond. Bernard Benstock's verdict on Joyce, that "Joyce the Dubliner remained aloof and often contemptuous of Irish civilization outside the Pale" (Benstock 1), simplistic as it sounds, cannot be refuted. Also, the musical metaphor of "mighty symphony" suits Joyce's masterpiece *Ulysses* far better than it does Dickens. A Dublin project, comparable to Dickens's conquest of London, is being sketched out almost in the passage above. Dickensian inspiration also may have had a share in the comic excesses of *Ulysses*. The other forte of Dickens's art has to do with its caricature, Joyce argues, using the term in its "strict sense and without any malice" (185). The unforgettable characters that abound in Dickens all come with "one strongly marked or even exaggerated moral or physical quality" (185). In this consists his greatness rather than his weakness: "It is precisely by this little exaggeration that Dickens has influenced the spoken language of the inhabitants of the British Empire as no other writer since Shakespeare's time has influenced it" (186). Those affected by Dickens would obviously include Joyce, as evidenced by the much-noted similarity of his "Penelope" episode and Flora Finching's (and Mrs Gamp's) breathless speech (Kaplan 1968: 344-46; Bolton 245-48). Joyce exaggerated Dickensian exaggeration ad absurdum.

Other, relatively incidental echoes of Dickens in *Ulysses* can be identified, as well. In relation to *Bleak House*, rich with exaggerations at all levels, we find the appearance in "Wandering Rocks" of "Spontaneous combustion" in the narrative's reference to the burning of the steamer *General Slocum* in June 1904, which can be taken as a commentary on his predecessor's "journalism novel," discussed earlier. In a mildly outraged and amused tone the narrative refers to a newspaper report of a shocking incident that will soon be forgotten:

> Most brutal thing. What do they say was the cause? Spontaneous combustion. Most scandalous relevation. Not a single lifeboat would float and the firehose all burst. . . . Is that a fact? Without a doubt. Well now, look at that. And America they say is the land of the free. I thought we were bad here. (10.727-33)

"Is that a fact? Without a doubt," says "Mr Kernan," to whom these words are assigned, for so the newspaper says. Journalism, however, in "Aeolus" is found to be so much sound and fury signifying nothing. In one of the last headlines of the episode, questions are raised as to the veracity and specificity of a trivial "fact," to be answered by more questions that add up to pointless, meaningless gossip:

> WHAT? – AND LIKEWISE – WHERE?
>
> —But what do you call it? Myles Crawford asked. Where did they get the plums? (7.1050-52)

Unable or unwilling to be clarify the problems it raises, journalist rhetoric consumes itself in a manner analogous to the self-serving economy of spontaneous combustion of Dickens's Chancery. Not only this episode but the novel as a whole adopts a certain "journalistic" façade. Joyce's "journal" or one-day novel covers literally the sundry "facts" of a single day, more meticulous in its attention to details than any of the novels or journalistic essays of Dickens. Another echo of Dickens occurs in "Wandering Rocks" when the sartorial appearance of the dance master Maginni is given a Dickensian description reminiscent of the aging Regency dandy Mr. Turveydrop, to whose motto of "Deportment"[5] the narrator alludes: "Mr Denis J Maginni, professor of dancing & c, in silk hat, slate frockcoat with silk facings, white kerchief tie, tight lavender trousers, canary gloves and pointed patent boots, walking with grave deportment" (10.56-59). Later, in "Circe," Maginni adopts Turveydrop's motto as his own: "Fancy dress balls arranged. Deportment. The Katty Lanner step. So. Watch me!" (15.4043-44). Corley from *Dubliners*' "Two Gallants," who had regaled himself at a cheap Dublin eatery with "a plate of hot grocer's peas, seasoned with pepper and vinegar" washed down with "ginger beer" (*Dubliners* 42), reappears in "Eumaeus," his circumstances hardly improved. He borrows a halfcrown from Stephen, muttering words which encourage a comparison with Dickens's young crossing-sweeper: "I don't give a shite anyway so long as I get a job, even as a crossing sweeper" (16.203). In the same episode a reference is made to "circumlocution departments with the usual quantity of red tape and dillydallying of effete fogeydom and dunderheads generally" (16.534-36), which sounds like a "jazz" variation on a major theme in Dickens's *Little Dorrit*. At the level of style, too, Joyce pays homage to Dickens in "Wandering Rocks" by invoking a hallmark Dickensian device of repeating the characterizing word:

> Dust webbed the window and the showtrays. Dust darkened the toiling

> fingers with their vulture nails. Dust slept on dull coils of bronze and silver, lozenges of cinnabar, on rubies, leprous and winedark stones. (10.801-4)

Substitute "fog" for "dust" and one would instantly be reminded of the famous opening passage of *Bleak House*.[6] But the prose poem here takes lyricism one step further, garnishing the sentences with alliteration of "webbed the window" and with compound words creating syncopation through the trochee of "winedark," particularly in the sentence which precedes this "Dickensian" description: "Stephen Dedalus watched through the webbed window the lapidary's fingers prove a timedulled chain" (10.800). Alliteration of "w" is closed off with the trochaic "timedulled." This is sophisticated poetry more akin to the "sprung rhythm" of the English-born Jesuit poet Gerard Manley Hopkins than to Dickens's relatively predictable refrains, but it was Dickens who set the example of making the prose of novels dance with poetry.

Scattered and mostly incidental echoes of Dickens in *Ulysses*, however, are less important in themselves than for what they do in the novel in each particular context. Both "The Wandering Rocks" and "Eumaeus" are atypical of the rest of the novel in that they employ an apparently plain third-person narrative format perfected by the great masters (and mistresses) of the nineteenth century such as Dickens and George Eliot. Yet the very mode itself is put on stage by Joyce, in "Eumaeus" especially, by using it excessively to the point of robbing it of any novelty or freshness through a style of studied clumsiness. Allusions to Dickens in *Ulysses* suggest Joyce's recognitions of Dickens's importance but they also function as negative foils shedding light on Joyce's distinctive narrative artistry of interior monologue, which at once embraces and collapses the dialectic of the subjective immediacy of *Erlebnis* and the objective reflection of *Erfahrung*. To discuss this aspect of Joyce's artistry, however, we first have to look further east across the Channel, rather than lingering with English precedents.

"Indifferent, paring his fingernails"

Born to a Catholic family and educated outside Trinity College, Joyce was placed beyond the pale of the Anglo-Irish Trinity-bred literati, who had perversely assumed and usurped the right to define Irishness as archaic and hence politically innocuous "Celtic twilight" in their "Irish Literary Renaissance." Pitted against this dominant group, he had to look somewhere else for his allies. Internally exiled even before leaving his country, Joyce followed in the footsteps of Irish Catholic elites of the past centuries who had fled to France and other Catholic European countries. When he saw no chance of standing up single-handed to the combined forces of class, race, and influence, led by talented writers such as Yeats and Synge, paying tribute with his feet to the "Flight of the Wild Geese," he left Ireland behind to roam European cities for the remainder of his life. Paris, rather than Dublin or London, served as his virtual "home" until France fell to Nazi Germany. Yet discussion of Joyce's relationship to European literature has been too much overshadowed by the supposedly decisive influence of Henrik Ibsen on early Joyce's "naturalism" (attested to by *Dubliners*), even when the importance of Gustave Flaubert for Joyce is admitted (see Budgen 179-80; Reichart 61-62). This bias may be due in large part to the fact that the young Joyce's only published review in a London magazine (*Fortnightly Review*, 1 April 1900) deals with Ibsen ("Ibsen's New Drama"), where he asks hyperbolically, "whether any man has held so firm an empire over the thinking world in modern times" (*OCPW* 30). And then there is Richard Ellmann who tells us that "Joyce proved Ibsen's superiority to Shakespeare," while talking to a Viennese in Zürich (Ellmann 398). Ibsen, however, is a playwright, obviously enough, and not a novelist. Whatever Joyce the novelist may have learnt from Ibsen would not have included any specific techniques or skills pertaining to prose fiction. Now, an equally obvious feature of Joyce's novelistic habit is his avoidance of quotation marks, from *Dubliners* on, in indicating a character's speech. He uses dashes instead, which is to impose French publishing conventions on English prose. Surely, the controlled reticence of *Dubliners* seems akin to the impersonal and impassive ethos of Continental naturalism that is quite different from the verbose and opinionated narrators of Victorian novels. Yet *Dubliners* and *Portrait* maintain a careful modulation of narrator's commentary and neutral reportage largely through free indirect speech. This is something perfected by Flaubert and certainly not by Ibsen.

To take one short passage from *Dubliners*, here is Little Chandler of "A Little Cloud" nursing his wounded pride after meeting his old friend Gallaher:

> A dull resentment against his life awoke within him. Could he not escape from his little house? Was it too late for him to try to live bravely like Gallaher? Could he go to London? There was the furniture still to be paid for. If he could only write a book and get it published, that might open the way for him. (*Dubliners* 63)

The first informative sentence slides into indirect speech replicating the character's perspective, sentiment, and language (such as "live bravely"), which the narrator distinguishes from his own language, but without wedging in quotation marks into them or italicizing them. It thus articulates the narrative's qualified sympathy for the pathetic character. Joyce's effort to tread a fine line between closeness and aloofness stands in clear contrast to the garrulous narrator of *Middlemarch*, for instance, commanding the reader to make allowances for Dorothea, now widowed, as she meets Will Ladislaw again:

> But the mixture of anger in her agitation had vanished at the sight of him; she had been used, when they were face to face, always to feel confidence and the happy freedom which comes with mutual understanding, and how could other people's words hinder that effect on a sudden? Let the music which can take possession of our frame and fill the air with joy for us, sound once more—what does it signify that we heard it found fault with in its absence? (Eliot 1997: 592)

Joyce would never ask, "Why should Little Chandler, with his furniture still to be paid for, not indulge in a dream of escape, of success in London?" Instead, he lets the character articulate his thoughts in his own language, which George Eliot is averse to do. It is almost as if the narrator hushes Dorothea, just as she is about to reveal to herself (and to the reader) her inner feelings. Joyce clearly does not inherit this legacy of chaperoned narration. Nor does he abandon his characters to swallow their unspeakable woes by themselves, as does Hardy in *Jude the Obscure* (1895). In what would arguably be the novel's most pitifully gruesome scene, the elder son of Jude had just strangled his siblings and then killed himself, with the laconic message, "Done because we are too meny." The narrator, however, merely reports the parents' reaction, without caring to enter their distraught mind:

> Half paralyzed by the strange and consummate horror of the scene he let Sue lie, cut the cords with his pocket-knife and threw the three children on the bed; but the feel of their bodies in the momentary handling seemed to say that they were dead. He caught up Sue, who was in fainting fits, and put her on the bed in the other room, after which he breathlessly summoned the landlady and ran out for a doctor. (Hardy 325)

Hardy's last novel has more affection for the characters than the cold-blooded hard-boiled world of Hemingway, an offshoot of naturalism, yet the passage does seem to be heading in that direction. At stake here is a crisis of experience, of *Erlebnis* in particular, for the shock of the "strange and consummate horror" petrifies the subject's psychological response. Experience as *Erfahrung* is also hampered, for although an indictment of ruthless class society can be filed on the basis of this passage, the incident (as well as the relationship between Jude and Sue) is far too extreme to be representative of the "too meny" who are dispossessed. Joyce can be held responsible for many uncomfortable novelties, but indulgence in violent tragedy surely is not one of them.

Nothing eventful takes place in Joyce's *Portrait* but then its real drama unfolds in its language, which "grows" along with Stephen, as it were, stage by stage. For instance, the narrator's language by no means imposes itself on that of the young, adolescent, and sophomoric protagonist. To take a fairly plain example, here is the pre-adolescent Stephen at Clongowes, punished unjustly by Father Dolan. Painful as Dolan's pandybat on his palms was, it is his pride that suffers even more, which the narrative captures in a style attuned to the young pupil's vocabulary and syntax:

> It was wrong; it was unfair and cruel: and, as he sat in the refectory, he suffered time after time in memory the same humiliation until he began to wonder whether it might not really be that there was something in his face which made him look like a schemer and he wished he had a little mirror to see. But there could not be; and it was unjust and cruel and unfair.
>
> He could not eat the blackish fish fritters they got on Wednesdays in lent and one of his potatoes had the mark of the spade in it. Yes, he would do what the fellows had told him. He would go up and tell the rector that he had been wrongly punished. A thing like that had been done before by somebody in history, by some great person whose head was in the books of history. And the rector would declare that he had been wrongly punished because the senate and the Roman people always declared that the men who did that had been wrongly punished. (*Portrait* 44-45)

The text distributes sufficient indications throughout of its being a free indirect speech rather than a conventional third-person narrative. In addition to the simple "childish" words and phrases, and the paratactic conjunction overly relying on "and," the repetitions of "unfair," "cruel," "wrong," "wrongly punished" serve to underscore the mentality of young Stephen. The second sentence of the second paragraph, starting with a "Yes," which foreshadows the later celebrated "Yes" of "Penelope," aligns the narrator with the character. Linked arm in arm by the conditional "would do" and "would go," the narrator and the character march together to the rector in a "Roman" spirit of public heroism, as conceived by the young school boy's rudimentary and imprecise book-learning about the "senate and the Roman people." At this level of moderated, half-sympathetic, half-detached presentation of the character's views, sentiments, and limitations—so different both from the Dickensian technique of reducing a person's identity to a single trait and from the sort of learned commentary on a character's moral worth that George Eliot specializes in—Joyce's narrator practices the ideal of the artist remaining, in the words of Stephen now a university student, "within or behind or beyond or above his handiwork, invisible, refined out of existence, indifferent, paring his fingernails" (*Portrait* 181). Stephen's words allude to Flaubert's remarks in his letters, and Flaubert's style deserves a closer look.

Whether an "artist" can be "invisible" or "indifferent," hiding "within or behind or beyond" the words he writes is a question not so much of aesthetic philosophy as of narrative technique, a question, that is, of whether the writer can succeed in not leaving visible marks of his personal commitment or judgment in the manner of Victorian novelists. Joyce the author is invisible despite the heavily autobiographical details that make up the life of Stephen, yet his "indifference" is a tactful artistic device, learned from Flaubert, as the allusion above to the French master's correspondence seems to acknowledge. But one has to examine the prose style of Flaubert's fiction to fully appreciate the French writer's virtuosity. We take a passage from *Madame Bovary*, where Emma muses on the memories of her passion with her lover, with sweet and partly bitter regret:

> La rivière coulait toujours, et poussait lentement ses petits flots le long de la berge glissante. Ils s'y étaient promenés bien des fois, à ce même murmure des ondes, sur les cailloux couverts de mousse. Quels bons soleils ils avaient eus! quelles bonnes après-midi, seuls, à l'ombre, dans le fond du jardin! Il lisait tout haut, tête nue, posé sur un tabouret de batons secs; le vent frais de la prairie faisait trembler les pages du livre et les capucines de la tonnelle. . . Ah! il était parti, le seul charme de sa vie, le seul espoir possible d'une félicité! Comment n'avait-elle pas saisi ce bonheur-là, quand il se présentait! Pourquoi ne l'avoir pas retenu à deux mains, à deux genoux, quand il voulait s'enfuir? (Flaubert 157-58)

> (The river still flowed on, its ripples lapping slowly against the slippery bank. There they had so often strolled, listening to that same water murmuring over those same moss-covered stones. How brightly the sun had shone on them! How lovely their afternoons had been, alone in the shade at the bottom of the garden! He, sitting bare-headed on a rustic wooden stool, would read to her, the fresh breeze from the meadows ruffling the pages of his book, and the nasturtiums growing round the arbour. . . Ah! He was gone, the only light of her life, her only possible hope of any happiness! Why had she not grasped that happiness when it lay within her reach? Why had she not held onto him, with both her hands, on her knees, when he tried to leave? [Mauldon translation 110])

The first two sentences apparently initiate a conventional third-person narration, the first describing the locus and the second specifying its personal significance for the character. Yet the third shifts gear with a sudden "Quels bons soleils ils avaient eus!" fortified by an exclamation mark, to enter her subjectivity. Her reminiscence that follows sustains the openness of *passé imparfait* enabling the interchange or convergence between the narrator's informative statements and the character's subjective thoughts. The language used here, moreover, is saturated by *mots justes* not in any absolute sense surely, but in the relative, dramatic sense of their being Emma's kind of language, expressive of her own limited viewpoints and sentiments. In Flaubert, the subjective *Erlebnis* of the character, rendered into a communicable *Erfahrung* for others, achieves a polyphonic synthesis, singing two melodies and two registers simultaneously. English novels do not lack comparable examples to compete with Flaubert's *style indirect libre*, yet the difference in degree and effectiveness is undeniable. French prose permits a more unhampered usage of emotive punctuations and paratactic connections via semicolons. Above all, the verbal modality of *passé imparfait* has a nuance the monotone English past tense cannot replicate. This also means that the English language which Joyce had to use, in its "normal" shape, would resist his artistic ambition to be at once engaging and indifferent, visible and invisible. A notably Flaubertian passage in *Portrait*, such as the following, shows the strain of the more factual-logical-substantial language of Ireland's colonial master being stretched to imitate the language of Flaubert:

> Where was his boyhood now? Where was the soul that had hung back from her destiny, to brood alone upon the shame of her wounds and in her house of squalor and subterfuge to queen it in faded cerements and in wreaths that withered at the touch? Or where was he?
>
> He was alone. He was unheeded, happy and near to the wild heart of life. He was alone and young and willful and wildhearted, alone amid a waste of wild air and brackish waters . . . (*Portrait* 144)

Just about to be graced with the *Erlebnis* or "epiphany" of being captivated by a wading girl, Stephen's language wants to work itself up into lyrical elation. But the difficulties he faces is dramatized by the excessive repetition of "alone" or "wild" as well as of the deadpan single-note verb of "was," which lacks the multiple hints and suggestions of French past tense.

Right after Stephen apparently relishes the felicitous formulation of the ideal artist paring his fingernails, which he believes is his own but comes from Flaubert, his interlocutor Lynch blurts out, "What do you mean . . . by prating about beauty and the imagination in this miserable Godforsaken island? No wonder the artist retired within or behind his handiwork after having perpetrated this country" (181). Stephen (like Joyce) seeks to devise a way out of this impasse of the politically cramped colony eroding the autonomy of art. Yet a verbal "artist" can never escape from the labyrinth of politics, as long as he cowers before the colonial master's language. The way out is hinted towards the end of *Portrait*, in the sentence fragments of Stephen's diary, starting again in the language and manner of Pepys, as it were, articulating the voice of privacy, resettling the relationship between the private and the public realms through a more aberrant, deviant, and disobedient "English":

> Went to library. Tried to read three reviews. Useless. She is not out yet. Am I alarmed? About what? That she will never be out again. (*Portrait* 210)

The continuity between the last part of *Portrait* and *Ulysses* is announced by the signature towards the end of the former, "Dublin 1904 / Trieste 1914," and the triad of cities "Trieste-Zurich-Paris" at the end of the latter. In a sense *Portrait* also erects a triad of alliances, languages, and cities, of "Dublin-Trieste-Paris." From Paris if not as an address of residence, clearly as the capital of literary-textual republic, a different, alternative tradition could be tapped by Joyce, the "artist" stationed far off in the remote borderline location of Trieste, as he attempted to mould the language of Dublin's colonizers into new shapes and forms.

Stephen in *Ulysses* steps out onto the scene as a hybrid schizoid subject of *Erlebnis*, heralding in a new stage in the trajectory of "Flaubertian" free indirect style, which gave the reader a "fuller access to Stephen's consciousness via the interior monologue" (Cross 78) than Flaubert's narration. Furthermore, his "consciousness" converses in a version of familiar yet foreign English which appears at once something less and more than what it is:

> Stephen closed his eyes to hear his boots crush cackling wrack and shells. You are walking through it howsomever. I am, a stride at a time. A very short space of time through very short times of space. Five, six: the *Nacheinander*. (3.10-13)

The first sentence seemingly carries on the usual business of fictional prose of indicating what the character is doing, although the alliteration and internal rhyme of "closed," "crush," "cackling" and "wrack" create a more heightened poetic prose which no prose writer in the language before him ever dared or bothered to attempt. In doing so Joyce's sentence highlights the "Anglo-Saxon" roots of English, making it less familiar, turning back the clock to its atavistic past, unhooking it from its present seat of empowered language of the empire. It encapsulates the obdurate strangeness of English from the perspective of one for whom it is neither a native nor a foreign tongue. The second sentence, on the other hand, stumbles on its last word, "howsomever," which treads the borderline of received grammar (while allocating itself a greater, double sense not available in standard usage), as does the comma inserted after "I am" in the sentence that follows it. There could not possibly be a simpler means of disrupting the order and security of English than this disjuncture inserted between "I am" and the predicate, "a stride at a time." The principle of disjunctive conjunction, which we have earlier traced as pertaining to the conditions of the metropolis, now penetrates the very syntax of English, not only dramatizing the intermediary and interlinked experience of Stephen, but pushing the language off from its imperial homeland to the hyphenated interstices between colonial and foreign cities of Dublin-Paris-Zurich. "A very short space . . . times of space" rejects any predicate, or alternatively, it stands as a predicate of an absent subject, constituting in either case an absurd wordplay, or a "profound" philosophical conundrum, if one wishes to take it as such. All in all, the sudden striking movement from the normal-looking first sentence of the paragraph to those representing the subject's state of mind follows the model of Flaubert's narration. The styles of Dublin and Paris are thus hyphenated. Zurich, the German-speaking city, leaves its signature at the end, "Nacheinander" ("one by one"), appended to the equally deviant "Five, six" plus colon occupying the subject position of the sentence.

The estranged and estranging novelty of this and other passages in "Proteus," such as the "whitemaned seahorses, champing, brightwindbridled, the steeds of Mananaan" (3.57), which glues two or more words together at will, becomes even more conspicuous when compared with Virginia Woolf's first (and one of the boldest) exertions in experimental writing:

> The magnificent world—the live, sane, vigorous world. . . . These words refer to the stretch of wood pavement between Hammersmith and Holborn in January between two and three in the morning. That was the ground beneath Jacob's feet. It was healthy and magnificent because one room, above a mews, somewhere near the river, contained fifty excited, talkative, friendly people. And then to stride over the pavement (there was scarcely a cab or policeman in sight) is of itself exhilarating. (Woolf 152-53)

Thus in *Jacob's Room*, published in the same year as *Ulysses* and written by an author born and dead in the same years as Joyce, the form and plot deviate from the conventional norms of English novels. The language and the narration, however, do not stray too far from the technique of focalized presentation of characters' perspective balanced against topographical information, which Woolf's predecessors from Jane Austen to George Eliot frequently employ. Moreover, Jacob and her author have their feet on the ground, on the streets of their "magnificent" and "exhilarating" metropolis. Their London is essentially the same city in which Defoe and Dickens lived, wrote, and were part of. The place names Hammersmith and Holborn tower over the scene as literally "proper" nouns spanning and securing that leafy part of London as that which is proper to those who feel at home there. The city's uniqueness, character, and prestige, although far more subdued than in Dickens, constitute the essential backdrop of the actions and thoughts of the protagonist who is present in the passage in his proper-noun capacity. Jacob meets his early death in World War I, but the space (as well as the novel) retains his name, "Jacob's room." When he was alive, London used to be his, too, "Jacob's city."

The case with Stephen, however, is not as felicitous. "Porteus" dramatizes his soliloquy as he stands stuck on the non-property of Sandymount Strand beach: "Unwholesome sandflats waited to suck his treading soles, breathing upward sewage breath, a pocket of seaweed smouldered in seafire under a midden of man's ashes" (3.150-52). Sullied with the refuse of history, memory, offals, and a dead dog's carcass, he is stationed on a location that belongs neither exclusively to the English conquerors who had landed from the seas on the beach, nor to the ancient local Gaelic god Mananaan MacLir. The language used here would not allow Stephen to communicate with the latter, but the voice that speaks standard English does not fully represent Stephen either, as the previous episode with his anglophile employer Deasy shows. To Deasy's smug anti-Semitist remarks, Stephen's mute monologue responds by not responding:

> —They sinned against the light, Mr Deasy said gravely. And you can see the darkness in their eyes. And that is why they are wanderers on the earth to this day.
>
> On the steps of the Paris stock exchange the goldskinned men quoting prices on their gemmed fingers. Gabble of geese. They swarmed loud, uncouth, about the temple, their heads thickplotting under maladroit silk hats. Not theirs: these clothes, this speech, these gestures. (2.361-67)

"Not theirs . . . this speech" implies, "not mine this language of Deasy, which speaks itself through me," which, therefore, has to be made something different, something else, to be made his own, as in "goldskinned," "thickplotting" and "Gabble of geese." The memory of Paris also serves as crucial counterforce to Deasy's views. Speaking to himself from "Dublin-Paris," Stephen enacts not merely a Flaubertian *style indirect libre* but what came to be called "interior monologue." This, we contend, was initiated by another Parisian author, much less celebrated but one who deserves proper recognition: Édouard Dujardin.

Les Lauriers sont coupés

Between Flaubert and Joyce, Dublin and Paris, *Portrait* and *Ulysses* comes Dujardin. According to Ellmann, at a railway bookstall Joyce ran almost by accident into Dujardin's *Les Lauriers sont coupés*, which he avidly relished and studied (Ellmann 126). This is more than a passing episode in his life, and Joyce's respect for Dujardin needs emphasis, for it still tends to be stinted of full critical recognition. Walter Gabler leaves him out entirely in his preface to *The Lost Notebook* (Gabler i-x), while the collection of conference papers celebrating Joyce's French connections *Joyce et Paris 1902 ... 1920-1940 ... 1975* merely lists Dujardin's novel among "the books Joyce made reference to while in residence in Paris" with no separate article discussing its significance for him (*Joyce et Paris* 117-18). A critic studying Joyce's prose style such as John Porter Houston must surely come to terms with Dujardin's influence on Joyce, yet interestingly, Houston takes pains to disparage Dujardin's interior monologue as belonging to the "numerous crank attempts" of Joyce's "more naïve contemporaries" (Houston 102). Joyce himself shared no such contempt of later Joyceans for the French writer. Ellmann reports the private remarks Joyce made in his favour (Ellmann 95, 126). But a more crucial evidence is his letter written in 1917, that is, while he was still working on *Ulysses*, from Zürich to the French author, in which he introduces himself as "one who truly admires" his work and asks him to send him a copy of *Les Lauriers*, which he left at Trieste (*Letters* 2: 409). The letter was not delivered (Ellmann 411), yet it bears witness to the importance of the French novel for Joyce. Stuart Gilbert, who translated Dujardin and was a close associate of Joyce, had high opinion of the author as the first to experiment with interior monologue (Gilbert 10). Above all, Dujardin himself was grateful for Joyce's avowed recognition of what the Irish writer had learned from him, as we read in the latter's monograph, *Le Monologue intérieur*, where Dujardin acknowledges that Joyce perfected the technique whose innovation he nevertheless wished to receive credit for (Dujardin 1931: 20), even though the prevalent tendency is still to attribute it to André Gide (Lernout 34).

What in *Les Lauriers sont coupés* attracted the attention of Joyce can be demonstrated without difficulty. In this short novel, the reader overhears the passing thoughts and sentiments of a young male protagonist, a Parisian flâneur with money to spend and not committed to any occupation or relationship, as he moves about the metropolis. In what follows, he enters a restaurant and waits for his meal to arrive:

> Ainsi, je vais dîner; rien là de déplaisant. Violà une assez jolie femme; ni brune ni blonde; ma foi, air choisi; elle doit être grande; c'est la femme de cet homme chauve qui me tourne le dos. Sa maîtresses plutôt; elle n'a pas trop les façons d'une femme légitime; assez jolie, certes. Si elle pouvait regarder par ici; elle est presque en face de moi; comment faire? A quoi bon? Elle m'a vu. Elle est jolie; et ce monsieur paraît stupide; malheureusement je ne vois de lui que le dos; je voudrais bien connaître aussi sa figure; c'est un avoué, un notaire de province; suis-je bête! Et le consommé? La glace devant moi reflète le cadre doré; le cadre doré qui est donc derrière moi; ces enluminures sont vermillonnées, les feux de teintes écarlates; c'est le gaz tout jaune clair qui allume les murs; jaunes aussi du gaz, les nappes blanches, les glaces, les verreries. On est commodément; confortablement. Voici le consommé, le consommé fumant; attention à ce que le garçon ne m'en éclabousse rien. Non; mangeons. (Dujardin 1981: 12).

> (So I'm going to dine, and a very good idea too. Now that's a pretty woman over there; neither fair nor dark; a high-stepper, by gad; tallish, probably; must be the wife of that bald man with his back to me; more likely his mistress; somehow she hasn't just the married air; quite a pretty girl, really. She might look this way; almost exactly opposite me she is; what shall I? Oh, what's the good? There, she's spotted me. Really a pretty woman, and the man looks a bore; a pity I can only see his back; I'd like to have a look at his face too; lawyer, I should say, a family solicitor up from the country. Absurd I am! How about the soup? The glass in front reflects the gilded frame; the gilded frame behind me of course; those arabesques in bright vermilion, all scarlet flashes; but the light is pale yellow; walls, napery, mirrors, wineglasses, all yellowed by the gaslight. It's comfortable here, well-appointed place. Here's the soup, piping hot; waiter might splash some, better keep an eye on him. All's well; let's begin. [Dujardin 1938: 21-22])[7]

As one can see in this passage, in the way the sentences shift back and forth from first-person to third-person subject positions (e.g. "je vais diner" to "elle doit être grande"), the focalized descriptions accentuated by personalized punctuations of question marks and exclamation points, as well as the topic of detached yet wavering unrequited desire, all indicate that the novelistic stance of Dujardin (like many other French novelists coming after Flaubert) derives from the great master of free indirect speech. Yet unlike in the fastidious prose of Flaubert (or of *Portrait*, Joyce's most "Flaubertian" novel) the conjunction of details, paratactically added to one another by semicolons, are discrete, disjunctive, and digressive. The very first sentence makes one expect that the narrator would write on matters gastronomic, but eros intervenes, distracting him without guiding his desire to the woman, as it further slips to the miscellaneous facts of the restaurant's interior. The transition or the lack of it between the woman, his male partner, the ordered food, and back to the restaurant's interior dramatizes not so much an *Erlebnis* of the subject as its constant failure: his sensations are dispersed instead of being drawn into one impressive moment or tableau. Such paragraph formed entirely of disjunctive conjunctions that enervate the subject's capacity for sensory *Erlebnis*, much less a "moral" reflection on it as an *Erfahrung*, was attempted first by Dujardin. It flourished most spectacularly in Joyce's momentous metropolitan novel.

Ulysses, of course, is a long, complex, encyclopedic novel containing something much more than Dujardinian interior monologue. Newspeak in "Aeolus," drama-novel in "Circe," catechism in "Ithaca," a virtual anthology of English prose styles in "Oxen of the Sun," as well as the (deceptively) conventional third-person narratives of "Eumaeus" and "Cyclops," each addresses the question of how "English" a novel by a self-exiled Irish-Catholic author writing in Europe can or should be. The overhaul of English prose history in "Oxen of the Sun" alone, or the schizoid fantasy of shifting identities and realities in "Circe" (inspired in large part by Flaubert's *La Tentation de Saint Antoine*) protrude as monuments to a literary-stylistic will-to-power exercised over the inherited (and imposed) tradition of English prose fiction whose towering landmarks include Defoe and Dickens. But as far as the device of capturing the metropolitan experience from the standpoint of a self-absorbed but self-absent subject is concerned, the model of interior monologue provided by Dujardin echoes directly in those episodes depicting Bloom's peregrination in his city (episodes 4 to 6, 8, 11, and 13). The moment Bloom walks out of his house to begin his day, with a bellyful of pork kidney and after a happy stool, the narrative, after allotting the first couple of sentences to relating the action, moves straight into the character's thoughts, represented as a self-communicating monologue in the disjunctive and digressive manner of Dujardin:

> He crossed to the bright side, avoiding the loose cellarflap of number seventyfive. The sun was nearing the steeple of George's church. Be a warm day I fancy. Specially in these black clothes feel it more. Black conducts, reflects (refracts is it?), the heat. But I couldn't go in that light suit. Make a

picnic of it. His eyelids sank quietly often as he walked in happy warmth. Boland's breadvan delivering with trays our daily but she prefers yesterday's loaves turnovers crips crowns hot. Makes you feel young. Somewhere in the east: early morning: set off at dawn. Travel round in front of the sun, steal a day's march on him. Keep it up for ever never grow a day older technically. (4.77-76)

The compound words of the first sentence, "cellarflap" and "seventyfive" carry on the tense schizoid style of Stephen's monologue in "Proteus," but the relatively easy and simpler second sentence introduces the more mundane, physical realm of Bloom. His thoughts and feelings are first presented in normal English, but soon the subject of sentence is dropped ("Make a picnic of it," "Travel round in front of the sun"), and the character's mind begins to slide from one object or issue to another in an incidental, digressive, and disparate manner, as in Dujardin's restaurant scene.

The subject position of Bloom we shall discuss in chapter eleven below, yet what is clear for him, as well as for Stephen (and Joyce) is that English for this Jewish Dubliner is bound to be a foreign and familiar language, as he both belongs and does not belong (as others never fail to remind him) to the colonial capital, which in itself both is and is not an Irish city. The hyphenated local identity for Bloom holds a more tenuous and fragile lease than Stephen's, for no Dublin-Paris axis, no "Latin quarter hat" (1.519), can be summoned to bolster up his pride against a Deasy or the "Usurper" (1.744) Buck Mulligan. The relative security of the observations made by the young Parisian in Dujardin's restaurant scene contrasts itself to Bloom's disgust at other male Dubliners eating at "Burton restaurant," rife with "pungent meatjuice, slush of greens," to which he reacts with misanthropic derision: "See the animals feed. / Men, men, men" (8.651-53). Accompanying the disaffected as well as distracted Jew-Dubliner's solitary musings and muted self-discourse, Joyce takes the theme of the estranged urban subject first sketched by Dujardin and plays variations on it, running through all its chords and discords. The interior monologue of Joyce exposes "a certain diffusion or dilation of temporal experience" (Kumar 52), since time concedes no *Erlebnis* to the subject, as the slippery procession of sentences and sentence fragments dispels concentration on a single object or moment. This temporal diffusion has a clear spatial cause: Bloom's presence lacks the self-certainty of Dujardin's protagonist. Where he walks, eats, and rests is a tortuous question that follows him all throughout the novel.

Where walks Bloom? This question takes us to the next chapter where we will take a closer look at "his" city Dublin. But before we move on to that stage, we should also ask, where writes his author? "Trieste-Zurich-Paris / 1914-1921" is the final signature Joyce left on *Ulysses*. Whereas Trieste, Zürich, and Paris are indubitably real cities separately, no letter can be delivered to the compound address of "Trieste-Zurich-Paris." It is in between these cities, between English and other languages, that Joyce devised the many-voiced novel *Ulysses* (and later, *Finnegans Wake*). In Trieste he envisioned the work's shape and spirit, lecturing on Defoe and other masters of English literature, whose influence he could neither completely reject nor embrace as his own ancestry. The Trieste days are "without doubt the most important of all his life," according to Philippe Soupault, since "it was at this period that he detached himself definitively from our world in order to conceive the Joycean universe" (Soupault 110). The "Joycean universe," however, does have an anchorage in "our world," although no single city or nation can claim full allegiance or proprietary rights. *Ulysses* was published by an expatriate American bookseller in Left Bank Paris, "Shakespeare and Company / 12, Rue de l'Odéon, 12 / Paris / 1922," as the title page of the first edition states. Between Trieste and Paris the book came to shape, with the neutral Zürich providing a timely shelter to the wandering author during the First World War (Trieste belonged to Austrian empire at the time). The list of cities cannot stop here, however. Dublin acts almost as if it were the real protagonist of *Ulysses*. London, the capital of British Empire and the centre of English-language publishing business, draws its long shadow over Joyce, too, for it banished the first publication of the masterpiece to that obscure corner of the French capital, Rue de l'Odéon. "Trieste-Zurich-Paris," then, can be hyphenated further with "Dublin-Trieste-Zurich-(London)-Paris." Moreover, thanks to his indeterminate address between these cities and the respective traditions straddling and linking them, Joyce produced works that invite an internationalism of literary exchange. International cooperation, we recall, first came into being in the spirit of pursuing maximum profit, in the globalized city-system of international finance Defoe's Roxana benefitted from. The international network of the cities that enabled Joyce to subsist and create carries a utopian portfolio, however, since indigence, charity, and gift rather than profit, exchange, and business, take their place as the regular themes of Ellmann's biography of Joyce. When compared with Dickens's employment of European location and characters in his later novels such as *Little Dorrit* and *A Tale of Two Cities*, Joyce's *Ulysses* apparently is more insular as it tells stories of a single city Dublin, and a relatively small portion of it, at that, as we shall discuss in the next chapter. Yet its language, device, and technique hail from many other cities, including the London novels of Dickens.

But we must immediately modify our expression, "a single city Dublin," for this colonial capital can be singular but never quite single. "WHAT? – AND LIKEWISE – WHERE?", asks *Ulysses*. Which Dublin? Where in Dublin? The peculiar historical character of the host—if not the home—city Dublin has to be examined in greater detail, before we go further in our exploration of Joyce's heterogeneous metropolitan aesthetics.

CHAPTER TEN

DEAR DIRTY DUBLIN

"Hollandais? Non fromage. Deux irlandais"

In his letter sent to Sylvia Beach, the owner of the Parisian bookshop Shakespeare and Company that published *Ulysses*, Joyce comically alludes to his subjection to the British Empire, despite his exile:

> The British authorities, before exempting me from income tax on the ground of residence abroad, now want me to state my exact domicile. I have sent them a list of seven thousand addresses at which I resided since 1904. It seems I shall have to state a domicile in Paris and, as I cannot say that I have retained a room in the V. P. Hotel . . . I have no way out but to rent a room from you at 12 rue de l'Odéon. (Banta and Silverman 42-43)

Thousands of addresses for the author, yet the addresses of his novels know only one city: Dublin. Joyce left Ireland for good in 1904, but in his imaginative world he never left Dublin. Meanwhile, the Dublin of *Ulysses* and those works preceding it would largely disappear during the Easter Rising of 1916 (Duffy 37). Joyce's Dublin, frozen in time in the year of his last residence, 1904, nevertheless lived on, as a novelistic universe bustling, moving, stirring with life and foibles, enduring across the years, borders, and the numerous addresses of its chronicler's habitation. Dublin survived in Joyce's works, all the way to the digressive and dissonant world of *Finnegans Wake*. Exceptional in so many aspects, his final work nonetheless has not only an unmistakable "Gaelic"-Irish trajectory built into its framework as its title hints, but mixes its wordplay with local flavour, tuning on the key of "d" for Dublin (and drunkenness): "By the stench of her fizzle and the glib of her gab know the drunken draggletail Dublin drab" (*Finnegans* 436). Drunken, dirty, bedraggled Dublin, however, bids us to examine its historical profile, before we stroll around the town with Joyce.

Dublin in 1904 was a sickly, unwieldy, motley child of Victorian Dublin, with little left of the eighteenth-century Ascendency glamour it had once flaunted. Even the relatively resplendent Dublin of the eighteenth century, when compared with London or other major European capitals, had been predominantly a consumer city catering to the Anglo-Irish landlords who gathered there for society and pleasure (Cullen 1992: 262). Due to the relative weakness, if not virtual absence, of its indigenous burgher class of merchants and manufacturers, Dublin could not jump on to ride the tide of economic revolutions taking place towards the end of the eighteenth century. The downhill trend began in the 1820s, since after the Union with Britain in 1801 Westminster rather than Dublin became the high court of Irish politics (Somerville-Large 209). In the meantime, Belfast rose rapidly as a centre of manufacturing and shipbuilding to overshadow Dublin, where no competitive manufacturing hauled the city to join the Industrial Revolution (Cullen 1992: 271-77; O'Brien 9). By mid-nineteenth century, "Dublin had ceased to be 'the second city of the empire,' having been overtaken by Glasgow and Liverpool; two decades later Dublin ranked only fifth in a league of United Kingdom cities" (Hill 285). The decline of the colonial capital directly affected the Protestant elite of the city, who further suffered setback after the Catholic Emancipation (1829), which opened the doors to a significant and victorious Catholic presence in Dublin's streets, businesses, and municipal elections. Protestants voted with their feet by moving out to the suburbs beyond the jurisdiction of Dublin Corporation, notably Rathmines and Monkstown (Hill 382; Somerville-Large 216), forming a "number of prestigious pockets" (Somerville-Large 250) rigidly guarded against the encroaching masses of Catholics.

Although Dublin failed to profit from the manufacturing boom of the early nineteenth century, the city nonetheless benefitted from the other thrust of Industrial Revolution, the transport revolution, which was brought to Dublin by ambitious private entrepreneurs such as William Dargan, the organizer of the Great Dublin Exhibition of 1853 (Kilfeather 141; Somerville-Large 215). Metropolitan Dublin expanded thanks to the railways, but the central areas became increasingly derelict and déclassé. The north-eastern section of the city around Lower Gardiner Street and Summerhill, in particular, suffered most. Formerly a residential area for barristers, physicians, and other respectable professions, and often praised as "the real boast of the city," after these former residents crossed the Liffey to migrate to the southern suburbs, the district was taken over by lower-middle classes and sullied by the tenements and lodgings of the poor (O'Brien 12-14). The conditions of the Irish capital were quite shameful, even by contemporary standards. Streets reeked with horse dung and refuse, unemployment was almost a rule rather than an exception, and the mortality rate of Dublin enjoyed the unwelcome honour of being the highest among European and American metropolises in the last quarter of the nineteenth century (O'Brien 22, 67; Somerville-Large 264). Conditions were worsened as the poor flocked in from the countryside and spread out of the old slums of the Liberties to formerly respectable districts, transforming the city into a "metropolis for the poor" (O'Brien 7) who eked out a precarious living through casual labor in a stagnant "warehouse economy" (Kilfeather 141).

Is this insalubrious and infelicitous Dublin, then, the "home" of Joyce's novels, the permanent address haunting his thousand addresses? One is tempted to offer at least a tentative "yes" to this question, but it has to be a highly qualified affirmative. Dublin for Joyce always remained the Edwardian capital that existed before the Easter Rising, as we have pointed out earlier. But as important as this historical fixation is the boundary of his topography. Joyce dealt with this unappealing city and its glaring ills by turning away from the sites of both pompous affluence and abject poverty. "In geographical sense Joyce's Dublin was simply the Mountjoy Ward or more precisely that part of the Gardiner estate . . . which lay to the east of the line of O'Connell Street and North Frederick Street," Louis M. Cullen observes (Cullen 2009: 173). Outside this small segment of the inner city to the north of the river, "the vast comfortable districts spreading from Fitzwilliam Square southwards to Blackrock and Monkstown or south-westwards, served variously by railway and tram, to Terenure, is largely absent from Joyce's writing" (Cullen 2009: 178). That is, the portion of Dublin Joyce acknowledged as his own occupied the borderland between the South Side, boasting its stately Georgian Anglo-Irish squares, and the North Side, largely Catholic in character. In terms of social stratification, it precariously vegetated among the remnants of formerly affluent districts, which the Protestant middle classes had left many decades earlier, but which took pains to keep out of sight the squalid tenements near and around it. The extremes of the comfortable Anglo-Irish suburbs and the city's numerous slums, in sum, are erased from Joyce's map of metropolitan Dublin. To be fair, *Ulysses* summons some waifs of the urban poor or the representatives of the Protestant ruling block, as we shall discuss in this and subsequent chapters, but as a whole, Joyce's Dublin, including the famed Eccles Streets where Bloom and Molly live apart, occupies a chosen slice of Dublin, in a manner comparable to Dickens's attachment to City and Camden.

That selective area of Dublin holds absolute sway over the spatial landscape of Joyce's works. By contrast, given the importance of Paris for Joyce's biography, as well as his fictional aesthetics, Joyce's Parisian experience is surprisingly marginalized in Joyce's novels. At the end of *Portrait*, Stephen exultingly writes "Away! Away!", eager to yield himself to the "close embraces and the black arms of tall ships that stand against the moon," hearing voices that say, "We are your kinsmen" (*Portrait* 213). At the beginning of *Ulysses*, we see him returned, settled in a teaching job, and residing at a Dublin suburb. Scorning his own tribe, he had sailed to France, but Paris only thwarted his ambition. Memories of Paris flip past, but they reveal how insignificant and destitute he was there, a lonely foreigner reading Aristotle at "the library of Saint Genevieve . . . sheltered from the sin of Paris, night by night" (2.69-70), thanks to his empty purse. The young Irishman is flanked there by a Siamese reader: "By his elbow a delicate Siamese conned a handbook of strategy. Fed and feeding brains about me: under glowlamps, impaled, with faintly beating feelers: and in my mind's darkness a sloth of the underworld, reluctant, shy of brightness, shifting her dragon scaly folds" (2.70-74). The contrast with the cash-rich young Parisian of Dujardin could not be more poignant. The penurious student with no institutional affiliation, in his circumstances not that different from the Asian alien, struggles with the "sloth of the underworld" within his mind, and tries to wrench something out of it. Unlike the anonymous Siamese, Stephen, however, is as an Irishman treading the steps of his fellow countrymen who had fled from Ireland to France in the past. Earlier exiles, more illustrious than Stephen, haunt his memory at the bar MacMahon, named after a prominent descendant of the "Wild geese" who flew to France after the Battle of the Boyne (3.163-65). "[W]hen I was in Paris, *boul' Mich*'" (3.179), thus he wishes to recollect his Parisian days in "the most natural tone" (178), yet his memory gives him the lie: "With mother's money order, eight shillings, the banging door of the post office slammed in your face by the usher. Hunger toothache" (3.185-86). Indifferent to the tortuous history of the Irish Catholic exiles in France, Parisians have a good laugh at their expense, for *irlandais* pairs well with *hollandais*, a double insult to Irish Catholics, for it was the Dutchman William of Orange that had crushed their last political hope.[1] "She serves me at his beck," Stephen recalls a scene at the bar MacMahon:

> *Il est irlandais. Hollandais? Non fromage. Deux irlandais, nous, Irlande, vous savez? Ah, oui!* She thought you wanted a cheese *hollandaise*. (3.220-21).

The unflattering wordplay tossing *irlandais* onto *hollandais* may be entertaining, but it also shows that Irishness is an insignificant badge of identity to carry in the French metropolis. Stephen found Paris hardly hospitable or interested in the visitor from a cheese-like country somewhere out there. No *Erfahrung* can be extracted under such hampered circumstances, neither can there be any thrilling *Erlebnis* for Stephen "sheltered from the sin of Paris, night by night." Dublin, then, is where Stephen (unlike Joyce) cannot but return, not so much out of choice as out of necessity.

"The Grey block of Trinity"

Stephen in *Ulysses* is a returned, failed exile, whose circumstances have not met his wishes.[2] For someone lacking the good fortune of being born to the clan of Anglo-Irish elites, Stephen Dedalus would be considered relatively well off by contemporary standards to have a salaried job at all as schoolteacher. Yet his ambition can hardly be appeased by his occupation or his (lack of) accomplishments. Stephen grows most heroic (and clownish) when he takes on a contingent of Dublin's Anglo-Irish literati at the National Library to lampoon their sacred bard Shakespeare. Yet even then, his inner thoughts recall how abject, indigent, and unstable he is:

> —What is that, Mr Dedalus? the quaker librarian asked. Was it a celestial phenomenon?
> —A star by night, Stephen said. A pillar of the cloud by day.
> What more's to speak?
> Stephen looked on his hat, his stick, his boots.
> *Stepahnos*, my crown. My sword. His boots are spoiling the shape of my feet. Buy a pair. Holes in my socks. Handkerchief too. (9.942-48)

"What more's to speak?"—Stephen holds his ground in this half-comic campaign of assaulting Shakespeare's authority and authenticity, yet he is not invariably glib, eloquent, witty, or victorious. Moreover, his outfit has gaps and holes, concealed from his opponents perhaps but not from his self-consciousness. One uncontested property of his, his name (as was the case in *Portrait*) is a dubious asset. "You make good use of the name," one of them points out, "Your own name is strange enough. I suppose it explains your fantastical humour" (949-50). To this Stephen responds by sinking into mute soliloquy, ruminating on his failure to live up to his strange name:

> Fabulous artificer. The hawklike man. You flew. Whereto? Newhaven-Dieppe, steerage passenger. Paris and back. Lapwing. Icarus. *Pater, ait*. Seabedabbled, fallen, weltering. Lapwing you are. Lapwing be.(9.952-54)

Thus chants the fractured counterpoint to the elated final line of *Portrait*: "Old father, old artificer, stand me now and ever in good stead" (*Portait* 213). "Pater, ait" (Father, he cries), but the old father has not stood him in good stead. Dedalus is really Icarus, like a lapwing, not very good at flying away from his island. "Paris and back," yet Stephen finds himself not entirely at home in Dublin, either, for it has always been a strangers' city as much as his home, dominated by the presence and monuments of Anglo-Irish Protestants whose hegemony is represented by Trinity College, at the heart of Ascendancy Dublin's South Side. As Cullen notes, despite the significant changes in the city's class and sectarian characters, "the Georgian residential district of the south-east of the city avoided the blight" of decay and Catholic takeover, and the "classic squares of the eighteenth and early nineteenth centuries remained well-preserved and smart" on the eve of the Easter Rising (Cullen 1992: 276). The professions and high-ranking jobs were also under the control of Protestants, who maintained intellectual ascendency over the capital and the island as a whole through institutions such as Royal Dublin Society and the Royal Irish Academy, all with close ties to Trinity College (Somerville-Large 276). "In the medical and legal professions, according to the 1901 census, the non-Catholic elements exceeded 50 percent of the total in each case," Joseph V. O'Brien tells us. "Roman Catholics," furthermore, "were decidedly in the minority in banking (42 percent), engineering (32 percent), pharmacy (44 percent), and only had a slight majority as accountants" (O'Brien 40).

Stephen in *Portrait*, as a student of University College, is painfully aware how Trinity College, whose graduates colonized government positions and professions, symbolized the nation's cultural authority and intellectual capital. Its unrivaled hegemony profited from and perpetuated the colonial capital's general "ignorance":

> The grey block of Trinity on his left, set heavily in the city's ignorance like a great dull stone set in a cumbrous ring, pulled his mind downward; and while he was striving this way and that to free his feet from the fetters of the reformed conscience he came upon the droll statue of the national poet of Ireland. (*Portrait* 151)

The "grey block of Trinity" spawned no end of sons and friends, who now presumed to re-invent Irishness along an archaic Celticism transcribed into their language of (Hibernian) English. Stephen seeks to free himself from the "fetters of the reformed conscience," i.e. from the clutch of the "reformed" religion of Cromwell, William of Orange, and Defoe. Protestant hegemony has grown less virulent but more insidious: the Anglo-Irish have set up their own version of "nationality," as symbolized by the "droll statue of the national poet of Ireland" Thomas Moore, a Trinity graduate like many other card-carrying "Irish" writers. The person who commented on Stephen's surname above as being particularly suitable to Stephen's "fantastic humour" is also one of them, John Eglinton, born to a Protestant family, educated at Trinity, and now employed as assistant librarian at the National Library (Gifford 194). In fact, Eglinton is not exactly a full-fledged Trinity man. Economically second-class, he had paid for his education at Trinity as a sizar (i.e. through work-based scholarship), which left in him an inbred attitude of one who lives off his superior's tolerance and goodwill. "He laughed low: a sizar's laugh of Trinity" (9.30-31), notes Stephen with his razor-sharp sensitivity. He would probably never cease being a sizar even in his old age, withering into the clan of the "old sisars" who become "unbeurrable from age," as *Finnegans Wake* quibbles (*Finnegans* 162). Whereas Eglinton can be dismissed as a fawning lackey to the establishment, the "block" made up of those more properly endowed and empowered Protestants are far more menacing. W. B. Yeats treads on Stephen's consciousness ("Yeats admired his line" [9.304]), as does J. M. Sygne ("Synge has promised me an article for *Dana* too" [9.322]). The venerable name of Yeats is brandished by Buck Mulligan, another "sizar" figure, as he taunts Stephen: "Couldn't you do the Yeats touch?" (9.1160-61). Even G. B. Shaw, who took no part in the Irish Revival movement, hovers around the arena of Stephen's single-handed battle, as another "Irish" literary authority. "And we ought to mention another Irish commentator, Mr George Bernard Shaw" (9.439-40), says another assistant librarian there.

Against the combined forces of Anglo-Irish usurpers of Irishness, bent on safeguarding their "centrality as guardians and articulators" (Smyth 69) of cultural nationalism, Stephen braces himself by praying to, of all saints, the founder of Jesuits, in the midst of his irreverent oration on Shakespeare: "Ignatius Loyola, make haste to help me!" (9.163). Instead of the "old artificer" of ancient Greek mythology in *Portrait*, Stephen offers invocation to the arch warrior of Counter Reformation. Whether helped by Loyola's spirit or not, Stephen does carry on his campaign of ingeniously deconstructing the Bard. Stephen may have "thoroughly" challenged "the stereotype of the ignorant Catholic" held by the Anglo-Irish (Potts 163), yet it yields nothing besides. His performance does not add up to any meaningful action, politically and otherwise, as Stephen himself is clearly aware of: "One day in the national library we had a discussion. Shakes. After. His lub back: I followed. I gall his kibe" (9.1108-9). The episode joins the abortive *Erfahrung* of those "epiphanies" in *Dubliners*. What might have become a significant event ends incomplete, stranded on the border of prescribed reality which Stephen was supposed to have challenged. As an *Erlebnis* it lacks thrill, too, for the subject of experience is himself far too unstable and self-divided to relish the excitement of the moment. Eglinton may never wean himself of his "sizar's laugh," yet Stephen himself is no better than a "lub," a clown. Moreover, the echoes of Shakespeare's language, "I gall his kibe" from *Hamlet*,[3] hoist their flags inside his mind, undefeated. The last words of the episode are not his but Shakespeare's (from *Cymbeline*), and any political disturbance Stephen may have ignited at the library is daubed over with Mulligan's bawdy parody:

—*Everyman His Own Wife*
or
A Honeymoon in the Hand
(a national immorality in three orgasms)
by
Ballocky Mulligan (9.1171-76)

"His lub back: I followed," indeed, despite his sparking brilliance and heretical daring.

Meanwhile, Stephen-"Kinch" sulks but obeys Mulligan's orders: "My will: his will that fronts me" (9.1202). His subservience to Mulligan, from the very first episode on, derives from the fact that Stephen himself has no firm grasp of his own identity, that he fails to fully possess himself as a possessor of things. "I own, therefore I am"—this proposition epitomizes the individualist modernity advocated by Locke and Defoe. But for Stephen, the pronoun "I," far from occupying the subject position, grammatically and otherwise, of his thoughts, threatens to elude him:

I, I and I. I.
A.E. I. O. U. (9.212-13)

This mysterious and intriguing formula epitomizes Joyce's critical response to the economic views of possessive individualism upon which the private sphere, discussed in chapter one, is erected. Gifford's standard annotation decides that this wordplay "suggests both the continuity of the Aristotelian soul . . . and the discontinuity of the body and its molecules" (Gifford 206). The context, however, seems to encourage a more literal reading, namely, as the problem of indebtedness and accountability of the modern economic subject. "I, I and" fosters a proliferation of multiple subjects, so that one "I" can be free from the debt of the other "I." By

barreled beef" (497). Thus instead of "disobliging England" (498), the scheme would benefit both kingdoms. Joyce's "drove of branded cattle" carry on their backs the history of exporting prime beef to England, not to disoblige the masters, which Bloom's monologue both echoes and updates:

> Thursday, of course. Tomorrow is killing day. Springers. Cuffee sold them about twentyseven quid each. For Liverpool probably. Roastbeef for old England. They buy up all the juicy ones. And then the fifth quarter lost: all that raw stuff, hide, hair, horns. Comes to a big thing in a year. Dead meat trade. Byproducts of the slaughterhouses for tanneries, soap, margarine. (6.392-97)[5]

Roast Beef of Old England, the iconic picture of the French ogling at a wholesome chunk of English beef painted by William Hogarth, is given a mild but crucial twist to become "Roastbeef *for* old England," which seems more than appropriate as a description of the colonial trade of "exportation of barreled beef" to England, for "Liverpool probably." On the same scene of cattle and sheep driven to be slaughtered, the employee of the Royal Irish Constabulary has a laconic one-word comment: "Emigrants" (6.389). To the faithful servants of colonial power, cattle equal emigrants equal sound business; to Joyce, speaking through Bloom, dispatching the "drove of branded cattle" and slaughtering the "raddled sheep bleating their fear" point to the sanguine brutishness of colonial exploitation, embodied in Mr. Power of the Castle.

Dublin Castle, however, is no meat trader. Its chosen vocation is policing crime and death. Asserting his professional expertise in dealing with criminal violence, Power tells his fellow mourners inside the coach, "That is where Childs was murdered" (6.469), which becomes, thanks to the coincidence of the victim's name, an allusion to Swift's scheme of butchering the children of the poor. Quite fittingly, Power and Cunningham are involved in seeing off their dead acquaintance to the other world. The greatest nightmare for these gatekeepers of colonial power would be when the dead are not entirely dead, when the dead past returns to haunt, disrupt, and destroy the present status quo. "Hades" presided over by the agents of the Castle, therefore, recalls the tales of the "undead." The author of *Dracula* Bram Stoker was a Trinity-bred Anglo-Irish author with family connections to the Castle, and his novel bears the marks of Stoker's own Castle career in its format of intelligence gathering and its theme of paranoid policing, as Declan Kiberd observes (Kiberd 381-82). "Refuse Christian burial. They used to drive a stake of wood through his heart in the grave. As if it wasn't broken already" (6.346-48), muses Bloom in referring to those who have committed suicide such as his father. Driving a stake through a dead heart is also how the vampire-fighters kill the undead for good. Stoker's Van Helsing, the "great specialist" (Stoker 117) and Dutchman (i.e. an original "Orangeman") commands his crew of vampire slayers to take the "stake in your left hand, ready to place the point over the heart, and the hammer in your right" (215). Without such extreme measures, the "Un-Dead" will make "more of those Un-deads that so have filled us with horror" (214-15). The Count himself comes from somewhere far off in Eastern Europe, yet the author seems to transplant Irish history there almost, for in his country of Transylvania, "there is hardly a foot of soil . . . that has not been enriched by the blood of men, patriots and invaders" (21). Joyce's intertextual engagement with this novel written by the son of a Castle civil servant also pervades the "Oxen of the Sun" episode, which unfolds against the backdrop of the child delivery of Mina Purefoy, whose name recalls that of Mina Harker of *Dracula*, the antithesis to the lethally charming Lucy. Mina, a shortened form of Wilhelmina, is a name earmarked for a female Williamite "Orangewoman." Joyce's Mina, Mina Purefoy,[6] is connected to the Castle on her husband's side, according to Bloom in "Lestrygonians": "Theodore's cousin in Dublin Castle. One tony relative in every family" (8.361-62). That the child labour of this latter Mina is countered with an irreverent, noisy, rattling drinking party in this episode appears puzzling unless we see it from this angle of the skewered, harassed historical memory of those at the receiving end of the surveillance and state violence emanating from Dublin Castle. Stephen strikes the keynote by speaking of the "Lilith, patron of abortions, of bigness wrought by wind of seeds of brightness or by potency of vampires mouth to mouth" (14.242-44). The potency and fertility of Mina Harker (she becomes a mother towards the end of Stoker's novel) and Mina Purefoy are likened to the proselytizing potency of the "Un-Dead." This is to turn Stoker's sectarian politics against himself, by making these mothers of Protestant babies breeders of vampires.

While imagining Mina Purefoy's labour, Bloom spots a "squad of constables debouched from College street, marching in Indian file" (8.406-7), from which his thoughts slip to a vision of "horsepoliceman" (423) trampling down Nationalist protestors. "Prepare to receive cavalry. Prepare to receive soup" (413), he hears the sound of the armed colonial power mixed with his own hunger. "Police whistle in my ears still" (431) is intertwined with "Mrs Purefoy" at the hospital and the anti-Imperialist (pro-Boer) slogans of the students at Trinity protesting against their College's granting of honorary doctorate to the pro-Empire politician

Joseph Chamberlain:

> —Up the Boers!
> —Three cheers for De Wet!
> —We'll hang Joe Chamberlain on a sourapple tree. (8.434-36)

This is followed by a striking passage that overlaps the themes of eating (which Bloom's own famished condition invites), the physical colonialism of the Castle (invoked by the police, as well as by Purefoy family connections) and the hegemony of "Trinity's surly front" (8.476):

> Silly billies: mob of young cubs yelling their guts out. Vinegar hill. The Butter exchange band. Few years' time half of them magistrates and civil servants. War comes on: into the army helterskelter: same fellows used to. Whether on the scaffold high.
>
> Never know who you're talking to. Corny Kelleher he has Harvey Duff in his eye. Like that Peter or Denis or James Carey that blew the gaff on the invincibles. Member of the corporation too. Egging raw youths on to get in the know all the time drawing secret service pay from the castle. Drop him like a hot potato. Why those plainclothes men are always courting slaveys. Easily twig a man used to uniform. Squarepushing up against a backdoor. Maul her a bit. Then the next thing on the menu. And who is the gentleman does be visiting there? Was the young master saying anything? (8.437-48)

The "young cubs," despite their youthful radicalism, would be incorporated into the system upon their graduation, their Trinity degree ensuring them decent places in the government bureaucracy. Whatever their youthful sentiments may have been, they would later vote for the Empire's wars with their feet, "helterskelter." Such thoughts, names, and stock phrases from the public domain crowd into Bloom's consciousness, preventing its closure into an *Erlebnis* of a flâneur's encounter of the mob. The communal memory of the city's *Erfahrung*, on the other hand, lies scattered in (sentence) fragments, with no nodal point to gather them into any wise maxim. In this indeterminate state between the private and the public, Joyce inserts his tribute to the suppressed history haunting the Irish capital, particularly, the history of resistance against the British which occupies and punctuates Bloom's otherwise politically aloof mind: Vinegar hill stands for the Wexford rebels during the United Irishmen uprising and alludes to a nationalist song, "Whether on the scaffold high" (Gifford 169). The second paragraph levels a satire at the policing state itself, rather than the youthful radicals, showing how there is no real freedom of speech in the Hibernian metropolis, unlike in the metropolis of the British Empire. The colonial capital swarms with "Harvey Duff" figures, i.e. police informers, with the Castle penetrating even its most dreaded opponent the Irish National Invincibles ("Like that Peter or Denis or James Carey"), breeding betrayers such as Peter Carey, and gathering information even from the "slaveys" (lowest maid) of public eateries (Gifford 94-95; Comerford 49-50).

More interesting still is the mixture of resistance politics with eating. "Vinegar hill" is chosen from all other likely candidates because of its alimentary name, and the "Butter exchange" (the dairyman's guild of Ireland) band that took part in the rally likewise for the same reason. The connection between politics and eating is further developed, this time on the side of the dominant forces of surveillance, which "eggs" informers and then drops them when they turn too risky ("like a hot potato"). This joins the "menu" of tactics available to the colonial policing arsenal of "the castle." Meanwhile, the gratefully oppressed are content to remain oppressed as far as they can regale themselves with meat and ale. "Sloping into the Empire [buffet restaurant]" (8.599), Bloom chooses instead "the Burton" (8.650), where the typical wholesome English dish, "Roast beef and cabbage," or the typically tributary Irish "stew" entertains customers (8.668-69). He exits this eatery disgusted, with bloody words ringing in his ears as he walks along Grafton street, at the heart of Ascendancy Dublin: "Eat or be eaten. Kill! Kill!" (703). The Hibernian metropolis urges its dwellers to either "slope" into the Empire, or be eaten by the Empire, as cannon fodder and casual labourers. "Hungry man is an angry man" (662); therefore, a well-fed man will no longer be angry, even when steadily gobbled up by the "twoheaded octopus, one of whose heads is the head upon which the ends of the world have forgotten to come while the other speaks with a Scotch accent" (520-22)—the English head, on which the sun does not set, and the Scottish head particularly noisome for Irish Catholics due to its tentacles stretching towards them through Ulster.

"Parable of the Plums"

Our analysis of the innuendoes and hints of *Ulysses* so far should suggest one undeniable fact: the metropolis in Joyce's novel, in painful contrast to Defoe's and Dickens's London, is not a free, vibrant, open, dynamic, moneymaking capital of vigorous modernity. Nor do its complications encourage, unlike the Paris of Baudelaire, a refined, well-groomed, meandering, mesmerizing urban fantasy. It is a colonial city scarred by uncertain identity, uneven development, thwarted projects, and ever vigilant policing by paranoid state apparatus. Yet against these handicaps *Ulysses* takes actions, undeterred, undaunted.

"In the Heart of the Hibernian Metropolis," as the first headline of "Aeolus" goes, stands "Nelson's pillar," before and due to which the city traffic is clogged, a potent symbol in itself of the colonial hegemony of the English metropolis over Dublin:

> IN THE HEART OF THE HIBERNIAN METROPOLIS
>
> Before Nelson's pillar trams slowed, shunted, changed trolley, started for Blackrock, Kingstown and Dalkey, Clonskea, Rathgar and Terenure, Palmerston Park and upper Rathmines, Sandymount Green, Rathmines, Ringsend and Sandymount Tower, Harold's Cross. (7.1-4)

The names of the termini, mostly affluent suburbs occupied by Protestants south of the city such as Blackrock and Rathmines, are listed like so many subordinates, a motley crew with names at times shamelessly confessing their derivative status vis-à-vis the colonial overlord ("Kingstown," "Palmerston Park," "Harold's Cross"). Upon the political surface of Dublin, in addition to those marks of earlier colonization such as Trinity College founded by the Tudors and the various Ascendancy Georgian buildings, Nelson's pillar stands as symbol of Victorian British Empire.[7] Reacting to the overbearing presence of Nelson's pillar can take the form of a resentful sense of resignation, as well as disaffection. You hate it but you accept it as part of your unhappy city. Unless you can blow it up (which is what the Irish Republicans did in 1966 [Foster 584]), you put up with it, as a permanent fixture, like the English language you cannot but use. Or, you can choose to use such monuments of triumphant colonial power for your own purpose, irreverently, nonchalantly, and off-key. This is how the episode grapples with Nelson's pillar which stands for all that is grand and ugly about Britain's military domination of Ireland and other nations. "Dear Dirty Dublin" runs the headline of the episode's strategic turning point, which starts in a manner comparable to the first entry of the episode but in a different mode:

> DEAR DIRTY DUBLIN
>
> Dubliners.
>
> —Two Dublin vestals, Stephen said, elderly and pious, have lived fifty and fiftythree years in Fumbally's lane.
>
> —Where is that? the professor asked.
>
> —Off Blackpitts, Stephen said. (7.921-26)

The phrase "Dear Dirty Dublin" proclaims what Lefebvre calls the "right to the city," a right of the city-dwellers, however shabby their addresses may be or whether they own properties or not, to "appropriate" the city (Lefebvre 174). The key element which Lefebvre, as well as Joyce, emphasizes is that of play. The right to the city consists in the right to use the city as an *œuvre*, the city as a space not merely of utilitarian function or ornamented display but as a dynamic space of festive play, "overtaking use and exchange by gathering them together" (Lefebvre 172). Stephen elevates these two "elderly and pious" ladies into representative "Dubliners," bestowing on them their civic robe in calling them "vestals" notwithstanding their obscure residence near "Blackpitts." This bold "play" on Stephen's part is disturbed by his memory of street prostitutes accosting him, presumably around Fumbally's lane: "Against the wall. Face glistering tallow under her fustian shawl. Frantic hearts" (7.927-28). Such woman, too, deserve to be remembered as a Dubliner, yet the old ladies make for more likely candidates to become the "vestals" of the city, which may also account for the aged maidens presiding over the first ("Sisters") and the last story ("The Dead") of *Dubliners*. Stephen then narrates how these two elderly ladies choose to climb up the pillar "to see the views of Dublin from the top of Nelson's pillar" (7.931), which properly amounts to their exercising their right to appropriate the city as an *œuvre* to play in and on. Their outing also involves an "overtaking" of use and exchange, since they spend on the excursion their hard-earned money saved "in a red tin letterbox moneybox" (932). Moreover, as typical Dubliners, they need to satisfy their palate, as well as their eyes: "They purchase four and twenty ripe plums" (941) to eat with "one and fourpenceworth of brawn and four slices of panloaf" (939). This they carry up to the column, "grunting, encouraging each other, afraid of the dark, panting, one asking the other have you the brawn, praising God and the Blessed Virgin, threatening to come down, peeping at the airslits" (944-46). Stephen's narrative is interrupted by entries focused on Bloom, yet intermittently he goes on with his "*Parable of the Plums*" (1056-57), the upshot of which is that they accomplish their ascent, squat on top of the pillar, "peering up at the statue of the onehandled adulterer" (1017-18), and enjoy the sight as well as their juicy plums, "wiping off with their handkerchiefs the plumjuice that dribbles out of their mouths and spitting the plumstones slowly out between the railings" (1025-27).

One entry after, "HELLO THERE, CENTRAL!" brings back the names of the Protestant suburbs listed in the first entry, but now they lead to a rollicking word-play, with no respect paid to the "onehandled adulterer" and the Imperial power he symbolizes. "Hackney cars, cabs, delivery waggons, mailvans, private broughams, aerated mineral water floats with rattling crates of bottles, rattled, rolled, horsedrawn, rapidly" (1047-49), rolling into view as the entry ends, present the perspective of these ladies looking down on the city traffic from above. The final entry of the episode completes the text's ludic appropriation of Nelson's pillar, supplementing the title phrase of the first entry, "In the Heart of the Hibernian Metropolis," with an unlikely predicate:

> DIMINISHED DIGITS PROVE TOO TITILLATING FOR FRISKY FRUMPS. ANNE WIMBLES, FLO WANGLES—YET CAN YOU BLAME THEM? (7.1069-71)

In this wordplay, to the first names of the two ladies "Anne" and "Flo"(rence) are added "Wimbles" and "Wangles"—both alluding to giddiness (Gifford 153)—as the "frisky frumps" are vested now as full-fledged vestal virgins of Dublin, by virtue of having played with plums (matching "frumps") with their "diminished digits" on top of the monument honouring the hero of English military might, but now deprived of his proper name by Stephen to become the "onehandled adulterer." The professor "smiling grimly" concedes Stephen's wit: "Onehandled adulterer . . . That tickles me, I must say" (1072-73). "Tickled the old ones too," another listener of Stephens' "parable" says. In their pious, serious, but good-humoured "titillating" consumption both of their plums and of the city's colonial *œuvre*, the ladies have turned the "Hibernian Capital" into their "Dear Dirty Dublin."[8]

The *Erlebnis* of dizziness and sweet taste of plum these elderly ladies enjoyed on this most memorable trip of their lives has attained a status of communal *Erfahrung* of the city's vibrant traffic undeterred by the colonial landmark. Yet this is so only in the "parable," and not in the main narrative itself. The episode itself is marked by a graphic disjunctive conjunction, with headlines, interruptions, and noises dissecting Stephen's effort to finish his tale. In the two remaining chapters we shall examine, first, the debilitated vestiges of *Erlebnis* in *Ulysses* on the part of Bloom, the novel's resident flâneur-protagonist, and then, finally, the traces of disrupted *Erfahrung* in "Aeolus" and other episodes employing third-person narration.

CHAPTER ELEVEN

BLOOM AS FLÂNEUR

"Jewjesuit"

In the sequential order of *Ulysses*'s episodes, before Bloom comes Stephen. This simple and obvious fact has to be noted before we can discuss Bloom's character and deeds as a city stroller. The first part of *Ulysses* belongs to Stephen, who belongs in a skewered way to his society. The inter-subjective tension in the first episode—of Stephen turned into an outsider at his own dwelling by his guests Mulligan and Haines—lays down the condition, if not the necessary cause, of the intra-subjective tension of Stephen's schizoid monologue. In the second episode, one part of Stephen takes up his public duty as a school teacher hired by Deasy, while another part of him wanders off along his own mental landscape peopled with books he had read and with things pertaining to his private sphere:

> Across the page the symbols moved in grave morrice, in the mummery of their letters, wearing quaint caps of squares and cubes. Give hands, traverse, bow to partner: so: imps of fancy of the Moors. Gone too from the world, Averroes and Moses Maimonides, dark men in mien and movement, flashing in their mocking mirrors the obscure soul of the world, a darkness shining in brightness which brightness could not comprehend. (2.155-60)

The transition, or rather the lack thereof, is marked by a most apocryphal use of colons, "bow to partner: so: imps of fancy of the Moors," with the "so" disrupted in its conjunctive duty, just as Stephen breaks off from his rent-earning labour, by the colons that detains it before and after. Conversing with the dead heretics, "dark men in mien and movement" and attracted to their ironic mockery of brightness, Stephen nonetheless is nothing but a schoolmaster hired to care for the boys of well-to-do fathers. In the obfuscated narrative logic of *Ulysses*, Stephen precedes and prepares for Bloom's intra-subjective self-dialogues in this aspect of radical disjunction between the public and the private selves. No neat reconciliation of the two sides into a stable and secure subjectivity would be allowed either for Stephen or Bloom. This state of self-division serves as the essential cause and context of the novel's diverse verbal adventures.

As often noted, the two main figures brush past each other on more than one occasion (in episodes 6, 7, and 9), before they finally end up as a pair in the closing episodes. This tempts the reader to detect a teleological pattern in the plot of Stephen-Telemachus at last meeting his Odysseus-Bloom, in the "schematic" interpretation intent on establishing Homeric parallels. But the relationship breaks off when, in response to the older man's attempt to bind the younger to a business partnership, Stephen leaves Bloom's house. Such a bathetic ending, even apart from the slanders Molly has in store for Bloom in the final episode, debilitates any attempt to impose closure on the basis of Bloom-Odysseus' trajectory. A more plausible approach would be to regard Stephen and Bloom as Derridean supplements of each other (see Derrida 154, 235), in that the "trace" of unspoken, voiceless monologue left behind by Stephen produces the space in which Bloom presents his thoughts and fancies to the reader. For both, the voiced spoken words (even when they speak to each other) lack authenticity in contrast to the unspoken silent musings, since it is the authority of self-transcribing non- or anti-speech, the voiceless life of the mute but busy mind, that *Ulysses* persistently dramatizes and celebrates. In this speechless speech of the central characters, *Erlebnis* is driven to extremity, where no sharing or making common of the individual's isolated thoughts is sought or gestured. Or better still, it is speech that fails to add up to experience as either *Erlebnis* or *Erfahrung*, for instead of some remarkable events taking place to constitute a dramatic plot, all we have is a series of trivial, incidental, ephemeral occurrences.

The non-vocal mode of existence shared by Stephen and Bloom has greater importance than the anti-Semitism that affects not only Bloom but also Stephen, as when Buck Mulligan rails at Stephen, "O you inquisitional drunken jewjesuit!" (9.1159). Stephen surely stands apart from his fellow Dubliners in his freedom from racial prejudice, as pronounced by Deasy:

> England is in the hands of the jews. In all the highest places: her finance, her press. And they are the signs of a nation's decay. Wherever they gather they eat up the nation's vital strength. I have seen it coming these years. As sure as we are standing here the jew merchants are already at their work of destruction. Old England is dying. (2.346-51)

His effort to match this stereotype of sinister Jews bent on their "work of destruction" with real-life images takes Stephen back to the Jews he had seen at the Paris Bourse, quoted in chapter nine. They are money-dealers no doubt, but they matter more to Stephen as cases of resident aliens, belonging and simultaneously not belonging to their city. Stephen sees a reflection of himself in these Parisian Jews, but as for the Jewish Dubliner himself, his pork-loving palate—purchasing his breakfast meat from a pork-selling Jewish butcher, moreover—disqualifies him as a faithful member of the chosen people: "He halted before Dlugacz's window, staring at the hanks of sausages, polonies, black and white" (4.140-41). The narrator relishes the "s" sound of "sausages" exchanged between the client and the seller: "The ferreteyed porkbutcher folded the sausages he had snipped off with blotchy fingers, sausagepink. Sound meat there: like a stallfed heifer" (4.152-53). Critics wishing to highlight Bloom's specifically Jewish character have explained away his irreverent taste for pork as an instance of Joyce's "fine-tuned representations of a Jewish identity crisis that was fresh from the tensions of the Dreyfus Affair" (Davison 201), or that in spite of his truant palate, his mind is more properly Jewish in that "his speculative, sermonic, theologic, historic, mystic and fragmented thought . . . embodies the encyclopedic and discursive nature of Talmudic literature's view of Moses" (Nadel 97). Bloom is a citizen at odds with the social rubrics of his identity including that of his belonging to an ethnic minority. His Jewishness certainly thickens his isolation, yet the mode of his existence in the novel discourages hypostatization of his ethnicity. Rather than being a settled "character" with identifiable characteristics consistently speaking and acting in his (Jewish) character, "Bloom" moves around the novel as a signifier referring to a trace or space of thought fragments.

Bloom is rarely static or stable in every aspect. "Bloom is at his most vital in the world of process," writes Declan Kebard, for he is a "committed wanderer" who "knows that movement is better than stasis" (Kebard 2009: 82). The trajectory of this wanderer's pedestrian peregrination (with the exception of his joining the mourners at the funeral coach at Hades) is complicated by numerous diversions, detours, and stoppages, before his final return home. Bloom starts off from his home at Eccles Street north of Liffey and crosses the river to the Ascendancy capital. The north-south divide segregating the Catholic middle-class districts from the city centre boasting Protestant Anglo-Irish institutions and landmarks, apparently has a low-key role in the spatial backdrop of the novel, largely because of Bloom's sense of estrangement from both camps of Dublin, neither of which he is a fully qualified member. What it yields to the novel is the disdainful aloofness which gives Bloom an entry ticket to join neither the Jewish nor the Irish-Catholic nor the Anglo-Irish clan, but the clan of flâneurs. "To be away from home and yet to feel oneself everywhere at home" (Baudelaire 1964: 9) is the passion of the flâneur, according to Baudelaire, and Bloom's borderline status at the margins of races, as well as his unusual marital relationship, is one visible flâneur-like attribute: he feels estranged at home and feels at home in his estranged wanderings outdoors. Baudelaire celebrates the flâneur as a prototype of the modern hero by likening him to "a kaleidoscope gifted with consciousness, responding to each one of its movements and reproducing the multiplicity of life and the flickering grace of all the elements of life" (Baudelaire 1964: 9). Bloom surely reacts instantly and immediately to the "multiplicity of life" of his city, but whether any "flickering grace" emerges from either his "consciousness" or the external life he observes is not as certain. "Joyce's Dublin in 1904," according to Peter I. Barta, "is made for that intriguing creature of the European metropolis of the age, the mixture of the *flâneur* and the *badaud.* People have time on their hands: they do not seem to have full-time jobs, nor have they particularly pleasant and welcome homes to return to" (Barta 54). A more rigorous historical dating would make the flâneur an archaic, obsolete figure by the turn of the century even in his country of origin. The usage of the word, according to Priscilla Parkhurst Ferguson, can be traced to the early nineteenth century, when detached, solitary idlers were perceived as "something of a deviant in emerging bourgeois society" (Ferguson 25). The detached urban wanderer was made to stand for artistic creativity in the 1830s by writers such as Balzac, who downplayed his idling. As in so many other aspects, 1848 was a turning point, for apart from the lone exception of Baudelaire, the flâneur lost his prestige and habitat. "The urban renewal of 'Haussmmannization,' the manipulation of Parisian topography and accompanying economic activity" (Ferguson 32) forced him to retreat to the arcades. The advent of the Parisian arcades, therefore, *pace* Benjamin, denoted not quite the highpoint of the flâneur's career but foreboded his imminent demise. In the arcades, the "flâneur's dispassionate gaze dissipates under pressure from the shoppers' passionate engagement in the world of things to be purchased and possessed" (Ferguson 35). Bloom comes decades after the flâneur's retreat into the Parisian arcades, but he does display some key features of the flâneur, such as his constant movement, his idling, and his aloofness from the busy world.

As a remote kinsman or an atavistic revenant of the Parisian flâneur with gentlemanly sartorial appearance, Bloom commands that minimum degree of independence from utter indigence which would threaten the pleasure of leisurely strolling. Yet this independence involves his dependence on the world of business. His work as advertisers' agent provides him with economic security which the many unemployed wanderers of the city would envy. A telling point of comparison can be found in Lenehan of "Two Gallants" in *Dubliners*, whose unadorned prose of detached observation dissects the predicament of the poor sycophant roaming the high streets south of the river, with little cash to spare. Deserted by the other "gallant" Corley, he is thrust back to the humble reality of his meanness: "Now that he was alone his face looked older. His gaiety seemed to forsake him, and, as he came by the railings of the Duke's Lawn, he allowed his hand to run along them" (*Dubliners* 41). The Duke's Lawn is literally the Duke's and not his; he can only touch the cold railings guarding the protected realm. His mind being equally bare, with no stock of learning to fall back on, unlike Stephen or to a less extent Bloom, he has little in himself to erect his own mental enclosure.

> He walked listlessly round Stephen's Green and then down Grafton Street. Though his eyes took note of many elements of the crowd through which he passed they did so morosely. . . . The problem of how he could pass the hours till he met Corley again troubled him a little. He could think of no way of passing them but to keep on walking. He turned to the left when he came to the corner of Rutland Square and felt more at ease in the dark quiet street, the somber look of which suited his mood. (*Dubliners* 41-42)

Lenehan's strolling thus becomes a compulsory, inevitable choice: "He could think of no way of passing them but to keep on walking." Materially better off than the likes of Lenehan, Bloom has the composure of someone who feels relatively at home with himself in the respectable districts of the Hibernian metropolis. Compared with Stephen, moreover, Bloom's intellectual capital has just the right weight to keep his mind afloat without burdening it with abstruse meditations. A typical example would be his wry observations on Catholic mass, which sets him playing with words, but at the level of common average intellect:

> The priest bent down to put it into her mouth, murmuring all the time. Latin. The next one. Shut your eyes and open your mouth. What? *Corpus*: body. Corpse. Good idea the Latin. Stupefies them first. Hospice for the dying. They don't seem to chew it: only swallow it down. Rum idea: eating bits of a corpse. Why the cannibals cotton to it. (5.348-52)

This comes at a user-friendly portion, as it were, when placed side by side with the allusion-loaded animadversions of Stephen in "Proteus" or "Scylla and Charybdis." Bloom's mildly critical stance detaches him from the majority views of his Irish Catholic neighbours and puts him at that intimate but removed position in society which a flâneur cultivates. Bloom's eyes are also far more active and keen than those of Lenehan, appropriately enough for a flâneur participating in the life of the city predominantly thoroughly visual means. Although Lenehan's eyes also make "note of many elements of the crowd through which he passed," this "morose" gallant draws neither excitement nor pleasure from what he sees. Bloom, then, qualifies as a flâneur, albeit a belated member of the metropolitan species.

"Ikey Moses? Bloom."

However, a case for considering Bloom a flâneur proper faces some formidable objections. First to be noted is Bloom's inability to preserve his incognito, which for Baudelaire is a vital attribute of the flâneur whose expertise is "to be at the centre of the world, and yet to remain hidden from the world" like a "*prince* who everywhere rejoices in his incognito" (Baudelaire 1964: 9). Incognito is also crucial for Benjamin, for it furnishes the ground for the flâneur's potential transformation into a detective. The flâneur-detective knows the crowd without himself being known by them, hiding behind his "indolence" the "watchfulness of an observer" (Benjamin 2003: 22). This does not quite apply to Bloom, for already only a little way into the second episode of his outings on the streets of Dublin, his illusion of incognito is crushed, when he is instantly spotted, known, and accosted by M'Coy. "Wish I hadn't met that M'Coy fellow" (5.211-12), mumbles Bloom silently to himself. Dublin is a small town compared with London or Paris. Whereas in London the individual can hide among the vast, anonymous, and busy crowd constantly on the move, Dublin is different. Bloom cannot avoid, whether he wishes or not, running into acquaintances (Mrs. Breen, Nosey Flynn, finally Boylan), who interrupt his pleasure of anonymous rambling.[1] The impossibility of isolation in Dublin is used positively as a narrative device by the author, as each episode presents a group tableau, the most extreme instances being "Wandering Rocks" which packs the entire city centre with named individuals, or the orderly reappearance of characters on the surreal stage of "Circe." The upshot of this gregariousness is to diminish the focal centrality of Bloom as the undetected observer of urban life and to debilitate his sense of solitude. He suffers from the "great misery of not being able to be alone"—a phrase by La Bruyère which Poe uses as the epigraph for "The Man of the Crowd"—particularly in "Hades," where company is unavoidable. If "Hell is like London," as Shelley sang, Dublin is like Hell not so much in its depravity as in its compulsory companionship (think of Dante's Ugolino coupled with his foe Ruggieri, gnawing at the latter's skull for eternity [*Inferno* 32.124-29]). The novel makes no attempt to commiserate with Bloom's inability to remain anonymous. Being a multi-faceted novel, *Ulysses* activates other focuses and perspectives besides that of Bloom, a factor which also frustrates his incognito. Even before his hostile encounter with the "Citizen" in "Cyclops," Bloom emerges not merely alienated from other citizens but exposed to their surveillance. His identity and actions are known by others. Buck Mulligan, for instance, spots Bloom and shares intelligence concerning his behavior at the museum:

> —What's his name? Ikey Moses? Bloom.
> He rattled on:
> —Jehovah, collector of prepuces, is no more. I found him over in the museum where I went to hail the foamborn Aphrodite. The Greek mouth that has never been twisted in prayer. Every day we must do homage to her. *Life of life, thy lips enkindle.*
> Sudden he turned to Stephen:
> —He knows you. He knows your old fellow. O, I fear me, he is Greeker than the Greeks. His pale Galillean eyes were upon her mesial groove. Venus Kallipyge. O, the thunder of those loins! *The god pursuing the maiden hid.* (9.607-17)

His bantering tone notwithstanding, Mulligan's brandishing of his capacity to collect information is a sobering indication of how anonymity is contained and controlled by observing eyes in Dublin. The anti-Semitic jibes cannot be dismissed for sure, but the passage files a folder on Bloom underlining some key facts: his ethnicity, his connection (to Stephen's father), and his sensuality. Such pervasive practice of mutual detection no doubt owes considerably to the policing needs of the colonial capital, dominated physically and symbolically by Dublin Castle, the headquarters of administration and intelligence-gathering. Mulligan the "usurper," who befriends the English (such as Haines) and the Anglo-Irish elites, plays the informer, in addition to the quibbling clown. Parisian flâneurs, under the autocratic regime of the Second Empire, could revel in their scorn and disdain inside the arcades, mixing with shoppers, dandies, and demimondaines. Edwardian Dublin, however, offers no haven from outside reality, no interior space to cultivate daydreams.

The question of detecting an individual's identity in a metropolis does not necessarily require any special skill or power. In many instances, particularly before the consumer revolution brought about the era of cheap ready-made clothes, you literally wore your social status on your sleeves. Dublin in the first decade of the past century was no exception. Bloom is clad according to a gentlemanly dress code. As such he can enjoy a minimum degree of group anonymity, unlike those whose outfit makes them stand out instantly among the crowd, such as the "sandwich man," a species of walking human billboard that sauntered the boulevards of Paris in the nineteenth century, mostly to disappear by the 1870s (Hahn 172). In this outmoded minor metropolis of Dublin, Bloom the flâneur takes note of their presence with a mixture of patronizing pity and mild derision, regarding them as creatures clearly beneath him in the ladder of optical power pervading the city space:

> A procession of whitesmocked sandwichmen marched slowly towards him along the gutter, scarlet sashes across their boards. Bargains. Like that priest they are this morning: we have sinned: we have suffered. He read the scarlet letters on their five tall white hats: H. E. L. Y. S. Wisdom Hely's. Y lagging behind drew a chunk of bread from his foreboard, crammed it into his mouth and munched as he walked. Our staple food. Three bob a day, walking along the gutters, street after street. Just keep skin and bone together, bread and skilly. (8.123-30).

The silent letter "Y" leaves its mark in Bloom's consciousness as a signifier standing for, but also supplanting, the sandwich man. The human bearer of the letter, meanwhile, is reduced to a mere animate vessel feeding itself hastily. Reading religious meaning into their scarlet letters has something to do with Bloom's commiseration for them, yet there is no priest here to absolve them from their curse of having to walk the city's gutters to "keep skin and bone together, bread and skilly." Nor is there any respite to their wandering, since the wage-labour mechanism of having to earn three "bob a day" through their foot-sore peregrination is essential to their survival in the city.

Bloom's own walks in the city would take him to its more risqué, shady, and wretched corners in the later episodes ("Circe" and "Eumaeus"), encouraging the reader to trace out a semblance of sociological narrative logic in the progress of the novel. Starting off from the relative security of his middle-class house (even though the marital arrangement seems rather odd), he ends up after a day's trekking of the city's main thoroughfares at a brothel and a cabman's shelter north of the river, where he is forced to admit close proximity to the city's underclass pariahs. A much quoted passage supporting such a reading carries Bloom's (or Joyce's) eloquent reflections on the economics of city property:

> Cityful passing away, other cityful coming, passing away too: other coming on, passing on. Houses, lines of houses, streets, miles of pavements, piledup bricks, stones. Changing hands. This owner, that. Landlord never dies they say. Other steps into his shoes when he gets his notice to quit. They buy the place up with gold and still they have all the gold. (8.484-88)

It should be noted, in praising the felicity of the wordings of this mini prose poem, that unlike the sandwich men, the landlords who never die are not present in the episodes of *Ulysses*. This can be construed either as the author's reluctance to deal with the structural socioeconomic conflicts of his city (from which Dickens never shied away) or alternatively his wish to assign the city of his fictional world entirely to the less well-off common sorts (as he did in *Dubliners*). In either case, how much one can pursue a sociological interpretation of the novel depends to a large extent on how much importance one can place on Bloom's role as a protagonist exploring Dublin, since it would bring in other counterparts to the elements of a conventional novel. This is something we are wary of, as stated already: there is simply much more to this unique book than Bloom's adventure (or the lack thereof). The point is rather to emphasize the class or status distinctions encircling Bloom's identity, made manifest when he comes across those urban characters with clearly differential and often inferior social markers. In "Lestrygonians," the "lunchtime" episode, he runs into a "dotty" man (8.299-303), which Bloom certainly is not. In the same episode, the recurrent mention of a "blind stripling" also adds spice to Bloom's survey of his urban environment:

> The blind stripling tapped the curbstone and went on his way, drawing his cane back, feeling again.
>
> Mr Bloom walked behind the eyeless feet, a flatcut suit of herringbone tweed. Poor young fellow! How on earth did he know that van was there? Must have felt it. See things in their forehead perhaps: kind of sense of volume. Weight or size of it, something blacker than the dark. Wonder would he feel it if something was removed. Feel a gap. Queer idea of Dublin he must have, tapping his way round by the stones. (8.1104-11)

"Poor young fellow!" can hardly be taken to be an outburst of a heartfelt Blakean pity, as Rainford wishes to see it (Rainsford 202-3). For one thing, it is immediately tempered by his sense of detached wonder or intellectual curiosity as to how the "eyeless feet" get about the city at all. For another, the passage affirms a clear "gap" between the stripling's "queer idea of Dublin" and Bloom the able-bodied flâneur's expert knowledge of his city.

The novel, however, does not leave Bloom to enjoy the subject position of a flâneur undetected and undeterred by others, going about the metropolis, serenely contemplating like Boz the oddities and peculiarities of familiar scenes. The shape of the text hints otherwise. The paragraphs of those episodes recording his thoughts are ruffled, shattered, broken. The eighth episode jettisons overboard Bloom's interior monologue carefully developed for four episodes (counting from "Calypso"). The full gamut of the discordant deconstruction of prose—at all levels of paragraph, sentence, phrase, words, punctuation—will be performed in "Sirens," after two distinctive experimental modes of "Scylla and Charybdis" and "Wandering Rocks." Yet it is significant that the narrative-cum-monologue mode that focuses on Bloom through a series of flâneur-like episodes breaks down in the last of its sequence, offering a self-criticism of the dilettantism and complacency of Bloom's posing as flâneur. "A committed wanderer" on the move he may wish to be, but the novel chooses to disrupt the flow of his movement. After "Lestrygonians" the narrative focus would drift away from Bloom, to thrash him, at the end of Part Two, with untold number of torments in "Circe." The novel's distancing from Bloom starts off with a mini foreshadowing of "Sirens" in the eighth episode:

> Ah.
> His hand fell to his side again.
> Never know anything about it. Waste of time. (8.579-81)

The stifled cry of "Ah" plus full stop leaves not much space for the subject's meditations. The sentences that follow do little to garnish the emotions denoted by the single-word sentence "Ah." A "dotty" sound it becomes, in more senses than one. Sentences go apart and grammar acts amiss a few lines later:

> Stop. Stop. If it was it was. Must.
> Mr Bloom, quickbreathing, slowlier walking passed Adam court.
> With ha quiet keep quiet relief his eyes took note this is the street here middle of the day of Bob Doran's bottle shoulders. (8.592-95)

Periods play havoc on the first sentence, stopping it arbitrarily, while commas in the second, apparently coming to succour Bloom's troubled breath, would offer no service in the third sentence as words follow one another breathlessly. That all this confusion is due to his spotting Blazes Boylan, the macho lover of his spouse, further undermines the implicit assumption of distinction he sought to enjoy as a flâneur. Here comes someone far superior to him in potency and daring, undoing the self-confidence of the musing rambler rudely, though rhythmically, as the episode reaches its end:

> No. Didn't see me. After two. Just at the gate.
> My heart!
> His eyes beating looked steadfastly at cream curves of stone. Sir Thomas Deane was the Greek architecture.

> Look for something I.
> His hasty hand went quick into a pocket, took out, read unfolded Agendath Netaim. Where did I?
> Busy looking.
> He thrust back quick Agendath.
> Afternoon she said.
> I am looking for that. Yes, that. Try all pockets. Handker. *Freeman*. Where did I? Ah, yes. Trousers. Potato. Purse. Where? (8.1178-89)

Jostled by the random phrases and clauses uprooted from their context (as in "Sir Thomas Deane was the Greek architecture"), the pronoun "I" dangles without the complement of predicates, as in "Look for something I" or "Where did I?" When the first-person subject finds an anchor, it is only in his physical body, or rather, his trouser pockets—"Handker. *Freeman*. . . . Trousers. Potato. Purse." The subject is dismantled into these stray nouns referring to the things he possesses, to the formula "I own, therefore, I am" of possessive individualism.

"Better detach. Ow!"

In Bloom the nineteenth-century flâneur disintegrates by being re-integrated to the body of lower as well as upper organs. For the flâneur basking in the phantasmagoria of the arcade or Parisian boulevard, his eyes, as well as his walking feet, have predominance over other organs. His optical sensitivity, which easily relates him to the clan of detectives and spies, is what matters most. He takes in the sights of the metropolis primarily as spectacles. Visual possession predicated on dispossession entails not activating the body's tactile capacity: see but never touch. Should the viewer's hands follow the dictates of the enticed eyes, she would become a shoplifter, as was the case with Moll. The desire tickled by the pleasure of the flâneur's observation should mobilize his eyes only. One recalls, for instance, how in Baudelaire's "À une passante" in a flash of moment the poet captures the details of the lady's dresses, hems, and legs. The erotic excitement, moreover, consists largely in that instantaneous eye contact, vanishing in the blink of an eye. The charm of the "fugitive beauté" has as much to do with that evanescence as with the handsome face or slender legs of the supposed widow. Bloom, by contrast, has restless eyes absorbing the objects offered to them, but he is a creature made up of other organs besides: stomach, intestines, anus, and phallus. These organs assert their right to be recognized and respected, as much as his eyes. In so far as he is burdened with his bodily demands, Bloom has to forfeit the title of flâneur, of one literally enjoying the leisure with the aloofness of a dandy who keeps his body covered and controlled behind his smart outfit.

The counterpart to Baudelaire's depiction of "love at the last sight," as Benjamin puts it, in *Ulysses* is "Nausicaa." Pushed off from his central place after "Lestrygonians" for four consecutive episodes, in the last of which ("Cyclops") he had to physically flee hostile xenophobic drinkers, Bloom shares the stage of the next episode "Nausicaa" with Gerty, roughly half and half, thanks to whom he regales himself with masturbation. The fact that the two are immobile in this setting on Sandymount strand, away from the city centre, rather than walking the noisy streets of the metropolis, should first be mentioned as an obvious difference from Baudelaire's sonnet. This arrangement induces a prolonged free indirect speech focalized on Gerty, packed with references to the tawdry romanticism of women's magazines. It also gives Bloom's body ample opportunity to come out of the shackles of the optical-sartorial regime of a well-dressed flâneur, of one who sees but never touches. When the narration is taken over by Bloom's familiar monologue style, we realize that while Gerty was talking to herself (and to the reader), Bloom's hand was busy pleasing his male organ. Eyes are still crucial, for they form an optical-phallic nexus that turns the items of Gerty's intimate clothing into a phantasmagoria of erotic excitement:

> [H]e could see her other things too, nainsook knickers, the fabric that caresses the skin, better than those other pettiwidth, the green, four and eleven, on account of being white and she let him and she saw that he saw and then it went so high it went out of sight a moment and she saw that trembling in every limb from being bent so far back that he had a full view high up above her knee where no-one ever not even on the swing or wading and she wasn't ashamed and he wasn't either to look in that immodest way like that because he couldn't resist the sight of the wondrous revealment half offered like those skirtdancers behaving so immodest before gentlemen looking and he kept on looking, looking. (13.724-33)

The narrator's prose elicits and encourages both characters to indulge in sensuous fantasy, the man avidly relishing the details of the spectacle, the woman elated by her exhibitionist daring. He "couldn't resist the sight of the wondrous revealment," just as the poet in "À une passante" is excited by the glimpse of the passing woman's legs revealed under her long dress. But the visual encounter is evanescent and transitory, although longer and more sustained than that of Baudelaire, despite Gerty's wish to sustain her reverie:

> Was it goodbye? No. She had to go but they would meet again, there, and she would dream of that till then, tomorrow, of her dream of yester eve. She drew herself up to her full height. Their souls met in a last lingering glance and the eyes that reached her heart, full of a strange shining, hung enraptured on her sweet flowerlike face. She half smiled at him wanly, a sweet forgiving smile, a smile that verged on tears, and then they parted. (13.760-65)

The voyeuristic formula of "he kept on looking, looking," as well as the romantic eloquence of "last lingering glance and the eyes . . . hung enraptured on her sweet flowerlike face," however, are both supplemented or superseded by the busy work of the gentleman's naughty hand. First comes the disappointment at the truth of Gerty's limbs when she stands up to "her full height": "Tight boots? No. She's lame! O!"(771). More shocking still, at least to the earlier readers of the novel, is the consequence of Bloom's truant organ's ejaculation: "This wet is very unpleasant. Stuck. Well the foreskin is not back. Better detach. / Ow!" (979-81) This "Ow!" registers a different order from the "Ô" of the last line of "À une passante": "Ô toi que j'eusse aimée, ô toi qui le savais!" ("O you I might have loved, as well you know!" [Baudelaire 1993: 189]). It stands apart indeed from any previous works of literature in the Western tradition, with its obscene outburst puncturing not merely the literary decorum of *belles lettres* but the grammatical regulations of English language itself. Its subversive force exceeds that of D. H. Lawrence's four-letter words, doing duty in otherwise proper language as guides to the author's attempt to elevate sexuality onto a quasi-spiritual terrain. In one scene in *Lady Chatterley's Lover*, the gamekeeper teaches a lesson to his master's wife on the difference between "fuck" and "cunt": "Fuck's only what you do. Animals fuck. But cunt 's a lot more than that. It's thee, dost see: an' tha 'rt a lot besides an animal, aren't ther?—even ter fuck! Cunt! Eh, that's the beauty o' thee, lass!" The lady seems to agree since she does not retort, as she kisses his "unspeakably warm, so unbearably beautiful" eyes and runs home in elation, with the narrator commenting, "the world seemed a dream; the trees in the park seemed bulging and surging at anchor on a tide, and the heave of the slope to the house was alive" (Lawrence 178). This is poetic to the point of overstatement, yet perhaps Connie's sexual satisfaction merits such description, if not her lover's rather rude compliment. Joyce, on the other hand, leaves the "Ow!" unattended or unredeemed—a monosyllable as alien to cerebral language as the phallic organ's unseemly shape is to human face.

Yet it is through and in language that Bloom and Gerty meet and mingle, despite the physical distance and disparity between their two respective discourses. The focalized narrative of Gerty in one passage adopts the non-standard compound words typical of Stephen or Bloom's monologues:

> One moment he had been there, fascinated by a loveliness that made him gaze, and the next moment it was the quiet gravefaced gentleman, selfcontrol expressed in every line of his distinguishedlooking figure.(13.540-3)

It is as if Gerty admitted Bloom to her world, or as if Bloom's idiomatic style penetrated her language. This compliment Bloom also returns, after both the girl and his orgasm have disappeared, by peppering his style with sentimental phrases and rhythm reminiscent of Gerty's style:

> O sweety all your little girlwhite up I saw dirty bracegirdle made me do love sticky we two naughty Grace darling she him half past the bed met him pike hoses frillies for Raoul de perfume. (1279-81)

Words such as "sweety" signal Bloom's entrance to the world of Gerty's sentimentalism. Although the covering of innocence is quickly mangled by the internal rhyme of "dirty," "sticky," and "naughty," as well as the disheveled syntax of "she him half past the bed met him," the popular romanticism of Gerty's language resonates in Bloom's monologue particularly in its yearning for the improbable, fictive, false object of love ("Raoul de perfume"). Even so, this tantalizing convergence of Bloom's and Gerty's idiomatic signature on the surface of the text—"sticky we two naughty" together—does little to bridge the physical distance between the two immobile would-be lovers. More significant is the structural homology between Bloom and Gerty in the way the former's erogenous zone eludes or fails the phallic domain while connected to other organs. Bloom's penis bears the "sticky" reminder of how he climaxed thanks to Gerty's naughty exhibitionism, yet as a subdued secretive masturbation it is an anti-climax. No triumphant phallic homily on the meaning of "cunt" and "fuck" can ensue, for instance, from this abortive *Erlebnis* of Bloom's autoeroticism. Ecstasy and shudder of ejaculation partake of the attributes of *Erlebnis* understood most simply as a subject's experience of a memorable sensory moment. Lawrence's Mellors seeks (with his author's encouragement) to uplift the *Erlebnis* of sexual consummation into an *Erfahrung* of sexual wisdom; Joyce's Bloom fails to cross the threshold of erotic *Erlebnis* proper. But Bloom has his compensations. His other organs pursue their separate pleasures apart and away from his phallus, whose dominance is half-denied even before the brutal feminization of Bloom in "Circe."

"In one hole and out behind"

Bloom the able-bodied male adult has a serviceable sexual organ, no doubt, but when we first meet him, stomach seems to be his principal organ. His day begins with his delectable breakfast of juicy pork kidney, and the high point of his outdoor sauntering in the city is reached at lunch time. As he finally settles on the place and menu for his midday meal, with his bellyful and after his glass of burgundy, his thoughts wander off to those happy days when his relationship with Molly was more delightful and succulent:

> . . . Mawkish pulp her mouth had mumbled sweetsour of her spittle. Joy: I ate it: joy. Young life, her lips that gave me pouting. Soft warm sticky gumjelly lips. Flowers her eyes were, take me, willing eyes. Pebbles fell. She lay still. . . . Hot I tongued her. She kissed me. I was kissed. All yielding she tossed my hair. Kissed, she kissed me.
>
> Me. And me now.
>
> Stuck, the flies buzzed. (8.907-10, 915-18)

The pathos conveyed by the melancholy endpoint of this musing—"Me. And me now"—may seem touching, accentuated by its objective correlative of "Stuck, the flies buzzed." But Bloom's estrangement from his wife is no news at this stage of the novel; moreover, it is something that he lives with, having adjusted himself to his cuckolded station, if not positively enjoying it. One clue to his snug acceptance of his diminished role in the marital arrangement is his vigilant, avid, and keen pursuit of pleasure on his own, away from home and off the beaten track of phallic conquests. The pleasure in the quoted passage is that of his palate, through which he articulates his erotic memory of those better days with Molly. The overriding sensation in his reminiscence, induced by his eating organ, is carried in his mouth—tongue, lips, spittle. Visual organs are also activated as he evokes the image of Molly's flowery willing eyes, yet they are superseded by the meeting of tongues, "Kissed, she kissed me." Eating and kissing, as in the expression "gumjelly lips," intermingle with each other to yield a compound profit to the hedonistic body, quite independently from any phallocentric erotic grammar. It may seem to some readers a recollection of "prelapsarian" and "Edenic" happiness (Henke 123), but the unctuous sensuousness of spittle tends rather to soil such notion of innocence.

Unlike the nineteenth-century flâneur, Bloom is a subject endowed with other organs besides his kaleidoscopic eyes. At the same time, he bears the distinctive birthmark of the flâneur (literally, the "loafer") in his rejection of work, discipline, and busy routine. Bloom's action in his first appearance

("Calypso") in the novel is that of releasing his body from the pang of hunger and the tension in his bowels. The familiar passages are worth another look, since the sequence is significant:

> Then he put a porkful into his mouth, chewing with discernment the toothsome pliant meat. Done to a turn. A mouthful of tea. Then he cut away dies of bread, sopped one in the gravy and put it in his mouth. What was that about some young student and a picnic? He creased out the letter at his side, reading it slowly as he chewed, sopping another die of bread in the gravy and raising it to his mouth. (4.390-96)

Eating and chewing take temporary precedence over his brain's activity. Only when the juicy meat melts in his mouth does his mind work itself into forming a question. The lethargic tempo of his mental movement, "reading it slowly as he chewed," also emphasizes the corporeal ballast holding down this thinking subject.[2] Conversely, one may say his body pushes his thinking downward, literally, as when he simultaneously reads and defecates towards the end of the episode: "Asquat on the cuckstool he folded out his paper, turning its pages over on his bared knees" (4.500-1). Holding "an old number of *Titbits*" (4.467), his brain rambles away into disconnected half-thoughts:

> Evening hours, girls in grey gauze. Night hours then: black with daggers and eyemasks. Poetical idea: pink, then golden, then grey, then black. Still, true to life also. Day: then the night.
>
> He tore away half the prise story sharply and wiped himself with it. (4.534-37)

Paragraph breaks here not because some conclusive reflection has been reached, but because his bowels have finished their work, at which point, the newspaper in its turn becomes a mere physical medium for wiping himself. From mouth to anus, other organs besides his brain (the organ of "logos") and phallus—between which a male body's phallocentric axis is formed—are active, potent, and stirring. Bloom, or Joyce speaking through Bloom, asserts this alternative view of human condition in "Lestrygonians":

> Nectar imagine it drinking electricity: gods' food. Lovely forms of women sculped Junonian. Immortal lovely. And we stuffing food in one hole and out behind: food, cycle, blood, dung, earth, food: have to feed it like stoking an engine. (8.927-30)

Unlike the immortal gods and goddesses, eating and defecating are of supreme importance to mortals, the body-machine ever repeating the movement of "in one hole and out behind."

In the second episode featuring his monologue, named "Lotus Eaters" by the author, Bloom muses on an Oriental life of lazy leisurely idling under sunny skies, a fitting fantasy of those living in this generally wet and chilly island, but specifically suitable to this Hibernian flâneur starting his daily peregrination with no particular wish to get busy instantly:

> The far east. Lovely spot it must be: the garden of the world, big lazy leaves to float about on, cactuses, flowery meads, snaky lianas they call them. Wonder is it like that. Those Cinghalese lobbing about in the sun in *dolce far niente,* not doing a hand's turn all day. Sleep six months out of twelve. Too hot to quarrel. Influence of the climate. Lethargy. Flowers of idleness. (5.29-34)

This utopia freed from business, the sweet taste of not doing anything, of "dolce far niente," a tropical paradise where men are at peace with one another thanks to their laziness and hot weather, lies at the opposite end of the work discipline of making ends meet which Deasy lectured on to Stephen as a distinctively English virtue. It also steers away from the Homeric source, for this Ulysses, far from fleeing the lotus-eaters' dangerous lethargy, desires its opiate dullness, envying the "heathen Chinese" who prefer "an ounce of opium" to having their soul saved, in tune with their carefree religion: "Buddha their god lying on his side in the museum. Taking it easy with hand under his cheek. Josssticks burning. Not like Ecce Homo. Crown of thorns and cross" (5.328-30). Bloom actively desires inaction, to eat the "flower of idlenss," yearning to move to the land of lotus-eaters, rather than shunning their potent temptation. Baudelaire the flâneur-lyricist cries out to eschew the demonic clutch of ennui, "Anywhere! Just so it is out of the world!" (Baudelaire 1970: 100); Bloom the flâneur and commercial agent fancies a life of torpor and ennui in this world.

What warrant there is for elevating, with Richard Brown, Bloom's admiration of laziness into a conscious "revolt of the intellectual or aesthete against the alienating tyranny of labor" (Brown 2002: 67), is questionable, since a rebellion entails political will-to-power, which Bloom shows no sign of possessing. But that the novel rejects the regular, regulated, regimented economy of work, and not merely through Bloom's idling, cannot be denied. Capitalism's shackling of humans with wage and rent can be resisted directly by envisioning an alternative order such as socialism, but it can also be sabotaged while staying inside the system. Recall how Farrington in "Counterparts" survives in his stifling workplace by stealing off to the pub as often as possible, and that Stephen in *Portrait* has yet to find himself an occupation or mission even towards the very end. The job he finds in the first part of *Ulysses* may be a relatively secure profession measured by the depressed economic condition of Edwardian Dublin, but he is as mentally absent from his teaching as he is physically present. The interior monologues which define and distinguish both Stephen's and Bloom's subjectivities in the narrative, in their simplest aspect, can be understood as forms of mental sabotage, of thoughts wandering off, loafing and idling, instead of submitting themselves to systematic or profitable reasoning. If there is a common principle working through the rambling phrases, it is, once again, that of disjunctive conjunction, which we have detected between the lines of Defoe's novel, except that this disjunction is far more disparate and far less amendable to articulating the characters' subjective experience into an *Erlebnis*. Better still, it is a disjunction that articulates a new state of subjectivity in which the organs experience their activity apart from the brain's reflective synthesis. Mouth, stomach, intestines, anus all go their separate ways away from the mental regime of the mind, sabotaging its regulation and asserting their own needs.[3] Bloom's is a body-without-organ, in Deleuze and Guattari's formulation, in that the thinking organ has such a poor control over the body. Or more precisely, his is a body with many organs, as his organs constitute "so many points of disjunction" (Deleuze and Guattari 1983: 12) of a subject not unified with itself.

A body with many organs makes a poor candidate for a proper flâneur, one who should be able to roam the streets, indefatigable because unhampered neither by social constraints nor by his own physical, bodily needs. Poe's "Man of the Crowd" is one such dynamo; yet even his pursuer, the narrator, a convalescent still recovering from sickness, displays surprising vigor as he follows the old man for two days on foot, without any break, both unfettered by their circulatory organs or physical necessities. At the other extreme stands, or rather scampers, the famished Lenehan in "Two Gallants," whose effort to assume gallant nonchalance of a flâneur is seriously impaired by the pang of hunger gnawing his body. Or we may recall Pepys' strong phallic urge in public spaces or during his public duties, which has to be relieved singlehanded or with the nearest partner available. Molly the thief disguised as a London gentlewoman is totally subordinated to her pockets which dominate her as if they were artificial economic organs appended to her appealing looks and deft hands. Bloom's peculiarity, his claim to distinction among the clan of flâneurs—soon to die off as urban thoroughfares made way to marauding motor cars—lies in the manner in which his subjectivity has no single control centre, be it eyes or stomach or phallus or brain or pocket. Experience as *Erlebnis* eludes him, unable to find any locus for concentrated shock or memorable sensation, but at the same time, this deficit is compensated by the porous mingling of his bodily organs with outside stimuli. Baudelaire mused on the ideal of losing oneself in the metropolitan crowd as something approaching a "divine prostitution of the soul giving itself entire . . . to the unexpected as it comes along, to the stranger as he passes" (Baudelaire 1970: 20). Joyce's Bloom embodies a non-divine, totally human giving of the bodily self to the city and its crowd. Or rather, one may say the city streets enter his senses, literally inhabiting his body as their own space:

> Grafton street gay with housed awnings lured his senses. Muslin prints, silkdames and dowagers, jingle of harnesses, hoofthuds lowringing in the baking causeway. Thick feet that woman has in the white stockings. Hope the rain mucks them up on her. Countrybred chawbacon. All the beef to the heels were in. Always gives a woman clumsy feet. Molly looks out of plumb. (8.614-19)

This Dublin high street, which approximates as best as it can the glittering boulevards of Paris or London, "lures his senses," as the feminine items on display instantly colonize his brain, pulling him back to the nodal point of his desire, Molly. But it leads to no phallic assertiveness or reconfirmation of his masculinity, but instead a tactile sense of Molly-like "plumpness" further numbs and subdues his thinking organ:

> A warm human plumpness settled down on his brain. His brain yielded. Perfume of embraces all him assailed. With hungered flesh obscurely, he mutely craved to adore.
>
> Duke street. Here we are. Must eat. The Burton. Feel better then.
>
> He turned Combirdge's corner, still pursued. Jingling, hoofthuds. Perfumed bodies, warm, full. All kissed, yielded: in deep summer fields, tangled pressed grass, in trickling hallways of tenements, along sofas, creaking beds. (8.637-44)

His brain yields to the pleasant sensation of voluminous softness, boosted by his olfactory illusion of smelling invisible perfume embracing him. His inner organs, however, claim their rights: the "hungered flesh" debunks the exquisite sensation of his brain to reduce it to one of mute "craving." Driven by his stomach, the erotic flare of the city dims and the syntax is punctured by the clamor within his body for food: "Duke street. Here we are. Must eat." Having heeded the demands of his organs, he resumes his strolling of the city streets, with soothing thoughts of fragrance, artificial and natural, dictating his steps. Bloom's different organs encounter one another as his body roams the city streets, or to put it differently, Bloom brings his whole body to bear on his interaction with the metropolis. Thanks to his body's articulation as a body with many organs over which no single organ prevails, his body has intercourse with the city in a radical mode of disjunctive conjunction.

"Ah no, that's the soap."

The bodily subject with many organs, not beholden to the lordship of any single organ within it, assigns no seat to a transcendental soul. What it gains from this somatic materialism is a release from mental and spiritual regime, a right to indulge in the bodily pleasures without shame or guilt. It can also presume to be more impassive and stoic in facing death, for freed from any intimation of after-life, particularly of the Christian teachings of "Ecce Homo. Crown of thorns and cross," it can feel less tormented by spiritual anxiety. Yet two negative consequences follow from this. The first has to do with the question of death and extinction of the living body; the second, that of reification, the dying of the living into things.

To begin with the question of death, first, we can assume the following argument. If a human being is just a body without soul, it only has corporeal attributes. When the body dies, therefore, it is a simple termination of bodily functioning and nothing more. This is the position stated, irreverently, by Buck Mulligan in the first episode. Stephen's mother is "beastly dead" (1.198), for there is nothing to distinguish human death from that of other mammals. "It's a beastly thing and nothing else," declares Mulligan, "It simply doesn't matter" (1.206-7). But of course it does matter to Stephen and to the rest of humanity apart from this blasphemous medical student. It mattered very much to Stephen's author. *Dubliners*, from its first to the last story, tells tales of ghosts haunting and plaguing the living in various forms, including the newspaper article reporting Mrs. Sinico's death in "A Painful Case," which shatters the self-enclosed confidence of the Nietzsche-reading Mr. Duffy, an intellectual kinsman of Mulligan. Joyce in *Portrait* reserves generous pages to address the issue not merely of death but of afterlife. Death is literally a "grave matter" in the second part of *Ulysses*, as one may infer merely from the procession of episodes. The bodily (dis)charging of "Calypso" and the pursuit of laziness dramatized in "Lotus Eaters" are interrupted by Dignam's death and corpse in "Hades." Bloom's interior monologue would be suspended in the next episode "Aeolus," with only "Lestrygonians" remaining as an uncontested episode giving full (and last) coverage of

Bloom-centered monologue. Before the (anti-)climax of "Circe" that tears apart Bloom's gentlemanly and masculine pretensions, "Hades" checks the flow of hedonistic materialism implicit in the first two episodes.

Generally adhering to agnostic (if not outright atheist) stance on death, Bloom seeks to contain the question of mortality within a naïve scientific frame. Death is death and corpse is just a corpse. "A corpse is meat gone bad. Well and what's cheese? Corpse of milk," (6.981-82), Bloom cleverly observes. A corpse, better still, enriches the soil, like other putrefying proteins:

> I daresay the soil would be quite fat with corpsemanure, bones, flesh, nails. Charnelhouses. Dreadful. Turning green and pink decomposing. Rot quick in damp earth. The lean old ones tougher. Then a kind of a tallow kind of a cheesy. (6.776-79)

In this associative argument, death is naturalized as a cyclical waste, discharged and decomposed to nourish the earth. The same logic informs Bloom's remark in "Hades" about burial, "An empty hearse trotted by, coming from the cemetery: looks relieved" (6.436-37). The graveyard becomes an open latrine in this formula, where funeral carriages ease themselves of their unseemly and smelly burden. This scatological trope is already registered at the end of "Calypso," whose last line, after Bloom's successful stool, is his exclamation, "Poor Dignam!" (4.551). This phrase reappears like a leitmotif whenever Bloom thinks of Dignam's death. It begs the question, however, of why anyone should take pity on the dead if death is a mere biochemical process of heart stopping and body rotting. Commiseration, sympathy, and mourning all presuppose some transcendental realm or residue over and after the physical death itself. One feels sorry and nervous about the dead because of some intimation that death may not be all that simple or clear-cut. A "moment of silence" is observed even in the officially atheist socialist regimes that presumably have eradicated religion and superstitions about soul altogether. Even without any positive belief that there might be something after death, the blunt arbitrariness of death instills discomfort and disquiet into Bloom the non-believer, "Dreadful. Turning green and pink decomposing," in the above quote, or in the comical version of being curious as to whether corpses make wind like living bodies:

> Must be an infernal lot of bad gas round the place. Butchers, for instance: they get like raw beefsteaks. Who was telling me? Mervyn Browne. Down in the vaults of saint Werburgh's lovely old organ hundred and fifty they have to bore a hole in the coffins sometimes to let out the bad gas and burn it. (6.607-

11)

This excremental reflection is also an attempt to keep death strictly confined to earth. Saint or no saint, a corpse is a subterranean substance that putrefies and disintegrates. Yet gas may leak invisibly as the chemical counterpart to the spirit, escaping from the coffin to haunt the living, even on this rare sunny and dry June day in Dublin. Spirit-gas leads to the insertion of "Hades" episode into Bloom's morning schedule, and haunts his walks in the shape of various memories of the dead loved-ones, especially his son, which draws a long shadow over his thoughts in the later episodes: "If little Rudy had lived. See him grow up. Hear his voice in the house. Walking besides Molly in an Eton suit. My son" (6.75-76). No placid scientific joke about rotting or farting corpses can possibly put to rest this painfully vivid vision of his son. Mortality is a conundrum as much for Bloom the creaturely hedonist as for Stephen the hyper-intellectual young man.

Another antinomy of asserting the rights of a many-organed bodily life untaxed by spiritual concerns is its tendency to succumb to the pressure or allure of commodified consumer society, where the commodity's "soul of value," as Marx puts it, eagerly seeks to take on an eerie life of its own as "embodied value" (Marx 1976: 143). Bloom may not be a resident representative merchant-burgher of the Hibernian metropolis, but he is neither a poor clerk on pitiful wages like Farrington nor a jobless sycophant like Lenehan. Even compared with the young schoolteacher Stephen, he enjoys greater financial security. He has money to spend, small sums as they may be, and corrosive economic worries are not among the major themes flipping past his wife's soliloquy at the end of the novel. The first thing in the morning he does is to exchange money for commodity, the pork kidney, which enters the bodily circulation of Bloom the consumer, to be transformed (in part at least) into his morning stool. The next purchase he makes, however, resists easy transformation, being a soap he bought at a chemist's. "Nice smell these soaps have. Pure curd soap" (5.501), he thinks, intending to use them at a Turkish bath nearby, but that plan having been abandoned the soap remains inside his clothes throughout that day, evening, and night, bulging awkwardly inside his pants as a useless lumber.

The persistent presence of the soap settled inside Bloom's trouser pockets, attached to the middle zone of Bloom's body, at once smoothes over and substitutes for Bloom's defective phallic subjectivity. Bloom's male organ has no dominant position, as we have seen above. He himself hardly seems particularly distressed by it, but instead accommodates himself to his inherently bisexual persona, as the oxymoronic nickname,

"Henry Flower Esq" (5.62), used on his billet-doux with Martha, indicates. To "Henry" the name of English (and French) kings is appended the disarming surname "Flower" (5.62). "Henry Flower" further leads himself to toy with the notion that the venerable Shakespearan name "Hamlet" refers really to a woman in disguise: "Male impersonator. Perhaps he was a woman. Why Ophelia committed suicide" (5.195-96). The easy life his daydreams conjure in "Lotus Eaters" wanders off into his fancying the happiness of castrated masculine animals, a notion inspired by the "crunching of gilded oats, the gently champing teeth" and their "full buck eyes" looking straight at him:

> Their Eldorado. Poor jugginses! Damn all they know or care about anything with their long noses stuck in nosebags. Too full for words. Still they get their feed all right and their doss. Gelded too: a stump of black guttapercha wagging limp between their haunches. Might be happy all the same that way. (5.215-19)

That putative happiness presupposes a certain version of masochism, soon manifested in Martha's letter. Calling him "you poor little naughty boy" (5.246-47), Martha tickles "Henry Flower" with her desire to give him physical pain: "I do wish I could punish you for that" (244). The effect of the illicit letter is instant, as it gives him the first (minor) orgasm of the day:

> . . . Language of flowers. They like it because no-one can hear. Or a poison bouquet to strike him down. Then walking slowly forward he read the letter again, murmuring here and there a word. Angry tulips with you darling manflower punish your cactus if you don't please poor forgetmenot how I long violets to dear roses when we soon anemone meet all naughty nightstalk wife Martha's perfume. Having read it all he took it from the newspaper and put it back in his sidepocket.
>
> Weak joy opened his lips. (5.261-68)

Drugging himself with a flowery language of masochistic pleasure, of her "tulips" thrashing his "cactus," he extracts a "[w]eak joy," a quick if feeble jouissance from the letter, in which his phallic prowess or penetration has no role to play otherwise than as a passive receptacle of delightfully painful sensations. But pain is pain, nonetheless. Other implications of the language of flower, its musical property in particular, we shall examine in the next chapter, but in the present context one has to take note of its insufficiency as a means of compensating for Bloom's lack of phallocentric self-certainty. A full-fledged masochism, however strong its joy may be, is something Bloom's many-organed body shuns. At this point the soap intervenes, to wash off all marks of gendered distinction between bodies, even of florid delight in pain. He envisions now a seamless liquid form of auto-eroticism immersed in water: "Also I think I. Yes I. Do it in the bath. Curious longing I. Water to water. Combine business with pleasure. Pity no time for massage. Feel fresh then all the day. Funeral be rather glum" (5.503-6). The intimation of death which he cannot evade in the next stop of his peregrination he seeks to counter with this soap-inspired non-phallic ecstasy, where the entire body, or rather the skin itself becomes the erotic organ inducing excitement, as the closing "epiphany" of the episode poetically evokes:

> Enjoy a bath now: clean trough of water, cool enamel, the gentle tepid stream. This is my body.
>
> He foresaw his pale body reclined in it at full, naked, in a womb of warmth, oiled by scented melting soap, softly laved. He saw his trunk and limbs riprippled over and sustained, buoyed lightly upward, lemonyellow: his navel, bud of flesh: and saw the dark tangled curls of his bush floating, floating hair of the stream around the limp father of thousands, a languid floating flower. (5.565-72)

This pleasant, soothing, orgasmic bath Bloom is not allowed to indulge in by his author; instead, he is made to bear the weight and volume of the illiquid soap on his body, as he moves about the city and its environs. When his "limp father of thousands" or his "languid floating flower" finally ejaculates in "Nausicaa," the "scented melting soap" re-asserts its mediating force. Expecting to smell his "Mansmell" (13.1036) and confirm his masculinity, he merely finds that the soap has expunged his virility inside his clothes:

> Hm. Into the. Hm. Opening of his waistcoat. Almonds or. No. Lemons it is. Ah no, that's the soap. (13.1042-43)

At the centre of his body sits the soap, instead of his masculine organ, and the natural odour of his manliness has been usurped by the artificial perfume of the purchased ware.

Henry Flower the feminine man can be exceptionally sympathetic to women's predicament, such as child labour, as narrated in the mock-medieval style of "Oxen of the Sun":

> But sir Leopold was passing grave maugre his word by cause he still had pity of the terrorcausing shrieking women in their labour and as he was minded of his good lady Marion that had borne him an only manchild which on his eleventh day on live had died and no man of art could save so dark is destiny. (14.264-68)

Sir Leopold, if we can believe this narrator, commiserates with the natural woes feminine flesh is heir to. Moreover, his sharing of household duties, such as preparing breakfast for his spouse in "Calypso," could appeal to later readers as a prophetic image of gender-equal partnership. In the nightmare world of topsy-turvy fantasy which "Circe" enacts, however, his lack of phallic prowess becomes a topic lampooned remorselessly, first by making him a willing cuckold and liveried footman of his wife's lover Boylan (15.3756-67). To him is thrown nothing but the meager bone of voyeuristic pleasure: "You can apply your eye to the keyhole and play with yourself while I just go through her a few times," concedes Boylan the phallic man (15.3788-89). Grateful and content with his lot, Bloom ecstatically cheers Boylan as the latter makes athletic love to Molly:

BOYLAN'S VOICE

(*sweetly, hoarsely, in the pit of his stomach*) Ah!
Godblazegrukbrukarchkhrasht!

MARION'S VOICE

(*hoarsely, sweetly, rising to her throat*) O!
Weeshwashtkissinapooisthnapoohuck?

BLOOM

(*his eyes wildly dilated, clasps himself*) Show! Hide! Show! Plough her! More! Shoot! (15.3808-16)

One inevitable consequence of this and other debasements of Bloom in "Circe" is the impossibility of considering Bloom the main flâneur-protagonist of the novel. "Circe" conducts a final devastating reduction of Bloom's status and position within the novel, unleashed after "Lestrygonians" in different forms (making him a mere passing character from episodes nine to eleven and assaulting him in episode twelve). The part of the novel focused on Bloom's interior monologue is just one part, significant no doubt, but made unduly famous by subsequent "Bloom-worship" (such as the annual Bloomsday in Dublin), with little regard to the distancing, satirizing, and even brutalizing treatment his author metes out to him in other parts of the novel.

Any discussion of Bloom's *flânerie* cannot bypass "Circe," as the "nighttown"(15.1) is the climactic terminus of his wandering. The transformations that take place in this longest episode of the novel have to be taken not only as major statements in their own right but also as judgements on the characters introduced previously, including Bloom himself. Here Bloom is subjected to, among other things, a literal unmanning by Bella Cohen, now transformed into Bello the phallic woman and dealer in sex slaves. Bloom becomes an abject slave only too willingly:

BELLO

Dungdevourer!

BLOOM

(*with sinews semiflexed*) Magmagnificence!

BELLO

Down! (*he taps her on the shoulder with his fan*) Incline feet forward! Slide left foot one pace back! You will fall. You are falling. On the hands down!

BLOOM

(*her eyes upturned in the sign of admiration, closing, yaps*) Truffles!

> (*With a piercing epileptic cry she sinks on all fours, grunting, snuffling, rooting at his feet: then lies, shamming dead, with eyes shut tight, trembling eyelids, bowed upon the ground in the attitude of most excellent master.*) (15.2842-55)

This scene poses complicated questions, no doubt. The unflattering details apart, the grammatical denotation of the canine abject creature as a "she" is bound to be hardly palatable to contemporary political correctness, for it defines femininity in terms of subhuman servility. And the brutal deflowering of Bloom by Bella-Bello, in the auction scene that follows, seems almost gratuitous, however much one may wish to justify the ways of Joyce to the reader:

BELLO

. . . Swell the bust. Smile. Droop shoulders. What offers? (*he points*) For that lot. Trained by owner to fetch and carry, basket in mouth. (*he bares his arm and plunges it elbowdeep in Bloom's vulva*) There's fine depth for you! What, boys! That give you a hardon? (*he shoves his arm in a bidder's face*) Here wet the deck and wipe it round!(15.3087-91)

Gender and sexuality are obvious topics for discussion to ensue upon citing this passage, but the obviousness itself (of woman-vulva vs. man-"hardon") precludes perhaps any in-depth discussion. Bello's jeering challenge, "There's fine depth for you!" may also be something aimed at the academic reader, seeking to sniff abstruseness from "his" bare arms reeking with Bloom's wetness.

Equally, if not more important, is the fact that it all takes place in a thoroughly commodified context of selling female body for cash. Bloom first enters this underworld not unarmed but girded with his purse and purchased goods. "Bloom pats with parceled hands watchfob, pocketbookpocket, pursepoke, sweets of sin, potatosoap" (15.242-43), goes the "stage direction." Of these objects the soap is given an early prominence, as it speaks of the spurious magic of consumption, of love between the purchaser and the purchased thing:

BLOOM

I was just going back for that lotion whitewax, orangeflower water. Shop closes early on Thursday. But the first thing in the morning. (*he pats divers pockets*) This moving kidney. Ah!

(*He points to the south, then to the east. A cake of new clean lemon soap arises, diffusing light and perfume.*)

THE SOAP

We're a capital couple are Bloom and I.
He brightens the earth. I polish the sy.

(*The freckled face of Sweny, the druggist, appears in the disc of the soapsun.*)

SWENY

Three and a penny, please. (15.331-43)

In this scene re-enacting his morning shopping at the chemist, the soap emerges with glittering charm and glib eloquence, singing of the happy partnership of "Bloom and I." Yet instantly, the reality of monetary mediation of this "capital couple" raises its "freckled face," chiming in with the dull language of telling coins: "Three and a penny, please." Under the aegis of this commercialized world, illusions can be bought with small change, as illusory attractions of goods are manufactured by advertising agents such as Bloom. Quite fitting it is, then, that Bloom should meet a "nymph" of advertisement at "nighttown":

BLOOM

(*lifts a turtle head towards her lap*) We have met before. On another star.

THE NYMPH

(*sadly*) Rubber goods. Neverrip brand as supplied to the aristocracy. Corsets for men. I cure fits or money refunded. Unsolicited testimonials for Professor Waldmann's wonderful chest exuber. My bust developed four inches in three weeks, reports Mrs Gus Rublin with photo.

BLOOM

You mean *Photo Bits*?

THE NYMPH

I do. You bore me away, framed me in oak and tinsel, set me above your marriage couch. Unseen, one summer eve, you kissed me in four places. And with loving pencils you shaded my eyes, my bosom and my shame. (15.3253-65)

The sad melancholy look of the nymph cannot return Bloom's adoring gaze, and when she opens her mouth, shop talk pours out of it, dispelling any fantasy of romantic sentiment or lovemaking, which, as her second speech makes clear, are so many mercenary fabrications invented by Bloom himself. It is in this series of commodified erotic fascinations that Bella-Bello emerges, to rudely tear apart the façade of desire articulated and fulfilled through purchase. The scramble for the coins which the drunken Stephen listlessly hands Bella amplifies the hollowness of Bloom the flâneur's flirting with parcels, soaps, commerce, and commercialized erotics:

> *(Bella goes to the table to count the money while Stephen talks to himself in monosyllables. Zoe bends over the table. Kitty leans over Zoe's neck. Lynch gets up, rights his cap and, clasping Kitty's waist, adds his head to the group.)*

FLORRY

(*strives heavily to rise*) Ow! My foot's asleep. (*She limps over to the table. Bloom approaches.*)

BELLA, ZOE, KITTY, LYNCH, BLOOM

> (*chattering and squabbling*) The gentleman . . . ten shillings . . . . paying for the three . . . allow me a moment . . . this gentleman pays separate . . . . who's touching it? . . . ow! . . . mind you're pinching . . . are you staying the night or a short time? . . . who did? . . . you're a liar, excuse me . . . the gentleman paid down like a gentleman . . . drink . . . it's long after eleven. (15.3548-60)

With this another "Ow!" echoing Bloom's post-masturbatory "Ow!" in "Nausicaa," a cash nexus linking shillings to gentlemen to girls puts paid to the tradition of gentlemanly flâneurs roaming the streets incognito, indulging in fantasy, observing the other while threatened by none, with their subjective identities left intact and unmolested. Bloom's name, inserted into the last slot of the collective subject headed by Bella "squabbling" to grab the coins, has little resemblance to "Mr Bloom" walking "soberly, past Windmill lane" (5.1-2) through Westland row, with full breakfast sitting on his belly, and fancying an easy life of *dolce far niente*. In Dublin, as in any other modern city, *dolce* always comes at a cost, and when it is paid for, its sweetness begins to turn sour.

CHAPTER TWELVE

NARRATIO IN EXTREMIS

"Or the south a mouth?"

The florid language Bloom as "Henry Flower" dreams of suits his erotic fancy snugly, yet it flows through other channels as well, gray rather than rosy, cranking rather than mellifluous. In "Lotus Eaters," as much as he wishes to imagine himself as a Don Giovanni-like "Henry Flower," he has to tear off, under a railway arch, the envelop bearing his name on it to preserve the paltry secret of his epistolary liaison. This action drags into his mind the unlovely world of money: "Henry Flower. You could tear up a cheque for a hundred pounds in the same way. Simple bit of paper" (5.303-4). His invocation of finance and its numerical language calculated by the price of porter—"A million pounds, wait a moment. Two pence a pint, fourpence a quart, eightpence a gallon of porter" (307-9)—leads to the interruption of his monologue by a loud embodiment of real economy, a freight train rushing above his head:

> An incoming train clanked heavily above his head, coach after coach. Barrels bumped in his head: dull porter slopped and churned inside. The bungholes sprang open and a huge dull flood leaked out, flowing together, winding through mudflats all over the level land, a lazy pooling swirl of liquor bearing along wideleaved flowers of its froth.(5.313-17)

The wasteful leak of this liquid commodity, among other things, foreshadows Bloom's masturbatory leak in "Nausicaa," exemplifying in both cases a non-productive economy where no gain issues from the act of spending. In this regard it also relates to the other wasteful flow, a "huge dull flood" in its own right, inundating the city to vanish like so much forth: the word-mill of journalism.

Ulysses pays sardonic tribute to the close relationship between journalism and the novel, inseparable for both Defoe and Dickens as parallel discourses purveying experiential reality. In the narrative logic of *Ulysses* Part Two, the first three Bloom-focused episodes, closer to the first-person narration of *Erlebnis* (explored by Defoe), are given an abrupt check in the fourth, comparable to the porter-train's intrusion above, by a mock journalist discourse, which gestures towards the communal intention of *Erfahrung*, but instead debunks even its informative value by offering non- or stale news items that have no value to the consumer-reader of the arranged articles. A "lazy pooling swirl" of fortuitous information forms stray puddles throughout the episode, with all the headlines disjointed from the body. "Queen Ann is dead" (7.90) is a report that had once been new two centuries ago, while other headlines plead, "KYRIE ELEISON!" (7.559), or swear, "K[iss].M[y].A[rse]." (980). The most telling sample, however, of lampooning the bankruptcy of third-person narration, whether of newspaper reportage or novelistic accounts of experience, would be the following unnamable article headed by three question marks:

? ? ?

Lenehan said to all:

—Silence! What opera resembles a railwayline? Reflect, ponder, excogitate, reply.

Stephen handed over the typed sheets, pointing to the title and signature.

—Who? the editor asked.

Bit torn off.

—Mr Garrett Deasy, Stephen said.

—That old pelters, the editor said. Who tore it? Was he short taken?

On swift sail flaming
From storm and south
He comes, pale vampire,
Mouth to my mouth.

—Good day, Stephen, the professor said, coming to peer over their shoulders. Foot and mouth? Are you turned . . . ?

Bullockbefriending bard. (7.512-28)

The mute title at once registers and erases the rhetoric of journalistic prose, which always presupposes the reader's curiosity as to what, where, when, and how. Questions are indeed asked in the main body of the entry, but they are left astray, cut off from any meaningful context for those gathered in the newspaper office. Lenehan's question is simply ignored, while the editor's "Who?" is a mere laconic monosyllable. The content matters less than the margin being slightly torn off. The "professor" has two questions, which do not belong together. The centerpiece of the text, by contrast, is occupied by a verse, recited as Stephen's unvoiced monologue, which carries multiple layers of references in its own right (our earlier discussion of Bram Stoker would be one, for instance), but that this disjunction between title and content, as well as within the narrative content itself, glaringly dramatizes the failure of communication, and hence the aborting of information that occurs even at the heart of this news manufactory, is what we wish to emphasize in this chapter. Instead of having any journalistic value, the episode carries some minimal narrative value for the novel's action, for Stephen reappears after being absent for three episodes, having been sent there on errand by his employer in "Nestor," with the repetition of earlier phrases from "Telemachia" ("bullockbefriending bard" [2.431] as well as the verse) garnishing his presence as leitmotifs. One cannot say, even so, that the "novel" prevails over journalistic information, since the plot cares not to develop Stephen's action. He will wax most heroic two episodes later ("Scylla and Charybdis") at a different setting (National Library). Here Stephen's presence at *Freeman's Journal* office has no more significance than that of other characters, all floating in the vapid third-person narration Joyce assigns to this episode of punctured, severed, mangled journalism.

As *Ulysses* establishes new forms of literary expression, of which the interior monologue is the most prominent but by no means the only model, it also enlists various categories of literariness. "Intertextuality" would be a convenient term to describe this dialogue of forms and genres, most visible in the mini anthology of English prose unfolding in "Oxen of the Sun." But concerning other generic registers residing outside the canon of literary history, the relatively congruent or diplomatic interaction "intertextuality" implies may not be entirely applicable. In "Aeolus," which straddles, without bridging, the two terrains of journalistic information and narrative fiction, literariness as such is made strange, as these terrains are framed by an apparently transparent prose akin to newspaper reportage. Stephen's hallmark style of compound alliterative phrases in the above example of "Bullockbefriending bard" is literally left stranded like a stranger in this textual ambience, while the doggerel version of Hyde's verse occupies the centre stage like a ghost, invisible, silent to other characters, unconnected to other components of the entry. In another example, poetry, in all its proper foreignness, is turned into news and therefore into no-news at all, as words communicating no information are clustered together, under the heading of "Rhymes and Reasons":

RHYMES AND REASONS

Mouth, south. Is the mouth south someway? Or the south a mouth? Must be some. South, pout, out, shout, drouth. Rhymes: two men dressed the same, looking the same, two by two.

> . . . . *la tua pace*
> . . . . . . *che parlar ti piace*
> *Mentre che il vento, come fa, si tace.*

> He saw them three by three, approaching girls, in green, in rose, in russet, entwining, *per l'aer perso*, in mauve, in purple, *quella pacifica oriafiamma*, gold of oriflamme, *di rimirar fè più ardenti*. But I old men, penitent, leadenfooted, underdarkneath the night: mouth south: tomb womb.
> —Speak up for yourself, Mr O'Madden Burke said. (7.713-25)

This musing on the rhyme "Mouth, south" that will be inserted under the heading "? ? ?" ten entries later highlights an arbitrary pattern of words sharing the same phonetic property but without semantic links, and may seem to be in keeping with Stephen's self-consciousness about the English language which is both his and not his. Yet unlike in the final chapter of *Portrait*, or in "Telemachia," the subject asking the question, "Is the mouth south someway?" can be construed as another subject, or an impersonal (or third-person) narrator. Rhymes are likened to two men, but by whom? Who is quoting the Dante lines with excessive ellipsis? What is being announced here besides the fact that the ludic value of *pace-piace-tace* is cut off from the original context, as the ellipsis points attest? What does the entry "report" at the horizontal axis of the passage's progression, other than its separation from the vertical axis of intertextual allusions to Dante's *Commedia*? Or does the text simply pay tribute to Dante's Italian masterpiece, honored literally with italics? Is the "he" of "He saw them" Stephen or Dante or just any he, that impersonal third-person both journalism and third-person realistic narratives posit as the mediator of factuality? None of these questions can be answered with certainty although annotations can be appended on the provenance of the references (see Gifford 143-44). But understanding the allusions can be relevant only if the text is primarily concerned with Dante. It is and is not, sardonically and schizophrenically, for apart from the ellipsis that erases the original body, the English rhyme words "mouth south" return to assert their proprietary right, even to the point of gesturing towards a semantic closure, of giving meaning to the phonetic accident of sharing *-outh*: "tomb womb" is what "mouth sounds" means (or merely parallels). Even before that (non-)conclusion, the subject marker of the syntax is further complicated by the dissonance created by the first-person (singular-plural) statement of "But I old men," and the command, "Speak up for yourself," given by "Mr O'Madden Burke," which summons the text back from its poetic (or phonetic) reflections to its story-telling "novelistic" duty. In this state of

carefully crafted linguistic dissonance, no character, person, or subject can assume a position from which to experience what happens around him or what passes through his mind. Neither *Erfahrung* nor *Erlebnis* is conceivable in this disembodied, distracted (non-)focalization of narration that narrates not.

The montage-like collation of prose narratives over and above literary intertextuality is given a further contrapuntal variation in "Cyclops," where journalistic reportage, albeit in the service of double-edged satire, is adopted to revisit Ireland's historical trauma. The passage resurrects the tradition of heroic defeat rhapsodically, as the narrator reports the execution of Robert Emmet, the leader and martyr of the United Irishmen along with Wolf Tone. That Joyce lampoons Irish nationalism implicit in such statements as "*Sinn Fein*! says the citizen. *Sinn fein amhain*! The friends we love are by our side and the foes we hate before us" (12.523-24) can be readily recognized, but the bifurcation of "friends" vs. "foes" has a macabre relevance for this colonial capital, as the hanging, drawing and quartering of Emmet is described, with a minimal degree of stylistic disruption, in a factual third-person account. "The last farewell was affecting in the extreme" (525) is the opening sentence registering a news-like style, with its typical bombast spicing up its sensational value:

> From the belfries far and near the funereal deathbell tolled unceasingly while all around the gloomy precincts rolled the ominous warning of a hundred muffled drums punctuated by the hollow booming of pieces of ordnance. The deafening claps of thunder and the dazzling flashes of lightning which lit up the ghastly scene testified that the artillery of heaven had lent its supernatural pomp to the already gruesome spectacle. (12.525-31)

If Joyce's prose frames and satirizes the conventional third-person narrative which both journalism and novels employ to present a momentous event as an experience to the reader, he also takes advantage of the same convention to indict the sheer brutality of the political revenge the British exact on its enemies:

> Hand by the block stood the grim figure of the executioner, his visage being concealed in a tengallon pot with two circular perforated apertures through which his eyes glowered furiously. As he awaited the fatal signal he tested the edge of his horrible weapon by honing it upon his brawny forearm or decapitated in rapid succession a flock of sheep which had been provided by the admirers of his fell but necessary office. On a handsome mahogany table near him was neatly arranged the quartering knife, the various finely tempered disemboweling appliances (specially supplied by the worldfamous firm of cutlers, Messrs John Round and Sons, Sheffield), a terra cotta

> saucepan for the reception of the duodenum, colon, blind intestine and appendix etc when successfully extracted and two commodious milkjugs destined to receive the most precious blood of the most precious victim. (12.612-24)

The meticulous itemization of the instruments of quartering makes the pursuit of realistic (or naturalistic) reportage absurd, distracting the attention from the savage callousness of the executioner the first half of the passage emphasizes. But it also connects the Empire's modern industrial prowess to medieval atrocity, as the "various finely tempered disemboweling appliances" are "specially supplied by the worldfamous firm of cutlers, Messrs John Round and Sons, Sheffield," while aligning the addiction to factual detail with the obsession for measurement endemic to modern mechanical industrial civilization. This self-derisive mini-historical narrative demonstrates the novel's satirical appreciation of the validity of conventional third-person narration, which, as we have seen in discussing Dickens, had an intimate relationship with journalism in the nineteenth century. Objective representation of "outside" events does have a role, though one that comes debilitated by ambivalence and self-depreciation, in the vast array of styles which constitute *Ulysses*.

The narrative mode of *Ulysses* reverts from mock journalist reportage of "Aeolus" to Bloom-focused interior monologue for one more episode ("Lestrygonians"), to be superseded by the Stephen-focused Platonic dialogue of "Scylla and Charybydis," which in turn yields the stage to a third-person focalized narrative in relatively plain English prose of "The Wandering Rocks." The episode choreographs the simultaneous movement of numerous Dubliners, spatially discrete but all sharing the city's space, turned into one extensive ballroom full of dancers. Among the metaphorical dancers is a professional choreographer, a "Mr Denis J Maginni, professor of dancing & c, in silk hat" (10.56), but the show is stage-managed by the novelist himself. As its short narratives accumulate, "The Wandering Rocks" works itself gradually into a new type of metropolitan writing, unprecedented in any national tradition. Although it takes cue from Dickens's "cinematic" jumps from one scene to another, the "cuts" are linked not by an "economy of 'plot'" (Martin 43) disclosing secret links, say, of Amy Dorrit to Mrs. Clennam or of Esther to Lady Dedlock. Instead, this writing taps another Dickensian conception, that of spatial contiguity, of sharing the same city space unawares, which Joyce brings to an extreme point by depicting in a slow-motion "take" the simultaneity of the city's many characters living through the very same moments of the day. "The Wandering Rocks" shows the influence of Dickens's "spectacular effects" of "shock and euphoria of presenting apparently distinct but ultimately interconnected simultaneous events" (Brown 2002: 69). But the "shock and euphoria" in Joyce has more to do with the performance of narrative style than with plot development. The overall pattern of "the very reverend John Conmee S. J." initiating the first move of the episode and ending with the viceregal cavalcade of personages representing the British Crown seems to invite political interpretation, along the lines of what we have attempted in chapters nine and ten. Apart from those with Castle connections such as Martin Cunningham and Mr. Power (both from "Grace" of *Dubliners*), or the nameless "Constable 57C, on his beat" (10.217) or (possibly) the "onelegged sailor" (10.228) begging in the name of the Empire ("he growled unamiably: / — *For England...*" [10.230-32]), most of the figures appearing in each section belong to the majority group of Irish Catholics. The symbolism embedded in the statement, "The castle car wheeled empty into upper Exchange street" (10.972), intimates the hollowness of colonial power, in contrast to the concrete individual Dubliners who seem to have been liberated on this sunny June afternoon from the "paralysis" which the earlier collection of Joyce's tales diagnosed as the prevailing disease of the city's Catholic population. Boylan, among the most robust of them, walks side by side with the most burdened of them, the "H.E.L.Y's" sandwich men:

> Blazes Boylan walked here and there in new tan shoes about the fruitsmelling shop, lifting fruits, young juicy crinkled and plump red tomatoes, sniffing smells.
>
> H. E. L. Y'S filed before him, tallwhitehatted, past Tangier lane, plodding towards their goal. (10.307-11)

Organized around the juxtaposed and disparate trajectories of characters strolling, whether on business or for pleasure, the episode subscribes to the principle of disjunctive conjunction which we have identified as a major feature of metropolitan prose. Between and within the sections, narrative continuity is continuously ruptured and by being ruptured is connected: nothing binds Bolyan to the sandwich men, other than their contingent convergence in the city's open space. Moreover, no one character can claim proprietorship of this episode, unlike the two episodes preceding it, "Scylla and Charybdis" (steered by Stephen) and "Lestrygonians" (focused on Bloom). Thanks to its disruption of narrative focalization by regular rhythmic severance, "The Wandering Rocks" manages to depict a collective *flânerie* without any single individual flâneur acting as guide.

"The submerged tenth"

The tenth among the eighteen episodes of *Ulysses*, "The Wandering Rocks," is an interlude of sorts, exceptionally sunny, jocular, upbeat—transparent linguistically as well as thematically. Its harmony, however, is shattered by the radical atonality of the next episode, "Sirens." This initiates a stylistic polyphony of prose genres unfolding from episodes twelve to fourteen, after which we enter the surreal world of the fifteenth episode, where narrative prose has apparently surrendered its sovereignty to drama. But even in this nightmarish world in which gender roles are reversed and the dead are summoned, one feeler of the episode is stretched towards the actual nightmare of the city's political and economic woes. The introductory stage directions, as Bloom approaches "nighttown," include a "drunken navvy" (15.35) representing those proletarian Dubliners leading precarious lives, whom the novel's concentration on largely (lower-)middle class characters up to this point has so far helped to keep out of sight. Not having money enough to purchase proper penile ejaculation, the navvy discharges his bodily fluid out of his nose: "The navvy, swaying, presses a forefinger against a wing of his nose and ejects from the farther nostril a long liquid jet of snot. Shouldering the lamp he staggers away through the crowd with his flaring cresset" (15.134-37). Many steps above the navvy in income scale, Bloom enters the house of pleasure, but retreats back into the crowd when "he catches sight of the navvy lurching through the crowd at the farther side of Talbot street" (173-74). The navvy is one "man of the crowd" Bloom manages to evade, but Bloom the belated flâneur, like Baudelaire the flâneur-poet, cannot avoid running into a ragpicker. The ragpicker (*chiffonier*), spotted frequently in nineteenth-century Paris, inspired Baudelaire's eloquent sympathies in "Le Vin de chiffonniers."[1] Not so for Bloom: the encounter remains mute, rude, and farcical:

> (*He steps forward. A sackshouldered ragman bars his path. He steps left, ragsackman left.*)\
>
> BLOOM
>
> I beg.
>
> (*He leaps right, sackragman right.*)
>
> BLOOM
>
> I beg.

(*He swerves, sidles, stepaside, slips past and on.*) (15.222-29)

The ragman's unexplained silent action of blocking his path symbolically expresses his demand to be recognized and addressed by Bloom and his author. The dull politeness of "I beg" reveals the difficulty of confronting the likes of navvy, ragman, and other numerous members of the depressed colonial capital's depressed classes.

"Circe," however, seeks to do justice to the downtrodden and disabled of the city, its "submerged tenth" (16.1226) who had been so completely excluded in Joyce's previous fiction, *Dubliners* and *Portrait*. The wounds inflicted on their bodies by the colonial military machinery are audibly displayed: "Outside a shuttered pub a bunch of loiterers listen to a tale which their brokensnouted gaffer rasps out with raucous humour. An armless pair of them flop wrestling, growling, in maimed sodden playfight" (15.579-82). Sustaining various internal and psychological injury, the street prostitutes, properly belonging to Dublin's abject population, are also victims of the system. Yet they evince a "raucous" if "maimed" vitality which the armless discharged soldiers, like the snot-shooting navvy or the path-blocking ragman, also possess. "Bloom passes. Cheap whores, singly, coupled, shawled, dishevelled, call from lanes, doors, corners" (15.597-98), the direction tells us, before giving them a bawdy but articulate voice:

THE WHORES

Are you going far, queer fellow?
How's your middle leg?
Got a match on you?
Eh, come here till I stiffen it for you. (15.600-3)

Their sauciness being too much of a threat to the middle-class gentleman to be alluring, Bloom dodges them and heads "towards the lighted street beyond" (15.604), only to be greeted by a further raucous resurgence of animosity, this time between the navvy, now given voice as well as fierce nationalist animus, taking on singlehanded "two redcoats" (15.607) from the British army barracks blocking the arteries of the Hibernian capital, permitted by the authorities to taste the city's nighttime pleasures:[2]

THE NAVVY

(*gripping the two redcoats, staggers forward with them*) Come on, you British army!

PRIVATE CARR

(*behind his back*) He aint half balmy.

PRIVATE COMPTON

(*laughs*) What ho!

PRIVATE CARR

(*to the navvy*) Portobello barracks canteen. You are for Carr. Just Carr.

THE NAVVY

(*shouts*)

We are the boys. Of Wexford.

PRIVATE COMPTON

Say! What price the sergeantmajor?

PRIVATE CARR

Bennett? He's my pal. I love old Bennett.

THE NAVVY

(*shouts*)

The galling chain.
And free our native land. (15.612-31)

The navvy's drunken chanting of the nationalist ballad "Boys of Wexford" in front of the two privates, who do their best to ignore him, may not carry much political weight. Yet that the navvy speaks at all, raising his voice from the "submerged tenth" to high fifth fortissimo deserves to be noted as a sonorous example of the narrative's commitment to including *les misérables* of the Irish capital in its epic canvass.

With the two main characters finally paired up at "nighttown," the novel removes them to a "capman's shelter," again, in the region of the underclass Dublin, in "Eumaeus":

> Mr Bloom and Stephen entered the cabman's shelter, an unpretentious wooden structure, where, prior to then, he had rarely if ever been before, the former having previously whispered to the latter a few hints anent the keeper of it said to be the once famous Skin-the-Goat, Fitzharris, the invincible,

> though he could not vouch for the actual facts which quite possibly there was not one vestige of truth in. A few moments later saw our two noctambules safely seated in a discreet corner only to be greeted by stares from the decidedly miscellaneous collection of waifs and strays and other nondescript specimens of the genus *homo* already there engaged in eating and drinking diversified by conversation for whom they seemingly formed an object of marked curiosity. (16.320-30)

The built-in cracks in the narration such as "though he could not vouch for," and the foregrounding of clichés such as "waifs and strays and other nondescript specimens," create an effect of a Dickens prose shredded, recycled, and made threadbare. Dickensian in this reduced broken key are the figures appearing on the narrative's stage, such as the Italian ice-cream vendors (possibly kinsmen and descendents of Calvaletto of *Little Dorrit*?), in their typical mood of pugnacious brawling:

> Adjacent to the men's public urinal they perceived an icecream car round which a group of presumably Italians in heated altercation were getting rid of voluble expressions in their vivacious language in a particularly animated way, there being some little differences between the parties. (16.309-13)

The distance created by the highbrow, formal language (such as "vivacious" or "there being some little difference") from its lowly topic is a typically Dickensian humour-creating device. A more gruesome older version of Martha of *David Copperfield*, or of those sleepless females the Uncommercial Traveller runs into in his night walks, we see in the dark back alley of the Irish metropolis:

> The face of a streetwalker glazed and haggard under a black straw hat peered askew round the door of the shelter palpably reconnoitring on her own with the object of bringing more grist to her mill. (16.704-6)

Like Dublin itself, which had flourished during the heydays of the Ascendancy, these waifs and human strays, such as Gumley the "watcher of the corporation stones," had seen better times, "though now broken down and fast breaking up" (16.942-43). The novel acknowledges their distinctive presence, as it nears its terminus, of the "decidedly miscellaneous collection" of "nondescript specimens of the genus *homo*" to be found in the specific context of Dublin streets.

"Eumaeus" no doubt enlarges the social scope of the novel's characters, yet the style remains a problem for the reader, as it is narrated with an overtly contrived effort to sound "novelistic" in the conventional nineteenth-century manner. Its dubious third-person narration can be bewildering to the reader not only owing to its studied awkwardness but to its extensive consistency. The episode deals with the world of destitution short changed by a self-defeating attempt to embellish it with inept conventional literariness. A representation of the outside world nonetheless is brought forth in its gauche creaking language and despite the unreliable narrator who displays his inability to maintain narrative authority. For instance, the narrator wavers between alternative facts as in this recounting of Corley's speech:

> He was out of a job and implored of Stephen to tell him where on God's earth he could get something, anything at all, to do. No, it was the daughter of the mother in the washkitchen that was fostersister to the heir of the house or else they were connected through the mother in some way, both occurrences happening at the same time if the whole thing wasn't a complete fabrication from start to finish. Anyhow he was all in. (16.148-55)

Salient as the self-dismantling markers of "No" and "Anyhow" may be, it does tell a story about Corley, his jobless destitution. A Balzacian cross-reference to his earlier fiction also takes up a portion of this section, since this is the Corley of "Two Gallants," now no longer that flashy, dashing, young dandy preying on servant girls. "His friends had all deserted him," he tells Stephen. "Furthermore he had a row with Lenehan and called him to Stephen a mean bloody swab with a sprinkling of a number of other uncalledfor expressions" (145-48). Blunt realism spices his "doleful ditty" (144), for unemployment was a serious matter indeed for Dubliners at that time. "He was out of job and implored of Stephen to tell him where on God's earth he could get something, anything at all, to do." These words of his represent many other voices, whereas Bloom's or Stephen's monologues stand apart sui generis in their estranged complexity. The parallel with *Bleak House* we noted earlier—"I don't give a shite anyway so long as I get a job, even as a crossing sweeper" (202-3)—is no mere literary jest, since, despite obvious differences, on economic terms the jobless loafer begging coins from his acquaintances measures not incomparably taller than the harassed Victorian crossing sweep who nonetheless earns his living.

The prose of the episode, verbose but persistently throwing up evidence of cultural poverty through its awkward, cliché-ridden style (similar in conception to Gerty's portion of "Nausicaa") paradoxically achieves the status of deft artistry, however puzzling it may be to the reader. Its poor style can best be understood as being attuned to the theme of indigence and deprivation of the characters' circumstances. Stephen's drunken mind gradually wakes up to the pitiful reality of his family:

> Stephen's mind's eye being too busily engaged in repicturing his family hearth the last time he saw it with his sister Dilly sitting by the ingle, her hair hanging down, waiting for some weak Trinidad shell cocoa that was in the sootcoated kettle to be done so that she and he could drink it with the oatmealwater for milk after the Friday herrings they had eaten at two a penny with an egg apiece for Maggy, Boody and Katey. (16.269-74)

Words and details are piled as if to make up for the poverty of the family diet, in this example, as if every detail has to be relished to embellish the bare fare. Yet the stock of words runs thin, not abundant enough for the task of "repicturing" drab actuality. Sentences in this episode can gesture sudden emptiness of resource, as in the following example:

> That worthy, however, was busily engaged in collecting round the. Someway in his. Squeezing or. (16.681-82)

Full stops after "the," "his" or "or" may be construed as working out an eloquent deconstruction of the grammatical authority of English language in other more assertively experimental episodes such as "Sirens," but here they tell more of hiccupping stoppages and of the impasses that result from a strained effort to simulate literariness. Each episode of *Ulysses* appears a world set apart from the others in technique and style, but the lame language of "Eumaeus" holds an unflattering mirror up to the innovative styles of earlier episodes. The compound words, first employed in Stephen's monologues in Part I, fall short of the artistic effect of making strange, but retain a familiar dullness in examples such as "washkitchen that was fostersister" in Corley's focalized narration, or in "sootcoated" and "oatmealwater" in Stephen's reflections quoted above. Bloom's phrases, and the hedonistic worldview they subscribe to, are repeated here, but only to produce dull vapid sound: "Seeing that the ruse worked and the coast was clear they left the shelter or shanty together and the *élite* society of oilskin and company whom nothing short of an earthquake would move out of their *dolce far niente*" (16.1703-6). No sweetness is left in this recycled Italian expression. In sum, "Eumaeus" shows what a conventional depiction of Dublin might look like, when narration follows the footsteps of Dickens and other nineteenth-century writers, when the force of the glittering brilliance of technical experiments Joyce brings to bear on his city's shabbiness flickers and fades. What one might come up with would be a sequel to *Dubliners* at best, without its rigorous stylistic austerity, a portrait of Dublin faltering and lagging behind in its bid to become a "great metropolis" (514). "Eumaeus" admits the insufficiency of Joyce's experimental style for confronting the reality of his city, yet it also seeks to vindicate negatively the necessity of his stylistic tour de force with which Dublin's paralysis is overcome.

"In the ratio of 16 to 0 would be as 17½ to 13½"

The attempt at offering a representation of the city's poverty as an objective but sympathetic reality, as an engaged communal *Erfahrung*, overreaches itself in "Eumaeus." It is no coincidence that the most eloquent character of the episode is the dubious sailor, mixing bluff and spoof in his tall tales, at once presenting and debunking the classical mode of turning the experience of travel (*fahren*) to a community of listeners as *Erfahrung*. The "doughty narrator" (16.570), for instance, advocates foreign travel, on the authority of his rich experience, to those who most likely will never make one:

> The trip would benefit health on account of the bracing ozone and be in every way thoroughly pleasurable, especially for a chap whose liver was out of order, seeing the different places along the route, Plymouth, Falmouth, Southampton and so on culminating in an instructive tour of the sights of the great metropolis, the spectacle of our modern Babylon where doubtless he would see the greatest improvement, tower, abbey, wealth of Park lane to renew acquaintance with. (16.509-16)

England is now what Italy was to Flora and other insular Londoners, a land of wonder and plenty, which indeed it may appear to the regular members of the cabman's shelter in that particular corner of the Hibernian metropolis. This latter-day Crusoe, claiming familiarity with "our modern Babylon," has known the other races subjected to it. Speaking of his seafaring adventures, he is keen to extract for the benefit of his audience a lesson on the poor hygiene of the subordinate races:

> —There was lice in that bunk in Bridgwater, he remarked, sure as nuts. I must get a wash tomorrow or next day. It's them black lads I objects to. I hate those buggers. Suck your blood dry, they does. (16.670-72)

Crusoe's mortal hatred for the cannibals echoes dimly in the sailor's rabid racism, but equally notable is the fact that the seafarer's bluff resonates in Bloom, as the latter follows the sailor's suit in seeking to impress Stephen with his own tall tales, being "the more experienced of the two" (16.778). Sniffing Stephen's political predilections, he cooks up a yarn about his close encounter of Parnell. To convince Stephen that he had "enjoyed the distinction of being close to Erin's uncrowned king in the flesh when the thing occurred on the historic fracas" (16.1495-97), he invents a corroborating episode:

> His hat (Parnell's) a silk one was inadvertently knocked off and, as a matter of strict history, Bloom was the man who picked it up in the crush after witnessing the occurrence meaning to return it to him (and return it to him he did with the utmost celerity). (1513-16)

Not that it scores any impression on the younger man: "Over his untastable apology for a cup of coffee, listening to this synopsis of things in general, Stephen stared at nothing in particular. He could hear, of course, all kinds of words changing colour like those crabs about Ringsend in the morning burrowing quickly into all colours of different sorts of the same sand where they had a home somewhere beneath or seemed to" (16.1141-46). Communication of *Erfahrung* through storytelling, making the storyteller's experience the property of the audience, fails for this educated narrator as well as for the doughty, dubious mariner. Narration of the characters' experiences, which a novel in some form has to conduct, runs into a cul-de-sac in "Eumaeus," which thus addresses the "death of the novel" decades before the expression became fashionable.

"Eumaeus," however, is not the final episode of *Ulysses*. Molly's monologue revives in its own way the possibility of narrating her own emotional, bodily, social experiences as *Erlebnis*. Molly's reference to Moll Flanders, which we cited earlier, may be in keeping with the overall retro-mode of her first-person narration. To say so may almost amount to a sacrilege in some quarters, where "Penelope" is praised as the prophetic auspice of *l'écriture feminine*. Woman's voice in its most authentic honest guise should sound so? The predominance of matters sexual does justice to feminine desire but does so while restricting them to a particular version, more palatable to men than to women. Her desire for Stephen's young body, to take a typical sample, expresses itself with naked explicitness:

> I could look at him all day long curly head and his shoulders his finger up for you to listen theres real beauty and poetry for you I often felt I wanted to kiss him all over also his lovely young cock there so simple I wouldnt mind taking him in my mouth if nobody was looking as if it was asking you to suck it so clean and white he looks with his boyish face I would too in ½ a minute even if some of it went down what its only like gruel or the dew. (18.1349-55)

Her words, liberated from Victorian taboo as they certainly are, nevertheless drift towards "his lovely young cock," reinstating the phallus as the adored organ and object. The dividend feminist writing can extract from this picture of female desire cannot be large. Its undaunted bawdy talk apart, the porous seamlessness of the sentence can be seen as a new form of liberation from discrete boundaries and identities. But strictly speaking, not much is gained for femininity in terms of narrating her experience. As she stretches out on her bed, a great many of this sleepless lady's thoughts have to do with the wished-for actions of "could" and "would," as the above quotation shows. Events which took place in the past, particularly during her younger days in Gibraltar stored in her memory, lack clear demarcation and elude concentration on a moment of exciting or shocking incident which would enable it to stand out as *Erlebnis* from the continuum of time. She reminisces on her acceptance of Bloom's love, which ought to be a most memorable moment indeed in her life:

> I saw he understood or felt what a woman is and I knew I could always get round him and I gave him all the pleasure I could leading him on till he asked me to say yes and I wouldnt answer first only looked out over the sea and the sky I was thinking of so many things he didnt know of Mulvey and Mr Stanhope and Hester and father and old captain Groves and the sailors playing all birds fly and I say stoop and washing up dishes they called it on the pier and the sentry in front of the governors house with the thing round his white helmet poor devil half roasted. (18.1578-86)

The adamant insertion of the paratactic conjunction "and" leads her thoughts to glide to other names, facts, memories, and details. Her musings move along a continuous horizontal axis of digressive parataxis, conforming to a technique of distraction which disarms the subject's capacity for collected attention. But without any concentration of sensation, no *Erlebnis* is conceivable. The baffled "reader is denied any external point of view at all; the narrative voice seems to disappear, and we are left with Molly's monologue" (Whitley 44), Catherine Whitley states. Yet that monologue is "Molly's" only in a functional sense, for it passes through her and wanders off, instead of being controlled by Molly. Revolutionary it certainly is, in its radical presentation of subjectivity as a disjointed continuum; yet syntactically its radicalism is somewhat superficial. The clauses adhere quite conservatively to proper English grammar, as can be seen when punctuations and breaks are restored, as Derek Attridge demonstrates (Attridge 95-97).[3] Of course, removing all punctuations and apostrophes is a bold and clever device, but measured in terms of technical difficulty, it falls below many other episodes, above all that of the penultimate episode of this monumental book, "Ithaca." The last episode of *Ulysses* contributes to the gender balance of the novel, no doubt, but it addresses the task of renovating novelistic representation of experience by resorting to the easier alternative of digressive distraction.

The least likely candidate to join the chapters of any novel would be "catechism" or question-and-answer study guide, insofar as the novel should belong to a category of narrative prose with continuous paragraphs progressing along a recognizable trajectory. "Ithaca," however, brings narrative fiction to its extreme limit, or rather, drills the catechistic text into a resemblance of narrative. At the simplest level, the answers can "tell" what happened to the main characters:

> What did Bloom do at the range?
>
> He removed the saucepan to the left hob, rose and carried the iron kettle to the sink in order to tap the current by turning the faucet to let it flow. (17.160-62)

Even in this short response, the language of storytelling is affected by the peculiar format, so that it behaves in an objective scientistic manner to strictly exclude all emotional and affective words. "Ithaca" takes us back to the numerical language which Defoe employed in his novels. The mentality and worldview of numerals in *A Journal of the Plague Year* or *Roxana* helped to cleanse the rotting corpses or rotten earnings of their emotional shock or moral burden. It proved a strategy that discourses outside imaginative fiction gladly adopted, rather than the novels coming after Defoe. A strictly objective, measurable, recordable account of what did happen would distinguish itself as the factual "non-fiction" defined against fictions bent on adding sensational, emotional, moral effects to the narrated events. Exactly two centuries after Defoe's *A Journal of the Plague Year* (1722), *Ulysses* (1922) tackles Defoe's scientific, mathematical supplementation of formal realism, to examine, question, and disrupt its posture, confidence, and authority. "Eumaeus" stages a dying scene of conventional fiction. "Ithaca" coming after it, conducts an energetic counter-offensive against the antagonists of fictional narrative by penetrating and deforming their scientific pretensions.

Science asks and knows what it wants to know through measurement by dint of an impersonal language of numerals indifferent to human experience. "Ithaca" takes this impersonality to its extreme, by making scientific questions about the action of the main characters Bloom and Stephen to become overwhelmed by an overflow of answers, with excessive facts and figures exceeding the boundaries of the questions asked. To the simple question about the tap in Bloom's house, "Did it flow?" (17.163), is given a ludicrously detailed answer:

> Yes. From Roundwood reservoir in county Wicklow of a cubic capacity of 2400 million gallons, percolating through a subterranean acqueduct of filter mains of single and double pipeage constructed at an initial plant cost of £5 per linear yard by way of the Dargle, Rathdown, Glen of the Downs and Callowhill to the 26 acre reservoir at Stillorgan, a distance of 22 statute miles, and thence, through a system of relieving tanks, by a gradiant of 250 feet to the city boundary at Eustace bridge, upper Leeson street. (17.164-70)

The full passage, which is twice the length of this quotation, increasingly diverts the reader from what the question ostensibly wanted to know, "mocking the super-brain with a monstrous parody of its workings" (Kenner 167). Whereas the readers of a novel would be interested in the emotional and psychological reaction of Stephen to Bloom and vice versa, the questioning intellect of "Ithaca" has its eyes fixed solely on the measurable facts of their physical situation:

> In what directions did listener and narrator lie?
>
> Listener, S. E. by E.: Narrator, N. W. by W.: on the 53rd parallel of latitude, N., and 6th meridian of longitude, W.: at an angle of 45^{0} to the terrestrial equator. (17.2302-5)

The nautical terms allude, among other things, to the seafaring adventures of Defoe's protagonists (Crusoe, Singleton, Moll), whose ships carry them, or fail to do so, to their destination thanks to the accurate or inaccurate measurement of their position in the wide ocean. In "Ithaca" calculation has become severed from narrative and set on its own, devoid of human significance. Liberated from human experience, numerals couple with each other ad absurdum. "What relation existed between their ages?" (17.446), for example, is answered,

> 16 years before in 1888 when Bloom was of Stephen's present age Stephen was 6. 16 years after in 1920 when Stephen would be of Bloom's present age Bloom would be 54. In 1936 when Bloom would be 70 and Stephen 54 their ages initially in the ratio of 16 to 0 would be as 17½ to 13½, the proportion increasing and the disparity diminishing according as arbitrary future years were added, for if the proportion existing in 1883 had continued immutable, conceiving that to be possible, till then 1904 when Stephen was 22 Bloom would be 374 and in 1920 when Stephen would be 38, as Bloom then was, Bloom would be 646 while in 1952 when Stephen would have attained the maximum postdiluvian age of 70 Bloom, being 1190 years alive having been born in the year 714, would have surpassed by 221 years the maximum antediluvian age, that of Methusalah, 969 years.(17.447-58)

The numerical language at its acme and nadir, triumphant and self-destructive, measures the relationship between Stephen and Bloom, which of course is totally indifferent to and ignorant of their human relationship. The promiscuous coupling of words and figures terminate at the simple, self-complete, absolute silence of full stop.

> When?
>
> Going to dark bed there was a square round Sinbad the Sailor roc's auk's egg in the night of the bed of all the auks of the rocs of Darkinbad the Brightdayler.
>
> Where?
>
> (17.2327-31)

Thus run the last two questions and their answers. The black dot serving as the final full stop represents writing itself, as a trace or stain on the body of a blank page from which the whole book evolved and to which it returns. As such it is a black hole, the potent nowhere, alluding to the spacelessness of fictional space after this long duel with the language of numerals. No victor emerges in this engagement; no revival or even survival of authentic fictional representation is attained after some 2,331 lines of jocular deconstruction of scientific ethos. The episode may also be interested in political subtext, since the Anglo-Irish monopolized scientific research with an avowed intent of accomplishing an "Imperial Mission" through it (Gibson 231). But the exhaustive and exhausting parodic engagement, as was the case in the literary-cultural battle Stephen waged against the Anglo-Irish literary establishment in "Scylla and Charybdis," harvests no political benefit for anyone. The novel, however, goes on, refusing the finality or exhaustion of the dot, for one more episode, completely without any full stop, until the very last "Yes." In this regard "Penelope" possesses an indispensable value as the end that ends not. Defoe's novels, we recall, are never neatly closed off, often ending with unfulfilled promises of sequel. *Ulysses* erases the rational mentality Defoe's fiction toyed with, yet adopts its paratactic, disjunctive endlessness as it erects its vast but porous edifice.

"Why minor sad?"

Continuation and breakage, flow and stop, repetition and restart in *Ulysses*, however, should not be understood in the linear, teleological sense of a Hegelian surpassing of limits, of *Aufhebung* resolving intolerable conflict at a higher level. The task of rejuvenating representation, of re-presenting the social world "out there" without succumbing to the numbing forces of conventional fiction writing, surely leads Joyce's novel to discard one device and opt for another as it charts the lifeworld of a colonial metropolis fraught with contradictions. Yet no progress is made in terms of ideology, plot, or theme. Part Two does not replace and resolve Stephen's profuse mental cogitations of "Proteus," "Circe" does not bring to a grand synthesis whatever that came before it, "Penelope" cannot offer answer to all the problems exposed in the episodes preceding it. *Ulysses* has a spatial organization par excellence in that each episode occupies a distinctively separate "district" in this novel which is itself one vast, sprawling, vibrant metropolis of narrative forms. Time is stretched to its limit in this huge book, but more important is the separation and distribution of segments of the single day (and night) into discrete narrative worlds. The lateral spatial positioning of the episodes and their techniques, placed alongside each other in their own domain, imitates as a whole the uniquely metropolitan principle of disjunctive conjunction. Ruptures and breaks, new beginnings and sudden endings, unlike in Defoe and Dickens, are foregrounded in *Ulysses*. One may liken them to the elaborate, exquisite, hyperbolical prose poems attuned to the ideas of urban diversity and liberating contingency that Baudelaire dreamed of. The episodes belong together in the book, but they are also thoroughly independent, much more so than the collection of stories in *Dubliners*, due to their distinctive technical autonomy. What then is the status or nature of change, process, movement, and other attributes of temporality in this radically spatial novel? Music, figuratively and literally, provides the key to answering this question.

The "music" of language traditionally denotes repetition and variation of certain phonetic elements, crucial to poetry, but rarely is it applied to extended prose narrative. *Ulysses* remains one single exception. The disjunctive thought-flow of Stephen, for example, is held together at the phonetic level by syllables producing "s" (and "z") sound (marked with underline):

> <u>She</u> dan<u>ces</u> in a foul gloom where gum <u>burns</u> with garlic. A <u>sail</u>orman, <u>rust</u>bearded, <u>sips</u> from a beaker rum and <u>eyes</u> her. A long and <u>sea</u>fed <u>si</u>lent rut. <u>She</u> dan<u>ces</u>, cap<u>ers</u>, wagging her <u>sow</u>ish haun<u>ches</u> and her <u>hips</u>, on her <u>gross</u> belly flapping a ruby egg. (10.808-11)

When broken into lines the paragraph can very well be turned into a verse stanza, whose effect is to lend a semblance of formal unity, as in the urban poetry of Juvenal, Dante, Wordsworth, and Baudelaire discussed earlier in this book, to the dirty, noisy, shabby world outside. But Joyce's Flaubertian strategy of embellishing the ugly objects and insipid incidents with perfect word choice only forms one flank of the multiple "musical" approach of *Ulysses*. At the other extreme rings the grating sound of un-musical instruments, or the instrumental (non)-music of objects. Material objects making rhythmic sounds punctuate the apparently transparent third-person narrative in "Aeolus":

> Sllt. The nethermost deck of the first machine jogged forward its flyboard with sllt the first batch of quirefolded papers. Sllt. Almost human the way it sllt to call attention. Doing its level best to speak. That door too sllt creaking, asking to be shut. Eveything speaks in its own way. Sllt. (7.174-77)

The non-human sound of "Sllt" intrudes not only into the space between the sentences but into the very syntax itself, so that it appears like a grammatical element, as in "with sllt the first" or "wit it sllt to call," without of course signifying anything decipherable other than the fact that the printing machine is making such sound. Non-verbal and even non-human sounds yielding some recognizable pattern as the "sllt" in this example belong to a signifying order larger than that of verbal language, one that can be called the realm of music. Whether this should be classified as "noise" rather than "music" (Fischer 250) is not a vital issue, for this "music" is sufficiently a-tonal and non-standard to embrace noises. "Everything speaks in its own way" may very well be a slogan for the experimental music of Charles Ives (1874-1954), a contemporary of Joyce, and a great urban composer who sought to extract music from the variegated noises of modern American life.[4] Objects speak out aloud in *Ulysses*, for example in "Circe," not just the sonorous objects such as the "Gong" which goes, "Bang Bang Bla Bak Blud Bugg Bloo" (15.189), but completely dumb objects such as Bloom's soap we discussed earlier or the "Doorhandle" that exclaims "Theeee!" (2694). This premise of the universal semiotic sonority of objects disrupts the power of English language itself in "Sirens" from carrying on the task of third-person narration, while destroying its signifying capacity with rhapsodic dissonance. Experience as *Erfahrung* transmitted through storytelling meets its musical death, or, in Agamben's formulation, recedes to its babbling origin of sounds seeking meaning. Striding a step further than the cultivation of the "in-experiencable" non-happening in Proust (many of the reminiscences in his novel are putative and subjunctive) (Agamben 1993: 48-49), Joyce in "Sirens," rather than in the episodes featuring Bloom or Stephen's monologues as Agamben suggests, articulates the "infancy," or non-language, "anterior to and independent of language." Infancy, in this sense, does not converge with "the primary current of the *Erlebnisse*" (54-55), for there is no subject to navigate that current, no grammar to mould "Bang Bang Bla Bak" into significance. Nor is "sensuality of sound" in *Ulysses* (unlike in the first chapter of *Portrait*) "a 'sound sense' whose semiotic function attempts to recapture the purity of an experience unmediated by language" (Docherty 124). It is rather a sound sense contaminated, or better, conjugated by the impure sound of material civilization, promiscuously copulating with the corpus of the city's non-human sonority.

"Sirens" is one among the many episodes constituting the confederation of narrative states called "Ulysses," all fiercely independent although partaking of the common policy of renewing the techniques of novel-writing in English, calcified after two centuries of illustrious career (measured since Defoe). Its median position in the sequence of episodes, furthermore, makes it a less likely candidate to be considered the "last word" on the question of how English can be used to make itself both more and less than what it used to be in novels before *Ulysses*. Yet in tracing the vicissitude of the vestiges, variations, and deviations of third-person narration in its capacity to convey a sense of experience, "Sirens" does have a privileged place, as it registers one unsurpassable extreme in the novel's linguistic adventure. The so-called overture or prelude of the episode is certainly designed to absorb critical attention, as it lists the phrases to appear later in the narrative like a menu or blueprint, which however guides not, or rather which needs an expert guidance of annotation before its seemingly meaningless succession can be illuminated. The main fare itself, however, is no less dizzy in the way it creates dissonance of linguistic representations, even of those forms employed earlier in the novel, such as Bloom's interior monologue developed from episodes four to six:

> Bloom mur: best references. But Henry wrote: it will excite me. You know how. In haste. Henry. Greek ee. Better add postscript. What is he playing now? Improvising. Intermezzo. P. S. The rum tum tum. How will you pun? You punish me? Crooked skirt swinging, whack by. Tell me I want to. Know. O. Course if I didn't I wouldn't ask. La la la ree. Trails off there sad in minor. Why minor sad? Sign H. They like sad tail at end. P. P. S. La la la ree. I feel so sad today. La ree. So lonely. Dee. (11.889-94)

The language of flower in the earlier episode of Bloom's receiving the love letter from Martha addressed to "Henry Flower" is now syncopated and choreographed, as he attempts to write back to her. "La la la ree," above all, repeated twice with variation into "La ree," gestures at becoming a signifier without becoming one, as is the case with the "sllt" of "Aeolus," so that the signifying words such as "I feel so sad today" lose their semantic value before and after this non-language or music-language. It could even be that their meaning can be reversed, like the sad words sung in beautiful, soaring tunes. "Why minor sad?" or indeed, why sad sad? This seems to be what the episode implicitly asks. Music knows no tragedy, according to Deleuze and Guattari (Deleuze and Guattari 1987: 299). The music-language of *Ulysses* evades the tragic because Joyce creates out of it the joy of being minor, of being marginal on the borders of English and non-English. This is what Joyce in *Finnegans Wake* celebrated at a grand epic scale, but it is already bubbling forth in "Sirens," although unlike the multilingual hybrid alliance of the later work, here it is more of a generic hybrid of music and language, of word-sounds and sound-words.

"Why minor said?" we ask again. Bloom as Henry Flower never gets to see, touch, kiss or sleep with his lover Martha in *Ulysses*, yet in the quotation above, an elation and excitement derived from the "theme" (in the musical sense) of Martha is depicted in this experimental manner. It is a new, bold, regressive way of representing experience: The childlike "rum tum tum" or "la la ree" is juxtaposed to the mature virile subject's erotic fascinations of "You punish me? Crooked skirt swinging." The convention of English novel writing was such that even the child narrators speak proper adult language, often in a retrospective mode of a mature self relating his or her early days as in Dickens's *David Copperfield* and *Great Expectations*. Joyce's *Portrait of the Artist as a Young Man* begins as a portrait painted with a young male child's language, growing into teenage adolescent style and in the last chapter to a sophomoric undergraduate's bookish jargon. Striking as this stylistic conception is, it still follows the notion of progress, growth, maturation (or its failure). The "in-fantile" deconstruction of English in "Sirens," on the other hand, honors no such linearity. Bloom is proudly pre- or non-lingual, in the way he handles his physical-sexual inferiority vis-à-vis his wife's lover Boylan now denoted as "Jingle": "Jingle jaunted by the curb and stopped" (11.330). The word-play made possible by this felicitous transformation or reduction of Boylan to "Jingle" turns him into a miniscule "jingle" in subsequent variation as in "Jiggedly jingle jaunty jaunty" (579). "Jingle jaunty" in this repeated usage gains signifying function, as it refers to Boylan's better luck with Bloom's spouse: "Jingle jaunty. Too late. She longed to go. That's why. Woman. As easy stop the sea. Yes: all is lost" (639-42). But one should not heed merely to his renunciation stated in adult language. The apparent minor key of "Too late" and "Yes: all is lost" belongs to the grammar of an un-sad musical minor of "Why minor sad?", as the buoyant tune or beat or dance of "Jingle jaunty" sets the tone or leads the thought of "Bloom lost Leopold" (642), as the very next line cheers the supposedly dejected husband with further wordplay. "There's music everywhere" (11.964) in this episode. The "wavyavyeavyheavyeavyevyevyhair" (809) of barmaids turns the sober head of English grammar. Bloom's name becomes a musical theme in this giddy episode, variously stretched and reversed into "Bloom lost Leopold," "Bloom looped, unlooped" (704), or "Bloohimwhom" (309). All that is solid melts into dancing sound in the vision of the metropolis presented by "Sirens."

As the city is given a sonorous musical setting, Bloom's body becomes a sound-producing organ. Most scandalously, the last sound of this rapturous, boisterous episode comes from the nether hole of Bloom, who farts the episode to its finale:

> Prrprr.
> Must be the bur.
> Fff! Oo. Rrpr.
> *Nations of the earth.* No-one behind. She's passed. *Then and not till then.* Tram kran kran kran. Good oppor. Coming. Krandlkrankran. I'm sure it's the burgund. Yes. One, two. *Let my epitaph be.* Kraaaaaa. *Written. I have.*
> Pprrpffrrppffff.
> *Done.* (11.1286-94)

One may apply to this finale of "Sirens" what Steven Connor writes about "Circe." "The "ejaculatory language of the body" is an "articulation of a delinquent, one should even say, delinguent, violence upon the force and function of articulation itself" (Connor 118). This rather noisy, smelly, dizzy mingling of quotations, sounds, and thoughts, which Bevis reads as a "questioning amid commemoration" of nationalist politics (Bevis 255), nonetheless makes clear who the adversary is. With the last words of Robert Emmet, the United Irishman martyr, forming the counterpoint to Bloom's rude "ejaculatory" language of "Fff!" and "Rrpr," it makes for a potent bomb to throw at the snubbing nose of English language, "so familiar and so foreign," and of its novelistic tradition of sober accounting of social experience.[5] "Procreated on the ultimate ysland of Yreland in the encyclical yrich archipelago, come their feast of precreated" (*Finnegans* 605) *Ulysses*, this jazz-symphonic monumental novel, which stunningly compensates for the waning of both *Erfahrung* and *Erlebnis* through its radical play of precreating marks, letters, alphabets. Such a state of linguistic disjunction in *Ulysses* we propose to call *narratio in extremis*, extreme and/or dying narration. Narration dying a musical death that knows no tragedy can also be a rebirth of language into its in-fancy, communicating to us the incommunicable experience of living in the world of metropolitan modernity.

CONCLUSION

In discussing the relationship of the metropolis and experience in Defoe, Dickens, and Joyce we have sought to explore the manner or the mode in which the metropolis becomes a form, as well as the content, of experience. In Defoe's first-person narrative, hailing as it does from the emergence of the private sphere in Pepys's London, the metropolis informs and inhabits the very structure and syntax of his style, as disjunctive conjunction, in addition to providing the theme and direction of his plot, the pursuit of a life for and of the individual subject set against the background and forces of the public realm, which Moll's predatory forays into the urban crowd most graphically illustrate. Ideally, what the subjective standpoint of Defoe's narration can offer as sensory, physical, psychological *Erlebnis* is not only bolstered by its own authenticity, but, as in *A Journal of the Plague Year*, can approximate and simulate the authority of a shared, communal *Erfahrung*. Yet even in this boldest effort to extend the force of fictional experience to its borderland of non-fictional factuality, one sees the regular intervention or interruption of numerals and of statistic rationality, that erodes the grounds and necessity of verbal representation. This non-language of figures in *Roxana*, with close ties to the financial revolution which linked major cities by an abstract system of credit, inserts itself into the narrative matrix in place of the moral significance of her experience at the level of *Erfahrung*. With Defoe, the novel as a genre "rises" indeed as a potent voice of *Erlebnis*, of the personal, individual private experience which fascinates, compels, disturbs, and disrupts the conventional, communal, and collective wisdom associated by Benjamin with traditional tales imparting *Erfahrung*.

Writing in and for the different metropolitan context of a rapidly expanding Victorian London, Dickens adopted the public persona of "Boz" offering both *utile* and *dulce* in a prose that informs while marking itself and the objects described with characteristic features that highlight distinctive individuality, without however diminishing the voice of his self-appointed role of addressing the public as one of them. "Boz" is the name of this unique prose style: poetic, supple, dynamic, a veritable "poem in prose" of the metropolis. London is stylized, characterized, and portrayed in his works as a recognizable entity, not always or fully corresponding to the sprawling, bustling metropolis it had become.

Individuals, streets, squares, as well as that amorphous creature the urban crowd, come alive in his writing to convey vivid *Erlebnis*, while also offering to satisfy the demand for *Erfahrung* raised by the estranged, fragmented, depreciated individual lives in the metropolis. Giving sense to the city and the urbanized society most readers live in, however, is bound to compete with journalism's prolific representation of the current world as it is. As a writer speaking to the public, Dickens has to be engaged with topical issues, such as the complaints about Chancery delay in *Bleak House*, yet the novel has to be something else and more than the snapshots and skirmishes ephemeral periodical writings spawn. The mature Dickens's narrative revelation of interconnections between topics, scenes, classes, streets, and families elevates the immediacy of mere topicality into a symbolic *Erfahrung* about "life as such," yet its totalizing effects by no means succeed in controlling the discrete, disjunctive, disparate episodes, scenes, characters populating his thick novels. Similarly, in those novels dealing with travel, either geographical or historical or both (as in *A Tale of Two Cities*), the wisdom to be gained from travelling typically offers a negative *Erfahrung* revealing the vacuity of the journey itself, as in the second part of *Little Dorrit*, where lived truth of Marshalsea asserts its rights with vengeance. In Dickens the force of *Erlebnis* stored in the city's myriad, diverse, variegated faces tends increasingly to be reduced to an allegorical picture of death, desolation, despondence.

The transition from Dickens to Joyce requires one to sail across not only the rough Irish seas but the English Channel as well. Pitted against the entrenched block of the Anglo-Irish literati, the maverick son of Erin turned towards France. What inspired and strengthened him, years before publishing *Ulysses* in Paris, was the narrative models set up by Flaubert and Dujardin. Emerging from the Flaubertian *style indirect libre* of *Portrait*, which enabled the uneventful quotidian life to wear a semblance of *Erlebnis*, Joyce devised a new novelistic language inspired in part by Dujardin's interior monologue but more poignantly triggered by the tense schizoid stance of a genius born to a colonized Irish-Catholic milieu in which English is both the first language and an alien or even inimical tongue. Moving from the aesthetics of arrested plots constructed in a meticulously chiseled prose (of *Dubliners* and *Portrait*), the triumphant dissonance of aberrant English in *Ulysses* liberates the colonial capital from its subjugated disaffection and stultifying dereliction. What the novel gains in terms of stunning stylistic inventiveness, however, comes at the cost of disabling the main characters' capacity for experience, as both Stephen and Bloom are far too heterogeneous and centrifugal to be subjects of either *Erlebnis* or *Erfahrung*. Bloom the flâneur made up of other organs besides his perceptive eyes, lends his consciousness, body, and name to be played by the novel as it produces its musical eruptions and elations glistening like so many splinters of failed *Erlebnis* that know neither interiority nor sensory trance. Yet the Dickensian project of narrating the social exterior is also carried on over and below the regular pitch, in a self-deprecated mode which immunizes the complacency of ideological representation in "plain" proper English. The numerical mathematical modernity with which Defoe formed alliance meets its parodic death throes in the sheer excess of "Ithaca," which for us is the more moving conclusion than the breathless female bawdy of "Penelope."

In the last two episodes of *Ulysses*, the force of technical brilliance begins to exhaust itself. The fact that post-*Ulysses* Joyce spent his remaining years working on *Finnegans Wake*, painstakingly disfiguring or overloading every English sentence he wrote to make it something other, foreign, or Gaelic, is eloquent evidence of how *Ulysses* is a dead end, among others, for the metropolitan novel—both in the Dickensian mode of crowded thickness brimming over with clamorous conviviality and punctuated by scorching social satire, or the Defoesque mode of self-centered private sphere embodying the spirit of urban modernity in first-person narratives. From that Joyce twice or thrice removed from Dickens or Defoe, we are further cut off, despite or due to the accelerated domination of metropolitan civilization. "The great urbanization of *homo sapiens* occurred almost yesterday," states an introductory book on urban sociology (C. Fischer 5). What we have examined so far may correct this chronology, for the urbanization of human kind has a longer and a more complex time span than this statement assumes, at least in the case of London. But there is still a clear rupture diving us from the age of Defoe or even of Joyce. The great urbanization became universal almost yesterday, propelled by seismic catastrophes of the past century. As separated and linked as Joyce is from Defoe, so are we from Joyce, not to mention Defoe or Dickens.

Joyce died in 1941 during the first phase of the Second World War, before the atrocities of Auschwitz got into full swing, before the inconceivable catastrophe of Hiroshima heralded a new stage of scientific barbarism. The city architecture after the War, with the marginal exception of some rebuilt German historic towns flattened by Allied bombing, vied with each other to erase all pretentions to historical aesthetics. A rabid tyranny headed by developers and the construction industry transformed in no time the urban space into a paradise for fast cars, a limbo for anxious middling sorts, and an inferno not only for the poor (who be always with us) but for those we still harbor illusions about the human, cultural, artistic mission of the metropolis. As the great New Yorker Lewis Mumford lamented in his 1960s essay "The Disappearing City,"

> What has passed for a fresh image of the city turns out to be two forms of anti-city. One of these is a multiplication of standard, de-individualized high-rise structures, almost identical in form, whether they enclose offices, factories, administrative headquarters, or family apartments, set in the midst of a spaghetti of traffic arteries, expressways, parking lots, and garages. The other is the complementary but opposite image of urban scatter and romantic seclusion often called suburban. . . . As an agent of human interaction and cooperation, as a stage for the social drama, the city is rapidly sinking out of sight. (Mumford 1968: 115)

The city as a civic centre of active political culture already began to disappear in Pepys' and Defoe's London, even as it thrived as a money-making and pleasure-seeking arena for the private subject. Dickens's journalistic gestures did little to stem the tide of the privatization of urban experience. Any meaningful human relationship has to unfold in the margins and interstices, as is the case with Arthur Clennam and Amy Dorrit, away from the boom and bust of Merdle's muddled finance. Both Bloom's eventful daytime sauntering and his wild nightlife meet their demise at a sobering cabman's shelter, where Bloom plots to capture Stephen. And then the deluge: the shelling, bombing, killing in the metropolis, from Easter 1916 of Dublin to London under the Blitz to Hanoi under American napalm. And then the constructions or rather demolitions: extinction of history from London Docklands to Shanghai. The age of the anti-city can foster no imaginative intervention for the sake of human experience, whether of *Erlebnis* (trampled down by the utter monotony of the urban sprawl) or *Erfahrung* (locked off with gadgets and goods at the suburban private sphere). The aesthetic pastiche of postmodern architecture and cultural patois of the tourist industry towards the end of the past century did little to conceal the ugly truth of an urban sprawl riven by permanent class conflict. A few minutes' bus ride from white stucco London is greeted by a police line marking off a crime scene in some brown-black estate housing. The ancient East-West divide of London has become more complex, pervasive, and secure, but a knife stabbing in Camberwell (South London) or Edmonton (North London)[1] can never be answered by driving "Chelsea Tractors" (i.e. SUVs) or living in Kensington. Did the metropolitan private sphere of Defoe's H. F. really protect anyone from rampant plague? Can it insulate us from riots at Hackney? Just as the cash-rich Roxana ended up being tormented by the proletarian by-product of her past, and just as Dickens portended with such vehemence to his faithful readers: between the destitute and the distinguished, between Tom-all-Alone and Lady Dedlock, an unwelcome but indelible relationship is bound to be unearthed.

Even without being surprised by hidden familial, social, and legal interconnections which the metropolis has in store for the well-off, one suffers from the unsurprising woes waiting for us at home. The problem with metropolitan hedonism is that the fun never lasts long enough. Bloom's creaturely pleasures and risky nocturnal excitements are far too transient. The shabby sheltered soberness of "Eumaeus" succeeds the wild exuberance of "Circe." And then home, so to bed—for Bloom as well as for Pepys—with all the unresolved awkwardness of estranged marriage. For the descendents of Pepys and Bloom, the daily homecoming is to return to, in addition to failed human relationships, bills, debts, and the stalled careers the hyper-modern metropolitan world rewards us with. To the metropolitan soul, the universal human question of who should one live with is overlapped by the question of where in the city one should live. Marriages are held together as much by mortgages attached to a respectable address as by mutual affection or respect. This permanent burning issue of real estate presupposes the existence of the city as a meaningful, functioning, desirable social space, where life becomes worth living or at least work is worth the money. But it begs the question of where and whether the city as such exists at all. Those peopling the Square Mile queue each evening at Liverpool Station to flee London to their suburban gardens. The lorries jammed in the motorways of Mestre bear little resemblance to the tourist-crammed Rialto of the Serenissima. Joyce was celebrated and marketed in June 2011, as usual, in Dublin, but history seems indeed an on-going nightmare from which there is no waking up. Joyce Festivals or Bloomsdays hardly stopped the exodus of young Dubliners seeking employment overseas, for "wearily obvious" reasons, as the *Irish Times* put it,[2] with perhaps a lone Stephen Dedalus dreaming of an artistic career. Yet what can we do, really, when the money market thus wishes and dictates? Cities of the world have become more or less legitimate or adopted descendents of the City of London: cities of financiers and their rich clients, of Sir Robert Clayton and Roxana. Or perhaps one should say they are closer in spirit and shape, except for their waists, to those smug moneyed men on whose heads Dickens poured his venom in his letter to Douglas Jerrold:

> There were men there—your City aristocracy—who made such speeches, and expressed such sentiments, as any moderately intelligent dustman would have blushed through his cindery bloom to have thought of. Sleek, slobbering, bow-paunched, overfed, apoplectic, snorting cattle—and the auditory leaping

> up in their delight! I never saw such an illustration of the Power of Purse, or felt so degraded and debased by its contemplation, since I have had eyes and ears. The absurdity of the thing was too horrible to laugh at. It was perfectly overwhelming. (*Letters* 3. 482 [3 May 1843])

Pace Dickens—nay, *pace* Marx *pace* Mao—the Power of Purse rules from London to Beijing. "Sleek, slobbering . . . snorting cattle" as they may be, they have turned us all into cattle, to be fattened, occasionally flattered, but no more respected or recognized than the mute numbers lumped together in H. F.'s political arithmetic or the dizzy calculations of "Ithaca."

What rostrum still stands, then, for a novelist still presuming to write on the metropolis in our time? Is the dialectic of *Erlebnis* and *Erfahrung* still relevant for contemporary urban fiction? Both questions may sound gratuitous, for there is no end of novels published, marketed, shortlisted, and feted each year, the majority of which are likely to have adopted metropolitan backgrounds than to have their stories set in the countryside or country house. The thriving life of current novels as managed by publishing industry is strictly reserved for producers of user-friendly vendible goods. The experience of reading fiction, like other experiences of our time, has become strenuously categorized, segmented, programmed, and catered to, yielding dividends in the form of a pleasant self-gratifying feeling of mental exercise disguising intellectual and sensory torpor. Rodolpe Gasché, in tracking the genealogy of Benjamin's aesthetics of distraction proposed in the "Mechanical Reproduction of Art," alerts us to the fact that Kant was already conscious of distraction as an issue, but interestingly in relation to novel reading (Gasché 100). Reading novels, Kant writes, "in addition to causing many other mental discords, also has the result that it makes distraction habitual" (Kant 2006: 102). It is "a practice in the art of killing time and making oneself useless in the world," and as such is "naturally distracting and makes for *habitual absent-mindedness*" (Kant 2006: 78). This caustic verdict of Kant on fiction reading rings truer now more than in his own time. Defoe's fictions presumed and assumed the authority of real "history," Dickens turned his serial novels into a public forum, and Joyce recreated the city he left behind with a sparkling brilliance it rarely deserved. Habitual absentmindedness was surely what none of them sought to promote. Novels after Joyce, after Hollywood, after television, after computer games, are content or grateful to take up one corner in the Vanity Fair of our entertainment industry, for whom to be absent from one's self, to mix distraction with titillation, is the supreme virtue.

Two creative aberrations, from Latin Europe rather than the sales-driven Anglo-American fiction market, however, illustrate the on-going, if increasingly asphyxiated, pursuit of *Erfahrung* and *Erlebnis* in metropolitan novels: Italo Calvino's *Invisible Cities* (1972) and José Saramago's *Blindness* (1995). In the former, Marco Polo the great traveller entertains the Great Kahn with vignettes of the cities he has visited, or dreams of having visited. The *Erfahrung* of travel serves as the motif of this novel, which, however, displays its impossibility. The cities are static emblems or images, in essence, where nothing happens to the traveller-protagonist, who draws no "lesson" from them. The titles of each vignette, such as "Cities & Desire. 1" or "Cities & Memory. 3," signal their amenability to allegoresis, yet their numbered sequence yields no cumulative narrative value. What emerges instead is a view of seeing the city as an architectural layout, grid, pattern, or a detached aerial perception immune to the layered histories and communal lore of the city's *Erfahrung*, however full of eye-catching details they may be, as in "Cities & Signs. 2":

> Travellers return from the city of Zirma with distinct memories: a blind black man shouting in the crowd, a lunatic teetering on a skyscraper's cornice, a girl walking with a puma on a leash. Actually many of the blind men who tap their canes on Zirma's cobblestones are black; in every skyscraper there is someone going mad; all lunatics spend hours on cornices; there is no puma that some girl does not raise, as a whim. The city is redundant: it repeats itself so that something will stick in the mind. (Calvino 16)

This "redundant" city where people regularly turn mad evokes the plague-stricken city of Defoe, but the perspective is that of a passing traveller or tourist, more completely detached from it than the vigilant observer-resident H. F., with no reason or chance to subject himself to the *Erlebnis* of encountering wrecked humanity. Nor can the antics of the deranged be turned into a Dickensian humour, which, again, can only come from a communal familiarity with the city. The many intriguing and curious cities collected in this book, in fact, add up to a dirge lamenting the end of cities in our own day, of the cities ravaged, razed, erased, and oftentimes bulldozed by the Khans of our time: the combined "Power of Purse" of the banks, developers and construction industry. "I am collecting the ashes of the other possible cities that vanish to make room for it, cities that can never be rebuilt or remembered," Marco explains to Khan (52). It is a fitting remark for the age of the "great urbanization of *homo sapiens,*" when cities rise and die almost in the same breath. The fact that the narrator Marco has to gloss on his narrative to the reader-audience Khan, moreover, is due to the fact that there is no real communication between them. The isolation and solitude which Benjamin spotted in the writing and reading of novels have reached an absolute point. Marco speaks not the language of Great Khan, nor does the latter know any of Marco's Levantine languages. The storyteller resorts to various body languages and gestures, to which the auditor responds in kind. Yet even that game of mute communication would be cut off, with nothing but silence passing between them, since "in their conversations, most of the time, they remained silent and immobile" (33). One cannot but recall and relish, when things have reached this impasse, the dancing noises of Joyce's "Sirens."

A more serious and devastating vision of contemporary metropolis than Calvino's tastefully garnished fragments is thrust to the reader by our second example, José Saramago's *Blindness*. Interestingly, in the British literary scene, one year before Saramago's *Blindness* (1995) appeared, James Kelman's *How Late It Was, How Late* (1994), which won the Booker despite its strong demotic Glaswegian accent, also depicted the experience of turning suddenly blind. In Kelman's tale, the protagonist suffers blindness, in addition to his joblessness and exposure to police violence. Pitiless, drab, and demeaning the Scottish metropolis is to him already, and being blind rubs salt into Sammy's wounds, both mental and physical. But his new sensory deprivation provides the novel with an opportunity to pursue *Erlebnis* in its most extreme form. What greater shock can there be than to lose sight and experience all the ills an unassisted blind man has to go through in a crowded city? Yet by the same token, a blind *Erlebnis* is blind to the sensory benefits of *Erlebnis*. No thrill or excitement can delight the blind, but only sorrow, dejection, and no end of expletives occupy his soul. To take an almost random sample, here we see the narrator, justifiably of course, voicing Sammy's frustration in a tone and idiom focalized on the character:

> But how many crossings to the main road? How many wee streets before the big one! It was laughable, no knowing. There were all these things ye think ye've committed to memory but have ye! have ye fuck. He needed to ask somebody but how the hell do ye know somebody's coming when ye cannay see them and there's a lot of noise about, traffic and fucking the wind man, fuck sake that fucking wind, hell of a breezy. (Kelman 36)

In such passages the *Erfahrung* of coping with the city's "many crossings" and "many wee streets" is reduced to the *Erlebnis* of swearing, which the city of the propertied, protected, and privileged can easily dismiss as manageable misdemeanor. To one blind jobless male, society may turn a blind eye, but when an entire city turns blind, one by one, as in Saramago's astounding story, none can be complacent or safe. An infectious "epidemic of blindness" (Saramago 3), reminiscent of *A Journal of the Plague Year*, strikes at first a few victims, and then one by one everyone in the unspecified contemporary metropolis goes blind.

What the blind in Saramago's narrative have to grapple with is their physicality, above all. Their eyes have ceased to function, but other organs are as active as Bloom's bowels. The pathetic and bestial *Erlebnis* of turning blind gradually grows into an *Erfahrung* of communal blindness, as those early victims of the epidemic are first rounded up and kept a mental asylum, left to take care among themselves of their physical needs of eating, urinating, defecating, and copulating. The blind lead—and later exploit and kill—the blind, with the single exception of the ophthalmologist's wife, who may be the counterpart to Defoe's H. F. as she mysteriously and inexplicably remains untouched by the diseases but chooses to follow her husband by pretending blindness. Her husband, the medical professional, after managing to handle his toilet problem, knowing he was "dirty, dirtier than he could ever remember having been in his life," muses, "There are many ways of becoming an animal" (89). This *Erfahrung* of learning to cope together with blindness, however, has no promise of redemption. The demonic bleakness of the novel rejects Providence, content (if not delighted) to explore an infernal vision of hell-on-earth. "There is no salvation for us" (93), one character proclaims. All the while, "the lavatories were soon reduced, fetid caverns such as the gutters in hell full of condemned souls must be" (125). The outdoor toilet at 7 Eccles Street would beam with an angelic halo, in comparison.

After having thoroughly converted the asylum into a veritable inferno reeking with the stench of excrement, blood, semen, and corpse, the novel takes the main characters out to the city, now completely trampled down by the epidemic. This is a city, however, that is utterly severed from any pre-blind *Erfahrung*. Their past, as they discover, descends "without a guiding hand or a dog-leash, into the demented labyrinth of the city, where memory will serve no purpose, for it will merely be able to recall the images of places but not the paths whereby we might get there" (Saramago 206). To secure food, led by the doctor's wife whose eyes can still see, the group roams the city like "primitive hordes" (242). What they find is a nightmare version of contemporary over-consuming, over-littering cities:

> The rubbish seemed to increase during the hours of darkness, it was as if from the outside, from some unknown country where there was still a normal life, they were coming in the night to empty their dustbins, if we were not in the land of the blind we would see through the middle of this white darkness phantom carts and trucks loaded with refuse, debris, rubble, chemical waste, ashes, burnt oil, bones, bottles, offal, flat batteries, plastic bags, mountains of paper. (Saramago 293)

Towards the very end, in the last five pages or so, they begin to regain their eyesight, after two and half hundred pages of relentless description of desperation, frustration, and dehumanization. A respite of sorts is gained as the story ends, but the city as dump site and producer of rubbish is what it cannot but remain.

Among Calvino's numerous memorable cities, the one protruding above others is Leonia, utterly incapable of dealing with its waste, since "the more Leonia expels goods, the more it accumulates them; the scales of its past are soldered into a cuirass that cannot be removed. As the city is renewed each day, it preserves all of itself in its only definitive form: yesterday's sweepings piled up on the sweepings of the day before yesterday and of all its days and years and decades." Leonia's towering landfill has global consequences:

> Leonia's rubbish little by little would invade the world, if, from beyond the final crest of its boundless rubbish heap, the street cleaners of other cities were not pressing, also pushing mountains of refuse in front of themselves. Perhaps the whole world, beyond Leonia's boundaries, is covered by craters of rubbish, each surrounding a metropolis in constant eruption. The boundaries between the alien, hostile cities are infected ramparts where the detritus of both support each other, overlap, mingle. (Calvino 103)

The image of a dust pile at the centre of London broods over Dickens's last completed novel, *Our Mutual Friend*. The pile has grown since then to gobble up the metropolis itself. For Calvino, Saramago, and all of us who are yet alive, "Leonia" has broken out of the fold of fiction to become a stark, imminent reality. It is Roxana's Susan come to haunt us: for no protective private sphere can avail under such conditions, nor can finance help us transcend it. Appalled by these horrid pictures painted by Saramago and Calvino of the contemporary metropolis, we cherish anew the great monumental achievements not only of Defoe, Dickens, and Joyce, but also of those who came before Defoe: Pepys and Bunyan. Living in a metropolis for one's precious self like Pepys is what many desire, but the ongoing catastrophes of our cities bid us also to "look upwards" to the "Cœlestial City," like Bunyan's Pilgrims, even when the actual "Trade and Traffick . . . in Heaven" may dismay us. For more dismaying still is what reason without faith, faith in instrumental reason, has done and undone. As Terry Eagleton writes, "one simply cannot shake off the primitive conviction that *this is not how it is supposed to be*," when we see "the world" and the metropolis "in the light of Judgment Day" (Eagleton 123).

NOTES

Introduction

1. Comparison of two among them does have some precedents. Defoe and Dickens are given each a place in *The Journalistic Imagination*, whose first chapter goes to Defoe (Keeble and Wheeler 15-28) and the fourth to Dickens (58-73). Dickens and Joyce join other writers gathered by Dominic Rainsford, who finds Joyce in his critical treatment of Stephen to be "much a successor to Dickens, who was particularly committed and ruthless in his handling of 'Self'" (Rainsford 184-85)—a rather vague legacy, which most authors would can claim as theirs as well. Dickens and Joyce appear together in Matthew Bevis's study of the attitude to and use of public speech in the novels, such as Dickens's use of parliamentary speech in *Bleak House* (Bevis 114-18) and Joyce's of the rhetoric of Irish nationalism in "Cyclops" (248-55). John M. Warner wishes to adopt Joyce as a "grandson" of Defoe, in that both "envision history as a nightmare" (J. Warner 26). This genealogy flouts the nightmare of Irish history: Defoe eulogized as the "True-Born Englishman" William of Orange, who crushed the political hopes of Irish Catholics. Can Joyce be a "grandson" of English or Anglo-Irish writers, despite the antagonism and persecutions built into his Irish-Catholic lineage? This question, which Warner blithely evades, is the starting point of our discussion of Joyce.

2. Richard Wolin suggests that Benjamin's "Storyteller" was written as a dialogue with and rebuttal of Lukács's *Theory of the Novel* (Wolin 222-23), but it would be more to the point to see him rejecting the Marxist Lukács' canonization of nineteenth-century realists than the metaphysical Lukács' misgivings about the novel's redemptive potentials for a fallen age.

3. To compensate for the short shrift Balzac received from Alter, we corroborate Lukács' assertion about Balzac in his longest (and surely the most accomplished) work *Illusions perdues* (*Lost Illusions*), where characters are directly involved in the events, often faced with difficult choices, which the author never allows them to evade, as when Lucien has to judge and choose between loyalty to noble friendship and mercenary action for the sake of his mistress: "Lucien saw that he must choose between d'Arthez and Coralie: his mistress would be ruined if he did not slaughter d'Arthez in the big newspaper and *Le Réveil*. The unhappy poet returned home sick at heart, sat down by the fire in his bedroom and then read the book: it was one of the finest in modern literature. His tears fell on one page after another and he hesitated for a long time, but in the end he wrote a mocking article of the kind at which he was so skilful and laid hold of the book as children lay hold of a beautiful bird to pluck its feathers and torture it" (Balzac 452). Without the experience of reading Lucien's review, the reader can still be moved by his deed at the level of the "consistent context of experience" Kant speaks of.

4. Pierre Missac is not being entirely uncharitable in his strictures on Benjamin's distinction between story and the novel as something which leaves one "dissatisfied and in suspense": "Not only are the brilliant intuitions left in some sense to fend for themselves for lack of adequate foundation—a freedom they make excellent use of—but the thought does not always seem capable of mastering the problems it has set for itself" (Missac 32).
5. Alter seems to mean by "experience," which he never clearly defines, something resembling *Erlebnis*, to infer from such expressions as "shifting pulse of experience felt by the individual . . . in the urban zone" (Alter xi), or from his statement about Flaubert that his work is "in line with the new 'aesthetics of shock' that Walter Benjamin describes" (25). But *Erlebnis* is only one part of the pair, as we argue here. To merit the title of "experiential realism," a novel must balance *Erlebnis* with *Erfahrung*, instead of merely "conducting the narrative . . . through the moment-by-moment experience—sensory, visceral, and mental—of the main character or characters" (x).
6. Early usages of *Erlebnis* can be traced back to Hegel and Ludwig Tieck, but the word was generally interchangeable with *Erfahrung* (Sauerland 1-4), although Goethe's use of *erleben* in the sense of emotional intensity of experience is a notable precedent (8-9). Benjamin's emphasis on shock as a key semantic element of the term was his distinctive contribution (Sauerland 164).
7. Dilthey seems to have been ultimately dissatisfied with his concept of *Erlebnis*, since he came up with the notion of "Lebenserfahrung" in his later writings, which according to Michael Ermath was "more compatible with the objective and historical character of his later thought as a whole" (Ermath 226), characterized as it was by "reflection, articulation, repetition, general acknowledgement (within a community or tradition), and its own peculiar forms of method and proof" (227).
8. Our usage of *Erlebnis*, as that which generically adheres to first-person narration, goes further than its customary employment in German narrative studies, where from *Erlebnis* is derived *erlebte Rede* or free indirect speech, called so in the sense that it bridges and manipulates "Erlebnisdistanz" (see Stanzel 54-57, 127) between the narrator and the character.

Part I: Defoe

Chapter One. From the Private Sphere

1. Quotations from Pepys's *Diary* will be specified with dates, with the volume and page numbers given in square brackets.
2. By defining privacy as derivative residue, we wish to evade the extremes of Francis Barker's agonistic view of the private body as the "deadly subjectivity of the modern" (Barker 25) and James Turner's rejection of Barker's thesis by seeing in the Navy clerk's own humbler circle a reflection of Charles II's conscious "mingling of sex and power" (Turner 107). John H. O'Neil favors the latter viewpoint, arguing that Pepys' "will" to control pervades both his public and private lives (O'Neil 89). Pepys, in our view, has to be assessed in more modest

terms. He is far too self-divided, as we shall show shortly, to be seen as exercising lordship over his private life.

3. Another historian gives the following estimation, not very different from that of Stephen Inwood, that London's population grew "from perhaps some 75,000 in 1550 to 200,000 in 1600; thence to around 400,000 in 1650; and to some 575,000 in 1700" (Sheppard 126). Such growth largely owed to the heavy influx of immigrants from the provinces, mostly of two groups: "ambitious young men and women" and the "'subsistence' migrants, forced to leave their homes in desperation" (Inwood 160).

4. Works by Defoe, Dickens, and Joyce are cited in easily recognizable shortened titles, unless mentioned otherwise.

5. These terms borrowed from finance we will discuss in greater detail in chapters 3 and 4 below.

6. This and other passages in Locke's *Second Treatise of Government* should correct the overly idealist application of Locke's "individualism" to Crusoe's case handed down by Watt. More interested in the epistemological Locke of the *Essay Concerning Human Understanding* than in Locke the theorist of property, Watt merely states that Locke "constructed the class system of political thought based on the indefeasibility of individual rights" (Watt 62), without going into the crucial question of property. McKeon, likewise, refers only to Locke's *Essay* (McKeon 80-81), as does Richetti (Richetti 2005: 225). Novak, curiously, in discussing Crusoe, refers to Locke's remarks on money (Novak 2001: 549-50), instead of his theory of property rights.

7. Swift has his Gulliver, clearly with a satirical eye on such prudish or idealist view of the human body, make a point of mentioning how he took care of his urgent call of nature in the diametrically opposed situations of Lilliput and Brobdingnag: "I went as far as the Length of my Chain would suffer; and discharged my Body of that uneasy Load" (Swift 2005: 24), writes Gulliver in the former; "I went on one Side about two Hundred Yards; and beckoning to her not to look or to follow me, I hid myself between two Leaves of Sorrel, and there discharged the Necessities of Nature" (84-85), in the latter.

8. In *Grace Abounding to the Chief of Sinners*, Bunyan describes how his "own" thoughts were colonized by the thoughts and words of the "Tempter": "Sometimes it would run in my thoughts not so little as a hundred times together, Sell him [Christ], sell him, sell him; against which, I may say, for whole hours together I have been forced to stand as continually leaning and forcing my spirit against it, lest haply before I were aware, some wicked thought might arise in my heart that might consent thereto; and sometimes also the Tempter would make me believe I had consented to it, then should I be as tortured on a Rack for whole days together" (Bunyan 1998: 39).

9. Pepys clearly indicated that a major objective of his journal writing was to keep it strictly private, as can be seen in this last entry: "And thus ends all that I doubt I shall ever be able to do with my own eyes in the keeping of my journall, I being not able to do it any longer, having done now so long as to undo my eyes almost every time that I take a pen in my hand; and therefore, whatever comes of it, I must forbear; and therefore resolve from this time forward to have it kept by my people

in long-hand, and must therefore be contented to set down no more then is fit for them and all the world to know." (31 May 1669 [9.564-65])

Chapter Two. Paratactic Prosaics

1. By this phrase we mean the contradictory, inorganic, un-sutured textual connections effected by the force of overriding prose, although it can in part have a more substantial sense similar to Samuel Weber's "disjunctive convergence," which he uses to describe the relationship of space to time in Benjamin's Paris (S. Weber 231).
2. Even if we may not subscribe to Doug Underwood's rather cavalier assertion that Defoe's "Puritan plain speech sensibilities made him suspicious of ornate prose" (Underwood 50), one can assume his "sola scriptura" Dissenter background disposes him favorably towards parataxis, as it is the style characteristic of the Old Testament. On Biblical parataxis, see Auerbach 71-73.
3. Diametrically opposed to Defoe is John Cleland's *Memoirs of a Woman of Pleasure*, not only in its profuse depiction of sexual encounters but also in its hypotaxis, which cloaks its inevitably predictable subject matter, as the following illustrates: "He had now fixed, nailed, this tender creature with his home-driven wedge, so that she lay passive per force, and unable to stir, till beginning to play a strain of arms against this vein of delicacy, as he urged the to-and-fro constriction, he awakened, roused, and touched her so to the heart that, unable to contain herself, she could not but reply to his motions as briskly as her nicety of frame would admit of, till the raging stings of the pleasure, rising towards the point, made her wild with the intolerable sensation of it, and she now threw her legs and arms about at random, as she lay lost in the sweet transport; which on his side again declared itself by quicker, eagerer thrusts, convulsive grasps, burning sighs, swift laborious breathings, eyes darting humid fires: all faithful tokens of the imminent approaches of the last grasp of joy" (Cleland 154).

Chapter Three. The Ideal of Calculability

1. A good example of the older Puritan concept of time as the scourge chastising "vanities" is *England's Golden Watch-Bell. Summoning an Alarum to Death and Judgement* (1688-89): "Consider these things, all you that have as yet the Golden opportunity left by Time in your hands, and Kiss the Son least he be angry and ye perish in the way. Psal. 2. 12. for although the young man shine to day like the glist'ring of a Dove's neck, and dance like a bubble upon the Waves, yet too morrow he may set in the gloomy shades of Death and his place remember him no more. How many are there than sink suddenly into the blackness of night, and are laid up in the gloomy caves of during Darkness, till the Arch-angel's Trumpet rouze them from the long sleep, to appear with the rest gathered from the four Winds of Heaven, when they the least dream'd of leaving their Pageant Glories, when they thought they most securely hugged and embraced the trifling vanities of the lower World" (9).

2. See Harvey 240-42. Preoccupied as Harvey is with the problem of space, he does not give proper credit to the pivotal role of timepiece technology.
3. "Quantity is sublated being-for-self: the repelling one which related itself only negatively to the excluded one, having passed over into relation to it, treats the other as identical with itself. . . . Continuity is, therefore, simple, self-same self-relation, which is not interrupted by any limit or exclusion; it is not, however, an immediate unity, but a unity of ones which possess being-for-itself," says Hegel in *Science of Logic* (Hegel 186).
4. In Defoe's *Memoirs of a Cavalier* (1720), numbers of the dead attest to the relative humanity of the English Civil War, measured against the brutality of the Thirty Years' War: "[W]hat was this to Count *Tilly*'s Ravages in *Saxony*? Or what was our taking of *Leicester* by Storm, where they cried out of our Barbarities, to the sacking of *New Brandenburgh*, or the taking of *Magdeburgh*? In Leicester, of 7 or 8000 People in the Town, 300 were killed; in *Magdeburgh*, of 25000 scarce 2700 were left, and the whole Town burnt to Ashes" (151).
5. On Sir Robert Clayton Francis writes, "Some of the earliest of these new financial middlemen, or bankers, were scriveners, who *inter alia* drew up and organized bonds and mortgages or loans for their customers. One such was (Sir) Robert Clayton, the son of a Northamptonshire joiner, who was apprenticed to his scrivener uncle and in due course amassed a vast fortune and became Lord Mayor" (Sheppard 138).
6. Cf. "A Highwayman having met with a considerable Booty, gives a poor common Harlot, he fancies, Ten Pounds to new-rig her from Top to Toe; is there a spruce Mercer so conscientious that he will refuse to sell her a Thread Sattin, tho' he knew who she was? She must have Shoes and Stockings, Gloves, the Stay and Mantua-maker, the Sempstress, the Linen-Draper, all must get something by her, and a hundred different Tradesmen dependent on those she laid her Money out with, may touch Part of it before a Month is at an end" (Mandeville 1.88).
7. At the level of syntax alone, the run-on conversational tone of Roxana's "memoirs" has little in common with the didactic discreteness (and discretion) of Defoe the pedagogue in *The Compleat English Tradesman*: "He is to consider that the grand characteristic of a Tradesman, and by which his credit is rated, is this of paying his Bills *well* or *ill*. If any man goes to the neighbours or dealers of a tradesman to enquire of his credit, or his fame in business, which is often done upon almost every extraordinary occasion, the first question is, How does he pay his Bills?" (*Complete English Tradesman* 269)
8. Defoe's expertise in adopting political persona under disguise has a certain affinity to "the fictional" (Davis 173), but the quality and level of impersonation in *The Shortest Way with the Dissenters* (1702) belong to a different category from the sophisticated fictional impersonations of the mature Defoe, as any excerpt from the text would readily evince: "'Twou'd be more rational for us, if we must spare this Generation, to summon our own to a general Massacre, and as we have brought them into the World Free, send them out so, and not betray them to Destruction by our supine negligence, and then cry *it is Mercy*" (*PEW* 3.105). The barely concealed desire to agitate by inflammatory language ("a general Massacre" and "Destruction") gives away the impersonator's real political identity and his

agenda.

9. For instance, Sandra Sherman, intent on building an analogy between Defoe's "fictionality" and finance, suggests that "Roxana and Lady Credit emerge as sites in which Defoe, configuring the discourse of the market through a woman's capacity to sustain open-ended narrative, reflects on his own capacity to sustain generic indeterminacy" (Sherman 158). Such indeterminacy is robustly (over-)determined by the numerical language of finance both ladies speak fluently.

10. A current popular investment portal defines liquidity as follows: "1. The degree to which an asset or security can be bought or sold in the market without affecting the asset's price. Liquidity is characterized by a high level of trading activity. Assets that can be easily bought or sold, are known as liquid assets. 2. The ability to convert an asset to cash quickly. Also known as 'marketability.'" (http://www.investopedia.com/terms)

11. "Illiquid" is an investment term referring to that "which cannot quickly and easily be converted into cash, such as real estate, collectibles, and thinly traded securities" (http://www.investorwords.com), or to the "state of a security or other asset that cannot easily be sold or exchanged for cash without a substantial loss in value" (http://www.investopedia.com). Marriage fits these descriptions neatly: it inexorably involves real estate problems, and its breakup generally leads to loss in the (sexual and financial) value of the parties.

12. The violent death of Roxana's jeweller can be compared with the jewel-maker Cardillac's violent retrieval of his artifacts in E. T. A. Hoffmann's "Mademoiselle de Scudéri." Cardillac, the "first goldsmith in the world" (Hoffmann 209), resists the alienation of his handiworks by taking them back forcefully from those who carry them in the darkened night streets of Paris, killing the victims if necessary. Unlike Hoffmann's jeweller who conducts such bloody terrorist campaign against market economy, the jewel dealer in *Roxana* is already removed from the domain of skilled artistic labour, which inherently makes him dispensable. The expensive goods he carries have been separated from the illiquid world of qualitative labour to enter the world of liquidity, where one bearer or agent can be easily replaced by another.

13. A Goldsmith's bill was a major form of security during the early stages of financial capitalism. London goldsmiths became important in the sixteenth century as Henry VIII deposited his plunder from the monasteries with them. Banking functions evolved as they paid interests and granted loans on the security of gold and jewels they kept (Kindleberger 53-54). See also Inwood 341-44.

Chapter Four. "I" against the City

1. "All that is solid melts into the air, all that is holy is profaned, and man is at last compelled to face with sober senses, his real conditions of life, and his relations with his kind" (Marx and Engels 83). Coming between this dismantling of traditional illusions and the "sober" perception of reality Marx and Engels predicted, finance and its own mysticism of numbers obfuscate the "real conditions of life" more thoroughly than any ancient religion or superstition.

2. Stock market index of this period from *Robinson Crusoe* to *Roxana* presents a

clear picture of fluctuation in share value: spectacularly bullish, reaching from 80 in 1709 to 140 in 1719, extreme volatile defying measurement almost from 1720 to 1723, stabilized only in 1724 around 120, to settle at that range until 1726 (Neal 47-48).

3. "It took three to four generations," Maureen Waller writes, "for the Huguenot immigrants of the 1680s to become assimilated. Even then they remained justifiably proud of their separate identity and heritage" (Waller 274).

4. This early pamphlet of Defoe (1687) displays his ambition to present a systematic theory of finance, centuries before it became a thriving academic business, through a lucid exposition of the importance of clearance and liquidity for financial institutions: "A Bank is only a Great Stock of Money put together, to be employ'd by some of the Subscribers, in the name of the rest, for the Benefit of the Whole. This Stock of Money subsists not barely on the Profits of its own Stock . . . but upon the Contingencies and Accidents which Multiplicity of Business occasions: As for Instance; A man that comes for Money, and knows he may have it To-morrow, perhaps he is in haste, and won't take it to day: Only that he may be sure of it to morrow, he takes a *Memorandum* under the Hand of the Officer, That he shall have it whenever he calls for it; and this *Memorandum* we call a Bill. To morrow when he Intended to fetch his Money, comes a Man to him for Money; and to save himself the labour of Telling, he gives him the *Memorandum* or Bill aforesaid for his Money; this Second Man does as the First, and a Third does as he did, and so the Bill runs about a Month, Two or Three; and this is that we call *Credit*" (*PEW* 8.54).

5. Colin Nicholson puts the case wonderfully in these words: "[T]he stability of the ego is itself compromised when what was once a classically derived and coherent moral structure based on terra firma is called into question by new forms of capital liquidity increasingly held and passed in paper pledges of credit that were by definition and practice uncertain and socially unstable. Since self-hood and personality were now increasingly indentified through the tactics and strategies of exchange, while stock market encouraged fantastic self-projections that for some visibly materialized in the insignia of wealth, all things were flowing in ways never dreamed of by Heracleitus" (Nicholson 89).

6. On the emergence of London's class topography see Inwood 258-62 and Dorothy George 73. A clear index of social stratification of London spaces is provided by a modern statistical reconstruction of the distribution of the gentry and aristocratic households (in percentage) during 1693-94, which is as follows: West End 53.6%, Northern parishes 12.3%, City within the walls 10.8%, Metropolitan Middlesex 10.1%, St Margaret Westminster 6.2%, City without the walls 4.1%, Eastern riverside parishes 1.5%, Eastern parishes 1.4% (Spence 82).

7. "Capital is dead labor, that vampire-like, only lives by sucking living labor, and lives the more, the more labor it sucks" (Marx 1976: 342).

8. Bubonic plague and other diseases were unavoidable byproducts of population concentration in early-modern London. Numerous occurrences of plague are recorded before the Great Plague, which were often as ferocious if not more, with a total of nine disasters recorded from 1563 to 1666. A significant change took place in later plagues such as that of 1665 in terms of class and status composition of the

victims, as the mortality in the northern, eastern, and southern suburbs where the poor were packed together became far greater than the more socially-mixed City or the affluent western suburbs (Inwood 166-67).

9. In the restless busy metropolis of Seoul, South Korea, where I live and work, an average of 1.5 individuals die every day from car accident alone, with a hundred or more injured, according to the daily statistics on the electronic billboards of urban highways.

10. The characteristic features of Restoration London streets included, according to Christopher Hibbert, unfriendly shopkeepers, ill-paved streets, falling sign boards, filth in the gutters, as well as rushing coaches (Hibbert 145-47).

11. Many luxury shops moved west after the Great Fire to the Strand and Covent Garden. The New Exchange on the Strand housed shops catering to the nobility living in St. James (Waller 163).

Part Two: Dickens

Chapter Five. The "Boz" Style

1. "Je vais m'exercer seul à ma fantasque escrime, / Flairant dans tous les coins les hasards de la rime" ("Le Soleil" 5-6 [Baudelaire 1975: 1.82]) ("I practise my quaint swordsmanship along . . . Sniffing in corners all the risk of rhyme" [Baudelaire 1993: 169]).

2. This is not to deny the text's peculiarities, such as the truncated episodes' debunking of narrative conventions (stories are told but not developed), which Cheryl Krueger sees as expressions of the writer's wish to "escape from time and time-boundedness" (Krueger 296).

3. Karl Ashley Smith offers to "read" Dickens's London "as an Unreal City, a symbol made up of innumerable component symbols" (Smith 4), such as the "polluted but still flowing river" standing for "a whole society in need of renewal" (162). But these urban objects in their taut substantiality resist transformation into mere poetic symbols. Dickens is "not wholly a *flâneur*" confronting the Unreal City, as Jeremy Trambling emphasizes, for in his city there are "too many objects . . . from which there can be no separation" (Trambling 2009: 57).

4. That Dickens's prose is superbly vocal, resonant, and theatrical, has been pointed out by critics such as Deborah Vlock (Vlock 47-49). We propose to go a step further and claim Dickens wrote a veritable prose poem, with all the interesting contradictions this oxymoron contains.

5. A characteristic discussion of the topic of character in Dickens is Doris Alexander's biographical source study of characters, which identifies, for example, Leigh Hunt as the real-life model of Harold Skimpole (Alexander 42-48) or Walter Savage Landor as the model of Boythorn (49-53) in *Bleak House*.

6. "Measured by numbers of editions and adaptations, *Robinson Crusoe* and *Gulliver's Travels* have no rivals from this period. Over 70 different editions of *Robinson Crusoe* had been published by 1800; over 100 separate editions of *Gulliver's Travels* had appeared by 1815" (Zwicker 252), we are told, as if these

two novels jointly created a new fictional cosmos ex nihilo.

Chapter Six. The Man of the Crowd

1. I derive this expression from Deleuze and Guattari's discussion of the "block of becoming," which is "not an evolution" nor a "filiation" in that becoming "lacks a subject distinct from itself" existing "only as taken up in another becoming of which it is the subject, and which coexists, forms a block, with the first" (Deleuze and Guattari 1987: 238). Not only his sketches but Dickens's novels themselves may be understood to be such "blocks of becoming" as they constitute a dizzy succession of scenes, episodes, and characters, which nonetheless never disappear entirely but "coexist" in the later chapters or parts.

2. Dupin's faultless forensic analysis, in "The Murders in the Rue Morgue," shows no inkling of being affected emotionally by what he describes: "On the hearth were thick tresses—very thick tresses—of gray human hair. These had been torn out by the roots. You are aware of the great force necessary in tearing thus from the head even twenty or thirty hairs together. You saw the locks in question as well as myself. Their roots (a hideous sight!) were clotted with fragments of the flesh of the scalp—sure token of the prodigious power which had been exerted in uprooting perhaps half a million of hairs at a time. The throat of the old lady was not merely cut, but the head absolutely severed from the body: the instrument was a mere razor" (Poe 161).

3. London's sprawling horizontal expansion was enabled by the absence of fortification surrounding it (as in the Continental capitals or Dublin) as well as by the supply of cheap land (Sheppard 207). The development of West End squares was already completed by the eighteenth century (Inwood 257-62), and that of the respectable western suburbs of Bayswater, Notting Hill, Kensington followed in the 19th century. The status of the Northern suburbs of Somers Town and Camden, where Dickens as a young boy and young man lived, was a mixed one with lower-middle class elements dominating (Inwood 581). On the cultural politics of distinguishing London's landmarks and districts, see S. Joyce, chapter 1, "Mapping the Capital City."

4. Dickens's exploration of location-bound city characters is not confined to human residents. What ought to be counted among his best character sketches is this description of a "republican" swine of New York: "He is a free-and-easy, careless, indifferent kind of pig . . . as he seldom troubles himself to stop and exchange civilities, but goes grunting down the kennel, turning up the news and small-talk of the city in the shape of cabbage-stalks and offal, and bearing no tails but his own: which is a very short one, for his old enemies, the dogs, have been at that too, and have left him hardly enough to swear by. He is in every respect a republican pig, going wherever he pleases, and mingling with the best society, on an equal, if not superior footing, for every one makes way when he appears, and the haughtiest give him the wall, if he prefer it. He is a great philosopher, and seldom moved, unless by the dogs before mentioned. Sometimes, indeed, you may see his small eye twinkling on a slaughtered friend, whose carcase garnishes a butcher's door-post, but he grunts out 'Such is life: all flesh is pork!' buries his nose in the mire

again, and waddles down the gutter" (*American Notes* 86-87).
5. Gordon Riots was "London's biggest and most destructive civil disorder of this or of any subsequent century" (Inwood 401), and the casualties, nonetheless, during and after the Riots, were by no means negligible: "Twenty-one are known to have been executed and the Government admitted that 285 rioters had been shot by the troops and 173 wounded. It was subsequently admitted that these numbers were an under-estimate. A contemporary witness calculated that over 700 people lost their lives . . . [and] the damage done to property was incalculable" (Hibbert 162). See also Sheppard 255.

Chapter Seven. Journalist and Novelist

1. Journalism also inherits and supplants satire. The satirist "likes to imagine himself as isolated intellect, pitted against the city," yet if "everyone suffers alike from alienation, the satirist will find it hard to maintain his detachment" (Welsh 12), argues Welsh, whereas journalism criticizes society without posturing as an alienated voice. The uniqueness of Dickens lies in his never having assumed the role of a disaffected satirist. He wished to belong to the crowd, even as he chastised their folly.
2. One should also add to Dickens's journalist ventures his earlier stint as editor of *Bentley's Miscellany* (1837-39), broken up with no love lost between the two parties. See Drew chap. 5; Kaplan 1988: 97-103; Slater 91-96.
3. "Dickens's 'Young Men," such as George Augustus Sala and Edmund Yates, played important roles in the early years of *Household Words* (see Edwards 5-49). What mattered, as Drew cautions, is not so much that Dickens invariably controlled each issue of his weeklies as that his "desire for such control thwarted in his dealings with Richard Bentley, and lost in the trammels of the *Daily News*—was strong, even if the published results fell frequently short of his ideal" (Drew 106).
4. Mary Poovey makes inference from an "article in *Blackwood*'s in 1842," in her discussion of *David Copperfield*, that Dickens must have been counted as a "contributor" to "national" literature as understood by *Blackwood's* (Poovey 110), but this is to ignore the fundamental disapproval of the populist novelist by this status-conscious periodical.
5. Even in our own time, a venerable critic strongly attached to George Eliot echoes the voice of the magazine that befriended the learned novelist. The "organization" of Dickens's novels, according to Gillian Beer, is marked by "a profuse interconnection of events and characters so extreme as to seem to defy any overall meaning" (Beer 40).
6. It seems to have been so at least until late 1850s, to infer from *Judge Lynch (of America) His Two Letters To Charles Dickens (of England) upon the subject of The Court of Chancery* (1859), dedicated to Dickens, in appreciation of "the honest, but deadly and implacable hatred, which you have ever expressed and exhibited towards this monster of iniquity, 'the Court of Chancery'" (8).
7. Unlike in his novel, his *Household Words* grudgingly recognized the national event. As Sabine Clemm observes, the "Exhibition was simply too large a public

event to be omitted (Clemm 28).
8. According to Bigelow, Krook dies "because the market-system loathes a hoarder. Stoppage of circulation creates build-up, friction, heat" (Bigelow 596), but how the loathing of market directly affects the incident is not traceable in the novel. Grandfather Smallweed stretches out his hands to Krook's possessions only after the latter's death, not before it. Jeremy Trambling classifies the seven dramatized deaths in the novel into "interpretable" cases (Gridley, Jo, Richard) and unaccountable cases (Nemo, Krook, Tulkinghorn, and Lady Dedlock) (Trambling 1995: 82-83). But such distinction may be less important than to place them together as so many variations on the great theme of self-consuming anti-economy of Chancery.

Chapter Eight. Travellers and Strangers

1. Typically, the English visitors to the Santa Maria del Pianto in Naples, at the beginning of Radcliffe's novel are drawn to the "magnificence" of its portico, but their admiration is cut short by the appearance of a sinister stranger who they are told is an assassin (Radcliffe 1-2).
2. Such predominantly cultural interest in Italy was something of an anachronism for the well-to-do travellers by the mid-nineteenth century, who now went to Italy and other old Grand Tour destinations on medical pilgrimage. The various climates of Italy were matched as cures to various complaints, as the following passage in Edwin Lee's *Memoranda on France, Italy, and Germany, with Remarks on Climates, Medical Practice, Mineral Waters, &c.* (1841) exemplifies: "From the end of November to the middle of March, the climate of Florence is less adapted than any other in Italy to persons labouring under pulmonary, bronchial, or rheumatic complaints. It generally agrees with dyspeptic and nervous patients who seek mental recreation; and I have known it suit some patients with nervous asthma, better than any other Italian town. Such invalids should reside in that part of the city north of the Arno. . . . The weather in October and November is usually fine and warm. Invalids, on their way to winter at Rome, will frequently benefit more by remaining these months at Florence, than by proceeding at once to Rome. They should not return to Florence before April, at which period the weather is in general delightful." (Lee 130-31).
3. The dichotomy of inauthentic Italian tourist resorts and the authentic English home town is worked into a more complex pattern in George Eliot's *Middlemarch*. Dorothea, in the flush of her youthful idealism, marries the emotionally moribund Casaubon, whose meager worth she cannot fail to discover during her honeymoon at Rome. Rome itself appears to her a fitting image of her gloomy marriage, as "the city of visible history, where the past of a whole hemisphere seems moving in funeral procession with strange ancestral images and trophies gathered from afar" (Eliot 1997: 180). Yet the dialectic of the plot is such that here in Rome she begins to be stirred by that "eager Titanic life gazing and struggling on walls and ceilings" (181), which the bohemian spirit of Ladislaw embodies at least in part. Rome (and Ladislaw) is thus put in narrative and thematic opposition to the restricted world of provincial England (which defines Dorothea as Mrs. Casaubon), the latter

disturbed by the former to be enriched and enhanced.

Part Three: Joyce

Chapter Nine. Trieste-Zurich-Paris

1. Brown claims that "a much more ambitiously modern notion of the nation as being built out of ethnic diversity rather than purity" originates in Defoe and leads Joyce "to develop some of the highly important ideas about the separation between ethnicity and nationhood that feed into the making of the Bloom of *Ulysses*" (Brown 2006: 47) But given the tortuous history of Protestant suppression of the Catholics and of the Ulster Orangemen's struggle against Irish independence, it seems cynical and perverse to credit Defoe's non-essentialist attitude to Englishness in his encomium on William of Orange as an influence on Joyce.
2. Quotations from *Ulysses* follow the convention of Joyce scholarship of giving episode and line number of the Hans Gabler edition.
3. One may say that the "minimalist" minority use of English initiated by Friday is passed on, through Joyce, to the Anglo-Irish expatriate Samuel Beckett, whose prose wants to be less or least, as the carefully regulated slender vocabulary of *Molloy* (and his other works) shows. Here is how the novel ends: "My birds had not been killed. They were wild birds. And yet quite trusting. I recognized them and they seemed to recognize me. But one never knows. Some were missing and some were new. I tried to understand their language better. Without having recourse to mine. They were the longest, loveliest days of all the year. I lived in the garden. I have spoken of a voice telling me things. I was getting to know it better now, to understand what it wanted" (Beckett 176). English is made to appear here like an "acquired speech," familiar and foreign, not exceeding the accessible intermediate level of those learning English from Joyce in Trieste, or even that of Friday.
4. *Ulysses* has been compared with Defoe's *Journal of the Plague Year* in that it shares Defoe's "painstaking dedication in an attempt at distilling his narrative out of hard fact" (Pérez García 82), and that both works appear as "forged documents that recall attention to their form" (85). The former claim sounds superficial (for all novelists seek to do that to some extent), and the latter misplaced (for Defoe ostensibly seeks to conceal his work's fictionality).
5. "A leveling age is not favourable to Deportment. It develops vulgarity. . . . England—alas, my country!—has degenerated very much, and is degenerating every day" (*Bleak House* 193 [chap. 14]), laments Turveydrop, a "fat old gentleman with a false complexion, false teeth, false whiskers, and a wig." He has "everything but any touch of nature; he was not like youth, he was not like age, he was not like anything in the world but a model of Deportment" (190)
6. It also alludes to *Our Mutual Friend*, where dust, occupying a central place thematically and structurally, permeates the city's mood: "A grey dusty withered evening in London city has not a hopeful aspect. The closed warehouses and offices have an air of death about them, and the national dread of colour has an air

of mourning" (*Mutual Friend* 393 [book 2, chap. 15]). The same novel also flips past Bloom's "sotto voce" comment—"Our mutual friend's stories are like himself" (16.821)—made to Stephen concerning the boasting sailor in "Eumaeus."
7. This only published English translation by Stuart Gilbert smoothes over the disjunctive style of the original, although the differences between the two languages have to be held responsible in part. Sensitive to the shortcomings of the customary rendering of French into English, as can be seen both in the Flaubert passage above and this sampling of Dujardin, Joyce may be said to have "translated" French back to English in a more literal and alien mode, a case indeed of "foreignizing translation" which Lawrence Venuti champions (see Venuti 120-21).

Chapter Ten. Dear Dirty Dublin

1. On William of Orange's Irish campaign, see Simms 497-50.
2. Margaret McBride regards Stephen not merely as the autobiographical alter ego of Joyce, but as the implied author of the novel itself. "Stephen is the narrator who is 'all in all in all' of *Ulysses*," she states. "By creating the book, he completes his story, fulfilling himself as poet and also displaying his growth as human being" (McBride 60). Not having found any evidence, internal or external, to corroborate this view, we consider Stephen as a fictional character to be assessed strictly in terms of what the work depicts.
3. Hamlet comments to Horatio on the quibbling Clown in the graveyard scene: "By the lord, Horatio, this three years I have took note of it: the age is grown so picked, that the toe of the peasant comes so near the heel of the courtier, he galls his kibe" (5.1.116-18). The lines of this source text given as 151-54 by Gifford (Gifford 252) should be corrected.
4. On Dublin Castle and its method of policing, see Foster 469-70. The combined might of the city's barracks and Dublin Castle proved their worth during the Easter Rising. The rebels put the Castle under siege, but could not subdue it. Those resisting inside were soon relieved by the military enforcement from the city's barracks (Ó Broin 93-4).
5. Even in Bloom's concern for the leftover byproducts of "hide, hair, horns," one may read echoes of Swift's pamphleteer, who does not forget to add how those "more thrifty . . . may flay the carcass; the skin of which, artificially dressed, will make admirable *gloves for ladies*, and *summer boots for fine gentlemen*" (Swift 1984: 494-95).
6. Her surname "Purefoy," meaning "pure faith," suggests her French Protestant ancestry, which would make her a remote kinswoman of another possessor of fecund womb, Defoe's Roxana, mother of many children by many fathers. For Roxana, her nightmare of the "undead" has to do with the nightmare of her personal history, such as her first husband, who reappears in France as a hired soldier of the French king, as well as Susan, her daughter and former maid. The Van Helsing role in Defoe's fiction is taken up by Amy, who exercises her expertise in prevarication and secrecy to banish these revenants.
7. Jay Clayton points out that "the nineteenth-century London was internal to

Dublin, traceable in its monuments and street names, in the condition of its port and shipping industry, in its popular songs, and most important, in its language and culture" (Clayton 340). Replication of Nelson's Column in London's Trafalgar Square would be a salient example of this
8. Clayton sees Joyce influenced by and interacting with Dickens's *Martin Chuzzlewit* in this story, finding here a reference to the Monument in London in the latter, as well as Mrs. Gamp the midwife (Clayton 335). Plausible as his reading is, one significant difference lies in the plums: Joyce's Dubliners, unlike Dickens's Londoners, robustly satisfy their hunger and thirst. Physical consumption constitutes an indispensable part of their (political) appropriation of the city that seeks to "consume" them, as much for these "Dublin vestals" in "Aeolus" as for Farrington in "Counterparts."

Chapter Eleven. Bloom as Flâneur

1. For which reason, to credit the accidental, as Richard Lehan does, as the hallmark of Joyce's urban "grotesque" does not ring entirely true. "Joyce's imagination," Lehan writes, "builds upon the contrast between commonplace and happenstance (that is, coincidence) in the commercial city—all leading to a sense of the grotesque which is very different from the grotesque in the Victorian novel" (Lehan 252). People know each other rather too well, and chance encounters are far too predictable to be shockingly grotesque.
2. Similarly, in "Lestrygonians," eating precedes and leads thinking, as in the following example: "Hot mockturtle vapour and steam of newbaked jampuffs roly-poly poured out from Harrison's. The heavy noonreek tickled the top of Mr Bloom's gullet. Want to make good pastry, butter, best flour, Demerara sugar, or they'd taste it with the hot tea. Or is it from her? A barefoot arab stood over the grating, breathing in the fumes. Deaden the gnaw of hunger that way. Pleasure or pain is it? Penny dinner. Knife and fork chained to the table." (8.232-38)
3. It also sabotages the Taylorist regime which seeks to minimize the time spent on bodily activity, particularly at toilets. The monitored and controlled toilet in Taylorized factories, according to Tim Armstrong is "the site of a struggle between nature and culture, dirt and order, invisibility and visibility; between labour and capital, and correspondingly between two types of time, the time of the body and the time of the engineer" (Armstrong 65). In giving ample narrative space to Bloom's excretive activities in "Calypso," Joyce clearly sides with the "time of the body."

Chapter Twelve. Narratio in Extremis

1. Baudelaire finds a kindred spirit in the ragpicker he runs into in his city: "On voit un chiffonier qui vient, hochant la tête, / Butant, et se cognant aux murs comme un poëte, / Et, sans prendre souci des mouchards, ses sujets, / Épanche tout son cœur en glorieux projets" (4-8 [Baudelaire 1975: 1.106]). ("One comes upon a shaking ragman, who / Staggers against the walls, as poets do, / And disregardful

of policemen's spies, / Pours from his heart some glorious enterprise" [Baudelaire 1993: 217]).

2. As Greg Winston points out, "a calculated military policy continued to rely on and encourage the Dublin red-light district in order to appeal to young, single men" from Britain to enlist in the army, so that "in the spring of 1904 British authorities were permitting troops stationed in Dublin to spend free evening hours away from the barracks." It formed part of a desperate "recruitment effort during the final stages of the Boer War, when forces had become overextended across the empire" (Winston 107).

3. One cannot agree with Attridge's verdict that "the jumps and ellipses of Bloom's thought processes disclose a more eccentric and unpredictable mind" (Attridge 97), however. Molly's thought processes display—despite the conventional grammatical elements of "and I" or "I say" in the above quotation—as many jumps, ellipses, and elisions, in as eccentric and unpredictable a manner as that of Bloom's monologues.

4. Charles Ives, who worked full-time at insurance companies in New York and part-time as composer, eagerly translated his city life into music. As his biographers describe, "Ordinarily he got home from work about six-thirty and would arrive on the run, rush into the house, tear off his coat, collar, and vest, and hurry to the piano, where he would improvise and compose intently till he was called to supper" (Cowell and Cowell 40). A good example of his being inspired by the American metropolis would be his *Theatre of Chamber Orchestra Set*, which imitates Manhattan scenes. The first movement "In the Cage" depicts the animals at the Central Park Zoo. The idea of the second movement "In the Inn" was, according to the same source, "suggested by the sounds that come from inside the inn to the ear of a passer-by" (Cowell and Cowell: 169). Ives also was a "literary" composer in that he extensively and boldly used quotations, comparable to T. S. Eliot's and Joyce's compositions, using "musical reminiscence as a kind of stream-of-consciousness device that brings up old tunes with their burden of nostalgic emotion" (147).

5. However, that heretical writer with Anglo-Irish background Laurence Sterne's musical dismantling of English prose ought to be recognized as a major precedent of "Sirens." Tristram's broken fiddle, for Sterne, can find no other adequate transcription than the following: "Ptr . . . rr . . . ing—twing—twang—prut—trut——'tis a cursed bad fiddle.—Do you know whether my fiddle's in tune or no?—trut . . . prut.—They should be *fifths.*——'Tis wickedly strung—tr . . . a.e.i.o.u.-twang.—The bridge is a mile too high, and the sound-post absolutely down,—else—trut . . prut—hark! 'tis not so bad a tone.—Diddle, diddle, diddle diddle, diddle diddle, dum." (Sterne 297 [vol. 5, chap.15])

Conclusion

1. Both sadly typical murders involving teenage gangs, as well as the riots in Hackney and elsewhere, took place in summer 2011 as I write this final chapter in London.

2.http://www.irishtimes.com/newspaper/education/2011/0118/1224287750902.html.

BIBLIOGRAPHY

Achilles Tatius. *Leucippe and Clitophon*. Trans. Tim Whitmarsh. Oxford: Oxford University Press, 2001.

Agamben, Giorgio. *Infancy and History: The Destruction of Experience*. Trans. Liz Heron. London: Verso, 1993.

—. *State of Exception*. Trans. Kevin Attell. Chicago: University of Chicago Press, 2005.

An Agitator Anotomized: Or, The Character of an Agitator. London, 1648.

Albanese, Denise. "Mathematics as a Social Formation: Mapping the Early Modern Universal." In *The Culture of Capital: Property, Cities, and Knowledge in Early Modern England*, ed. Henry S. Turner, 255-73. New York: Routledge, 2002.

Alexander, Doris. *Creating Characters with Charles Dickens*. University Park: Penn State University Press, 1991.

All the Year Round 84 (1 December 1860).

Alter, Robert. *Imagined Cities: Urban Experience and the Language of the Novel*. New Haven: Yale University Press, 2005.

Armstrong, Tim. *Modernism, Technology, and the Body: A Cultural Study*. Cambridge: Cambridge University Press, 1998.

The Artificial Clock-Maker, A Treatise of Watch and Clock-Work, Wherein the Art of Calculating Numbers for Most Sorts of Movements is Explained to the Capacity of the Unlearned. London, 1700.

Attridge, Derek. *Joyce Effects: On Language, Theory, and History*. Cambridge: Cambridge University Press, 2000.

Auerbach, Erich. *Mimesis: The Representation of Reality in Western Literature*. Trans. Willard R. Trask. Princeton: Princeton University Press, 1953.

Backscheider, Paula R. *Daniel Defoe: A Life*. Baltimore: The Johns Hopkins University Press, 1989.

Ball, Michael and David Sunderland. *An Economic History of London, 1800-1914*. London: Routledge, 2001.

Bakhtin, M. M. *The Dialogic Imagination: Four Essays*. Trans. Caryl Emerson and Michael Holquist, ed. Michael Holquist. Austin: University of Texas Press, 1981.

Balzac, Honoré de. *Lost Illusions*. Trans. Herbert J. Hunt. London: Penguin, 1971.

Banta, Melissa and Oscar A. Silverman. *James Joyce's Letters to Sylvia Beach, 1921-1940*. Oxford: Plantin Publishers, 1987.

Barker, Francis. *The Tremulous Private Body: Essays on Subjection*. London: Methuen, 1984.

Baucom, Ian. *Specters of the Atlantic: Finance Capital, Slavery, and the Philosophy of History*. Durham: Duke University Press, 2005.

Baudelaire, Charles. *The Flowers of Evil*. Trans. James McGowan. Oxford: Oxford University Press, 1993.

—. *The Painter of Modern Life and Other Essays*. Trans. Jonathan Mayne. New York: Phaidon, 1964.

—. *Paris Spleen, 1869*. Trans. Louise Varèse. New York: New Directions, 1970.

—. *Œuvres complètes*. Ed. Claude Pichois. 2 vols. Paris: Gallimard, 1975.

Beckett, Samuel. *Trilogy: Molloy, Malone Dies, The Unnamable*. London: Calder Publications, 1959.

Beer, Gillian. *Darwin's Plots: Evolutionary Narrative in Darwin, George Eliot and Nineteenth-Century Fiction*. Cambridge: Cambridge University Press, 1983.

Behn, Aphra. *Love-Letters Between a Nobleman and His Sister*. London: Virago, 1987.

—. *Oroonoko and Other Writings*. Ed. Paul Salzman. Oxford: Oxford University Press, 1994.

Bender, John. *Imagining the Penitentiary: Fiction and the Architecture of Mind in Eighteenth-Century England*. Chicago: University of Chicago Press, 1987.

Benstock, Bernard. *James Joyce: The Undiscoverer'd Country*. Dublin: Gill and Macmillan, 1977.

Bevis, Matthew. *The Art of Eloquence: Byron, Dickens, Tennyson, Joyce*. Oxford: Oxford University Press, 2007.

Bigelow, Gordon. "Market Indicators: Banking and Domesticity in Dickens's *Bleak House*." *ELH* 67 (2000): 589-615.

Birdsall, Virginia Ogden. *Defoe's Perpetual Seekers: A Study of the Major Fiction*. Lewisburg: Bucknell University Press, 1985.

Berger, Harry. "The Pepys Show: Ghost-Writing and Documentary Desire in *The Diary*." *ELH* 65 (1998): 557-91.

Benjamin, Walter. *Charles Baudelaire: A Lyric Poet in the Era of High Capitalism*. Trans. Harry Zohn. London: Verso, 1983.

—. *Selected Writings*. Vol. 2. Part 1, *1927-1930*. Trans. Edmund Jephcott et al., eds. Howard Eiland and Michael W. Jennings. Cambridge: Harvard University Press, 2004.

—. *Selected Writings*. Vol. 2. Part 2, *1931-1934*. Trans. Edmund Jephcott et al., eds. Howard Eiland and Michael W. Jennings. Cambridge: Harvard University Press, 2005.

—. *Selected Writings*. Vol. 3, *1935-38*. Trans. Edmund Jephcott et al., eds. Howard Eiland and Michael W. Jennings. Cambridge: Harvard University Press, 2002.

—. *Selected Writings*. Vol. 4, *1938-1940*. Trans. Edmund Jephcott et al, eds. Howard Eiland and Michael W. Jennings. Cambridge: Harvard University Press, 2003.

—. *Gesammelte Schriften*. Vol. 2.1. Eds. Rolf Tiedemann and Hermann Schweppenhäuser. Frankfurt am Main: Surhkamp, 1977.

—. *Gesammelte Schriften*. Vol. 6. Eds. Rolf Tiedemann and Hermann Schweppenhäuser. Frankfurt am Main: Surhkamp, 1985.

Blackwood's Edinburgh Magazine 85 (May 1860).

A "Bleak House" Narrative of Real Life; Being a Faithful Detail of Facts Connected with a Suit in the Irish Court of Chancery . . . To Which is Added (By Permission,) Letters on Chancery Reform, By Locke King, Esq., M. P. London, 1856.

Bloom, Harold and Lionel Trilling ed. *Romantic Poetry and Prose*. New York: Oxford University Press, 1972.

Bolton, Matthew. "Joycean Dickens/Dickensian Joyce." *Dickens Quarterly* 23 (Dec. 2006): 243-55.

Bourdieu, Pierre. *Distinction: A Social Critique of the Judgement of Taste*. Trans. Richard Nice. London: Routledge, 1984.

Bowen, John. "Dickens and the Figures of *Pictures from Italy*." In *The Impact of Italy: The Grand Tour and Beyond*, ed. Clare Hornsby, 197-217. London: The British School at Rome, 2000.

Braverman, Richard. "Crusoe's Legacy." *Studies in the Novel* 18 (Spring 1986): 1-26.

Brown, Richard. "Joyce's Englishman: 'The Het'rogeneous Thing' from Stephen's Blake and Dowland to Defoe's 'True-Born Englishman.'" In *Joyce, Ireland, Britain*, eds. Andrew Gibson and Len Platt, 33-49. Gainesville: University Press of Florida, 2006.

—. "Time, Space and the City in "Wandering Rocks."" In *Joyce's "Wandering Rocks,"* ed. Andrew Gibson and Steven Morrison, 57-72. Amsterdam: Rodopi, 2002.

Budgen, Frank. *James Joyce and the Making of "Ulysses."* Bloomington: Indiana University Press, 1960.

Bull, Digby. *The Watch-Man's Voice, Giving Warning to All Men of the Dreadful Day of the Lord*. London, 1695.

Bunyan, John. *Grace Abounding with Other Spiritual Autobiographies*. Eds. John Stachniewski and Anita Pacheco. Oxford: Oxford University Press, 1998.

—. *The Life and Death of Mr Badman*. Eds. James F. Forrest and Roger Sharrock. Oxford: Clarendon, 1988.

—. *The Pilgrim's Progress*. Ed. W. R. Owens. Oxford: Oxford University Press, 2003.

Butt, John. "*Bleak House* in the Context of 1851." *Nineteenth-Century Fiction* 10 (1955-56): 1-21.

Calvin, [Jean]. *Institutes of the Christian Religion*. Trans. Ford Lewis Battles, ed. John T. McNeill. 2 vols. Louisville: Westminster John Knox Press, 1960.

Calvino, Italo. *Invisible Cities*. Trans. William Weaver. London: Vintage, 1997.

"Captain Speke's Adventures in Somali Land." *Blackwood's Edinburgh Magazine* 85 (May 1860): 561-80.

Chancery Delays, and Their Remedy. London, 1830.

The Character of a Diurnal-Maker. London, 1654.

Churchill, Kenneth. *Italy and English Literature, 1764-1930*. London: Macmillan, 1980.

Clayton, Jay. "Londublin: Dickens's London in Joyce's Dublin." *Novel: A Forum on Fiction* 28 (Spring 1995): 327-42.

Cleland, John. *Fanny Hill, or, Memoirs of a Woman of Pleasure*. Ed. Peter Wagner. Harmondsworth: Penguin, 1985.

Clemm, Sabine. *Dickens, Journalism, and Nationhood: Mapping the World in "Household Words."* New York: Routledge, 2009.

Comerford, R. V. "The Land War and the Politics of Distress, 1877-82." In *A New History of Ireland*, vol. 6, *Ireland Under the Union, 1870-1921*, ed. W. E. Vaughan, 26-80. Oxford: Oxford University Press, 1989.

Connor, Steven. "'Jigajiga… Yummyyum… Pfuiiiiii!... Bbbbblllllblblblblobshb!': "Circe's" Ventriloquy." In *Reading Joyce's "Circe,"* ed. Andrew Gibson, 93-142. Amsterdam: Rodopi, 1994.

Cowell, Henry and Sidney Cowell. *Charles Ives and His Music*. New York: Da Capo Press, 1983.

Cross, Richard K. *Flaubert and Joyce: The Rite of Fiction*. Princeton: Princeton University Press, 1971.

Cullen, Louis M. "Dublin." In *James Joyce in Context*, ed. John McCourt, 173-83. Cambridge: Cambridge University Press, 2009.

—. "The Growth of Dublin 1600-1900: Character and Heritage." In *Dublin: City and County: From Prehistory to Present: Studies in*

Honour of J. H. Andrews, eds. F. H. A. Aalen and Kevin Whelan, 251-77. Dublin: Geography Publications, 1992.

Curtis, Gerard. "Dickens in the Visual Market." In *Literature in the Marketplace: Nineteenth-century British Publishing and Reading Practices*, eds. John O. Jordan and Robert L. Patten, 213-49. Cambridge: Cambridge University Press, 1995.

Curtius, Ernst Robert. *European Literature and the Latin Middle Ages*. Trans. William R. Trask. Princeton: Princeton University Press, 1953.

Dampier, William. *A New Voyage Round the World: The Journal of an English Buccaneer*. London: Hummingbird Press, 1999.

Dante Alighieri. *Inferno*. Trans. and ed. Robert M. Durling. Oxford: Oxford University Press, 1996.

Davison, Neil R. *James Joyce, Ulysses, and the Construction of Jewish Identity: Culture, Biography, and "the Jew" in Modernist Europe*. Cambridge: Cambridge University Press, 1996.

Davis, Lennard J. *Factual Fictions: The Origins of the English Novel*. New York: Columbia University Press, 1983.

Defoe, Daniel. *A Journal of the Plague Year*. Ed. Louis Landa. Oxford: Oxford University Press, 1990.

—. *The Life, Adventures, and Pyracies, of the Famous Captain Singleton*. Ed. P. N. Furbank. London: Pickering & Chatto, 2008.

—. *Memoirs of a Cavalier.* Ed. N. H. Keeble. London: Pickering & Chatto, 2008.

—. *Moll Flanders*. Ed. G. A. Starr. Oxford: Oxford University Press, 1981.

—. *Robinson Crusoe*. Ed. Thomas Keymer. Oxford: Oxford University Press, 2007.

—. *Roxana*. Ed. John Mullan. Oxford: Oxford University Press, 1996.

—. *The Complete English Tradesman, Vol. 1*. Vol. 7 of *Religious and Didactic Writings of Daniel Defoe*. Ed. John McVeagh. London: Pickering & Chatto, 2007.

—. *Serious Reflections during the Life and Surprising Adventures of Robinson Crusoe*. Ed. G. A. Starr. London: Pickering & Chatto, 2008.

—. *Political and Economic Writings of Daniel Defoe*. Vol. 3, *Dissent*. W. R. Owens. London: Pickering & Chatto, 2000.

—. *Political and Economic Writings of Daniel Defoe*. Vol. 5, *International Relations*. Ed. P. N. Furbank. London: Pickering & Chatto, 2000.

—. *Political and Economic Writings of Daniel Defoe*. Vol. 6, *Finance*. Ed. John McVeagh. London: Pickering & Chatto, 2000.

—. *Political and Economic Writings of Daniel Defoe*. Vol. 7, *Trade*. Ed. John McVeagh. London: Pickering & Chatto, 2000.

—. *Political and Economic Writings of Daniel Defoe*. Vol. 8, *Social*

Reform. Ed. W. R. Owens. London: Pickering & Chatto, 2000.
—. *The Political History of the Devil*. Vol. 6 of *Satire, Fantasy and Writings on the Supernatural*. Ed. John Mullan. London: Pickering & Chatto, 2005.
Delays in Chancery Considered with Practical Suggestions for their Prevention or Removal. London, 1843.
Deleuze, Gilles and Félix Guattari. *Anti-Oedipus: Capitalism and Schizophrenia*. Trans. Robert Hurley et al. Minneapolis: University of Minnesota Press, 1983.
—. *A Thousand Plateaus: Capitalism and Schizophrenia*. Trans. Brian Massumi. Minneapolis: University of Minnesota Press, 1987.
De Vries, Jan. *European Urbanization 1500-1800*. London: Methuen, 1984.
Dickens, Charles. *American Notes and Pictures from Italy*. The Oxford Illustrated Dickens. Oxford: Oxford University Press, 1957.
—. *Barnaby Rudge*. The Oxford Illustrated Dickens. Oxford: Oxford University Press, 1954.
—. *Bleak House*. The Oxford Illustrated Dickens. Oxford: Oxford University Press, 1948.
—. *Christmas Books*. The Oxford Illustrated Dickens. Oxford: Oxford University Press, 1954.
—. *David Copperfield*. The Oxford Illustrated Dickens. Oxford: Oxford University Press, 1948.
—. *Dombey and Son*. The Oxford Illustrated Dickens. Oxford: Oxford University Press, 1957.
—. *Great Expectations*. The Oxford Illustrated Dickens. Oxford: Oxford University Press, 1948.
—. *Hard Times*. The Oxford Illustrated Dickens. Oxford: Oxford University Press, 1955.
—. *Little Dorrit*. The Oxford Illustrated Dickens. Oxford: Oxford University Press, 1953.
—. *Martin Chuzzlewit*. The Oxford Illustrated Dickens. Oxford: Oxford University Press, 1951.
—. *Nicholas Nickleby*. The Oxford Illustrated Dickens. Oxford: Oxford University Press, 1950.
—. *Oliver Twist*. The Oxford Illustrated Dickens. Oxford: Oxford University Press, 1949.
—. *Our Mutual Friend*. The Oxford Illustrated Dickens. Oxford: Oxford University Press, 1952.
—. *Pickwick Papers*. The Oxford Illustrated Dickens. Oxford: Oxford University Press, 1948.

—. *Sketches by Boz*. The Oxford Illustrated Dickens. Oxford: Oxford University Press, 1957.

—. *A Tale of Two Cities*. The Oxford Illustrated Dickens. Oxford: Oxford University Press, 1949.

—. *Uncommercial Traveller and Reprinted Pieces*. The Oxford Illustrated Dickens. Oxford: Oxford University Press, 1958.

—. *The Letters of Charles Dickens*. Eds. Graham Storey et al., 12 vols. Oxford: Clarendon, 1964-2002.

—. *The Speeches of Charles Dickens*. Ed. K. J. Fielding. Oxford: Clarendon, 1960.

Dilthey, Wilhelm. *The Formation of the Historical World in the Human Sciences*. Vol. 3 of *Selected Works*. Eds. Rudolf A. Makkreel and Frithjof Rodi. Princeton: Princeton University Press, 2002.

—. *Introduction to the Human Sciences*. Vol. 1 of *Selected Works*. Eds. Rudolf A. Makkreel and Frithjof Rodi. Princeton: Princeton University Press, 1989.

—. *Poetry and Experience*. Vol. 5 of *Selected Works*. Eds. Rudolf A. Makkreel and Frithjof Rodi. Princeton: Princeton University Press, 1985.

Docherty, Thomas. "'Sound Sense'; or 'Tralala'/'Moocow': Joyce and the Anathema of Writing." In *James Joyce and the Difference of Language*, ed. Laurent Milesi, 112-27. Cambridge: Cambridge University Press, 2003.

Donne, John. *The Complete Poetry and Selected Prose of John Donne*. Ed. Charles M. Coffin. New York: Modern Library, 1994.

Doody, Margaret Anne. *The True Story of the Novel*. London: Fontana Press, 1998.

Drew, John M. L.. *Dickens the Journalist*. Houndmills: Palgrave Macmillan, 2003.

Duffy, Edna. "Disappearing Dublin: *Ulysses*, Postcoloniality, and the Politics of Space." In *Semicolonial Joyce*, eds. Derek Attridge and Marjorie Howes, 37-57. Cambridge: Cambridge University Press, 2000.

Dujardin, Édouard. *Les Lauriers sont coupés*. Paris: Le Chemin Vert, 1981.

—. *We'll to the Woods No More*. Trans. Stuart Gilbert. New York: New Directions, 1938.

—. *Le Monologue intérieur: son apparition, ses origines, sa place dans l'œuvre de james joyce*. Paris: Albert Messein, 1931.

Eagleton, Terry. *Reason, Faith, and Revolution: Reflections on the God Debate*. New Haven: Yale University Press, 2009.

Earle, Peter. *The Making of the English Middle Class: Business, Society and Family Life in London, 1660-1730*. London: Methuen, 1989.

Edwards, P. D. *Dickens's "Young Men": George Augustus Sala, Edmund Yates and the World of Victorian Journalism*. Aldershot: Ashgate, 1997.

Eliot, George. *Middlemarch*. Ed. David Carroll. Oxford: Oxford University Press, 1997.

—. *Romola*. Ed. Andrew Brown. Oxford: Oxford University Press, 1994.

—. *Scenes of Clerical Life*. Ed. Thomas A. Noble. Oxford: Oxford University Press, 1985.

—. *The Journals of George Eliot*. Eds. Margaret Harris and Judith Johnston. Cambridge: Cambridge University Press, 1998.

Eliot, T. S. *The Complete Poems and Plays of T. S. Eliot*. London: Faber and Faber, 1969.

Ellison, Katherine E. *Fatal News: Reading and Information Overload in Early Eighteenth-Century Literature*. New York: Routledge, 2006.

Ellmann, Richard. *James Joyce*. Oxford: Oxford University Press, 1982.

Easson, Angus. "A Novel Scarcely Historical? Time and History in Dickens's *Little Dorrit*." In *History and the Novel*, ed. Angus Easson, 27-40. Cambridge: The English Association and D.S. Brewer, 1991.

England's Golden Watch-Bell. Summoning an Alarum to Death and Judgement. London, [1688-1689].

Ermath, Michael. *Wilhelm Dilthey: The Critique of Historical Reason*. Chicago: University of Chicago Press, 1978.

Evelyn, John. *Diary of John Evelyn*. Ed. William Bray. 3 vols. London: Bickers and Son, 1905.

Ferguson, Priscilla Parkhurst. "The *Flâneur* on and off the Streets of Paris." In *The Flâneur*, ed. Keith Tester, 22-42. London: Routledge, 1994.

Fielding, Henry. *Joseph Andrews and Shamela*. Eds. Douglas Brooks-Davies and Thomas Keymer. Oxford: Oxford University Press, 1999.

Fischer, Andreas. "Strange Words, Strange Music: The Verbal Music of "Sirens."" In *Bronze by Gold: The Music of Joyce*, ed. Sebastian D.G. Knowles, 245-62. New York: Garland, 1999.

Fischer, Claude S. *The Urban Experience*. New York: Harcourt Brace Jovanovich, 1976.

Fisher, Carl. "'The Rage of the Street': Crowd and Public in Defoe's *Moll Flanders*." In *Historical Boundaries, Narrative Forms: Essays on British Literature in the Long Eighteenth Century in Honor of Everett Zimmerman*, eds. Lorna Clymer et al., 73-86. Newark: University of Delaware Press, 2007.

Flaubert, Gustave. *Madame Bovary*. Ed. Béatrice Didier. Paris: Librairie Générale Française, 1983.

—. *Madame Bovary*. Trans. Margaret Mauldon. Oxford: Oxford University Press, 2004.

Flint, Christopher. *Family Fictions: Narrative and Domestic Relations in Britain, 1688-1798*. Stanford: Stanford University Press, 1998.

Flynn, Carol Houlihan. *The Body in Swift and Defoe*. Cambridge: Cambridge University Press, 1990.

—. "Defoe's Idea of Conduct: Ideological Fictions and Fictional Reality." In *The Ideology of Conduct: Essays in Literature and the History of Sexuality*, eds. Nancy Armstrong and Leonard Tennenhouse, 73-95. New York: Methuen, 1987.

Foster, R. F. *Modern Ireland 1600-1972*. London: Penguin, 1988.

Gailhard, J[ean]. *The Present State of the Princes and Republicks of Italy with Observations on Them*. London, 1671.

Gabler, Hans Walter. Foreword to *The Lost Notebook: New Evidence on the Genesis of "Ulysses" by James Joyce*. Eds. Danis Rose and John O'Hanlon. Edinburgh: Split Pea Press, 1989.

Gallagher, Catherine. *The Industrial Reformation of English Fiction 1832-1867*. Chicago: University of Chicago Press, 1985.

Gasché, Rodolpe. *Of Minimal Things: Studies on the Notion of Relation*. Stanford: Stanford University Press, 1999.

Gay, John. *Walking the Streets of Eighteenth-Century London: John Gay's* Trivia *(1716)*. Eds. Clare Brant and Susan E. Whyman. Oxford: Oxford University Press, 2007.

George, M. Dorothy. *London Life in the Eighteenth Century*. Chicago: Academy Chicago Publishers, 1984.

Gibson, Andrew. *Joyce's Revenge: History, Politics, and Aesthetics in "Ulysses."* Oxford: Oxford University Press, 2002.

Gifford, Don and Robert J. Seidman. *Notes for Joyce: An Annotation of James Joyce's "Ulysses."* New York: E. P. Duttton, 1974.

Gilbert, Stuart. *James Joyce's Ulysses*. New York: Alfred A. Knopf, 1931.

Gilloch, Graeme. *Myth and Metropolis: Walter Benjamin and the City*. London: Polity Press, 1996.

Goodlad, Lauren M. E. *Victorian Literature and the Victorian State: Character and Governance in a Liberal Society*. Baltimore: Johns Hopkins University Press, 2003.

Habermas, Jürgen. *The Structural Transformation of the Public Sphere: An Inquiry into a Category of Bourgeois Society*. Trans. Thomas Burger. Cambridge: MIT Press, 1989.

Hahn, Hazel. "Boulevard Culture and Advertising as Spectacle in Nineteenth-Century Paris." In *The City and the Senses: Urban Culture*

Since 1500, ed. Alexander Cowan and Jill Steward, 156-75. Aldershot: Ashgate, 2006.

Hanssen, Beatrice. "Language and Mimesis in Walter Benjamin's Work." In *The Cambridge Companion to Walter Benjamin*, ed. David S. Ferris, 54-72. Cambridge: Cambridge University Press, 2004.

Harding, Desmond. *Writing the City: Urban Visions and Literary Modernism*. New York: Routledge, 2003.

Hardy, Thomas. *Jude the Obscure*. Ed. Patricia Ingham. Oxford: Oxford University Press, 2002.

Harris, Margaret. "What George Eliot Saw in Europe: The Evidence of her *Journals*." In *George Eliot and Europe*, ed. John Rignall, 1-16. Aldershot: Scholar Press, 1997.

Harvey, David. *The Condition of Postmodernity: An Inquiry into the Origins of Cultural Change*. Oxford: Blackwell, 1989.

Healey, Christina L. "'A perfect Retreat indeed': Speculation, Surveillance, and Space in Defoe's *Roxana*." *Eighteenth-Century Fiction* 21 (Summer 2009): 493-512.

Hegel, G. W. F. *Hegel's Science of Logic*. Trans. A. V. Miller. Atlantic Highlands: Humanities Press International, 1989.

Heidegger, Martin. *Basic Writings*. Ed. David Farrell Krell. London: Routledge, 1992.

Henke, Suzette A. *James Joyce and the Politics of Desire*. New York: Routledge, 1990.

Hibbert, Christopher. *London: The Biography of a City*. London: Penguin, 1977.

Hill, Jacqueline. *From Patriots to Unionists: Dublin Civic Politics and Irish Protestant Patriotism, 1660-1840*. Oxford: Clarendon, 1997.

Hobbes, Thomas. *Leviathan*. Ed. Richard Tuck. Cambridge: Cambridge University Press, 1996.

Hoffmann, E. T. A. *Tales of E. T. A. Hoffmann*. Eds. and trans. Leonard J. Kent and Elizabeth C. Knight. Chicago: University of Chicago Press, 1969.

Holmes, George ed. *The Oxford Illustrated History of Italy*. Oxford: Oxford University Press, 1997.

Household Words 209 (March 1854).

Houston, John Porter. *Joyce and Prose: An Exploration of the Language of "Ulysses*." London: Associated University Presses, 1989.

Hume Brown, P. *History of Scotland: To the Present Time*. Vol. 3: *From the Revolution of 1689 to the Year 1910*. Cambridge: University Press, 1911.

Hunter, J. Paul. *The Reluctant Pilgrim: Defoe's Emblematic Method and Quest for Form in "Robinson Crusoe."* Baltimore: Johns Hopkins University Press, 1966.

Hylton, Stuart. *A History of Manchester*. Andover: Phillimore, 2003.

Investopia.com. http://www.investopedia.com/terms

InvestorWords.com. http://www.investorwords.com

Inwood, Stephen. *A History of London*. London: Macmillan, 1998.

The Irish Times. http://www.irishtimes.com/newspaper/education

Jagodzinski, Cecile M. *Privacy and Print: Reading and Writing in Seventeenth-Century England*. Charlottesville: University Press of Virginia, 1999.

John, Juliet. *Dickens's Villains: Melodrama, Character, Popular Culture*. Oxford: Oxford University Press, 2001.

Johnson, Samuel. *Samuel Johnson's Dictionary: Selections from the 1755 Work That Defined the English Language*. Ed. Jack Lynch. New York: Levenger Press, 2002.

Johnston, John H. *The Poet and the City: A Study in Urban Perspectives*. Athens: University of Georgia Press, 1984.

Jones, Emrys. *Metropolis*. Oxford: Oxford University Press, 1990.

Joyce et Paris 1902 ... 1920-1940 ... 1975: actes du cinquième symposium international James Joyce, Paris 16-20 juin 1975. Eds. J. Aubert and M. Jolas. Paris: Éditions du CNRS, 1979.

Joyce, James. *Dubliners*. Ed. Jeri Johnson. Oxford: Oxford University Press, 2000.

—. *Finnegans Wake*. New York: Penguin, 1967.

—. *A Portrait of the Artist as a Young Man*. Ed. Jeri Johnson. Oxford: Oxford University Press, 2000.

—. *Ulysses*. Ed. Hans Walter Gabler. London: Bodley Head, 1984.

—. *Letters of James Joyce*. Ed. Richard Ellmann. 3 vols. London: Faber & Faber, 1966.

—. *Occasional, Critical, and Political Writings*. Ed. Kevin Barry, trans. Conor Deane. Oxford: Oxford University Press, 2000.

Joyce, Simon. *Capital Offenses: The Geography of Class and Crime in Victorian London.* Charlottesville: University of Virginia Press, 2003.

Judge Lynch (of America) His Two Letters To Charles Dickens (of England) upon the Subject of The Court of Chancery. London, 1859.

Juvenal. *Juvenal and Persius*. Trans. G. G. Ramsay. Loeb Classical Library. Cambridge: Harvard University Press, 1940.

Kant, Immanuel. *Anthropology from a Pragmatic Point of View*. Trans and ed. Robert B. Louden. Cambridge: Cambridge University Press, 2006.

—. *The Critique of Judgement*. Trans. James Creed Meredith, rev. and ed. Nicholas Walker. Oxford: Oxford University Press, 2008.

—. *Kritik der Urteilskraft*. Vol. 10 of *Immanuel Kant Werkasugabe*. Ed. Wilhelm Weischedel. Frankfurt am Main: Suhrkamp, 1974.

Kaplan, Fred. *Dickens: A Biography*. New York: William Morrow and Company, 1988.

—. "Dickens' Flora Finching and Joyce's Molly Bloom." *Nineteenth-Century Fiction* 23 (Dec. 1968): 343-46.

Keeble, Richard and Sharon Wheeler eds. *The Journalistic Imagination: Literary Journalists from Defoe to Capote and Carter*. London: Routledge, 2007.

Kelman, James. *How Late It Was, How Late*. London: Vintage, 1998.

Kibbie, Ann Louise. "Monstrous Generation: The Birth of Capital in Defoe's *Moll Flanders* and *Roxana*." *PMLA* 110-5 (1995): 1023-34.

Kiberd, Declan. *Irish Classics*. London: Granta, 2000.

Kilfeather, Siobhán. *Dublin: A Cultural History*. Oxford: Oxford University Press, 2005.

Kindleberger, Charles P. *A Financial History of Western Europe*. New York: Oxford University Press, 1993.

Krueger, Cheryl L. "Telling Stories in Baudelaire's *Spleen de Paris*." *Nineteenth-Century French Studies* 30 (Spring-Summer 2002): 282-300.

Kumar, Udaya. *The Joycean Labyrinth: Repetition, Truth, and Tradition in Ulysses*. Oxford: Clarendon, 1991.

La Mettrie, Julien Offray de. *Machine Man and Other Writings*. Trans. Ann Thomson. Cambridge: Cambridge University Press, 1996.

Latham, Robert. *The Diary of Samuel Pepys*. Eds. Robert Latham and William Matthews. Vol. 10: *Companion*. London: HarperCollins, 1995.

Lawrence, D. H. *Lady Chatterley's Lover and A Propos of "Lady Chatterley's Lover."* Ed. Michael Squires. Cambridge: Cambridge University Press, 1993.

Leavis, F. R. *The Great Tradition: George Eliot, Henry James, Joseph Conrad*. London: Chatto and Windus, 1948.

Lee, Edwin. *Memoranda on France, Italy, and Germany, with Remarks on Climates, Medical Practice, Mineral Waters, &c.* London, 1841.

Lefebvre, Henri. *Writing on Cities*. Trans. Eleonore Kofman and Elizabeth Lebas. Oxford: Blackwell, 1996.

Lehan, Richard. *The City in Literature: An Intellectual and Cultural History*. Berkeley: University of California Press, 1998.

Leonard, Garry. "Holding on to the Hear and the Now: Juxtaposition and Identity in Modernity and in Joyce." In *James Joyce and the*

Fabrication of an Irish Identity, ed. Michael Patrick Gillespie, 39-51. Amsterdam: Rodopi, 2001.

Lernout, Geert. *The French Joyce*. Ann Arbor: University of Michigan Press, 1990.

Locke, John. *Two Treatises of Government*. Ed. Peter Laslett. Cambridge: Cambridge University Press, 1988.

Lucas, John. "Past and Present: *Bleak House* and *A Child's History of England*." In *Dickens Refigured: Bodies, Desires and Other Histories*, ed. John Schad, 136-56. Manchester: Manchester University Press, 1996.

Lukács, Georg. *The Theory of the Novel.* Trans. Anna Bostock. Cambridge: MIT Press, 1971(a).

—. *Writer and Critic and Others Essays*. Ed. and trans. Arthur Kahn. London: Merlin, 1970.

—. *Probleme des Realismus I: Essays über Realismus*. Vol. 4 of *Georg Lukács Werke*. Neuwied: Luchterhand, 1971(b).

—. *Zerstörung der Vernunft*. Vol. 9 of *Georg Lukács Werke*. Neuwied: Luchterhand, 1962.

Lynch, Deidre Shauna. *The Economy of Character: Novels, Market Culture, and the Business of Inner Meaning*. Chicago: University of Chicago Press, 1998.

Makkreel, Rudolf A. *Dilthey: Philosopher of the Human Studies*. Princeton: Princeton University Press, 1975.

Mandeville, Bernard. *The Fable of the Bees: Or, Private Vices, Publick Benefits*. 2 vols. Oxford: Clarendon, 1924.

Marx, Karl. *Capital: A Critique of Political Economy*. Vol. 1. Trans. Ben Fowkes. New York: Vintage, 1976.

—. *Capital: A Critique of Political Economy*. Vol. 3. Trans. David Fernbach. New York: Vintage, 1981.

Marx, Karl and Friedrich Engels. *The Communist Manifesto*. Harmondsworth: Penguin, 1967.

Maxwell, Richard. *The Mysteries of Paris and London*. Charlottesville: University Press of Virginia, 1992.

Mayer, Robert. *History and the Early English Novel: Matters of Fact from Bacon to Defoe*. Cambridge: Cambridge University Press, 1997.

McBride, Margaret. "*Ulysses" and the Metamorphosis of Stephen Dedalus*. Lewisburg: Bucknell University Press, 2001.

McKeon, Michael. *The Origins of the English Novel*: *1600-1740*. Baltimore: Johns Hopkins University Press, 1989.

"The Mill on the Floss." *Blackwood's Edinburgh Magazine* 85 (May 1860): 611-23.

Miller, D. A. *The Novel and the Police*. Berkeley: University of California Press, 1988.

Miller, J. Hillis. *Charles Dickens: The World of His Novels*. Cambridge: Harvard University Press, 1958.

Missac, Pierre. *Walter Benjamin's Passages*. Trans. Shierry Weber Nicholsen. Cambridge: The MIT Press, 1995.

Misson, Maximilian. *A New Voyage to Italy: With a Description of the Chief Towns, Churches, Tombs, Libraries, Palaces, Statues, and Antiquities of that Country*. London, 1695.

Moretti, Franco. *Atlas of the European Novel 1800-1900*. London: Verso, 1998.

—. *The Way of the World*. Trans. Albert Spragia. London: Verso, 1987.

Mumford, Lewis. *The Culture of Cities*. London: Secker & Warburg, 1938.

—. *The Urban Prospect*. London: Secker & Warburg, 1968.

Nadel, Ira B. *Joyce and the Jews: Culture and Texts*. Basingstoke: Macmillan, 1989.

Nägele, Rainer. "The Poetic Ground Laid Bare (Benjamin Reading Baudelaire)." In *Walter Benjamin: Theoretical Questions*, ed. David S. Ferris, 118-38. Stanford: Stanford University Press, 1996.

Neal, Larry. *The Rise of Financial Capitalism: International Capital Markets in the Age of Reason*. Cambridge: Cambridge University Press, 1990.

Nicholson, Colin. *Writing and the Rise of Finance: Capital Satires of the Early Eighteenth Century*. Cambridge: Cambridge University Press, 1994.

Novak, Maximillian E. *Daniel Defoe: Master of Fictions*. Oxford: Oxford University Press, 2001.

—. *Realism, Myth, and History in Defoe's Fiction*. Lincoln: University of Nebraska Press, 1983.

Nugent, [Thomas]. *The Grand Tour: Containing an Exact Description of Most of the Cities, Towns, and Remarkable Places of Europe*. London, 1749.

Ollard, Richard. *Pepys: A Biography*. London: Allison & Busby, 1999.

O'Brien, Joseph V. *"Dear, Dirty Dublin": A City in Distress, 1899-1916*. Berkeley: University of California Press, 1982.

Ó Broin, Leon. *Dublin Castle and the 1916 Rising*. New York: NYU Press, 1971.

O'Neil, John H. "Samuel Pepys: The War of Will and Pleasure." *Restoration: Studies in English Literary Culture 1660-1700* 19 (Fall 1995): 88-94.

"Orange and Lemons." *Household Words* 210 (1 April 1854): 145-50.

Owens, W. R. Introduction to *Political and Economic Writings of Daniel Defoe*, vol. 8, *Social Reform*, by Daniel Defoe. London: Pickering & Chatto, 2000.

Patten, Robert L. *Charles Dickens and His Publishers*. Oxford: Clarendon, 1978.

Peck, John. *War, the Army and Victorian Literature*. Basingstoke: Macmillan, 1998.

Pepys, Samuel. *The Diary of Samuel Pepys*. 11 vols. Eds. Robert Latham and William Matthews. London: HarperCollins, 1995.

Pérez García, Diana. "Imagining Memory: *Ulysses* and *A Journal of the Plague Year*, or the Novel of the Inventory." In *Critical Ireland: New Essays in Literature and Culture*, eds. Alan A. Gillis and Aaron Kelly, 81-87. Dublin: Four Courts, 2001.

Petty, Sir William. *Five Essays in Political Arithmmetick*. London, 1687.

Plantinga, Theodore. *Historical Understanding in the Thought of Wilhelm Dilthey*. Toronto: University of Toronto Press, 1980.

Pocock, J. G. A. *Virtue, Commerce, and History: Essays on Political Thought and History, Chiefly in the Eighteenth Century*. Cambridge: Cambridge University Press, 1985.

Poe, Edgar Allan Poe. *The Complete Tales and Poems of Edgar Allan Poe*. London: Penguin, 1982.

Pooley, Roger. *English Prose of the Seventeenth Century, 1590-1700*. London: Longman, 1992.

Poovey, Mary. *Uneven Developments: The Ideological Work of Gender in Mid-Victorian England*. Chicago: University of Chicago Press, 1988.

Potts, Willard. *Joyce and the Two Irelands*. Austin: University of Texas Press, 2000.

Pred, Allan. *City-Systems in Advanced Economies: Past Growth, Present Processes and Future Development Options*. London: Hutchinson, 1977.

Price, Richard. *British Society, 1680-1880: Dynamism, Containment and Change*. Cambridge: Cambridge University Press, 1999.

Radcliffe, Anne. *The Italian*. Ed. Frederick Garber. Oxford: Oxford University Press, 1998.

Rainsford, Dominic. *Authorship, Ethics and the Reader: Blake, Dickens, Joyce*. London: Macmillan, 1997.

Rasmussen, Steen Eiler. *London: The Unique City*. Cambridge: MIT Press, 1982.

Reader, John. *Cities*. London: Heinemann, 2004.

Reichert, Klaus. "The European Background of Joyce's Writing." In *The Cambridge Companion to James Joyce*, ed. Derek Attridge, 55-82.

Cambridge: Cambridge University Press, 1990.

Richetti, John. *Defoe's Narratives: Situations and Structures*. Oxford: Clarendon, 1975.

—. *The English Novel in History 1700-1800*. London: Routledge, 1999.

—. *The Life of Daniel Defoe*. Malden: Blackwell, 2005.

"Rights and Wrongs of Women." *Household Words* 210 (1 April 1854): 158-61.

Ross, Michael L. *Storied Cities: Literary Imaginings of Florence, Venice, and Rome*. Westport: Greenwood Press, 1994.

Saïd, Suzanne. "The City in the Greek Novel." In *The Search for the Ancient Novel*, ed. James Tatun, 216-36. Baltimore: The Johns Hopkins University Press, 1994.

Saramago, José. *Blindness*. Trans. Giovanni Pontiero. London: Vintage, 2005.

Sauerland, Karol. *Diltheys Erlebnisbegriff: Entstehung, Glanzzeit und Verkümmerung eines literaturhistorischen Begriffs*. Berlin: Walter de Gruyter, 1972.

Schiller, Friedrich. *On the Aesthetic Education of Man: In a Series of Letters*. Eds. and trans. Elizabeth M. Wilkinson and L. A. Willoughby. Oxford: Clarendon, 1982.

Schwarz, L. D. *London in the Age of Industrialisation: Entrepreneurs, Labour Force and Living Conditions, 1700-1850*. Cambridge: Cambridge University Press, 1992.

Schwarzbach, F. S. *Dickens and the City*. London: Athlone, 1979.

Scott, Sir Walter. *The Heart of Mid-Lothian*. Ed. Tony Inglis. London: Penguin, 1994.

—. *Waverley*. Ed. Andrew Hook. London: Penguin, 1972.

Shakespeare, William. *Hamlet, Prince of Denmark*. Ed. Philip Edwards. Cambridge: Cambridge University Press, 1985.

Sharrock, Roger. "Modes of Self-Representation: Herbert of Cherbury, Kenelm Digby, Pepys." *The Seventeenth Century* 3 (Spring 1988): 1-16.

Shatto, Susan. *The Companion to "Bleak House."* London: HarperCollins, 1988.

Shattock, Joanne. *Politics and Reviewers: The "Edinburgh" and the "Quarterly" in the Early Victorian Age*. Leicester: Leicester University Press, 1989.

Shelley, Percy Bysshe. *Shelley: Poetical Works*. Ed. Thomas Hutchinson, corrected by G. M. Matthews. Oxford: Oxford University Press, 1970.

Sheppard, Francis. *London: A History*. Oxford: Oxford University Press, 1998.

Sherman, Sandra. *Finance and Fictionality in the Early Eighteenth*

Century: Accounting for Defoe. Cambridge: Cambridge University Press, 1996.

Simmel, Georg. *The Philosophy of Money*. Trans. Tom Bottomore and David Frisby, ed. David Frisby. London: Routledge, 2004.

—. *Simmel on Culture: Selected Writings*. Eds. David Frisby and Mike Featherstone. London: Sage, 1997.

Simms, J. G. "The War of the Two Kings, 1685-91." In *A New History of Ireland*, vol. 3, *Early Modern Ireland 1534-1691,* eds. T. W. Moody et al., 478-508. Oxford: Clarendon, 1991.

Slater, Michael. *Charles Dickens*. New Haven: Yale University Press, 2009.

Smith, Karl Ashley. *Dickens and the Unreal City: Searching for Spiritual Significance in Nineteenth-Century London*. Houndmills: Palgrave Macmillan, 2008.

Smyth, Gerry. *Decolonisation and Criticism: The Construction of Irish Literature*. London: Pluto Press, 1998.

Somerville-Large, Peter. *Dublin*. London: Hamish Hamilton, 1979.

Sommerville, C. John. *The News Revolution in England: Cultural Dynamics of Daily Information*. Oxford: Oxford University Press, 1996.

Sorensen, Janet. "'I Talk to Everybody in Their Own Way': Defoe's Economies of Identity." In *The Economic Criticism: Studies at the Intersection of Literature and Economics*, eds. Martha Woodmansee and Mark Osteen, 75-94. London: Routledge, 1999.

Soupault, Philippe. "James Joyce." In *Portraits of the Artist in Exile: Recollections of James Joyce by Europeans*, ed. Willard Potts, 108-18. Seattle: University of Washington Press, 1979.

Spence, Craig. *London in the 1690s: A Social Atlas*. London: Centre for Metropolitan History, Institute of Historical Research, 2000.

Stanzel, Franz K.. *Theorie des Erzählens*. Göttingen: Vandenhoeck & Ruprecht, 1979.

Starr, G. A. *Defoe and Spiritual Autobiography*. New York: Gordian Press, 1971.

Sterne, Laurence. *The Life and Opinions of Tristram Shandy, Gentleman*. Ed. Ian Campbell Ross. Oxford: Oxford University Press, 2000

Stoker, Bram. *Dracula*. Ed. Maud Ellmann. Oxford: Oxford University Press, 1996.

Stow, John. *A Survey of London, Reprinted from the Text of 1603*. 2 vols. Oxford: Clarendon, 1908.

Strype, John, *A Survey of the Cities of London and Westminster . . . Written at first in the Year MDXCVIII by John Stow . . . Now Lastly Corrected,*

Improved, and very much Enlarged: And the Survey and History brought down from the Year 1633 . . . to the present Time. London, 1720.

Swift, Jonathan. *Gulliver's Travels*. Eds. Claude Rawson and Ian Higgins. Oxford: Oxford University Press, 2005.

—. *Jonathan Swift*. Eds. Angus Ross and David Woolley. Oxford: Oxford University Press, 1984.

Thackeray, William. *Barry Lyndon*. Ed. Andrew Sanders. Oxford: Oxford University Press, 1984.

—. *Vanity Fair*. Ed. J. I. M. Stewart. London: Penguin, 1968.

Thompson, E. P. "Time, Work-Discipline, and Industrial Capitalism." *Past and Present* 38 (1967): 56-97.

Tomalin, Claire. *Samuel Pepys: The Unequalled Self*. London: Penguin, 2002.

Trambling, Jeremy. *Dickens, Violence and the Modern State: Dreams of the Scaffold*. London: Macmillan, 1995.

—. *Going Astray: Dickens and London*. Harlow: Pearson Longman, 2009.

Turner, James Grantham. "Pepys and the Private Parts of Modernity." In *Culture and Society in the Stuart Restoration: Literature, Drama, History*, ed. Gerald MacLean, 95-110. Cambridge: Cambridge University Press, 1995.

Underwood, Doug. *Journalism and the Novel: Truth and Fiction, 1700-2000*. Cambridge: Cambridge University Press, 2008.

Venuti, Lawrence. *Translator's Invisibility: A History of Translation*. Abingdon: Routledge, 2008.

Vlock, Deborah. *Dickens, Novel Reading, and the Victorian Popular Theatre*. Cambridge: Cambridge University Press, 1998.

W. D. *The Artificial Clock-Maker, A Treatise of Watch and Clock-Work, Wherein the Art of Calculating Numbers for Most Sorts of Movements is Explained to the Capacity of the Unlearned*. London, 1700.

Waller, Maureen. *1700: Scenes from London Life*. New York: Four Walls Eight Windows, 2000.

"War and Progress in China." *Blackwood's Edinburgh Magazine* 85 (May 1860): 525-42.

Warner, John M., *Joyce's Grandfathers: Myth and History in Defoe, Smollett, Sterne, and Joyce*. Athens: University of Georgia Press, 1993.

Warner, William B. *Licensing Entertainment: The Elevation of Novel Reading in Britain, 1684-1750*. Berkeley: University of California Press, 1998.

Watt, Ian. *The Rise of the Novel: Studies in Defoe, Richardson and Fielding*. London: Chatto and Windus, 1957.

Weber, Max. *Economy and Society*. Eds. Guenther Roth and Claus Wittich. 2 vols. Berkeley: University of California Press, 1992.

Weber, Samuel. *Benjamin's–Abilities*. Cambridge: Harvard University Press, 2008.

Welsh, Alexander. *The City of Dickens*. Cambridge: Harvard University Press, 1971.

West, John B. "Krook's Death by Spontaneous Combustion and the Controversy between Dickens and Lewes: A Physiologist's View." *The Dickensian* 90 (Summer 1994): 125-29.

Weston, H. W. *Chancery Infamy; Or, A Plea for an Anti-Chancery League*. London, 1849.

"Where Are They," *Household Words* 210 (1 April 1854): 152–58.

Whimzies: Or, A New Cast of Characters. London, 1631.

Whitley, Catherine. "Gender and Interiority." In *Joyce and the City: The Significance of Place*, ed. Michael Begnal, 35-50. Syracuse: Syracuse University Press, 2002.

Williams, Raymond. *The Country and the City*. Frogmore: Paladine, 1975.

Willis, Mark. "Charles Dickens and Fictions of the Crowd." *Dickens Quarterly* 23 (2006): 85-107.

Winston, Greg. "Barracks and Brothels: Militarism and Prostitution in *Ulysses*." In *Bloomsday 100: Essays on "Ulysses,"* eds. Morris Beja and Anne Fogarty, 96-114. Gainesville: University Press of Florida, 2009.

Wolin, Richard. *Walter Benjamin: An Aesthetic of Redemption*. New York: Columbia University Press, 1982.

"The Wolf at the Church Door." *All the Year Round* 84 (1 December 1860): 177-80.

Woolf, Virginia. *Jacob's Room*. Ed. Kate Flint. Oxford: Oxford University Press, 1992.

Wordsworth, William. *The Prelude 1799, 1805, 1850*. Eds. Jonathan Wordsworth et al. New York: Norton, 1979.

Wright, Laura. "Speaking and Listening in Early Modern London." In *The City and the Sense: Urban Culture Since 1500*, eds. Alexander Cowan and Jill Steward, 60-74. Aldershot: Ashgate, 2007.

Zimmerman, Everett. *The Boundaries of Fiction: History and the Eighteenth-Century British Novel*. Ithaca: Cornell University Press, 1996.

Zwicker, Steven N. ed. *Cambridge Companion to English Literature 1650-1740*. Cambridge: Cambridge University Press, 1998.

INDEX